P9-CRR-308

INDIAN TIME

A Year of Discovery
with the Native Americans
of the Southwest

SIMON & SCHUSTER
New York • London • Toronto • Sydney • Tokyo • Singapore

SIMON & SCHUSTER
Simon & Schuster Building
Rockefeller Center
1230 Avenue of the Americas
New York, New York 10020

Designed by Deirdre C. Amthor

Manufactured in the United States of America

1 3 5 7 9 10 8 6 4 2

Library of Congress Cataloging-in-Publication Data
Fein, Judith (Judith Lynn)
Indian time : a year of discovery with the Native Americans of the
Southwest / Judith Fein.
p.   cm.
1. Pueblo Indians—Social life and customs. 2. Pueblo Indians—Phi-
losophy. 3. Pueblo Indians—Public opinion. 4. Public opinion—
United States. 5. Fein, Judith (Judith Lynn)—Diaries. I. Title.
E99.P9F38 1993   93–13957
973'.04974—dc20   CIP

ISBN:0-671-79576-7

To the universe, for providing me with a complicated, funny, crazy, difficult life that I can write about . . .

To Paul, for being my life partner and a cross between Buddha and a stand-up comic . . .

To my friends and family (in no special order) who received the letters—Mickey, Hank, Patsy, Lonnie, Marla, Peter, Jessie, Dick, Rahla, Carl, Joyce, Mae, Jay, Ceil, Dale, Marlan, and sometimes Arnold, Gail, Ginette, Paul, and Odile . . .

To my film and television agents, Byrdie and Ian, who shared my excitement and pushed me to turn fact into film . . .

To my friends in L.A. who are always so supportive of me . . .

To all my friends in the Southwest who appear in the book and all those who do not, but who are still fascinating to me . . .

To Allan K. for godfathering the book . . .

To my book agent, Arthur, for his vision . . .

And to my editor, Michael Korda, who came into my life as a blessing . . .

Contents

On May 1, 1991, I left Los Angeles on assignment. I was hired by a television station to research, create and write a dramatic series that takes place among the Pueblo Indians. I was introduced to a Pueblo screenwriter, and we became writing partners.

I came from Los Angeles for a job, and I arrived with a secret: I was phobic about so many things that I could no longer count them. I *thought* I was in northern New Mexico to get a good TV story but, in actuality, I was there to get a life. The Indian reality was so different from my urban existence that it challenged all of my previously held beliefs and knee-jerk behaviors.

My growth and learning were crazy, funny, profound, scary and sometimes overwhelming. I began to write long letters home about them and, since I was pressed for time, I photocopied the letters and sent them to a group of family and friends who I thought would be receptive to them.

The response to the letters was very strong, and I began to understand that my people back home were actively sharing my experiences with me. First they asked me if they could show the letters to their friends and friends of friends. Then they began urging me to publish them.

I resisted the idea for a long time, because the letters were so intensely personal and because I was afraid they would betray or reveal too much about my tribal friends. I was at a feast day at Jemez Pueblo, and I decided to ask an elder Indian man what it was appropriate for me to write about. He sat silently for a long time, looking out the window, past the adobe houses, to the vast desert beyond. Then he looked at me and answered, "You can write anything, as long as it's the truth."

It dawned on me then that I could be a bridge person—helping to connect the culture I come from with the culture I was thrust into. I could take readers with me on my fabulous journey to the contemporary indigenous people of the Southwest. They could meet my Indian and Hispanic friends, go to feast days with me, bake in the summer and shiver in the winter at the amazing ceremonies. And they could be astounded, as I was, to learn that all of this goes on today.

I took great pains to conceal my friends' identities and to exclude details of their lives that were too intimate for ink. I calmly informed them all that I was writing a book about them, but that they were "protected."

To my astonishment, almost all of them insisted that I use their real names and *include* those details. They wanted to be presented in my letters and in my book as they really *are*, not as people would like them to be. Also, if my descriptions and appraisals of them were wrong, so be it—they were only *my* version, and reality can be seen from many different angles. I was humbled by their humility and generosity.

This book is faithfully based on my letters. Although the letter format is gone, I hope you will consider this work as a long letter to you, my reader.

I won't pretend that this is *the* truth, but it is *my* truth, and I present it to you the best way I know how.

Judith Fein

INDIAN
TIME

1
Horizontal Woman in a Vertical World

Early May, 1991

It's hard to be in northern New Mexico, sent by a Los Angeles TV station to research and write a series on contemporary American Indians, when you're an extremely fearful person. The altitude is 7500 feet and it's hard for a sea-level resident like me to breathe here. There are hideous bugs lurking everywhere, the diet is fatty and meaty and I'm a vegetarian, everyone is in love with nature and I am a child of concrete, brick, and glass. Everything is *high up* here—the mountains, the Indian ruins I have to visit, the city of Santa Fe itself—and I have a horror of heights. As a matter of fact, I lied to the producers and said I wanted to drive to Santa Fe in order to "drink in the scenery." The truth is that I would rather die than get in a plane. Why can't things be at ground level? I feel like a helplessly horizontal person in a vertical world.

Worst of all, my supposed Indian writing partner, Lenny Smallfeather, disappeared three days after my arrival. He was supposed to introduce me to people, accompany me to the Indian Pueblos, and plan the television series with me; instead, he has informed me that he is busy working on another project and I have to fend for myself. When I tell this to people, they smile and say, "Good luck." I think they mean, "Bad luck." Apparently, Indians do not easily take Anglos into their circles or their confidence, because they have a history of bullshit and betrayal at the hands of whities. To add a little pressure to the cooker, my husband, Paul, is apprehensive because he has left behind his work and life in L.A. to accompany me. I have to do something to get our stay here off to a good start.

I guess I should be grateful that I had even three days with Lenny before he took off. He is a small, wiry Indian man of about fifty with dark brown skin, big brown eyes, and a wavy gray mane that is as thick as the hair of a horse. I know this because I ruffled his hair playfully, trying to disguise my resentment, and called him "Birdhead." The name stuck.

Lenny Smallfeather, alias Birdhead, looks vaguely Hispanic and is very articulate and clever. He dresses like a rag-picker, and pretends not to be concerned with appearances, but I laugh when I catch him discreetly ogling pretty women. He has had two white wives, and four children. He is one of the few Native Americans in the country who writes screenplays professionally, which is why we were paired up to write together.

The first day in Santa Fe, Lenny invited us to a forty-second birthday party at the home of his cousin Ron. "It's at Mesita, about a two-hour drive," Lenny said. "Will it be fun?" I asked. "FUN?" Lenny said, scrunching up his face in disgust. "How do I know if it will be fun? I just asked you to go." Birdhead brooks me no margin.

We left Santa Fe and drove south past Albuquerque toward Laguna Pueblo. There are nineteen Indian Pueblos in New Mexico, the hardy remains of the more than ninety indigenous villages that were extant when the Spanish arrived. The word "pueblo" means "town" in Spanish, and it referred to the fact that the local Indians lived in tight-knit communal villages with adobe houses.

The incursion of the Europeans wreaked havoc on the Indian way of life. It was a spiritual, moral, financial, emotional shock to their systems. In the name of Christianity, and using conversion by force, the *conquistadores* did everything they could to destroy the Indian lifestyle. Most of the Pueblo Indians today have Spanish names and are good Christians and look somewhat Hispanic. This is because there was so much rape, marriage by force, and willing intermarriage. It is very difficult to trace a clear, pureblood Indian heritage for the Pueblo people of today. But they are certainly pureblood in their cultural identification. A little bit or even a lot of Spanish blood makes no difference in that arena.

There are five villages that make up the Pueblo of Laguna, and Mesita is one of them. There was a vigorous wind blowing in our direction, and when we got out of the car, we got a mouthful of New Mexico dirt. As I wiped the grainy earth from my lips, I felt a rising excitement. Most Americans think of Indians as frozen in time—living in tepees on the Great Plains in the late eighteen hundreds. They imagine horses and war clubs, peace pipes and feathers, and a hearty meal of fresh buffalo ripped apart at dinner time. I, like my fellow compatriots, had no idea of what contemporary Native American homelife was like.

Ron's house appeared before us: a one-story, sand-colored, earthen rectangular structure with exposed rounded wood beams called *vigas.* As we walked toward it, Paul commented on the impressive number of yelping dogs and laughing children. I was busy feeling apprehension at my first Indian birthday party, but Ron and his wife were so friendly that I immediately felt at home.

The furniture was threadbare and poor, there was obviously not much income from Ron's job as a substitute teacher, but the dining room table groaned with Jell-Os and salads and cakes and two huge aluminum pots of chili. It was the first time we had ever tasted this New Mexican staple, and everyone was curious to know how we would like it. Paul and I exchanged looks: it was made with red meat. We politely scooped a daub of red chili onto our plastic plates and then soaked it up with pieces we tore from a big round bread. We had much more bread than chili. Paul smiled and seemed to enjoy it. I could hardly taste it because I was too busy wondering if the meat were going to kill me on the spot or wait a while to clog my arteries and give me a slow, lingering death.

We were the only white people at the party, and we tried to keep a low profile. We *tried*, but we didn't succeed. Paul stood in the kitchen, surrounded by children wearing T-shirts and sneakers, imitating Michael Jackson and then doing a stand-up routine. Lenny had instructed me not to ask questions in Indian country, but I'm extremely inquisitive by nature and I found it impossible to restrain myself. I knew enough not to ask personal questions, so I tried to keep it general. There was so much I wanted to know. "What's that a picture of?" I asked the old woman on the rocker next to me, pointing to a colorful painting of *kachinas,* who represent different supernatural aspects of the created world. "Oh, just something," she answered, rocking rhythmically and looking into the fire in the fireplace. You might think her answer would discourage me, but it didn't. I asked about the house, the furniture, the jobs everyone had, the weather, the wind, clothes, and recipes. God knows why I wanted recipes, since I can't even boil an egg. I could see Lenny wincing and then shaking his head. "White people. They're all the same," Birdhead was probably thinking.

Every time Paul and I finished the food on our plates, Ron or his wife would urge us to fill up again. We had tried and survived the red chili and they insisted that we sample the green. I began to wonder if the Indians were one of the lost tribes of Israel, because the food fixation is very common in Jewish houses.

When we could eat no more, we were shuttled outside for games. Children and adults played together, with the grown-ups laughing and teasing as much as, if not more than the kids. We had a choice of horseshoes, breaking balloons, or charades. We chose the latter, and I was thrilled when I won. I was given a huge pink plastic comb and a set of tiny foam makeup brushes as a prize. The other participants were also given prizes. For coming in second, or third, or for being a good sport. "Interesting," I inscribed in my mental notebook. "There are no losers here. Everyone plays very hard, but there is no real competition."

Unlike the dominant culture that surrounds them, Pueblo Indians are taught to think of the group first. Individual accomplishments are not emphasized and active, joyous participation in communal sports, games or activities is more important than winning. And, if someone does win, it is considered bad form to brag about it.

It was starting to get chilly by late afternoon, so we went inside again. Lenny, who is a storyteller, gathered all the children around him and told them how, when he was their age, his grandma used to tell him stories in the evening in front of a warm fire. He especially loved the stories about Coyote, the wily, manipulative animal who sometimes outsmarts the other animals and other times is too smart for his own darn good. Coyote is an omnipresent character in Indian folk legends, much like Brer Rabbit is for southerners, except that Coyote is also a sacred being, and has aspects of the human and the divine.

Lenny leaned forward in his chair and began to tell a tale about Coyote trying to be like Buffalo, and wanting to eat what Buffalo eats and roam where Buffalo roams instead of being content to be Coyote. The children paid attention, but I found my mind wandering. I knew there was a "message," but I didn't get it. It is nonlinear storytelling, which means that the narrative is not straightforward and chronological the way our tales are told. The details are often extraneous and pull the story off in a direction that makes me lose the thread. I knew that Indian culture and beliefs are handed down through sto-

16

ries, since there is no written language, and I marveled that something so accessible that children could understand it would be so inaccessible to me.

When Lenny was done, Ron distributed bingo cards and, at the end of each round, gave candy and household products and gadgets to the winners. At the end of the last game, he stood up and thanked all the guests for being there with him to celebrate his birthday. *He* made the food, *he* planned the entertainment, *he* invited the guests, *he* gave all the gifts, but *we* were thanked. He made it sound as though our presence was an important gift, and he singled Paul and me out and told us to make his house our house and come back. When we left, as we were walking toward our car, the family pulled at our arms and begged us to sleep there. Although we did not take them up on their offer, we had the feeling that they really meant it. This was our first brush with Pueblo hospitality.

When we were dropped off at our little *casita* on the south side of Santa Fe, within walking distance of nothing and part of a huge compound surrounded by a red clay wall, Lenny mumbled something about there being a "sweat" in honor of my arrival the next night. Birdhead never tells me anything directly and never offers explanations. Instead of "There's a sweat for you tomorrow night," followed by an explanation of what a sweat is, he murmured, "I guess I'll be meeting you around five for the sweat."

The following evening, it was very chilly on the hilltop where the sweatlodge was located. The sweatlodge is made of a frame of bent willow bows, covered by layers of tarps, and it is shaped like a small domed igloo. It is the Indians' church or synagogue. It is there they go with brother tree and brother stones (the tree to make the wood for the fire and the stones to hold the heat) to pray to Grandfather or Father, the Creative Spirit in the universe.

The sweatlodge ceremony consists of four rounds of prayer and thanksgiving. Between rounds, the participants exit the sweatlodge through a flap and cool off by hosing down with freezing water. All of the worshippers are called *brothers* and *sisters*, part of the universal family.

During the first round, Grandfather is greeted, and all the creatures of the earth are blessed. The second round is devoted to praying for *human* relations and asking that they be blessed. The third round is to pray for healing of the heart, mind, body, and soul of all creation.

17

And the fourth round is in case the participants have forgotten anything. It is the last chance to talk about a difficult situation or ask for a blessing. This fourth round is as far as the worshippers can go into the realm of the Spirit, and now they must return to living their lives. Hopefully, through intimacy with Grandfather in the womb-shaped sweat, they have been reborn and renewed, fortified and strengthened, clearer about the purpose and meaning of their lives.

I arrived early at the sweatlodge with Lenny because he was running the sweat. There were several other people there, sitting around an outdoor fire about ten feet from the sweatlodge. They were all talking, exchanging friendly banter, but Lenny didn't introduce me and it was just as well, because I was too preoccupied to remember names anyway. I was worried about going into the sweat. I didn't even know what I was frightened of; just a sort of generalized anticipatory anxiety.

We all sat there, looking at the wood fire in the outdoor fire pit, and soon I began to feel much warmer, physically and emotionally. There was something bonding about sitting together, watching the same fire and the large stones that were heating up in the flames. I was drawn into the talk, the joke-telling, the grunts and laughs and groans of social conversation. And then, suddenly, the chatting died down. I looked around—had there been some sign or signal to stop talking? It was as though a breeze whispered and everyone heard it. It was time for the ceremony to begin.

A man with long white hair, wearing a breechcloth around his groin area, was in charge of the stones. He drew a path in the earth that led from the fire in the outdoor fire pit to another fire pit dug into the ground inside the sweatlodge. Then he carried the stones on a shovel into the fire pit in the lodge. Birdhead told us that we could not walk across the path that had been drawn once the sacred stones were carried in. "You must go all the way around if you want to cross from one side to the other," he said with utmost seriousness. Although I hadn't seen him change, he, too, was now wearing a breechcloth, and his behavior was much less casual and more formal.

The logs were then carried into the sweatlodge and placed atop the stones in the fire pit. All of the other people began to strip off their clothes, discreetly, behind shrubs and trees. They came back draped in towels. The men's were around their loins only. The women covered their whole torsos.

I am not great about nudity. I wore a bathing suit and wrapped the towel around that. It was a sort of emotional contraceptive.

When we were all appropriately attired, we were given an order to enter the holy sweatlodge. One by one, the participants got down on all fours, and crawled into the sweatlodge through the open flap. As each entered, he or she spoke the words, "To all my relations." It acknowledged the connectedness of the individual person to the whole universe. Birds and animals and snakes and insects were given life by mothers and fathers. They breathe and live as we do. They manifest the wonderment of creation. They come from Mother Earth, the same as human beings.

Once inside the sweatlodge, it was an inferno. Lenny happily told us that the stones were new and they gave off a special intense heat. I was already grappling with the long car trip from Los Angeles, little sleep, and the altitude. Even without these excuses, it was like being trapped in total darkness in the world's hottest sauna. I could feel the sticky sweetness of everyone's sweat around me. I bore it for about ten minutes. When I whispered hoarsely in the dark that I needed to leave, Lenny asked if I could wait until water was poured on the fire. I said yes. I lied. I could not bear it another second. I sat there in the pitch-black as sticks were passed to us all and water was thrown on the fire to make steam, which made it all hotter. Everyone else was praying and thanking Grandfather for the sweat, and they all sounded grateful, relaxed and at peace. I was huddled next to all these people, but I felt completely apart. I saw FEAR in front of me like a monster. I thought I would pass out or die or have a stroke. But I know how urgent it is for me to face down FEAR, so I just sat there. I kept telling myself over and over that heat is a friend, and that I was all right.

When I finally crawled outside into the night air, I noticed that six people crawled out after me. I guess I was wrong in assuming that all of them could bear the heat. Maybe I was just an average coward, and not so different after all. Nonetheless, as I shook from the shock of the freezing hose-off, I decided that I would not go back into the sweatlodge for the next three rounds. I had faced the fear monster in the form of heat for as long as I could, and for this day, my courage retired. But it was plenty scary out there alone after everyone else went back in. As Arnold, a Cochiti Indian and drum-maker, crawled back in, he joked, "It sure is hard being an Indian." And I'm not an Indian, so I found it even harder.

There were biting bugs out there. Then the cold got colder. I heard strange, unidentifiable noises in the night. I had this weird fear that something awful was going to happen to me. I decided to hold on to the outside of the sweatlodge for support, and I clung to the tarps, hugging them. I heard the rumble and mumble of prayers inside, and realized that although it probably came easily to all the people inside the sweatlodge, I do not know how to pray. It was useless for me to try, as I didn't have the vaguest clue of how to do it. I heard singing inside. I could not sing. I didn't have a song in my heart. I decided to concentrate instead on the fact that it's okay for me to be an outsider— it's nothing to be ashamed of. I often FEEL like an outsider in life. Now I get to BE one. As the communal hum inside the lodge got louder, and tighter, and more unified, as the prayers were whispered and I could barely hear them, I just felt MYSELF and what that self feels like and how even though that self is alone, and separated, that self reaches out toward others (the sweatlodge I clung to) in silent support and for support.

Lenny had assigned me a job when he came out during one of the rounds. I was the flap monitor. I was to lift the flap and let people out between rounds. The signal for me was the word "Owa," which someone would call out. Also, if anyone needed to exit for an emergency, I would also hear "Owa" and I was to immediately lift the flap.

Easier said than done. The flap was so damn heavy I could hardly lift it, and even in this I needed support. What in the world could I do alone?

I sat out there some more in the cold night. I didn't know what to do with my mind.

Time passed. I was shaking from the cold, and my neck was sore from whipping around every minute or two to make sure a wolf or coyote wasn't sneaking up on me. The singing quieted down. And then I heard Lenny's voice from inside the sweat say, "Does anyone else have a song? Does anyone OUTSIDE have a song?" I have no idea what possessed me, but I dug up the only religious song I could remember from my childhood synagogue days— HAYVENU SHALOM ALECHEM. I half-lifted the flap, because that was all I could manage, and I stuck my head into the sweat. I began to sing those words, in a loud and rather melodic voice. I usually have a dreadful voice, but I liked the way it resonated in there. And most of all, my head felt really warm, while the rest of my body was flip-flopping around behind me, freezing in the night. So I kept my head in there, a sort of disembodied head, singing the words over and over and over. I thought, "they must all think I am nuts." But it didn't stop me from singing. Five

20

times. Ten times. Repeating those words from my childhood, the words people sang as they were leaving the synagogue. Words of brotherhood and peace. And soon other people began to join in. Finally, when I felt I had stayed and sung as long as I could, I pulled my head out.

The next day, I entered the makeshift offices of the Institute of American Indian Arts and asked Beaver, the outgoing, pretty, rotund Indian receptionist, if I could see Lenny, who was working there. He was cheerful and buoyant as he bid me farewell. He was leaving New Mexico to do research. The producers of my TV show agreed to let him go. "After all, he's an Indian and he knows all of this stuff already" they said. "You go find it out for yourself." So Lenny was gone, and there I was, alone in Indian country. How would I make inroads into this alien culture without a guide? How would I ever meet people and penetrate the surface that is presented to tourists?

I went home and was just about to succumb to panic when the phone rang. "Hi, this is Beaver. How would you like to go to Jemez, my Pueblo, for a wedding?" For someone who didn't know how to pray, I was sure having beginner's fortune!

There were several hundred people present at Jemez Pueblo, all dressed very casually in summery clothes. A wood fire was burning high on a hill, a flute player made soft melody, and brick-red cliffs towered dramatically all around us like nature's own cathedral. The bride and groom, Laura and Steve, stood in traditional Indian dress— she, short and beautifully plump in buckskin, he, as tall as a Brobdingnagian, in a feathered Chippewa headdress. I jabbed at Paul's elbow in excited anticipation. "A real, traditional Indian wedding," I whispered. "Not quite," he whispered back. A white minister appeared and the couple was married with a very conventional church ceremony that included reading from the Bible. If I closed my eyes to the Indian clothes, I could have been back in Los Angeles.

This is very typical of the Pueblo way. After the initial conversion by force, the Pueblo people embraced Christianity. Indian dress and rituals were incorporated into Christian observances. There was a melding and a blending of the two ways which still goes on today as Indian tribes are assaulted by evangelists of every stripe.

After the ceremony, we felt a bit shy, since we didn't really know the bride and groom. We tried to sneak past the reception line, but Laura and Steve held on to our hands and looked us in the eyes and

21

thanked us so, so much for being with them and begged us to come to the reception. Once again we experienced Indian hospitality, and realized how central it is to the Pueblo way of life. A white person may *feel* like a stranger, but is certainly not treated like one.

We tried to blend in. We followed all of the guests' cars around the dirt road that circles the tan and rust adobe houses of Jemez Pueblo. Paul cheerfully honked on our horn the way the Pueblo people honked on theirs. When in doubt, we just do whatever everyone else is doing. Finally we ended up in the Jemez civic center where many speeches were made, offering the couple advice and philosophy which we all would do well to follow. The bride and groom chose a *madrone* and a *padrone*—an older married couple who would be there for them as guides when they needed advice or comfort or support.

And then the food! Tables and tables of home-cooked dishes, all prepared by the relatives. This is the Pueblo way of entertaining—everyone chips in. There were many kinds of red and green chili, and they ranged from spicy to mouth-on-fire. I was so hungry that I threw up my hands, gave up being a vegetarian, stood on line like everyone else, and helped myself to the meaty dishes. The guests all ate until they were puffed up, and still the food tables groaned. Our forks and spoons had hardly made a dent.

When we left the reception, we encountered the Indian flute player from the wedding ceremony standing on the porch. Suddenly we were talking, and I started asking questions of him and I stopped myself. Even though the Indian culture is so different and there is so much I want to know, I must get out of the habit of doing this—banging into an Indian person, asking him/her questions, and then splitting. *He* didn't seem offended. *I* just felt it was the wrong thing to do. It was the white way, which they resent. They end up telling you something, any old thing, answering the questions any which way, but not telling you anything really important. For that, you have to hang around a bit. Well, I vowed not to do it again. But it's hard to learn. Old habits are hard to break. Plus they are reassuring when you come up against silences. They lead you out of the silence. I don't know how to stand quietly with another person without talking, the way Native Americans do.

We headed out of the Pueblo and saw a small sign saying "pottery for sale" on a house, so I hinted very unsubtly and very repeatedly until Paul stopped. We went inside, and we were admiring some round polychrome pots when the owners of the house, Fay and Michael, came in. He was sweet and low key, but she was a real dynamo in a flaming red blouse with short, bobbed hair. They offered us cold drinks and then began to tell us about their lives. Both of them had been working in low-level government jobs, but they had pulled back from the external workaday world and started potting, which is a good Pueblo way to spend one's days. Fay's narrative soon got very personal. I guess she could say to outsiders what would have been inadmissible to her neighbors. She was born at another Pueblo, and she had been the victim of much jealousy and vengeance because she was an outsider and not a native to Jemez. There is a very strong sense of place, she told us, and a xenophobic exclusion of people who come from somewhere else. According to Fay, people are resentful when someone else gets ahead—even if it means a new truck or car. There is a pull toward the status quo and homogenization. Pueblo people are, above all, communal. The individual is subordinate to the group. People are supposed to blend into the community and no one is supposed to stand out.

Although this was extremely interesting to hear, and I was trying to acquire a factual, unromantic acquaintance with Indian life, it was still disturbing. I felt like I was eavesdropping or catching a glimpse of taboo sex. Indians are so very private, and Fay was opening up that secret world.

We spent the night in a small motel in Albuquerque and crashed out when we hit the bed. The altitude change makes you very tired. The following morning we got up and flopped into a restaurant for breakfast. It was very crowded because it was Mother's Day. There was a long wait. I asked two women on a bench if they could move over and let me sit. They opened like the Red Sea, and I dove in between them. Just to make conversation, I wished them both a happy Mother's Day. They told me how many children they had and we chatted a bit and soon Paul was waving exultantly to me that he had gotten a table. Just as I was getting up to go, something possessed me to ask the Indian woman to my right if she wanted to share our table. She would have a long wait and we already had a table. She declined, declined again, and then finally accepted. Thus began the meeting with Reina and her husband, Drew.

At first I thought Drew was somehow impaired. He was a big man, with a basset-hound face. He spoke very little, and seemed unresponsive. But as Paul said, to get anywhere with Indians you have to give them time. Because just at the moment when white patience gives

23

out, Indians' kick in. Drew kicked in when he started to drop hints about HIS mother on Mother's Day. At first he said very little, and Reina was urging him to talk, but he wouldn't. Something came over me and I asked him if I could play a little guessing game with him. It was a shot in the dark, but somehow it worked. I sort of tuned into Drew on a deeper level and trusted the intuitive information I was getting about him. I asked him if his mother was an artist, and he nodded yes. I suggested that his mother was perhaps a potter, and again he nodded. Then I really dug in and inquired whether Mom found old pottery shards and did something special with them. Drew's eyes lit up and he stared at me in amazement. On and on the game went, with Drew nodding and bobbing his head excitedly, and then suddenly it all came to life, and I got Drew's story. He was reluctant to tell us, because he didn't want to brag.

Drew comes from Acoma, a Pueblo that sits on top of a thousand-foot-high mesa—and because of its majestic elevation it is called Sky City. The adobe homes of the Indians blend into the sandy color of the mesa, and going there is a voyage back in time, because many of the inhabitants still live the old way with few modern conveniences. Acoma is known worldwide for its fine-line pottery, meticulously painted geometric designs that are intricate and eye-dazzling.

Lucy M. Lewis, THE potter of Acoma, is Drew's mother. As the famed potter Maria Martinez is to San Ildefonso, Lucy M. Lewis is to Acoma. Lucy found pottery shards from her Indian ancestors, and, inspired by their beauty, she revived the art. She is now well into her nineties. Drew is also a well-known potter, as are his eight brothers and sisters. Contrary to what we had been told about not being invited to Indians' houses, by the time we had finished our blueberry pancakes, the Lewises invited us back to theirs. We were beginning to realize that what people told us to expect was not THE truth; it was just THEIR truth.

We arrived back in Santa Fe, and I sat with my head in my hands. "What now? How am I going to write the television series? Where do I go from here?" The phone rang. "Hi, this is Beaver. Put on your dancing shoes. We're going to a powwow at Jemez. I'll meet you there."

Beaming, we drove the hour and a half back to Jemez again. It was nice feeling that the road was familiar and we knew our way. We drove past the wedding site and arrived at the powwow, amid the ruins of a magnificent seventeenth-century abbey. It's hard to admit that the religious oppressors could leave such beautiful footprints in the bloody sand. Anyway, the powwow was being held in honor of Mother's Day, and Indians from all over came to play the communal drums, dance, meet, and eat. Beaver had, in understated Indian fashion, neglected to mention that her parents were the sponsors of the event. So as the other visitors lined up to buy Indian fry bread and lemonade, we were greeted by Beaver, wearing buckskin and a breastplate with some animal skins hanging from her long braids, and whisked past everyone else to the sponsoring family's outdoor tables. Then we were once again stuffed with food. Perhaps on a deeper level, the Pueblo people are wary of outsiders, but on a social level, they are extremely giving and welcoming.

There must have been a thousand people at the Jemez powwow. Beaver's family asked us nothing about ourselves. They simply accepted us. They introduced us around and treated us like adopted guests. I remarked that Beaver's last name, Toya, seemed to be shared by almost everyone we met. "Sure," said Beaver, "we're all related. That's the way it is at the Pueblos. One big family."

We were given a blanket and we plopped down next to the drummers, and all around us were people who spoke of contemporary matters in a contemporary mode, except that they were dressed in feathers and bells and colorful powwow dress. We watched the jingle-dress dancers with their tinny ornaments jumping and clinking in the summer breeze, the eagle dancers soaring and swooping with their outstretched feather wings, and the fancy dancers spinning and jumping athletically. We listened to the high-pitched, hypnotic song of the drummers grouped around several huge powwow drums; each man held his own drumstick but they all shared together in the beating and playing.

One of Beaver's cousins approached me and asked if I knew the story behind the jingle dress. I confessed that I had never even *seen* a jingle-dress dance before. She told me that a long time ago, there was an old man who fasted for four days to help his sick granddaughter. During the long fast he had a vision, and the Creator showed him how to make a jingle dress. He made it, and when his granddaughter wore it, she got well. At the time of the old man, the jingles were made of shells. Today, spindle folded tobacco can tops are used.

Beaver arrived on the blanket and beckoned to me. "It's an *intertribal*—for people of any tribe. You can dance now," she said. My

25

mind flooded with a tidal wave of fears. I wasn't ready. I didn't know the steps and I couldn't follow the complex rhythms of the music. I would stick out with my white face among all the fudge-colored dancers. I would be ridiculous. And yet I wanted to dance. To throw my fears to the fates and just join in. "Go ahead," Paul urged me. Should I? Shouldn't I? I politely declined.

After the sun had set on the powwow, we drove to Albuquerque to see the performance of Belinda James, an Indian ballerina who lives in New York. As we chugged along the freeway, I mused about how lazy we get in L.A. and how reluctant we are to drive for several hours on a whim. Here, our interest in what is going on makes us oblivious to the time and effort expended in getting anywhere. We have become very mobile.

As we drove along, the only other name of an Indian ballerina I could conjure up was Maria Tallchief. Indians are not, by and large, integrated into mainstream white culture. They have lived as second-class citizens, without money or access to our artistic institutions. Without high-level professional training, it has been difficult for them to achieve the high standards of professional performance. All too often, for Indian performers, no matter how great the talent, it has been a case of do-it-yourself. I was anxious to see Belinda James's work because she had struggled for years to get access to the best possible training.

We arrived in the experimental theater for the dancers' showcase. We were given standing room, because there were no seats. "I don't like standing for performances. I wish we could sit," I said to Paul. I had barely spoken the words when an elderly couple, seated next to where I was standing, got up and left. Right at the beginning of the show, as though they were delivering the seats to us! We sat through the first act, and as we walked back to our seats after the intermission, I formulated another wish. "I'd like to have two seats with a better view." Was it possible? A woman motioned to me and pointed to two empty seats that had somehow materialized in front of her. It was Belinda James's mother.

The show began again. Belinda came on. At first we could only see her in the penumbra. She is about five feet ten inches tall, very lithe, very very elegant. And she began to move, to do sculptural modern ballet in toe shoes. She arched her back, on the floor, on all fours— I began to gasp. Her body is taut, like violin strings. She is all tension-release-tension. Every moment between movements is a mesmerizing still-life. Every gesture is a full extension; she has full range of movement in every centimeter of her body. She has perfect concentration, she cuts space like a high priestess, and she subordinates her ego completely to the piece.

After the show, we went backstage to meet Belinda. We were so overwhelmed with her performance that we hugged and kissed her and told her how marvelous she was and she got all shy and crumbly. She had dislocated her arm during the performance and popped it back in, and now it was beginning to swell. I have always thought of dancers as martyrs. Real dancers are. I wondered what had given Belinda, a Southwestern Indian woman, the desire to enter the rarefied world of ballet. And, even more curious, why she chose to do the muscular, angular Horton technique wearing toe shoes? Belinda explained to us why she uses toe slippers in her ballet work. "I was raised on a Pueblo," she said, "and those formative years were very important to me. When I first saw toe slippers they reminded me of deer's hooves, and I knew I had to dance that way."

As we were talking, a weird thing happened. My mind floated to a white doctor I had met in Santa Fe who worked in the Indian hospital. I wondered what the quality of medicine was like for Indians today, and I made a mental note to call him and speak further to him. Suddenly I blinked with incredulity as the very same doctor showed up. It turned out that he was Belinda's doctor and he came to see her dance.

I decided to secretly continue my little mental adventure. "I wish we could spend more time with these people," I said to myself. Poof! We were invited by Belinda to go out for drinks with her friends. I sat across the table from a big, hefty, mighty Pit River Indian woman artist from northeast California named Jean La Marr. She is one of the few Indian women printmakers in the country. We began to talk, and she told me that the California gas and electric company had stolen her people's land and now the Indians have no light because they can't afford to pay the electricity bills to the people who stole their territory. Much of their language and customs are gone, but they are trying to preserve what is left by any means possible. How come I lived in California and I never knew this? I had never even heard of Pit River Indians. I had a sudden thirst to know more and more and more about the Indian culture. It went beyond mere curiosity for a television show.

We arrived back at our *casita* in Santa Fe at 2:30 A.M., and I lay awake for a long time in bed. Once again my mind began to churn.

27

How would I find out more? What was the way into this culture? I was awakened by the phone. I picked it up. It was Filiberto Kuru'es, a dark, handsome, mysterious-looking Pasqua Yaqui man. He had gotten our number from Beaver. He was the first Indian to be certified from a medical school—-he is a dentist who dropped out to pursue an artistic life. "Do you remember me?" he asked.

Of course I remembered him. I had met him at the Pasqua Easter ceremonies last spring in Arizona. I had been very impressed by Filiberto, who walks between a twentieth-century city life, crass and materialistic, and his people's spiritual life, where he dwells in peace with the Flower People of Yaqui lore and observes ceremonial seasons and cycles that are in harmony with nature. The Pasqua Yaqui Indians have such extended ceremonies and preparations that it is hardly possible to hold down long-term jobs in the "real world." How can you tell your boss at IBM that you need two months off to pray and prepare? So, most of them work as garbage men. They pick up rags and recycle what other people throw away. They live communally and in poverty. But they trade it for spiritual cohesion and spiritual wealth.

Filiberto is Yaqui, but he is no garbage man—he knows how to make a bridge and prepare a crown! He is also, apparently, the fantasy object of more than one single woman. With his black skin, black hat, and black cloak, he looks every bit the Indian Don Juan! Filiberto does not make polite chitchat. Either he plays with words and makes puns, or else he speaks in mystical Indian lingo, words shrouded in metaphor and mystery. He is not the first Indian I have met who speaks like this. I think it is a way of Indians giving white people what they think white people want to hear—a sort of bogus Indian wisdom. It conforms to the white notion that every Indian over the age of forty is a wizened medicine man and when he speaks, eagles soar overhead and flutes play in the background. It is also a way for Indians to hide what they really feel and think. "I wish he would get real," I think. "I wish he would speak from the heart."

I have no idea how it happened, but suddenly Filiberto was speaking about his feelings. He told me about a serious back problem he has to contend with. "I have been a slave to it," he said. "But I've got a choice where to put my attention." I paused when Filiberto said this. He decided that he was going to focus on something other than his pain. Healing is a DECISION. Maybe I could DECIDE not to pay attention to fears. I would try to remember that.

Paul was in the kitchen, making blue-corn pancakes for breakfast. "Hey, Paul," I said, "what's going on here? We were told how difficult it was going to be for us in Indian country. How come we had been invited by Beaver to a wedding and then a powwow? Why did Fay open up to us? How did I 'get' the information about Drew's mother just by looking at him? How come we got seats at Belinda's performance? Why did Belinda's doctor show up when I was thinking about him? How come I wished for it and Filiberto just got real? All I have to do is THINK about something and it materializes. Why? Can you tell me why?"

"Nice consistency," Paul said, as he mixed the batter. He licked his finger and smiled. My husband Paul was acting like an Indian!

2

The Right Heart

We've been so busy lately that I completely forgot to be worried, which is very unlike me. After only a few weeks, there is an uncanny sense of HOME here. It's not our place, but we've met so many people and gotten such an abundance of invitations that we already have a feeling of belonging. The invitations come from everywhere—Indians at Pueblos, the maintenance man, people we meet while eating somewhere, friends of new friends who call out of the blue. It is a great relief to talk endlessly and words like "deal" and "agent" never come up. I realize what a drain it is on the spirit to be caught up in the Hollywood machinery. Here, the spirit is a frequent subject of conversation. So are credos. Who you are is determined by what you believe.

Our Indian friends say you can be a fool sometimes. You do not have to act perfectly. You're not God. It's absurd to think you are, or to play at it. You have to have a "right heart" . . . and after that, you are only human. People aren't always judging you. What a soothing thought.

"What are you doing?" I ask Filiberto, who sits in a corner at a gallery opening, watching a drunken man badgering an exasperated woman.

"Just watching a man act like a fool."

"Why don't you intervene?" I inquire.

"I don't have to *do* anything. What goes around comes around."

"You mean the woman will eventually deck him? Or a security guard will drag him into the men's room and shove his head in the bowl?"

Filiberto laughs. "All I know is that if someone acts poorly, it will come back to him," he says. "The way he's behaving, that man is just giving himself enough rope to hang himself."

"Filiberto," I say, as I watch the dentist-philosopher, draped in black, shifting his position on his chair and wincing, "are you in pain?"

"I'm looking at the paintings," he answers.

The Grand Inquisitor is itchy; I grill Filiberto a little more.

"How come you left your own reservation? Why did you come to Santa Fe?"

Filiberto grins. "I guess I came here for a healing."

Filiberto is not the only one. Many people seem to come to Santa Fe for healing. I can't quite get the story straight, but there is some sort of energy vortex here. It is supposed to be one of the earth's power spots. The first week as I was walking through La Posada Inn, I met a manager, and within moments he told me the tale of his healing. How he wandered the earth under a cloud of depression, metaphorical knife to the throat, wanting to do himself in. He came here and thought it was a huge mistake. He sat on a park bench and wept for himself and for his inability to enjoy life. And then it was as if the town held up a mirror to him. It is so very intense here. He saw that he was really anchored in a doom and gloom mindset, and he brought this baggage with him wherever he went. And when he saw himself as he really was, in a flash IT happened. What all the years of therapy had failed to effect. He began to let go of old patterns, of the doom and gloom mindset. Now it has been three months. He is joyous. And yet sometimes, he looks over his shoulder, mourning for a part of himself that is gone. The depressed part. He has found new impetus and new life here. This is a common story. People run out of money, out of steam, out of job ideas, but it is here the healing journey begins. I wonder if it is because of the presence of the Indians in the environs. Secretly, I wonder if the healing journey will happen to me . . .

Tonight we go to have dinner with Arnold Herrera, about fifteen minutes outside of Sante Fe. Arnold, an open-faced man with a halo of gray hair, gestures a lot when he speaks . He is a drummer from Cochiti, a Pueblo that is known for drum-making. Arnold writes traditional Pueblo songs. Arnold sings. He is always smiling and laughing. Nothing appears to bother him. I tell Arnold that he seems to walk the face of the earth lightly. "No," he corrects me, "I walk it with intention. I know where I am going. If I walk over a man and my heart is right, maybe *he* is in the wrong place."

Arnold's wife is on an extended condolence call, so he is alone with his three boys. Suddenly, as he speaks, he grows serious and stops laughing. His voice gets lower, and Paul and I almost fall from the edge of our seats as we lean forward to hear him.

Arnold starts talking about death. "I don't know what to say about things like that. Our Maker has a plan for us all. But I know how we Indians act. We go and take the family in. They just move in with us. We rent out their old house or apartment. We make them feel useful and important and make their life busy and meaningful, or else the wife follows soon after the husband."

Arnold speaks of solitude, and how important it is. He writes many of his songs when he goes high into the mountains to gather aspen wood to make his drums. He writes songs when he is on the road. He speaks Keres, and it seems to be a multi-tiered language; there is a "daily language" and a very sophisticated literary language that the respected elders use to speak to each other. There are many descriptive words for things in the natural world. For example: there is a word for "sun that spreads its beams," another for "sun that showers its light to the earth," another for "sun that spreads out across the horizon." This comes from thousands of years of close observations of nature. Paul remarks that because ours is an acquisitive society, we have only one word for things in nature—tree, sun, moon, sky, grass. But we have many names for things you can BUY—for example, we don't just say car, but Chevy, Mercedes, Volvo, Honda, etc. Suddenly English seems so impoverished. I long to understand more of nature and to know how to open my eyes and really see it. I stand in the middle of it, surrounded by so much, and see so little. I notice that tonight's sunset is shades of white and gray. The colors of a Persian cat. "Good," says Paul. "Usually you don't even notice that there *is* a sunset!"

Arnold tells me about his father, who was crippled, but who did not see himself as a cripple, and who did not act like a cripple. He dragged his leg behind him and climbed the mountains to hunt. He ran all over the Pueblo, leading a full life. His mind conquered his body. And this was Arnold's living lesson—"Indians teach by example," he says. Now every day Arnold gets up smiling, he sings, because his mind has been trained to conquer adversity. In fact, he doesn't even see it as adversity. It's just part of life.

Arnold grows silent for a moment. Paul gestures to me to sit and enjoy the peace, but I am possessed by the Grand Inquisitor and begin to ask questions. Arnold laughs at me. "You're not a Wanna-Be, like some Anglos," he says. "You're a Wanna-Know!!" Then he tells me a tale of his father's deathbed. His father was the elder responsible for half of Cochiti. And on his deathbed he pointed his finger at Arnold and designated him as next in line, even though Arnold was third from the eldest, and not the eldest child. Now Arnold has to assume that role. If someone calls from Cochiti and needs help, he must be there. If there is a dispute, a problem, he is on call. An honor, yes. But also a tremendous, relentless responsibility.

"Tell me about your grandfather," I beg Arnold. I have no idea WHY I want to know everything. Ever since I arrived here, I have developed an insatiable NEED TO KNOW. "I'm driven by curiosity," I whisper to Paul. "Tell me to stop asking questions." Paul shrugs. "Birds have to fly and fish have to swim," he says.

"Ah, my grandfather," Arnold says, and his eyes moisten with affectionate memory. "When I was young, my grandfather said to me, 'Look to the land to the east of Cochiti.' " Arnold remembered the words, but had no idea what his grandfather meant. "Many years later," Arnold continued, "a man arrived from Guadalajara in Mexico and told me that he had found an important paper in the museum there and had a photocopy with him. He showed it to me, but I couldn't understand it. It was in an old form of Spanish, no longer in use. The paper was finally translated in the Spanish department at a university in Colorado. It proved that the land to the east of Cochiti was appropriated by Uncle Sam, and never sold. It still belonged to Cochiti. Many years of bureaucratic maze-work in Washington later, twenty-five thousand acres have been returned to Cochiti. Now I finally know what my grandfather meant."

Arnold's house is a sty. Lenny's apartment is a sty—with piles of clothing, papers, and half-eaten food. The inside of his refrigerator looks like it has been ransacked and abandoned by a pack of ferocious rats. House after house is a cluttered, messy junkheap. But after ten minutes with the inhabitants, the surroundings dissolve and it just doesn't matter. I guess cleaning and housekeeping aren't top priorities. "That's why you like Indians," Paul says, very clearly referring to the fact that even if I were homeless, I would have someone cleaning for me once a week.

I decide not to pay attention to this assault on my missing domestic gene, and focus instead on the word "Indian." What, in fact, is the politically correct word to use? Some people insist on using "Native American," but I find this to be a big mouthful. Other preferences include "Tribal Americans," and "Indigenous People." Then there are those who are comfortable with the word "Indian" and refer to themselves that way, even though they know that the name "Indian" was given to them at the time of Columbus when it was erroneously assumed that the *Niña, Pinta,* and *Santa Maria* had landed in the Indies.

It suddenly occurs to me that the problem is not unique to Indians. What should we call our dark brothers? Blacks? Afro-Americans? Negroes? And how do we designate the descendants of the Spanish in the New World? Hispanics? Latinos? Chicanos? Mexicanos? Of course there is a problem with names, because there is a problem with identities. They are all minorities and their self-definition is often at odds with the definition given to them by the dominant culture.

"What should I call you?" I ask Arnold, trying to be culturally sensitive, and hoping he will give me a definitive answer. But Arnold just shrugs.

"Look, it's easier for me to say 'Indian,' so is it okay if I use that term, knowing that I do it with a 'right heart'?"

Again, Arnold shrugs. "Call me Arnold," he says simply.

When we leave Arnold's house, I tell Paul that I wish we could have stayed all night. There is so much I want to learn.

"But it's midnight. Enough. You asked so many questions you might as well be a writer on 'Jeopardy'!" he exclaims.

"I wish I could ask more."

"Tomorrow."

"No, tonight."

Paul smirks, thinking I am being ridiculous, but as soon as we walk in the door, the phone rings: an answer to my wishes!

"Can you talk?" asks Don, an older man who suffers from insomnia and likes to phone instead of watching late-night talk shows.

I lie back on the sofa contentedly, throwing Paul a triumphant look.

Don has lived with Indians for years, and he calls to share his insights with me. Although I have never met him, we have established a phone relationship. As he talks, it sounds like he's sipping through a straw.

"When whites come to Indian land, they have to leave their white thinking behind them. Completely. There's a lot out there for them, if they can learn to discern the fakes. There are a lot of fake medicine men out there. Just learn how to listen."

34

The Right Heart

I try to listen and not to talk. I try not to ask too many questions. But I can't seem to do either. I wonder: if you don't talk, how in the world are you supposed to make conversation? If you're a quiet blob, why would anyone talk to you? If you don't ask questions of people, you end up talking about yourself, which is totally boring. So if you don't talk about *you* and you don't ask about *them*, what in the world do you speak about?

"Indians are tuned in to the natural world," Don tells me. "Much more than white people are."

I tell Don that I think white people are handicapped. They are cut off from their five senses. "Yes," he says. "They live in their heads. Their heads are so full of stuff their senses are literally cut off."

When I go to bed, I try to be kinesthetically aware. What do I smell? Taste? Hear? See? Feel? Before I know it, I have fallen asleep.

When I awake, Paul brings me breakfast and a newspaper in bed. He has circled a strange event: "Painting with Aborigines from Australia." I smile up at him: he knows just what I like!

"Come on," he says. "Adventures with other indigenous people!"

We arrive at a dirt area next to a local museum that has been cleared for two very dark-skinned aboriginal men who are doing dreamtime paintings. Those of us who show up are invited to help. Do I? Don't I? Is my life going to be ruled by my handicap of fear? Am I going to stand on the quay and watch the ship of life sail away? I decide to act like Arnold's father and pretend I don't have a handicap at all. I walk forward and join in.

A few other people pick up brushes and begin to paint dots under the artists' direction. I sit down next to an aboriginal man wearing a broad-brimmed hat. Dinny, as "my" painter is called, indicates a color and an area to fill, and then I have to make dots with twigs or the back-end of a paintbrush. Dinny indicates, through summary gestures, if the dots should be closer, or if I should fill in more of the area.

About two minutes into the dot-making, it occurs to me that this is not just about painting, but a sort of meditation is going on. All the other white painters dot and then drift away, but I stay, and try to have a little conversation with Dinny in his language—Walpri. There are a few white translators, all pretty supercilious, and they explain, with painful condescension, that the paintings tell creation stories, and that the painters don't "own" the stories any more than parents "own" a child.

35

"You mean Dinny is the caretaker for the stories that are being painted today?" I ask.

A translator nods.

"He watches over the stories, making sure they are told correctly, ensuring their survival?"

He nods again.

I knew it! I knew they weren't just dots!

In Dinny's culture, the word for "knowledge" is the same as the word for "hear." In other words, it is an oral culture, and you "get it" by listening. (Aha! This comes up again! The transmission of information and a set of values through stories, just as in the Pueblo Indian culture.)

The aboriginal creation stories are told to the children once a year. If they don't listen and recall, they have to wait another year to get it. So a story is an event, and the listening becomes very important.

To the aboriginals, time is not linear. The Creation myth they paint is happening now, and the painters are part of it. In the execution of the painting, they actually participate in Creation. Their paintings, like their language, are not symbolic or iconic. What I am working on is not a picture of two brothers; it IS the two brothers. Each painter creates the story anew as he paints it. He is both the creator and the caretaker: the artistic parent.

Part of the reason for the aborigines' visit to the United States is to meet with Navajo medicine men and compare sand paintings. As I continue making dots, I ask Dinny if he's excited about meeting his Indian counterparts. The translator indicates that perhaps Dinny and his friend won't go to meet the Navajo after all. They don't like to go to others' ceremonies. They don't like to intrude. They just like to paint.

I feel very privileged to be allowed to paint, and very humbled by the opportunity.

"You don't have to feel humble," Dinny says to me through his translator. "Just paint."

I concentrate. I focus. I finish the white dots and begin to make dots in pink. Time goes by and I no longer notice where we are or who is around. When I look up, Dinny is nodding at me.

"Palala," he says.

I squint at him. "Palala?"

"Very good painting," says the translator.

I can't remember a compliment that makes me feel this proud. "Hey,

Dinny, I'm doing palala work, huh?" I squeal. I make a few more dots, and ask him, very hopefully, "Palala?"

As the painting nears completion it is announced that it will go on sale for a thousand dollars.

"Don't I get a discount for having worked on it?" I ask Dinny.

"No. The price goes up for you. Don't you ordinarily have to pay to go to school?"

I put the last dot on the canvas, and it begins to hail. What timing! As Paul and I run to the car, I hear an Indian man telling a tourist that this is a male rain—heavy and violent. Soon the gentler female rains will come and then it will be the end of the rainy season.

As we drive home, I tell Paul I think it's odd that I painted all day and he stood and watched.

"It's not odd," he says, "it's the way we are. You throw yourself into things. You get absorbed by the dots and the task. I stay back a bit and get the overall view."

I like that description. As we pull into the compound where our *casita* is located, I look up and I notice the sky. There is a 180-degree panoramic view. To the right, it is steel gray and stormy. In front of us, it is blue and full of white clouds. To the left, moderately gray and awash with clouds. Like three different paintings at the same time. Nature's triptych. I've been alive all these years, and it takes coming to Santa Fe to notice that there is a sky!

In the evening, we are invited to supper at the home of Lilly and Mark, a very wealthy couple who moved here from Malibu, and who have a custom-built home, in the shape of a moon, with views of the desert and mountains from every room.

"Why are you so interested in *Indians*?" they ask me.

"Well," I answer, nibbling on a piece of jalapeño quiche and twirling my fork around delicate pieces of exotic salad, "I think they have answers to questions I don't even know how to ask."

Lilly grunts disapprovingly and asks me if I would like a tour of the clothing stores in town.

"Judie recycles," Paul tells her politely, meaning that I'm still wearing my prom dress for formal occasions.

"The Indians here aren't very interesting," Lilly continues. "They have no money and there's a big drinking problem."

She has made up her mind in advance about most things. When people do that, there is no room for anything new to come in. Her husband, Mark, is very stubborn, but he seems to be willing to open his mind. He starts off the meal saying that I should stop being so obsessive in my search to understand the Indian way of thinking and living. And if I am afraid of things, I should back off. The best thing for me would be to write superficially and commercially about the Indians, finish the TV project, and get on with my life. But by the end of the evening, when I have told Mark about sweatlodges and powwows, about drum-makers and conversations about death, his eyes grow wide.

"I wish I had done that when I was your age," he says. Then, out of earshot of Lilly, he leans forward across the table and whispers to me. "Go for it. Learn everything you can. Forget your fears. Really dive in there. I'm rooting for you. Don't be like us. All we know about Santa Fe is the shops and restaurants."

Lilly goes into the kitchen and I tell Mark that we are having a hard time with the food at the Pueblos. "You see, Paul and I are not meat eaters. When we go to the Pueblos, we are offered chili and it's made with red meat and lard and we don't know how to handle that. It's a great insult not to eat, so we eat and then feel lousy afterwards. Boy, it's a treat to eat here and not have to deal with the saturated fats of animal flesh."

Mark nods understandingly as Lilly arrives with the next dish: chateaubriand!

The next morning I get up and nervously wonder how I am going to proceed with my Native American research. I had been compiling a list of names of Pueblo Indians who sounded fascinating, but what was I supposed to do: just pick up the phone and call them? I had been told time and again that Indians do not play by white rules, and they certainly wouldn't be receptive if I called them on the phone. I'd have to go there in person.

"Try it anyway," a little voice tells me. So I gulp a few times, wet my whistle with two cups of herbal tea, and dial the first name on my list: Mary Sena. My handwritten notes are so illegible, that I can't even decipher why I wanted to contact her.

"I'm glad you called instead of coming by," she says. "I'm very busy and if you knocked at the door, I wouldn't have time for you."

Another white stereotype of Indians shattered. And, within minutes of talking to Mary, a second stereotype bites the dust. Indian women are supposed to be nurturers who spend time in the kitchen as

The Right Heart

they laboriously and lovingly prepare endless quantities of food. Mary is an Indian woman who HATES TO COOK. (She must be related to me.)

Although Mary does not spend time in the kitchen, her time is certainly accounted for. She has five kids, is a grandmother, and she and her sister have cows.

"It's actually lucky you found me here at all. We've been out all morning trying to find our cows; we just lost two of them."

In addition to field and foyer, Mary also drives a school bus, eats lunch every day with her kids, grows or farms (What's the right word? What's EVER the right word?) alfalfa and corn, makes pottery and embroiders, and is trying to revive the old style of this art at her Pueblo. In addition, she is preparing her crafts for the eight northern Pueblo crafts show this summer. I volunteer to help her in the fields, or to come to school, or ride on the bus, or whatever. I can hear her smiling on the other end: what use would this urban Anglo be to her?

Even though Mary protests vigorously that she has no time to speak to me, she opens up and begins speaking very readily.

Mary says her Pueblo, like all the Indian villages, used to be governed by a chief, war captains, and a traditional religious leader called a Cacique, but the dominant culture imposed their own form of government. Running the day-to-day affairs of the Pueblo is an appointed council of nine men. Mary has been put down, degraded, and insulted by them. She takes a moment of silence and then goes into detail.

"My first husband was a non-Indian from Oregon. The marriage didn't work out. I kept growing and I finally left him in the dust. He is still trying to grow up."

Another pause, and then she continues.

"I virtually raised our children alone. It was very difficult for me. I went to the tribal council for help because they have many benefits to bestow in the form of money, grants, and housing. But I got none of those benefits, and they told me it was because I married a white man. Worse than that, they told me I had to leave my Pueblo altogether. I should follow my white husband to Oregon and have him provide for me.

"I was completely trusting, and I believed what the council told me. I packed up my children and my belongings and followed my husband to Oregon. Then my mother called me from the Pueblo. She told me that the council members' own kids married non-Indians and they

39

were given houses at the Pueblo!! She told me to her to come back home. Well, I couldn't come right away, because I had set up my family in Oregon.

"As soon as I could, I came home to my Pueblo, but nothing had changed. Again, no home was given to me. I was miserable. I finally got a family home—a run-down adobe near the Plaza that only my sister had been living in. There was a terrible storm, and my little children were there in that house with me. The roof leaked and one of the walls fell in. Cold air was coming through the poorly sealed windows. I cried all night and then went to the council again and asked them for help. They said no—I wasn't needy enough. There were lots of people with children who were needier than me."

"That's awful," I say, commiserating, but Mary doesn't seem to hear me.

"I guess they didn't like me," Mary says. She reflects a moment. I can hear her thinking. I keep waiting for her to sigh, or take a deep breath, but none of our Indian friends here react that way. They grow silent, and you know they are thinking and feeling.

"They didn't like me because they didn't like my father. He died about twelve years ago. About the time I married my second husband, Paul, who is Cree. My father was an outspoken man. He was a traditionalist. He said we Indians should keep to our own ways. Our old ways. Our old form of religion and government. They punished me— they punished my kids for that. They also punished my father and his father before him."

There is another silence. Although Mary doesn't say anything, I know that she is reliving the pain of the experience.

"Then they started building new homes at my Pueblo," Mary continues. "I applied. They turned me down, but said I was on top of the list for the next round. The next round came and the next round and the next, but my name was never on the list.

"I got really ANGRY at the injustice. But if I confronted someone on the council, he would always say that was what the *others* wanted. No one would take the blame. They would throw it onto others.

"Nothing has changed," Mary insists. "People who marry outsiders are on probation for five years by the council to see if the new spouses take to the Pueblo life. With my second husband, who is Cree, it's been FIFTEEN YEARS and still he is on probation. They're still punishing me."

Mary explains to me about the council. "It's made up of all men, and men are told not to show their feelings. You never know how they feel. They just go along, following the strongest party, and the strongest party is corrupt. The council does things for its own good, out of greed."

People at Mary's Pueblo are angry, but Mary says she is not angry any more. She learned to accept things. Anger only hurts her. When people are mean to her, she treats them nicely. It drives them nuts.

As Mary speaks, I remember something that happened to me when I first came to California after living for many years in Europe and Morocco. I moved into a huge apartment complex while looking around for more permanent quarters. There was a nasty old man who lived there whom everyone hated because he got on their nerves and drove them crazy. He was bitter and mean. He yelled and groused. I decided to be exceedingly nice to him. Every day I talked to him, and asked him about himself and his kids and his life. Over time, he just melted. When I left the complex, he came to say goodbye and told me how much he liked me and would miss me. It was a human experiment. The memory links me to Mary.

"Many times," Mary continues, "my Cree husband has been tempted to pack it in and leave the Pueblo, but I say no, because that's just what the council wants. This is my land. My people. Even if they do this to me, they are my people."

"If there is such resentment of the council, how do they stay in power?" I ask Mary.

"They talk down to people and scare them. This is how they maintain their power. Through power tactics and intimidation."

I take a deep breath, trying to absorb what Mary has to say about self-government at her Pueblo in particular and at Pueblos in general. Far from the rosy Shangri-Las I would like them to be, they are rife with corruption, favoritism, political factionalism and male chauvinism. On a spiritual and ceremonial level they are perfect little islands in the middle of America, but when it comes to social and interpersonal problems, they are part of the mainstream archipelago.

We talk a bit about artists. Mary tells me that at Indian Market in August in Santa Fe, rich people come from all over the world to buy from the best Indian artists. They come before 6 A.M. and wait by the booths. By 9 A.M. everything is sold. The Indian artists ask outrageous prices and people pay them. The artists are getting corrupted by money. They will do anything for money. Sell anything. Their work and art suffer from it. (Hey! Might as well be Hollywood!)

"It makes me sad," she says. "We have our Indian ways, and that's something more important than anything money can buy. It's sad what happens to my people. I will not charge too much at Indian Market. I feel that I am rich and I have everything.

"Money corrupts my people. My Pueblo has a million dollars in the bank. Can you imagine that? There is so much that needs to be done, but the council just wants to keep it sitting there. They say they need it in reserve in case they ever get sued. Sued?! Why worry about that when our people are running around hungry."

There is a long silence. I am not sure, but I think Mary is crying now. Crying? She surprises me again when she breaks her silence with a laugh.

"I'm the only cowgirl at the Pueblo, " she tells me, giggling. "In the old times, a lot of families had cows. But the grandfathers died off and a lot of the grandchildren had jobs and couldn't keep the cows. They sold them or ate them. I'm glad my sister and I still have cows. It's important because it makes us self-reliant. The council preaches self-determination, but doesn't act on it. Cows help make you self-sufficient. We have just enough beef for our families. The council doesn't even know the meaning of the words 'self-sufficient.' "

"You are very lucid," I tell Mary. "Very clear-thinking."

"I HAVE TO BE clear-thinking," Mary says forcefully. "I have to pass this on to my kids." Like all Indians I have met, she is excruciatingly aware of the generations to come.

"Cows are tiring, dirty," Mary continues. "The council doesn't like that I keep cows. They ask each other: 'Where does Mary get the time and money to do it? She doesn't have the education to do all of this.' They resent the fact that they can't beat me down. I don't mind getting dirty. When it comes to getting down on their hands and knees, to getting dirty, the council can't do it."

For the first time, an Indian person really talks to me about Indian squalor. Kids don't know how to clean their rooms. No one teaches them. Their parents live in filth. It is something you have to be taught.

I am confused as Mary talks. Indian ceremonies are so powerful— why don't they help people to act better in their daily lives?

"After all," Mary says, "Indians are just people."

A busy day goes by. I am sitting in the *casita,* guzzling a cold glass of lemonade and wondering which Native American person I should speak to next, when the phone rings.

"Hi, this is Filiberto. What's news by youse?"

The Right Heart

I like him so much better now that he has stopped using elliptical speech; Indians think this is what whites want to hear, and it keeps them from speaking directly.

When they do speak directly, it is remarkable to me. They share with you their innermost feelings and beliefs. They will tell you what they stand for. It's right-down-to-the-basics, and the system they operate by is very coherent so it is easy for them to situate themselves vis-à-vis any given situation or problem.

The problem at hand is that Filiberto is trying to get a grant for an Indian project. He is banging his head against a bureaucracy, and the bureaucracy won't budge.

"I momentarily got unbalanced and thrown by it. All the waiting, the stalling, the procedures. But all I need is a reminder of who I am and where I come from, and I get back into balance again."

Filiberto dips into that incredible font of discipline and patience that Yaquis have, and that all reservation Indians seem to share. It helps him deal with the frustrations of daily life. I realize that this is the problem with the "me" generation. It's not that we are so smug and selfish. The problem is that when there is any real problem or adversity, we do not have the tools to deal with it. Our upbringing was permissive, and we are not equipped with patience and discipline. My grandparents' generation, which came from "the old country" in Europe, learned how to deal with hardship. My parents' generation learned too. I am trying to learn patience and discipline when it comes to dealing with my fears and emotions. But I do not have an Indian reservation and its set of values to fall back on. It is hard to pull back from your emotions and tough things out.

Filiberto speaks to me about Yaquis and their interpretation of Christianity. The cross symbolizes MOTHER for them. "During our Easter doings, we carry the cross. Symbolically—and symbolism is at the core of our society—we carry the mother who has suffered for us all. In the middle of the cross is the heart. The cross symbolizes the four sacred directions and each direction points to one of the world's principal religions. The Yaqui had stories of Bethel before contact with Christianity. It is part of our creation myth of coming out of a tree. So when we met with Christianity, there were many similarities already—like the fact that Bethel equals Bethlehem."

As Filiberto speaks, I recall the time I spent with the Pasqua Yaquis in Arizona, attending their Easter ceremonies. I FELT everything Filiberto is talking about when I walked with the wailing woman, fol-

43

lowing the man who carried the cross. I felt the woman power, even though I could not articulate it at the time. The Yaquis bring a pagan sensibility to Christianity. They keep both worlds going. They have a deep, direct relationship to the story of Christ, and I experienced with great intensity their interpretation of the suffering, the pain, and the enlightenment and catharsis it brings.

"Now tell me about death, Indian-style," I ask Filiberto, without bothering to use any transition in our conversation. His mind is extremely fluid and nonlinear and he doesn't need any transitions, so this is just fine.

"The plants give up their lives so that we may eat. And the beautiful animals sacrifice themselves and lay down their lives so that we may eat too. There is a reason for these deaths, then, in the scheme of things," he tells me.

"Fine. And in the scheme of things, why do people die?" I ask him.

"The experiences we have and the feelings we feel are passed along in the genes. This is why, when we have a strong emotion or know joy, we can really FEEL them—they have been lived before and are now part of the gene pool. We can recognize them and experience them fully—because they have been experienced before. So when we die, our experiences are passed on too. Does this make sense to you?" Filiberto asks.

"Maybe." I think to myself. I resolve to ask other Indians what they think about death. How do they understand human death so that they can make peace with it?

When I get off the phone, I call my two television producers in Los Angeles. They sent me here to write a story that is loosely based on the life of Carl Hammerschlag, a white doctor who came to work with the Indians, and whose life was turned around by contact with them. I begin to wax eloquent about all I am learning and how deeply it is affecting me. I hear a judgmental silence on the other end of the phone.

"Cool it," the main producer says to me. "You don't have to understand it all. After all, there IS a white point of view too in our series. You have an Indian partner to present the Indian point of view. When Lenny gets back, he'll explain it to you."

I hang up the phone, and realize that I feel bad. Hurt. Disappointed.

"Those feelings are part of your gene pool," Paul tells me.

I determine to keep on probing and learning. In my heart, I know that part of it is to satisfy the work requirements of the television series. But I have a growing awareness that a lot of the learning is intimate, personal, for me, and for my development as a human being.

"Paul, do you think that I can ever learn from our Indian friends how to get over my fears?"

"I hope so," he says, but I'm not sure he's paying attention. There are ants in our kitchen and, with his closed fist, he is offing them.

At night, we go to a Native American video showing at the Center for Contemporary Arts. First up is Jean La Marr's *Double Visions*— a two-video installation about Indians' attitudes toward the celebration of Columbus discovering America. The Indians in the room, of all ages and walks of life, are unanimous in their reaction to the advent of Columbus. THEY were on these shores when Columbus came. THEY discovered HIM. And he was a plunderer, a rapist, the ignominious man who set in motion the colonial brutalization and murder of the indigenous population. He was also the man who harmed and destroyed Mother Earth. To the Indians, these are not idle words. They really think of the earth as their mother. Biologically. It is their mother who gave them life and they love and protect her.

"Yes," Paul comments under his breath, "but then why do they throw garbage on her?"

"I guess they aren't perfect. They're just human beings," I say, having learned a bit from Mary. It is becoming increasingly apparent to me that Paul, although he appreciates it, is a lot less romantic about Indian life than I am.

In the video room, an Indian man stands up and points out that different peoples have different creation myths. The arrival of Columbus in America is the white American creation myth. It reassures us and makes us feel connected to this land. Couldn't we find another, slightly more noble, story?

On the way home, I comment to Paul about how strange the weather is in northern New Mexico. As I speak, I am proud that I am becoming aware of the forces of nature around me. One minute it is sunny, and we dress in summery clothes. Then, suddenly, the sky blackens and it rains. Aha, you think, rainy weather. We sort of bundle up and then presto! the sun shines. So we are sweaty and dragged down in our bulky clothes by the humidity. We shed the clothes and then, of course, it starts to rain again.

Today is the third day of rain and thunderstorms. Brazen zigzag lightning cuts the sky like some experiment in a school science lab gone wacko. Thunder booms and shakes our little *casita*. I snuggle closer to Paul in bed.

"Hey, Paul," I tell him, "we are really lucky."

I show him an article in the newspaper teaching non-Indians about going to a Pueblo. There are rules about behavior. There are lists of tourist organizations that, for a fee, take non-Indians to the Pueblos and show them around. There is even the possibility of eating in a real Indian house.

"We get to bypass the tourist route. With very little effort we have gotten straight to these wonderful people. We're lucky, lucky, lucky. Aren't we?"

There is the sound of thunder coming from the bed next to me. Actually, it's the sound of Paul snoring.

He hasn't heard a word I've said.

3

Visiting the Ancient Ones

A call comes with an invitation to fly to New York City to teach a playwriting workshop. I was selected from many, many candidates, the pay is good, it would certainly be fun, and it's an opportunity to share what I know with other people who are eager to learn it. I tell them I will get back to them in an hour, after looking at my schedule.

First I wander around the *casita,* mumbling to myself. Then I hound Paul. Next I look in the mirror, force a rictus-like smile, and repeat over and over again: "I can do it, I can do it." But the truth is, I cannot do it. There is no way I can pick up a boarding pass, walk down the tunnel of doom, strap myself into a seat, and fly, suspended 40,000 feet in the air, trusting a pilot who was probably out carousing the night before, is perhaps emotionally unstable, and most likely has suicidal tendencies.

Feeling tremendous defeat, I pick up the phone and lie, saying I cannot come to New York because it's the same weekend as my cousin's wedding. I don't even *have* a cousin who is getting married. I'm just a coward.

"You'll get over your fears one day," Paul reassures me.

"How? How? Can you tell me that?"

"Maybe you'll outgrow them."

"Sure. Ha. I've never even outgrown adolescent acne."

"Well, then you'll learn how to overcome them."

"Fat chance. I've sampled more therapies than I've eaten Chinese dishes in my life."

I slump onto the grotesquely uncomfortable sofa in our tiny living room, and I notice that my breathing is labored. As a matter of fact, I can't draw a decent breath. It's the altitude, sucking up my oxygen. I get fearful, imagining myself in an iron lung.

The phone rings and it is Lenny Smallfeather, checking in from out-of-town. I am surprised he still remembers that he is my writing partner. I try to have a normal conversation with him, but I'm too panicky, so I tell him that I can't breathe. Instead of commiseration, I get a stern command.

"Stop taking your breath for granted!"

"What?"

"Breath is the gift of life. It's the difference between a cadaver and a vital being. Have you said 'thank you' to the Creator today for giving you breath?"

"Why should I say 'thank you' for my breath when I don't have any?"

When I hang up with Lenny, I grumble a few "thank yous" and eventually I leave the iron lung of my imagination and resume my life.

"Welcome back," Paul says with a smile. Whenever I am overcome by fear, I retreat. He says it's like living with an empty space.

The phone rings and it is Don, whom I still have never met.

He starts musing about his life with Native Americans.

"You know, Indians are very repressed. They have so many cultural taboos. That's why when they break out, they lose all control and go nuts. Alcohol is one example of this. Seeing a drunk Indian is not a pleasant sight. Their eyes glaze over, they become inarticulate, they are really gone. That's why many freeze to death outside or, staggering, fall to their deaths from mesa tops where they've lived all their lives. In fact, like winos and people from the Mongolian race, the Indians are missing an enzyme needed to break down alcohol and process it. It gets into their system in its pure form and packs an awful, deadly punch."

He says this in a very matter-of-fact way.

"I really love Indians, but it took me time to understand their ways. It's a whole different culture. Do you know, for example, that much of the Indian humor consists of putting you on and telling you things that are not true?"

I give a verbal nod. I, too, have found this to be the case. I have begun to wonder if much of what anthropologists transcribe so faithfully from Indian informants isn't a colossal joke that is taken seriously.

"When white folks get with Indians," Don continues, "all they want to do is ask questions, but you have to let go, slow down, down, down and get into their reality instead. They can sit and watch a cloud as it forms and dissipates. There's nothing to say about it, so they sit in silence. They are comfortable with that silence; the same silence makes us squirm. Sometimes, it's appropriate to just be at peace with them, and sit there. Watch a cloud, a mountain, a child. Let the questions in your mind go a bit.

"You see, the Indians are always watching you, to decide if they can trust you. If you come at them like an anthropologist, forget it. They're sick of being prodded and picked over. If they trust you, they'll talk to you. They teach by parable. If you are patient, they just may answer the question you were going to ask, without your having to ask it.

"Anglos have trouble listening. In a conversation, they are always busy thinking about what they are going to say next. Indians are not like that. When they talk, they talk, and when they listen, they really listen."

I sit in the minuscule kitchen, flicking ants off the table, sipping an herb tea, and trying to take in what Don has just told me. I hear a light *tap, tap* on the door, and Filiberto is standing there, dressed all in black.

"What's *doin'*?" I ask him.

"Everything that's not *don'ting*," he answers.

I tell him that I have been reading about Mayan/Aztec/Toltec culture before I fall asleep at night. He knows much about it, having studied Meso-American culture for years. His details are precise and fascinating. He knows as much as the experts I have been learning from. The more I speak to Filiberto, the more astonished I am by the breadth of his knowledge. But he comes on so quietly—in fact, he doesn't come on at all. It really takes time to learn the value of people, and then it's overwhelming. What you see is decidedly NOT what you get—you get much, much more. Judging people at first sight or even at first meeting is an absurdity. Let the onion unpeel and then— mmmm—yum-yummmmm—savor that delicious onion!

In the evening, we go to see *Tilai*, an African film, with Beaver. It has been recommended by several Indian friends. It's a tribal film, an indigenous film, a sparse Greek tragedy. As the film progresses, I become increasingly aware that she is tuned into the film on a different level from me. She leans over and whispers to me with comments like "Yeah, right, they'll listen to their father. Sure. Sure." Or "Oh, boy, is she gonna get it for that one!" Afterwards, we go to the Zia Diner and talk about it. When Paul quietly asks if she feels a familiarity about the film, she immediately pipes up that it has much in common with village life, and she gives some examples— the autocratic father, the fact that when one person in a family does something it influences everyone else in the family and changes the balance. She speaks at length about the suffocating closeness of the village, the fact that everyone knows everything, and the use of the land.

"Didn't you see?" she asks me. "In the film they use the earth to plow, to make huts, to make mortar."

In truth, I was following the story and the characters; I hadn't even noticed.

Then Beaver speaks about herself. How her father had been very autocratic and she ran away from home at the Pueblo at age sixteen. She went to an Indian reservation near San Diego and then landed, as a hippie, in Los Angeles. Years later, she came back to the res with a guy, and because her family liked HIM they figured she must be okay because HE liked HER.

Once again, we hear of the xenophobia of the Indian villages. Beaver's mother came from Zia and her father from Jemez. Because of ancient tribal rivalries, her mother could not live at Zia with him— so they had to go to his Pueblo, Jemez. The more Beaver speaks, the more it sounds like the film. Of course she responded differently from me! I wasn't exactly watching Long Island on the screen!

I look at the calendar next to my kitchen table, which Paul and I use as a desk, and I realize that we have been in Santa Fe for almost three weeks. I stand up to get a glass of cold water and I see Paul, in the doorway, laughing at me.

"What's so funny?" I ask.

"YOU," he answers. "You're walking like a ninety-year-old woman."

"Well, you know about my legs," I chide him.

"Oh, your legs. Of course!" he says, and laughs again.

I guess it's time to confess "the leg story," which started this morning. I got up and ow! I could barely drag my legs out of bed.

"Paul, get up! There's something wrong with my stumps!" I cried.

Paul rolled over in bed and grunted,"Hey, Jude, it's Charley Horse."

Of course! Instantly I flash back to what I did yesterday and the reason for the aching limbs becomes clear. It all began with a noon meeting I had scheduled with Dr. Doug White Wolf in an Espanola restaurant. All I knew about him was that he is an Indian educator, and he agreed to meet me.

"I'll come along," Paul tells me as I'm running out the door. He worries when I drive because I have no sense of geographic orientation.

At 12:20, with Paul at the wheel, we still have no sense of geographic orientation, and we are chasing our tails around Espanola, so I call Doug.

"I thought my directions to the restaurant were pretty explicit," he says.

"I guess I'll never be mistaken for an Indian scout," I joke.

I'm feeling a little miffed with Paul for insisting upon driving and then getting us lost. But when I return to the car, a severely nervously impaired man is leaning in the car window, drooling on Paul. Dear Paul is very decent and patient about it, and I love him for that so I forgive him.

There is a screech of brakes, and Dr. Doug drives up to meet us. I expected a gray-haired Indian elder, but instead I see an attractive man in his late thirties with shoulder-length thick black hair and honey-colored skin. (Indians are many shades, you know.)

Doug is so amazed that we couldn't find the restaurant by ourselves that he doesn't even trust us to follow him. We go, instead, to a cheapo New Mexican restaurant in the immediate environs. The food is very good, with the usual oozing red and green chiles sliding over our food, onto our plates, and down our chins.

As soon as we sit down, Doug starts to talk. Another silent Indian? Ha! This is the first time in my life that I have to ask my interlocutor to slow down, because I can't follow what he is saying.

Doug has spent years formulating his ideas about a way to revamp Indian education. The Anglo-American school system does not suit Native Americans, which is why so many of them drop out or do poorly at it. Indians must be taught the way they have always been taught. Doug breaks it down into five channels of learning. They go by so fast that I am not sure I remember them. (Even Paul is interrupting him at every turn with questions.) There is community learning (which includes family). There is spiritual learning (which includes rites and ceremonies). There is the mythological (which includes the storytelling from the oral tradition). There is nature. And there is . . . there is . . . well, there is one other category.

Doug is a highly intelligent man. He has lassoed the English language, and he drags it this way and that way. He is well versed in any subject you can name. As he explains it, he is a generalist in an era of "specialists." People are focused on the narrow field they have to know about. Indians have always had to know the skills it took for survival in nature. They were all, in a sense, generalists.

When we finish lunch, Doug directly but politely asks if HE can drive, and he takes over the wheel of our car. Within minutes we leave the town of Espanola behind us. We are now on the reservation of Santa Clara, and Doug's whole body language changes. He relaxes totally into the setting. We see small, hand-painted signs on the houses that read: "Pottery for sale." I control my hand from pressing on the door handle and my body from flying out of the car to shop.

The houses get more primitive, and therefore more attractive to my eyes. They are made of adobe, and the lines are very simple. We are now in the older part of the Pueblo, around the Plaza. I can see in the backyards the beehive-shaped ovens, called *hornos*. Just as I think we are getting out to walk, Doug heads even farther away.

Now we are at the Puye cliffs. I scan my brain and vaguely remember that these are prehistoric Indian ruins. Meanwhile, Doug, Paul, and I are chatting, and it is no light banter. The level of discourse is high, the rhythm is chaotic, the content is dense, the feeling is intense. We cut right to the bone and saw through each subject. Secretly, I am both proud and dismayed. Proud because I gave up any "agenda" with Doug, didn't take a notepad, and so the conversation is wonderfully free. Dismayed, because here we are again, plying him with questions.

We get out of the car, and the majestic ruins of the cliff-dwellers are above us and all around us. They are the color of sand, barely discernible to the untrained eye, and spread out under the afternoon sun. Doug tells us that he hasn't been to the ruins in a long time, and that he knows them well because he worked there as a kid. The minute we hit the ruins, he says, "This is where the people of Santa Clara used to live." I feel my heart race faster. My God! These cliff-dwellers were Doug's ancestors. The Anasazi. The Ancient Ones. For the first time, we are visiting ruins with a man whose roots are right in the ruins.

I make a big to-do about it, saying that the anthros tell us they don't know what happened to the cliff-dwellers, who mysteriously disappeared. Doug says it's nonsense, there was no mystery at all, and that they probably moved down from the hills because the source of water dried up, and they traveled on. He assures us that they were people who moved on every three generations anyway. Puye had been a particularly large community, so they stayed about three hundred years and then continued on.

We start climbing the hills to reach the ruins. We visit the lowest level, the cavelike houses, some with burnt ceilings from the fires. I comment that these dwellings really seem more sophisticated than modern houses, since no building at all was required—nature provided the framework and the architecture.

I'm babbling away, having a grand old time, and then, suddenly, we come to IT. A three- or four-story VERTICAL ladder, hanging there. And my heart drops. This is the way up to the next story. A woman is standing at the top of the ladder, hyperventilating. I look away.

My old fear of heights wells up inside of me.

"Ignore the fear," Paul whispers to me.

"Ignore it?! Do you think I am kidding? When I lived in Europe, rather than fly, I had to take *ships* to come home and visit my family!"

"Well, there are no ships here."

"Very funny."

Once again, I have come face-to-face with one of the paradoxes of life. Here I am, ecstatic to be with Dr. Doug, but mortified that, metaphorically speaking, there is only one way to get to the next level and it's by climbing right through FEAR. Doug quickly tells me that there is a long way around the mountain, a back way, that's all on terra firma. But my mind is made up. I will not be a coward. I will face MR. FEAR. I firmly grip the rails of the wooden ladder, feeling as brave as Joan of Arc.

I make it up one rung! Yay! Two rungs! Yay! Paul is already at the top, and he is calling down hints like: "Don't look behind you! Just concentrate on the rung in front of you!" And Doug is pacing around, seemingly bored by my travails. I am making excuses, loudly, a mile a minute. And then I stop making excuses, because I am heaving with fear. Finally, rung by rung, and following Paul's words, I make it to the top! Brava! You can imagine how elated I am and how the conversation flows like water because of the relief. We are on top of the ruin, walking around the houses,and Doug explains how Puye was probably like the Pueblo of Taos is today—a multi-story structure. He talks to us about complex irrigation and water drainage systems. We see the Pueblos in the distance, because it is a clear day, and we discuss how, in days of old, they probably had fire signals from Pueblo to Pueblo. I bemoan the fact that sign language and smoke signals are gone. Doug doesn't seem at all bothered by this. He shrugs and says that the times change, and what is necessary changes. There used to be smoke signals, and now there are computers. (The Pueblo philosophy that one should "accept the good change" echoes in my ears.)

I comment to Doug that this is a FEMALE ruin. I have no idea where THAT comes from, but I know it to be true. Doug nods. He knows it to be true too. It is docile, not bellicose. Gentle. You can feel the presence of women and children there. We talk about Chaco Canyon, the ruins I am dying to visit. I am almost afraid, because I know the power there is so strong. He confirms it. And he tells me how the presence of humans in recent years has altered two rocks at Chaco Canyon which form one of the most sophisticated solar calendars and observatories known to man. I am sad. I know of this place. I have heard of the two rocks. A strong wind kicks up.

And then, as laws of physics are wont to do, they suddenly present themselves at the most awkward times: what goes up must come down. The wind is blowing with gale force now, and suddenly there is a ladder for me to DESCEND.

"Doug," I ask him, "is there anything you are really afraid of?"

He scrunches up his face, thinking.

"Bugs? Snakes? Remnant dinosaurs?"

He shakes his head no.

I stand on the top of the ruin, flanked by two ostensibly fearless men, and I have to make a leap of faith to get going down this vertical horror with visions of being blown off to the horizon. Doug descends first. He stands on the ground and chimes in with Paul: "Keep your body close to the rungs. Don't look back." I breathe so loudly that Paul thinks it is the wind. No, it is *moi*, exhaling with a vengeance on each rung. Paul is now calling down: "Only eight to go . . . seven . . . six . . . five . . . three . . . two . . . ONE." I am down. I thank God, I am ready to get on my knees, I have made it.

I start to breathe normally as Doug tells us about the volcano that was responsible for this mountain. It was estimated to be over 29,000 feet high, and it was between one million and five million years ago. He picks up a piece of aerated lava—called "tuffa"—and it is very light. Almost like a Hollywood rock.

We are all chatting amicably and Doug is answering our queries and then—I cannot tell why this happens, but it happens—there is ANOTHER ladder to descend. Huge. Leading from security into the chasm of death. Doug says he is sure there must be a back way down, but this time I AM FIRM. I declare that I will like myself much better if I do it. And I do. Of course there is a repeat performance of panting and clinging and the coaching of the two men as though I were in labor. But the result is that I *do* like myself better when I arrive on the ground.

We then get into the car, with Doug driving, and head into a lush forest. There is a park ranger, and then another ranger, and we have to pay an entry fee. I am amazed that every Indian we meet is related to Doug. He asks solicitously about their families and we drive on. "We're all one big family," he says, smiling.

Now all civilization is behind us. Doug points out a sacred mountain. It is one of four sacred mountains. He confirms what we heard from Arnold about there being a special language that is accessible only to the elders. (Arnold speaks Keres and Doug speaks Tewa. Among the Pueblo people of the Rio Grande, there are three Tanoan dialects spoken. They have very mellifluous names: Tewa, Towa, and Tiwa. Keres is an entirely separate language.) Doug explains the multi-leveled nature of his language beautifully. The same stories are told at different times in your life and have different meanings for you when you are a child, when you are an adult, and when you are fifty or sixty. The story deepens, the language to tell the story deepens, and you get closer to the mystery of language, breath, and life. How wonderful! A culture with something to look forward to as you age, instead of the degradation our culture brings.

This day is a very special day. As we drive, I spot a hornytoad, a hawk killing a squirrel and, with a swoosh, lifting it by its throat and carrying it away, seven doe, and a blue bird. This is most extraordinary since I, like Woody Allen, usually see nothing special in the natural world ("Nature? It's just things, eating other things!"). I guess I am learning to open my eyes.

We alight from the car and stand in front of one of many lakes in this forest. Doug starts to salivate. He is an avid trout fisherman, and tomorrow the lakes will be stocked and a big tournament will begin. He is going to enter, and he describes how they will fry the trout with parsley and herbs and yum . . . yum . . . he is already licking his lips. Paul and he start to discuss fishing techniques—my generalist husband can discuss anything too.

Suddenly I get an idea. I clam up, and I nudge Paul to do the same. "Let's practice silence," I urge him. "Let's try to *hear* nature."

We hear one twitter of a bird, and then Doug starts talking. He continues to babble with us for the rest of the day. There is no silence. Another stereotype broken forever. Another plan of ours (to be silent) gone awry. Oh, well. Go with the flow.

It is wonderful to see Doug here in the forest, where his ancestors used to hunt. He is free and happy, like an unfettered kid. He tells us that when he was a young boy, he used to come with his friends and hide out behind the trees. They watched the lakes being stocked with fish. The minute the adult stockers were gone, they dove into the water, fishing with their hands, throwing fish at each other, carrying pails of trout home.

Suddenly Doug clears his throat, and we understand that it is time to get back in the car and go home. Paul hints four times about wanting to taste that trout, but Doug will do it on his own time. He tells us how unusual it is for him to have time free from his consulting work, and how rare it is that he spends time with people like this. We know this to be true and are very flattered and grateful. It was supposed to be a quick lunch . . . and instead, I learned a great deal, and got myself a good, solid case of Charley Horse. In my legs, and in my mouth!

We leave Doug, and I am so talked out that I vow never to speak another word in my life. We see signs about pottery and unusual *objets*, and I gesture to Paul to stop. We do. I have done no shopping so far, so it's a minor indulgence. We pull up next to a tiny house that serves as a store.

The storekeeper, Enrico, comes to greet us. I think he is Indian, but it turns out he is Hispanic—it is often extremely difficult to tell the two cultures apart. He shows us the famed black-on-black Santa Clara pottery and how it is made, and then shows us a new kind, which his wife makes. It is similar in form, but highly glazed, made with somewhat fewer processes, and much cheaper. I immediately break my vow of silence.

"Tell me, Enrico, do the potters at Santa Clara mind that you are making your own pottery in a similar style to theirs?"

"No, no, nobody minds."

"I guess you must have a lot of good Indian friends."

"Sure. Sure. Everybody is my friend," Enrico tells me.

"Do they come from nearby at Santa Clara Pueblo?"

"Sure. Sure. They come from everywhere," he says with a grin.

When Enrico's wife, Elsie, arrives in the room, we learn a more tempered truth. It turns out Enrico knows a lot of Native Americans . . . from a distance. There is very little blending of the two cultures, because from the time the Spanish landed on these shores, one people became the conquerors and the others were the conquered. These wounds do not heal quickly.

Enrico is an extremely talkative man, and he sighs and says he and his wife would love to go sell their pottery in Santa Fe, but they have no one to watch their shop.

"I'll do it!" I volunteer exuberantly.

"You're a store owner?"

"No, not exactly," I hedge.

"A salesperson?"

"Well, I once sold Kool-Aid on a street corner when I was a kid."

"Then how come you want to watch our shop?"

"I don't know," I answer. "Because you need it."

For some reason, Enrico and Elsie are overwhelmed by the offer. They immediately declare that we are their friends forever. They ply us with food. They take us on a tour of their house. They show us Elsie's pottery workshop. And then Enrico really opens up his heart and tells us about his true love—lowriding. He begins to talk with passion about the lowriders of New Mexico, and he offers to introduce me deep into the culture of lowriding. It all started after World War II when Mexican-American men came home from the service and combined their innate love of vehicles, their unique cultural perspective, their newfound money, and their army-trained mechanical abilities to create a new folk art. They began to customize cars, going for a slick, low, and ultra-streamlined profile. They lowered the wheelbase to the point where it barely cleared the ground, and attached "skid plates" which sent out a glory of sparks when it didn't. Today, lowriders cruise the streets in their customized "rides"; they are hip, proud, visible, and outrageous. It can cost twenty, thirty or forty thousand dollars to revamp a car which then requires endless maintenance. But the end result is the fulfillment of a fantasy.

Enrico ceremoniously shows us a Chevy he remodeled, on the cover of a lowrider magazine. It is gorgeous and we wax enthusiastic. Now we are Enrico's friends for life. He insists on getting us dinner reservations at the famed Rancho de Chimayo.

"We tried to get in, but it's all booked, Enrico."

"Booked? There is no booked."

He picks up the phone, talks in Spanish, and the deed is quickly done.

"How do you know the people there?" I ask him.

Indian Time

"We're all one big family," he answers.

One big family. That's the second time I have heard that in one day. It is a concept that is unknown to us in Los Angeles, where we each exist in isolation.

So thanks to Enrico, we eat at the converted farmhouse which is Rancho de Chimayo. It is the descendant of a Spanish settler who owned the farm, which turns me off, because I am now resentful of the entire Spanish culture for bothering the Indian people ("bother" is a gentle word for massacre). The food is good, but I can barely take another New Mexican or Mexican meal. I pine for the days when I was a vegetarian.

On our way home, we stop to catch the last round of Indian bingo on the Tesuque reservation. I think it will be a folksy way to end the evening, but we are stunned by how huge the operation is! It is totally mechanized, satellite-linked to other games at other reservations. The last time I played bingo, I had a card in front of me and some colored plastic chips. This game is unrecognizable. The "caller" announces which configuration is necessary to win. I have never heard of *any* of the configurations. It is a completely high-tech game, played with utter seriousness. As I look out over the vast room, all I see are waves of expressionless people (mostly white). Each one brandishes huge, oversized highlighters over a dozen or so paper bingo sheets and there is not a peep in the room. I withdraw, happy that we are not playing and glad the Indians get the money from these games. It's Vegas with no glitz whatsoever.

During the night, I have intense, colorful dreams about this new culture I am encountering. Images of cliff dwellings and pottery intertwine with bowls of chili and bingo games. It is hard to believe that I am only a long day's drive from Los Angeles.

In the morning, I go to a swap meet. There are very few vendors there, since it is an off-day, and almost no shoppers. I have a long talk with a woman who looks like Heidi. She home-educates her kids, touts her lifestyle as the last bastion of free enterprise (all barter; no taxes paid and no interest earned in a bank), and she tells me how she left her job making door panels for GM and hit the road with her hubby and kids. Now they barter everything except food and gas, and sometimes they even barter that. They eat out sometimes, and otherwise they study and sell their wares and see the country. She has antique Indian artifacts, and she tells me how she doesn't know much about what

58

they mean, but they *feel* very powerful. She hasn't sold any of them and she's secretly happy about that. Somehow it makes her feel secure just *having* them.

"I never cared much about the Indians until I met a few of them," she tells me.

I meet a vendor who was studying constitutional law, when he realized how beautiful and perfect it was, and how it didn't apply to everyone. This was when he became sympathetic to Indians and underdogs and left the world of law to sell at swap meets. He now has Indian artifacts and a thick book on Pueblo Indians which I keep flipping through as we talk. We are like two pots, boiling over with enthusiasm.

I buy a bread from an Indian from Santo Domingo Pueblo, and this leads to a private demonstration of how he makes his pottery. I ask why there is a broken line on each pot. He starts to say they are "spirit holes" but then he catches himself, shuts up, and I respect that. I know that many Indians have been instructed not to tell anything to us palefaces. We are not high on their list of trustables.

In the evening, there is an art opening at the museum of the Indian school. It is a very provocative exhibit about the nude in Indian art. The Indians have become so puritanical that they have obliterated the nude body. (By reputation, Indian men are very sexual, but they keep it all very private.) Now it comes splashing back in bold color, in traditional beadwork, in "White Women." Why is there such a fascination with white women? Is it the same reason we all dated black men—attraction to the "other"?

Maybe it is deeper than that. Maybe it is the culturally inculcated sense of inferiority that has been pummeled into Native Americans. In a dominant culture where Indians cannot belong, white women are a fantasy, an affirmation of potency and acceptability, the ultimate prize. They are trophies. Bagging a white woman means taking one away from a white man, being equal to or better than a white man. The whole notion of what has been perpetrated on the Indian psyche makes me shudder. Apparently it makes Indian women shudder as well, for their entries in the show are pretty strong stuff. They also object vehemently to the use of the nude as *Playboy* fantasy objects. There is a very definite feminist consciousness among the Indian artists.

A woman standing next to me coos that her favorite piece in the show is a *Playboy* centerfold, traditionally beaded and laid on a traditional skin. Mine is a white woman with a buffalo head. It reminds me of the Indian attitude to the hunt. You must blend with the animal, feel what it is thinking, understand it, know it, *be* it, in a moment of ecstasy and union before it yields to you, to feed you. It is the hunt. It is sex.

There is also a room of Indian student art. Much of it is strong, original, and reasonably priced. I really would buy . . .

At the opening is an Indian artist (his work is not represented) with a lot of attitude. When all of the white people are gone he approaches me and begins to bait me. He pries me, and when I answer, he forces me into asking him questions. Then he refuses to answer or tries to rebuff or humiliate me.

"Hey, I'm not the enemy," I say gently.

He smirks.

I try to understand that he has probably been very hurt by the white world, and I am just emblematic to him.

The next day is Open House at the Santa Fe Opera. Beautiful grounds, lots of fresh air, and only one black family among the thousands of people. Indians? You'd have to be a scout to find one.

Filiberto comes with me, and I don't have to mention the fact that he is in the minority. "Hide and seek. Find the Yaqui," he says, as he pulls his broad-brimmed hat low over his head.

As part of the entertainment, a New York psychoanalyst and jeweler is talking about the history of jewelry-making. He says that when he picks up a bracelet from ancient Egypt or Greece, straight out of a crypt, he can feel the way the old goldsmith worked. Just as a woman who knits knows her own stitches, and if she put her knitting down she could tell if someone else picked it up and continued it, so it is with jewelry-makers. You can tell the direction the smith worked in, the pressure, etc. He shows some of his own pieces—they cost about $8000 a piece—and they are lovely, delicate, finely wrought.

Filiberto, who is also a jeweler and a doctor, jokes with the psychoanalyst.

"What's the difference between a patient and gold?" Filiberto asks the shrink. The analyst shrugs good-humoredly.

"At least gold is malleable!" Filiberto answers.

The analyst and Filiberto exchange a smile, and the analyst confides that this is the first time he has ever spoken to an Indian. I begin to understand what our Indian friends mean when they say they are "invisible" in the fabric of American culture.

Visiting the Ancient Ones

After the opera, we stop at the largest of the local swap meets. It is huge. Enormous. You can just dive in and buy, barter and look for hours. I meet two men from Nigeria of the Yoruba tribe and I have an extended talk with them. Filiberto is tickled because I lived in Lagos for a while, and as soon as I start to talk, I fall into the "pidgin English" patter that one uses in Nigeria. "I no be shamed." "You no be shamed?" "No, I done swear, I no be shamed."

In the last year or so, Yoruba beadwork has been dumped on the American market. It is very distinctive and easy to recognize— bold colors, faces with the noses and eyes in relief, snakes, lizards, and the like. These pieces seem to be knockoffs, probably washed in urine and then rubbed in dirt to make them look old. But the last wave of Nigerian beadwork was the real thing. I think the early pieces were family heirlooms carelessly sold off by children and grandchildren who no longer care about traditions.

"Selling their culture," Filiberto says. "One day they will be sorry. Some things cannot be replaced. Once they are gone, that's it forever."

Then he lifts the cuffs of his trousers and shows me two mismatched socks.

"Like that black sock. I lost one at a laundry, and I never could replace it. So what's the weather like in Lagos?" he asks, with no transition.

I tell him about my days in Lagos when Nigeria was under military rule. The total chaos, the highway robbery with machine guns stuck in your face, the whites who thought I was nuts for plunging into African culture, the fear, the mosquitoes, the malaria, the danger ("You done be in danger from the minute you get up in the morning, before your feet even hit the floor"), the public executions on the beach where the executed are tied up to oil drums, the traffic, the crowds, the long lines, the longer lines, the squalor, the humor, the women who wanted to make cornrows in my hair. All of this comes flooding back as I talk to Filiberto.

"I guess you took your war club in your suitcase," he says.

"Nah," I respond, trying to sound casual. "Just some drip-dry clothes and anti-malaria pills."

As I sit here writing, there are now several pottery sherds on my desk before me. I picked them up at the Puye ruins. When I first touched them, a zing of recognition went through me—almost as though I had been there, hundreds and hundreds of years ago, looking down from

61

that mountain and across the green expanse. Doug told me that the spot where I found them had probably been a refuse heap. What? Throw away these perfectly good sherds? I decided to take them home with me.

I have learned that everything in Indian community life is done with intentionality. I wonder if the pots were thrown away because they were broken, or if the Indians were instructed to throw away the pots when they moved on in their migrations.

There is a knock at the door, and it is Jim Terr, a local satirical songwriter. "Come on," he says, "you've seen the Indians, now take a look at the cowboys."

He drives us to his hometown, Las Vegas, New Mexico, for the Rails and Trails Celebration. The local highlight is tossing cow chips, if that gives you any idea. But the highlight for me is Richard Bodner, poet.

We all sit under a tent. The wind is kicking up pretty strongly, and the tent flaps make a loud thwopping noise. Richard Bodner assumes the identity of S. Omar Barker, a deceased poet, pioneer of the West, and native of the environs of Las Vegas. Richard is adorable—with two big dimples and a small overbite, a short black-and-gray beard, a weather-beaten sweat-stained cowboy hat, and worn leather vest.

First he talks anecdotally about crossing the plains and reaching Las Vegas and the life of the late 1800s. He jokes about Texas as being a way station en route to New Mexico and speaks rhapsodically about nature and the lost buffalo. He tells of his best friend and brother leaving for the First World War; he knew it would never be the same again when his brother came back. And then he quotes from Barker's poems. Suddenly it leaves the realm of the anecdotal and seems to come from deep inside. He speaks of a boy's need to have his own mountain, one that fires his poetic imagination. And funny, but Richard and Omar really blend in that verse.

I feel tears come to my eyes as I listen to the poems that flowed from S. Omar's soul. And I get tears in my eyes as I watch Richard—for I feel his passion and love for poetry. I can only imagine how difficult it must be to live in the nineties as a poet and storyteller. It's hard enough being a screenwriter!

After the show, farmers come up who knew the real Barker, and they trade stories with Richard. It's as though Central Casting sent over a few farmers from their roster. They really wear overalls and have Okie faces and twangs and sturdy bodies.

I've been so absorbed by the Indian culture that when I look around me at the people in Las Vegas, I begin to wonder where the Indians are.

"They're busy doing Indian things," someone tells me.

"What are 'Indian things'?" I ask.

"I don't know. Sitting in a tepee. Shooting buffalo. Smoking a peace pipe."

It is amazing that Las Vegas is so close to the Indian Pueblos, and yet the image that persists is one of Plains Indians during the last century. It's an image drawn from Hollywood movies, and not real life.

Jim Terr takes us for a ride around his hometown, past the Victorian houses, into the mountains where sudden surprising prairies look like nineteenth-century England, past horses, and farmhouses, and finally to a Jewish cemetery. I certainly never knew that Jews had been here in the 1800s as merchants. Their names—Teitlebaum, Kahan, Goldblatt—are written in English, with messages sometimes in Yiddish. And then Jim passes his own father's grave. He died in 1986. A doctor. Seventy-six years old. Liver cancer. Nothing more is said. I wonder what is behind that silence. I guess I'm beginning to learn to listen to silences.

On the way back to Santa Fe, I take my glasses off and prepare to lean back for a little snooze when I see a watermelon pit on the floor. I reach for it, and the watermelon pit scurries through my fingers and down my hand. It is some awful black bug. I scream, and Jim's car almost careens off the road. I guess I must remember to wear my glasses when I pick anything up from now on!

In the evening, there is a call from Filiberto.

"How about coming to the Coyote den for dinner?" Then he howls.

I laugh, understanding that he means the famed Coyote Cafe.

"The treat's on the French," he says, meaning that a Frenchman has invited him, and he has invited me.

"Are you inviting me because you know I speak French?"

"Because I know you're hungry."

"Well, Filiberto, I'm *always* hungry, but I suspect there's another reason you're inviting me."

"I hear you know about the Native American Church."

"Well, " I say, "I've been to a peyote ceremony and I know people who are active in the Church, and I've been to the home of a Roadman, and my friends in the Church have prayed for me during their tepee meetings, and I have a lot of respect for the Church, but I wouldn't say I *know* about it."

"Then let's just say you're coming to appease your appetite."

We sit outside on the patio. There is a French journalist there named Jean-Maurice, and he is looking for info on the Native American Church. He wants to write an article. For the first time in my life, I find myself "pulling an Indian." When questions are asked of me, I get elusive, evasive, and downright secretive. I just don't want to tell him what I know. He is just after "stuff" for a story. He wants to go to a ceremony. I feel that the members of the Native American Church have the right to be left alone. They have been persecuted for their religious beliefs, for using eagle feathers, for using peyote—which is not a drug, but highly revered "medicine" to them. I don't want to connect Jean-Maurice to anyone I know in the Church; I want to protect them.

When I get home, I can't sleep. It bothers me all night and into the next day. Somehow this journalist, Jean-Maurice, has stirred some very deep feelings in me. He is after "the goods," as I have been and as many non-Indians are. Well, Indians are ingenuous and you can get at least some of "the goods" if you are friendly and persist enough. But so what? It doesn't mean much to you without the cultural context, without having LIVED it, and it just ends up in an article or book and people clap you on the back and say how much they like your writing and voilà, the Indians are ripped off once again.

I call Filiberto and tell him how I feel about it.

"Jean-Maurice is a man you introduced me to, and I'd like to do you a service, but I just can't oblige you. I don't want to reveal any names or anything I know."

I am afraid Filiberto is very disappointed in me, but after a brief pause, I can FEEL him smiling over the phone line.

"You've learned something from the encounter," he tells me.

"Fine. And I think you are wasting your time with Jean-Maurice!" I tell him.

"We don't see people as a waste of time," Filiberto reminds me. "If Jean-Maurice can relate to the good parts of Indian life, if he can write and show that Indian people are different from what others think they are, then it's worth it."

"I guess that's why you think I am worth it . . ."

He smiles again. I can feel it.

In the afternoon, Paul and I drive north and stop off at the Santuario of Chimayo, which is supposed to be a sort of mini Lourdes. I guess in my mind's eye I imagined us gaping at the faithful and clicking away on my camera. I have never been much of a believer in healing places.

The reality is very different from my judgmental expectations. It really is a holy place. The church is very small, picturesque, with a little wooden house and a bell on top—perhaps the house is for the bellkeeper.

Inside there is the main chapel, with a very simple Jesus wrapped in a mustard-yellow loincloth at the main altar. People pray quietly. In an adjacent rear grotto is a shallow pit of holy earth, and people lean down, take a pinch or a fistful, and carry it away or rub it on themselves. This is the earth where the sacred cross was found. On the walls are renderings of the church, poems about the spot, paintings done by hands connected to hearts. The prayer candles glow brightly and because this chamber is small, they heat up the room.

Next to the grotto with the healing earth is a larger grotto, and the heat from the candles is almost stifling. They seem to burn through you, to your personhood. The room is lined with pictures of Gulf War soldiers, and prayers are hung from all the walls. The paintings get more expressionistic. One is done in red. Abandoned crutches hang on the walls. One sailor, who came back alive from Operation Desert Scam, has left his white Seabee hat as an offering. There are Christs in ceramic and plastic of every shape imaginable. Big, broad ones, shaped like the Buddha. Scrawny ones. Garish ones. Christs in earth tones. Small glass installations with rosaries and medals. The place is so holy one cannot help but be struck by it. I am moved to tears. This small spot on the face of the earth is invested with so many prayers of desperation, longing, thanksgiving. The outpourings of the human heart.

I have had many conversations with Lenny Smallfeather about my inability to pray. Once he instructed me to go into a closet, lock the door, and chant "father, father, father," until I learned how to pray. But it never worked. I just started sneezing from the mothballs.

Here in the grotto at Chimayo my cheeks are red from the heat of the candles—but also red from embarrassment. In the midst of all this prayer, which lingers after the people who pray have gone, how can I still be so dumb, so unable to offer anything up from my heart to a power larger than I?

"Prayer is healing and healing is prayer," Lenny often told me, but I shrugged, uncomprehending.

"Who do I pray TO?"

"Do it and you'll find out."

I have tried to pray to the Universe, but I am not sure that the Universe hears me. I'm not even sure what the Universe IS.

We go to see the famed weavings of Chimayo and then on to San Juan Pueblo. We drive past the church, pass the tiny hub of buildings, to a house on the outskirts to meet with Claire and Lorenzo Mendeza. Lorenzo is an important Indian leader. Claire is an outgoing, highly verbal woman with a wonderful wild streak. She offers us huge slices of watermelon and we begin to talk. We chitchat for a while, and I understand that underneath her ebullient surface is a lot of suffering.

"My parents separated when I was young," she tells me. "I was very outspoken and emotional, and the people at my conservative Pueblo looked askance at me and my sister. We were always outsiders."

She takes a bite of watermelon, cracks a joke, and continues.

"Then I married some jerk. After that was over I fell in love, got married again, and my husband died in an auto accident."

In her retelling of this tragic soap opera, she is very matter-of-fact.

"Now I am with Lorenzo, and I have been for many years. That's my romantic story."

Lorenzo sits there affably, saying very little, and she half-playfully berates him for his lack of emotional connection. As we speak, their tiny grandson runs around, playing with toys, dropping them, and bouncing onto my lap for hugs.

"Nice house," I comment, always uncomfortable with lulls in the conversation.

"It started as a trailer, and we extended it out," Lorenzo explains. "We basically built it by ourselves, with help from some wetbacks."

The front two rooms are expansive and sparse—white painted adobe with *bancos* (benches) and *nichos* (niches) built in. Indian pottery and rugs are scattered artistically and tastefully around the rooms. But a trip to the bathroom reveals that each successive room farther back in the house is more full of junk and squalor than the one before. I stop looking. I stop caring. This is the way things *are*. It doesn't mean anything. Neatness is a bourgeois detail. Besides, who am I to pass judgment? I'm hardly Hannah Homemaker myself.

In the bathroom, I fill up water pistols and squirt them up and down the grandson's shirt. He squeals delightedly.

I decide that I will not be anthropological. Yes, my "job" is to learn about Indian culture, but I will not rip these people off. I will have no agenda. We will discuss whatever comes up. There is nothing I WANT to KNOW.

We continue to eat watermelon and chat. Like Dr. Doug, Claire is more verbal than I am. The problem she expresses is a universal one that has nothing to do with being "Indian"—namely, how do emotionally expressive people relate to repressed ones? Especially when they are married.

Claire has been very introspective about her outgoing nature. She has come to realize that she drew people to her out of need. She looks at her own past and analyzes it. She thinks it was a very painful childhood. Lorenzo, who had no parents and was raised by his grandfather and aunts, sees the past as ideal. No matter what the "objective" reality of having no parents, to him it was idyllic.

"So," I ask Lorenzo, "was it really so good on the planet you came from?"

Claire laughs uproariously. I laugh uproariously. Lorenzo just smiles. I act cynical, but deep inside I wonder if Lorenzo, in all his denial, is better off than Claire and I are. He creates a scenario that makes him happy.

When we get up to leave, Claire smiles at me and says: "Well, you sure are brave and peppy."

Brave? Me? The closet phobic? The Fearful Wonder? Does she know who she is talking to?

4

Why I Owe the Pueblo of Sandia a Watermelon

Early June, 1991

"Meditation!" Paul exults. "That's how you're going to get over your fears."

"I am?"

"Sure. You go inward and quiet your mind. You can't be relaxed and phobic at the same time. It's not logical."

He presents me with a book on meditation that he bought at a Buddhist bookstore. I begin to practice in the living room of the *casita*. I count "one" as I breathe in and "one" as I breathe out. Then, I count "two" in and out for my second breath. "Three" in and out for the third breath. I go back to "one" when my mind wanders, and start all over again.

"Well?" Paul asks.

"I've been meditating for twenty minutes and I can't get past 'two.'"

We pack it in and head back to San Juan Pueblo for the high school graduation party of Lorenzo and Claire Mendeza's son Timmy. Timmy is going to Stanford this fall, he's a computer science whiz, he's tall, cute, and has a winsome smile, even though he seems to be a bit shy.

When we arrive at the Mendeza house, Lorenzo is outside barbecuing steaks. This time we solve the red-meat problem by bringing our own chicken breasts. We also bring a watermelon, as it is customary to bring food when you go to someone's house, especially if you are going to eat and there is a party. This is part of the communal spirit. The food is always accepted willingly, but no one says "thank you." I suppose that when you are part of the human family, you're supposed to provide some comestibles without thanks.

Timmy is in a back room most of the time, reading. He comes in a few times, wanders around, and then disappears. None of his friends has come, and he is probably bored. His male siblings set up a volleyball net and amuse themselves, and Timmy is so low-key that it's hard to believe the whole party is for him.

There is no specific time set for the celebration. People come trickling in all day. As soon as they arrive, Lorenzo or Claire urges them to eat. The food consists of red chili stew, posole, hamburgers, hot dogs, deli meats, cut-up vegetables, cakes, and watermelon: a real blending of Indian and non-Indian culture. As usual, there is no alcohol. People sit at the dining room table and eat. When they are through, they generally leave the party. And then the next guests arrive and eat.

The mood at the table is jocular and lighthearted. I sit with five adult sisters, who tell me they grew up in a house with two brothers— and all seven of them lived in two rooms with their parents. Their mother looks hardly big enough to give birth to an egg, let alone all these kids.

I joke about my sisters and me fighting like cats and cats, and they look at me oddly. They all seem to get along. At 4½ of them per room! We would have been hauled away for sororicide!

I walk outside and sit with Lorenzo and his friend Charles from San Ildefonso, who immediately invites me to come and visit him at his Pueblo. This hospitality is typical behavior for Pueblo people, but it is so atypical for me that I never take it for granted. I try to implement my new resolve: (1) don't ask questions; (2) don't offer advice; (3) be comfortable with silences. By the time I have finished listing these new rules of behavior, they are broken!

After several hours of benign chitchat, Lorenzo suddenly starts talking about his boyhood and telling me that when he went to school, he was only exposed to the *white* view of history.

"There's more than one way of seeing American history," he says.

"You mean the true way, and the Anglo way?"

He nods and continues.

"I never even knew there was a successful Pueblo revolt against the Spanish occupation in 1680. I wrote my big paper on the Louisiana Purchase. Can you imagine? If I'd have known, I would have written about our leader Popé and my people's rebellion."

He also never ate with utensils before going to school in Santa Fe.

Indian Time

At the Pueblo, his people simply used a bowl and scooped up the food with two pieces of bread—sort of shoveling it together. When he went to school, he was taught etiquette for eating out: "Use knives, forks, and don't slather butter over your whole piece of bread at once."

Lorenzo laughs at the memory as he scoops up chili with two pieces of bread, and his fork sits unused on the table in front of him. Then he continues his story.

"The most upsetting thing at school for all us Indian kids was that there was one piece of bread per kid per meal. We complained, but no one did anything about it. So finally we got together and baked bread in the school ovens ourselves so we'd have more. We Indians really love bread!"

Lorenzo, like all the Indians I have met who are middle-aged or above, speaks with great nostalgia about the old times.

"Our uncles and grandfathers used to make rows with the tractors, and we kids would run behind and plant corn in the rows. It was great fun. At noon, the women would come with food, and the men would sit and scoop it up with bread. Now the men drive home for lunch, the farm work is mechanical.

"Last season I decided to plant corn with a digging stick, the old way, and the corn is good. Look over there—"

I look obediently. Irrigation ditches run alongside the fields. The farmers have only to divert the water they need to grow their corn.

Lorenzo takes a bite of his hamburger on pita and points across the way.

"That old stone building, now a warehouse, is where I grew up with my grandmother. In my whole life, I've moved my habitation maybe a hundred yards. And you, you've probably lived in a hundred different cities."

Like many other Indians, Lorenzo lived in that stone house, and, simultaneously, he also lived in another house closer to the Pueblo Plaza, the hub of communal and ceremonial life. Like other children, he was raised by aunts, grandmothers, and grandfathers.

The whole world is so close to Lorenzo—his family, the siblings he grew up with, the hills, the house he grew up in. I know none of this. My childhood is across the country in a small town. I visit it only in memory.

Lorenzo is very easygoing and casual. He has an open face. He is quiet but warm and friendly. When Claire comes outside and sits down, the whole energy changes: she is a powerhouse.

Why I Owe the Pueblo of Sandia a Watermelon

She starts to talk about Timmy. He had a very hard birth, he lost oxygen, and Claire and Lorenzo were told he would be retarded. Claire thought for a day and said, "Fine, if he is retarded, so be it. But he will be the smartest retarded kid they've ever seen!" I tell her that her ACCEPTANCE of things is marvelous. She says that although she is an educator, after all these years, she realizes you can't teach that kind of equanimity to people. She truly believes it is genetic. "You are born with a peaceful or agitated character, and that's it, folks!" she says, laughing. I silently agree, wondering if Claire knows how it really feels to be agitated. . . .

She talks about Timmy's birth and Timmy's growing up without ever mentioning her own difficulties. Timmy was four before he spoke a word. The first thing he said was: "Watch out, you stupid asshole!"—the words he had heard Claire scream to a driver who almost killed them.

Claire tells the stories with vivacity and humor, but without dwelling on the angst, the pain, the suffering. It's obvious she isn't Jewish. I try to imagine how the stories would be told where I come from. The story wouldn't just hop along. It would pause and linger on the NO OXYGEN, the possible RETARDATION, the NOT SPEAKING FOR FOUR YEARS, the man who ALMOST KILLED THEM. And I realize how these emphases make up a worldview that it is almost impossible to change with the adult logical mind.

Paul and I feel it is time to leave, even though no one says anything. We have been at the party for three hours, and everyone else has been coming and going. We stand outside, under the impeccable sky with the cumulus clouds.

"Hope you enjoyed your day at the Pueblo," Lorenzo says, as he and two of his friends accompany us to our car.

"Hope Timmy enjoys Stanford as much. Hope he comes back home to live here when he's done."

"We have to find a way to create more jobs to keep kids on the Pueblo."

"How do you do that?" I ask.

Damn it! Why do I have to ask? If I shut up, he'll tell me anyway!

"There's no gas station, no laundry, no grocery store, nothing here," Lorenzo says sadly. "All the money goes OUT, and nothing stays at the Pueblo. It takes capital, it takes confidence, it takes belief in oneself."

I babble something about "It will come . . ." but no one responds. They don't have those polite tics of conversation. I see that they are

71

really worried about the Pueblos. They want to make a future so the children who go away to school have something to come back to—in terms of work. Then they can remain and participate in the ceremonial life. This, after all, is how the Indians have stayed intact after murder, massacre, and conversion.

In the evening, Paul takes the car to research a newspaper story he is writing, and Sam the maintenance man volunteers to drive me to go shopping. Sam is a tough, hunky Hispanic, who sports a tattoo, dresses all in black with a few skulls and crossbones, and wears a cowboy hat. His voice has a singsong lilt. He drinks a lot. He sells dope. Yet, when I ride in the car with him, he crosses himself every time we pass a Catholic church, out of respect.

"Sam," I say, "I hope I don't offend you if I ask you something about your past."

"Three hundred women, all of 'em beautiful," he offers, laughing.

"How do you feel about what your ancestors did to the Pueblo Indians?"

"Hey, man, I'm responsible if I run a red light or nick a Mercedes."

The conversation comes to an abrupt end.

In the morning, Lenny is back in town, and comes to visit, bringing along his little daughter from his second marriage. With her huge black eyes, she looks like she just walked off a Kean painting.

"You never told me you had a three-year-old daughter."

"I have a whole tribe."

"Johnny Appleseed," I whisper to Lenny.

"Hmm?"

"You just keep walking over white women, planting your seed everywhere."

He laughs. We have adopted a mode of teasing each other.

"Hey, got a bagel?" Lenny asks me. "My daughter sure likes Jewish food."

As she eats, Lenny looks at me and smiles. "I know that since I left you alone here you must have accumulated a lot of questions. Stopping those questions would be like trying to stop a moving train, so I'll encourage you to write them down and when I have time in the future, I'll try to answer them."

"Why 'in the future'?" I ask. "What's wrong with now? Or tomorrow? Or the next day?"

"Sorry," he says as he flicks his hair back off his forehead, "but I'm giving some workshops and I have to plan them."

"Lenny, your first allegiance is to researching and writing this TV show with me."

"Gotta go," he says, and is gone. I try not to gnash my teeth because it's bad for the porcelain crowns.

Because Lenny is so busy with his own agenda, Paul and I accept an invitation to go to Oklahoma with Beaver for Red Earth.

"What's Red Earth?" I ask, but I don't get a specific answer from anyone.

"It's a good trip for you to learn from," Filiberto says with approval. "The Pueblo Indians are the richest Indians, the most entrepreneurial. Their water and hunting rights are intact. They have inhabited the same locales without interruption. Their costumes are elaborate. Other tribes are displaced, poor, they don't know how to market their goods."

"Is the same true of your tribe, the Yaquis?"

Filiberto gets proud and defensive when I mention his tribe.

"We are poor, we have been displaced, we only have homegrown costumes—but we have maintained our secrecy and exclusivity. And we want it that way. We wouldn't trade what we have for anything."

Rationalization or truth?

Paul and I leave Santa Fe for Oklahoma in a government van, provided by the Institute of American Indian Arts, with Beaver at the wheel. She is going to be our guide and hostess. Laura Fragua, her friend and cousin, whose wedding I went to when I first came, is also along. It is a clash of wills from the get-go. Beaver wants blasting rock music. I can't stand it coming from the speaker behind my ear. I ask her to just play it up front. She doesn't like the "balance" —it sounds too tinny to her ear without the rear speaker. Then I want the window closed and she wants it open. I want to stop to eat and stretch, but she wants to drive straight through.

"There's a party in Oklahoma City and there'll be some handsome Indian guys. I want to get there."

When we cross the Texas border, I feel sympathetic to Beaver's plight of being single, and I propose that we all get out of the car and make a little ceremony to pray that Beaver meets a guy. We offer up some cornmeal and we all give Beaver our blessings and wishes. Even though we joke a bit, Beaver and Laura take the prayer session very seriously.

"Thanks, guys," says Beaver. "I really appreciate the support. When we get to Red Earth, I'm going to make sure you meet everyone. You're going to have a great time."

We arrive in Amarillo, Texas, and suddenly there are tornado warnings and a storm with flash flooding. On the radio, there is an advisory against driving. I ask if we can spend the night in a motel in Texas, and Beaver almost lops my head off. Holding the wheel makes her a total tyrant.

Finally, when Beaver is absolutely blinded by the pelting rain, she grudgingly pulls into a motel. At the check-in counter, Beaver asks if we can simplify things by laying out money for her motel room with Laura. She says she will pay us right back. We make the mistake of agreeing. The minute the motel bill is paid, suddenly Beaver pleads poverty. I don't like this, because Beaver has brought along enough money for the trip. It's hard to accept playing the sucker.

This is not the first time we have had this experience in the Southwest. Because you are white, you are expected to have money. When you sit at a restaurant table with Indians, they often get up and leave, kicking in a dollar here and a dollar there. You are left to foot the rest of the bill. If you lend them money, you kiss it goodbye. I was warned by every white person I met when I arrived in Santa Fe, but I poohpoohed it. It has proven true, alas. It creates much resentment.

In the morning, we set out for Oklahoma again, and I sit in the back with Laura, trying not to pay attention to the shattering rock music. At first Laura is very quiet, but then, after an hour or so, she begins to whisper to me.

"I feel split," she confides. "I have been trying to educate myself, because you know that we were lied to in school. I understand what the coming of the Spanish did to the Indian people. But yet, I am Christian, and Christianity is the religion imposed by the Spanish. How can I practice the religion of oppression? So what is my religion? Indian? Christian? Who am I?"

Laura, who is a wonderful sculptor, painter, and potter, is as sensitive as she is artistic. "How can we NOT feel divided?" I look at her face: it is haunted.

The music is now heavy metal. I listen to Laura's low voice against the head-banging background. She tells me that Christianity has messed up the Indian way of life, and turned Indian against Indian. Her own grandmother was whipped publicly by the Indian council for practicing Protestantism—a variant religion on the Catholic Pueblo.

"It makes you crazy," she says, half to me and half to herself. "At the Pueblos, one Christian group is intolerant of the other, and yet all of them are practicing adopted religions, religions that were forced down their throats."

"Enough to make you schizo," I concur, and then, suddenly, Laura leans in closer to me.

"Why do people hate Jews so much?" she asks.

I felt myself blush. It is an innocent question, but it brings up a great deal of feeling—defensiveness, "otherness," resentment. I, who have so little religious affiliation, suddenly feel myself very identified with my own tribe. I cannot really answer her question. I feel the same bewilderment that all oppressed people must feel. Why DO people hate Jews? Is it really because they said Jews killed Christ? Is it envy? Because Jews were successful? Rich? Tall? Short? Fat? Dark? Is there a real reason at all?

"I guess it's the same reason people hate Indians," I tell her.

She nods. I nod. She looks down. I look down. It is clear that neither of us understands.

"We're heeeere!" Beaver yells exultantly as we arrive in Oklahoma City. We check into a suburban motel, where Beaver had been promised a special rate and a shuttle to drive us back and forth to Red Earth in the downtown area. Both prove to be lies. After our room is changed three times, Paul crashes out on the bed. Beaver and Laura check out to find a cheaper motel and we decide to trust the crooked-toothed promise made by the sleazoid management that they will rectify the situation.

The Oklahoma visit really begins to deteriorate now. The weather sucks, it is either pouring or unbearably humid, the management lies and never provides us with transportation, the city is totally unappealing, the architecture is hideous, the food ranges from blech to sub-blech, the people are slow, and Beaver disappears with the van that was supposed to be provided to show me around. Since Beaver never calls us from her new motel, we have no idea where she is. We are twenty minutes out of town, taxis are expensive and hard to come by, we have no transportation anywhere. As for Beaver's offer to show us around and introduce us to everyone, it is about as sincere as a white treaty.

While *my* van is somewhere in Oklahoma City, we try to get around. Red Earth is a fairly new, albeit well publicized, annual Indian event. It is a combination art show, powwow, and reunion for Native Americans from all over the country. There are tables set up in a huge convention center, and Indian artists sell their arts and crafts. There are some fine works of art and some touristy trinkets. The economic climate in the country is beginning to turn really sour, and the vendors are very anxious to sell so they can put on a new roof or fix their cars. They seem focused and not very chatty. It is not conducive to meeting people. For the first time since our arrival in the Indian world, we meet no one.

"Let's practice ACCEPTANCE," I propose. "Let's pretend we are Claire Mendeza, and make the best of things."

"Fine. The city is famous for barbecue, so how about we get some?"

"Great."

Paul and I picture ourselves covered in barbecue sauce, crawling in barbecue sauce, picking up dripping pieces of chicken as comfort food. Wrong. The only thing we can find is benign ready-made slices, served neatly on a plate. All the fun of the slurp is gone.

We spend my birthday stranded in the cold and rain till 1 A.M. trying to get a cab, while Beaver is shaking her bustle all over Oklahoma City in "my" van, in God-knows-which-motel. I am furious! And then we get a call that Lenny's mother died suddenly and I can't get back for the funeral because dear Beaver is off somewhere partying and I have no way to return. I keep hearing reports that Beaver is having a ball, Beaver is meeting men, Beaver is really enjoying herself. It takes a lot to control myself from hiring a snuffer to eliminate the Beaver problem.

As for Oklahoma City, all the brochures and pamphlets brag that when the territory was opened up to settlers, there was such a rush that the city was made in one day. If you ask me, it looks it! I also have a bad taste in my mouth about Oklahoma, because it is here that all the Indians were forced to come, pulled off their reservations, herded into "Indian Territory" at the behest of the U.S. government. The infamous "Trail of Tears" led to Oklahoma— all those Cherokees forced to walk hundreds and hundreds of miles, as they dropped off and died along the way to "civilization." What must the Cherokee have felt as they left their sacred lands and their way of life behind them? Did they curl up in the beneficent arms of their Creator and pray for better times? Did they believe, even then, that what goes around comes around? To me, Oklahoma City is aptly summed up in the words of a bragging doorman: "Yeah, it's the best here. We've got great hospitals and a terrific doctor who does sex change operations but I can't remember his name."

Even on such a bad trip, there are always good parts—namely, the powwow. There are about two thousand dancers registered for the Red Earth indoor powwow. The convention center is packed. When they announce the grand entry parade, we are caught by complete surprise. The only experience I have ever had like this is when I first stood on Second Mesa, in Hopiland, and watched the masked *kachinas* coming up over the horizon. Half-men and half-spirits, they flooded the dusty plaza like the rays of dawn. Here in OKCity it is two thousand Indians in full regalia who suddenly appear on the convention center floor. There is a startling, almost overwhelming array of brilliant colors, feathers, bells, headdresses, as wave after wave of Indians pour in. The seven drum groups, some of the best in the world, have been brought in especially for the occasion. The heartbeat drumming is hypnotic. And just when you think the convention center can't hold another burst of color, another fan or feather, more Indians pour in. The floor of the huge convention center is completely covered with dancing Indians. Facepaint, staffs, feathered bustles, women's jingle dresses, shawls— it transports you back to another era on the Great Plains, and you witness the outpouring of love that Indians have for their Creator and for Life. Not far in the distance, you can almost hear the stampede of buffalo. It is hard to believe that you are indoors, in Oklahoma City, a plane trip from Wall Street, Hollywood, and Beverly Hills!

The second day of Red Earth, there is a dance competition. The august, elegant ladies in their simple dresses, walking with great pride and dignity during the women's dances. The traditional dances where the older men, imitating birds, seem to be in a trance, while the younger ones show off for the judges. The women and their shawl dances—twirling and spinning, and some, too, in a seeming trance. The clinking of the silver ornaments on the women's dresses as they shake in time to the rhythm during the jingle-dress dancing. And the sometimes-chaotic, sometimes-wondrous spins and twirls of the fancy dancers. The music is thumping, dancing, pounding, regular as a heart, and wild as the imagination. The dancers are all former champions, the lights in the convention center are used for dramatic effect, and it is some of the best dancing I have ever seen. "Dance is the breath of life made visible," Lenny once told me, and I am beginning to believe it is true.

Before this trip, I never really appreciated powwows, and tended to dismiss them as sloppy Sunday afternoon entertainment. Now I see them as a time for the children to learn from the Old Ones, to reaffirm faith, to dance the dance of the earth, to pass on traditions to the young, to socialize, to fall in love. I quite like powwows after all. There are Indians whose lives revolve around the powwow circuit; it's their religion. They travel from gathering to gathering, entering in the competitions, perfecting their dancing, winning prizes, or just coming along for support.

Three, four days go by. We hang out, sweat in the humid rain, try to figure out where Beaver is and how we can get back to Santa Fe. The morning of our supposed departure, there is a message at our motel: Her Royal Beaverness is reportedly sleeping in, hung-over. She'll call us at some later time and tell us when she will pick us up. End of message. Paul and I are gnashing our teeth, and to hell with my crowns!

There is a light tapping on our door and when Paul opens it, Laura is standing there.

"Nice of you to visit," Paul says sarcastically.

"I hope you had a good birthday," she says to me.

"Sure. I had a blast. A BLOW-OUT. I hope my birthday is like this *every year*."

She reaches into her pocket and hands us money. "I want to reimburse you for the motel you paid for," she says.

Paul and I look at each other, surprised.

"Beaver has abandoned me, too, and I need to get back just like you do. Some friends are driving me to New Mexico in their truck, and I'd like to invite you to hitch a ride with us."

"Sorry," I say to Laura, and I mean it. "I guess I confused you with Beaver just because you are cousins and friends. You're really very decent, and none of this is your fault."

"You won't like me so much when I tell you that my friends who own the truck are all loaded up with sculpture. There's no room in the driver's compartment. We have to lie in the back of the truck for the ride home. Well, I'll wait for you guys outside."

I almost get whiplash as I shoot a look at Paul.

"Ride for ten hours, lying down in the back of a truck?"

"They call their trucks 'Indian Cadillacs.' Let's consider it an adventure."

"I'm terrified. It will be dark. Closed in. The truck door will probably be locked so we can't get out. If we get murdered, no one will hear us yell."

"I'm sure it will be very different from your imagination, and much better."

We get into the back of the truck, and the door is shut behind us. It is EXACTLY LIKE my imagination. Paul generously encourages Laura to squeeze into the driver's compartment and assures them all that we will be fine on the floor. I lie prone on the metal floor, feeling the bumps of the road beneath me and the lashing of rain above me. Lightning and thunder shake the truck and it is safe for me to howl, because no one can hear me.

As we ride along, I begin to think of Beaver, all comfy-cozy in bed, sleeping off her partying. I realize that although it does not usually surface, I have a tremendous warehouse full of anger. And, worse yet, I hold on to it. I try to meditate, reason, push it away, but the anger sticks. It lasts, in all of its intensity, for the entire ride home. I realize that it eats me up, but the anger has a will of its own. I am SEETHING about Beaver. I cannot think of anything else. *Bump. Bump. Bump.* My God, are we driving over *barrels*?

The only respite from my anger is a few pit stops, when we get to meet the driver of the truck, Tim Shay, who just won first place for sculpture at Red Earth. He is accompanied by his girlfriend, Wilma Mariano, a sculptress who works in a bronze foundry.

We all start talking about Red Earth, and I mention that I am appalled by the fact that during the gorgeous, moving powwow, there was much jingoism and glorification of "the fighting boys." Hunky, handsome Indians in Marine uniforms sat in the lobby. A statue of an Indian dressed in military regalia and holding a machine gun was presented as a gift—it's a model for a proposed memorial to Native American veterans.

I listen quietly while Tim tells the genesis of his own anti-war feelings. He is the first Indian we've met who isn't gung-ho military.

"In the army, I asked myself the question: what is the value of a human life? I thought about it a lot and decided that the only attack that is justified is in your own backyard, when someone threatens life and property."

"How come so many Indians support the military? They're second-class citizens in this country. What are they fighting for? Oppression of other second-class citizens around the world?"

Tim nods, understanding my passion.

"Indians pride themselves on being warriors. They haven't subjected their feelings to reason in this area. They haven't yet experienced a collective disgust for war."

"The *conquistadores* did a great job on the Indians," I reflect aloud
in a wash of sarcasm. "They brought Christianity and rammed it down
their throats. The Indians adapted so well, I even saw the requisite Indian gospel singers at Red Earth."

I turn to Laura.

"You're right. It's enough to make you schizo," she says.

When I finish my diatribe, we get back in the truck and bump along
toward home. We are dropped off, like two garbage bags, at the *casita*. We hug Laura and Tim and Wilma, really grateful to them for
helping us out.

"If you hear from Beaver, tell her I'm on the warpath," are my final words.

"I thought you're a pacifist," Tim teases me.

Yeah, right.

In the morning, when we roll our aching bodies out of bed, we leave
for the village of Paguate at Laguna Pueblo, to pay a condolence call
to Lenny.

We arrive late in the day. We have been to his mom's before. As a
matter of fact, she had invited us to come and stay there, and we were
going to take her up on her generous offer. But death is a train with
its own secret timetable.

We stop off to buy food—including bagels—since Lenny and his
mom always liked bagels. Lenny looks tired when we arrive. Indian
funerals are very intense. They go on for four days. Almost all day and
all night, with women cooking outside in the backyard on three fires,
cooking inside, serving, all the village coming, the prayers, the visits
to the cemetery, the feeding of the living and the dead, and tribal doings of which I have no knowledge.

Apparently, at birth, the Mother of All provides each person with
a guardian spirit and a soul. When a person dies, the guardian spirit
and soul leave the body but remain in the home of the deceased for
four days. After this time, they travel to the entrance of the underworld and are selected for one of the four underworlds. The most vir-
tuous enter the rainmakers' world and come back to visit the Pueblos
in the form of clouds.

Why I Owe the Pueblo of Sandia a Watermelon

We walk into the house. It is strange. The back room, where his mom used to sit, is all cleared out. Instead of furniture, there are big dishes full of food on the floor. Perhaps some of it is food for the deceased, because when I erroneously start to bring it into the kitchen to help "clean up," one look from Lenny tells me to put it right back where it is.

This is the end of the fourth day of the funeral rites. We act very serious, the way we think you should behave during a condolence call. But no one else is as dour as we are. A food feast is going on in the kitchen. Relatives are clustered around, picking the meat off a chicken, stuffing in stews and puddings and fruit and posole. It is all very good-humored, and Paul and I change our *modus operandi* and begin doing a little impromptu comedy routine. The audience is very appreciative.

"Have you ever been to a Feast Day?" they ask us.

We shake our heads no.

"You be sure and go to the Sandia Feast," they say.

"What's a Feast Day?" I ask, biting my tongue for asking yet another question.

The relatives leave, imploring and exhorting Lenny to get along with his siblings now that both parents are gone. He says little, and nods.

Alone with Lenny, he is warm, open, and quite talkative. He tells us how he was the one who found his mother when he came to visit. She was sitting in her chair, her head thrown back, with juice and toast still held in her hands. She must have been sitting down for a light meal. She was obviously very peaceful, and she just went to sleep. Lenny says that when he arrived he saw the room flooded with light, and knew the holy spirit was there. It just reaffirmed his faith that life and death are continuous.

As he speaks, we can see the swallows building their nests outside. They carry sticks and mud from the roadside to the eaves of a neighboring house. Other swallows are tucked into their nests. We can see their heads protrude. Life, death, swallows, food—it's all a great confusion to me. I listen to Lenny, as I listen and listen everywhere in Indian country, hoping I will get answers. I know that life answers are supposed to emanate from within, but somehow they are not forthcoming.

Suddenly Lenny's siblings come in. I offer condolences and try to make contact with them, but they are very cold to me. I clam up and stare at my food. Paul tries to make conversation, but he, too, is rebuffed. Then we try to greet them in tandem. Once, twice, three strikes and we are ready to be out of there. Lenny's younger brother says quite openly that it's time for the family to be alone. Goodbye, Smallfeather family. Goodbye, Mother Smallfeather. May you have a safe voyage to the Other Side. May you come back as a cloud.

The next morning, we take the advice of Lenny's relatives and head for Sandia Pueblo. We have learned that when you get a message in Indian country, listen to it. We stop off at a small trading post to ask directions. A charming, friendly white woman who works there stares at us as though we are nuts.

"Sandia? Why would you want to go there? It's a very small, traditional Pueblo. It won't be interesting to you. Don't bother. None of the Anglos go there."

Aha! That is the voice of temptation saying: "Don't go, don't go, go back to your *casita* in Santa Fe and relax. You're tired from all this running around. Turn on the TV. Read a book. Stick with what you know. Don't go out of your way and inconvenience yourselves."

I turn to Paul when we get outside the trading post.

"Do we listen to this woman, or to Lenny's relatives?"

Paul heads toward Sandia Pueblo. Our marriage is like that: a lot of things we just don't have to discuss. As we learn to trust our instincts, we get further along in the remarkable maze of life.

Sandia Pueblo is set against the dramatic background of the Sandia mountains. When we arrive, there are dozens and dozens of cars parked in the dirt—Indians who have come to visit from other Pueblos. A white man tells us that if we are hungry, we can go to eat at someone's house. He disappears into a house and we walk on. How can he just stroll into someone's house like that? I'm afraid that a blast of ire would send us hurling backwards!

"Let's just try it, Judie. If we make a mistake, we make a mistake."

"We'll make a spectacle of ourselves."

"Luckily no one knows us. At least we'll make an anonymous spectacle."

We walk past the dusty central plaza and stop in front of a stucco house with about ten people sitting on the porch. Paul nods to them, opens the front door and walks in, holding the door open for me. I gasp at his audacity, and reluctantly follow. Once the door closes behind me, I am terrified. Here I am in a strange house, knowing no one, making an idiot out of myself.

The living room is full of people, just sitting around. The decor is the usual—Indian pottery and pictures, some ceremonial objects, blankets and baskets. There is a little friendly banter. A few tots play on the floor. We peek into the kitchen. There, at a long table, people are eating. It is very awkward, and no one acknowledges our presence. We back into the living room again and sit down, trying to make polite conversation.

"Nice pottery," I say.

"Lovely painting," Paul adds.

Then the conversation dies.

One by one, the people in the living room get up and walk into the kitchen as others come filing out. The living room is empty, except for the two of us. An old woman comes out and asks, "Who is next?"

Paul and I look at each other. "Do we dare?" We timidly step into the kitchen and sit down at the long table. We look in front of us and see red chili stew, green chili stew, chicken, sweet bread pudding, sweeter bread pudding, potato salad, mashed potatoes, posole, fresh fruit, bread, Jell-O, lemonade. Someone puts a plate down in front of me.

"You see," Paul whispers, smiling. "You didn't have to be afraid. It's fine for us to be here. You can relax now."

I take a deep breath and exhale slowly. Yes, I guess it is all right. Just as I am reaching to help myself to food, a woman asks, "Sooooo, who you do know?" I freeze. Everyone at the table turns to look at me. No one is chewing. No one is eating. My mind races: Who do I know? I know my friends and family and . . . God, help me . . . no one in this house or even in this village! I stutter and stammer, trying to fake an answer.

The woman persists: "Are you a friend of someone here?"

Again, everyone turns to look at me expectantly. There is a long silence. I would be a terrible prisoner of war. I would be useless in an interrogation room. I break down. "I'm really sorry. I don't want to offend you. Someone told us we could just come here and eat."

The woman looks at us for a long minute, and graciously brings more food to the table. "Here. Enjoy!"

There is some conversation at the table, of the trivial kind, and we eat ourselves sick. By now the living room is filling up with more hungry people, so we get up from the table and leave. We've got the hang of it! We heard the name of a villager mentioned at the meal, and we go straight to the man's house. We walk boldly inside.

"Hi," I say, "we'd like to see Sam."

"Sam isn't here," says Sam's wife, "but please sit down and eat with us." So we do. Everyone at the table is a friend or relative of Sam's. They are solicitous of each other's health and well-being. They talk about mutual acquaintances, and a friend who died. I take a forkful of chili, and I almost choke with shame. What am I doing at this house, where I was not invited? How could I dare take advantage of the hospitality of poor people?

I slink out of the house and it is raining. I overhear a woman saying that a friend of hers sold her jewelry to pay for Feast Day food. I stand in the rain, feeling that I have been mindless and disrespectful, but not knowing how to make amends. The rain drips down my face and drenches my clothes.

Suddenly I hear a drumbeat and look up. A huge line of dancers comes onto the Plaza for the corn dance—which is really the rain dance. We see the elders all in white, who do the singing in a chorus. Then the oldest boys, girls, women, and men arrive, followed by the children. The women wear black *mantas* with much jewelry and colorfully painted *tabletas* (headpieces) in their hair. They dance barefoot. The men are bare chested; they also wear jewelry and white kilts. In their hair, they wear parrot or macaw feathers. On their arms, they sport green bands. The longer I look at them, the more details I see on their outfits. The younger girls wear white feathers, instead of wooden *tabletas*. The men all have bells on their ankles. They carry rattles—the sound symbolizes the rain. And evergreen branches—for growth and eternal life, I guess. The dancing is at once totally incomprehensible and completely clear: they are dancing for their crops, for good health for all humans, animals, and plants, and for long, happy lives.

I guess they must dance well, because they have been rewarded with rain. Pools of mud formed on the Plaza, but the barefoot dancers don't even seem to notice. They dance and pray on Mother Earth and beneath Father Sky, who blesses them with rain.

Beyond the Plaza are booths to buy pottery and jewelry. We go there between dances. We stay all day, and see about five or six rounds of dances. We begin to notice that there are two different groups of dancers—the Squash or Winter group and the Turquoise or Summer group. They belong to different moieties and wear different colors—yellow ocher for squash and blue-gray clay for turquoise. Each moiety, or half, governs Pueblo affairs for six months of the year. Together they make up a whole.

Suddenly, as I watch, I have my first "experience" of a dance. I can feel the drum vibrating through my body. It is *inside of me*. I feel the rhythm of the dance. When the long mysterious pole with macaw feathers is passed over the dancers I know it is a blessing and purification and I feel blessed and purified too.

It has taken many rounds and many hours of watching the dancers for me to begin to feel this—but now, sympathetically, I am participating too. It's so wonderful when I can get out of my head and FEEL! I'm tired of thinking! We are all so damn cerebral.

I listen carefully as an old woman tells us about Santo Domingo Pueblo, where the water dried up recently and people had to haul water from the next town. I pay rapt attention as she speaks of parts of San Juan Pueblo, where they have no electricity or running water at all. "Funny," she says, "the U.S. has all that money to spend abroad and this is how we have to live at home."

I muse that the war against the Indians is still being fought, in so many subtle ways.

Suddenly a kid comes running up to Paul—Arnold Herrera's kid. "Hey, I remember you," he bellows. "You guys came and talked to my father. Yap. Yap. Yap. You were pretty funny."

I guess that's a compliment. He takes us to Arnold and his wife, Elisa. They, in turn, introduce us to three-quarters of the Pueblo and then invite us back to their friend Mike's house to eat. I am hesitant to go in, because we have already eaten, uninvited. "Come on," Elisa urges us, pulling my hand for me to follow her. "You're our guests. It's fine."

Once again we wait in the living room and chat and then, when the kitchen table empties, we eat our fill until chili is coming out of our pores and we smell like it! The woman next to me at the table, a Cherokee, has blue eyes and blond hair.

"Surprised?" she asks, when she sees me staring at her. "We Indians come in all shapes, sizes, and colors."

She tells me she came from a very poor family. She had fourteen brothers and sisters, and they all lived in two rooms. Beds, beds, everywhere. They are all on excellent terms, and they never even thought of themselves as poor.

Suddenly, as I sit there, receiving so much from people who have so little, I hatch the idea of going back to L.A. and making a Feast Day. Turning off the security system, opening our fifteen locks and letting people in. Isn't this the way it is supposed to be? Why do I feel comfortable here, and uncomfortable in a world where everyone is always talking about deals, jobs, and money?

We walk outside into the Pueblo night. A large group of teenage boys stands in a circle talking. The circle is such a natural Indian form—it represents a world where there is no beginning and no end, and where all things are connected. Standing in a circle, the boys can all see each other and listen to each other. In our world, when kids just kick and hang, they would *never* stand in a circle or any other form.

We watch the circle, smiling, and then, just as we are getting ready to go, it happens again. We must have some kind of invisible magnets! Ernie, Mike's brother, walks up to us and starts to talk. He tells us about his role in the ceremonies, and why it is a great responsibility. He must be here for the ceremonies, so he cannot live away from his Pueblo. It is a commitment for life: he will have to stay at the Pueblo forever to fulfill it. He tells us about the rain ceremony, and how he feels blessed because they brought rain today. He is a big bruiser, but his voice is soft, mellow.

Arnold approaches silently, and Mike starts to sing songs to him, to share with him. Gentle songs, tender songs. He tells us that when boys come home from war or the service, the medicine society takes them for four days of ceremonies to cleanse them of anger and violence. Then they sing gentle songs that exhort the boys to love, to love each other, not to harbor hate. Mike continues talking for about an hour. Talking and singing. We are amazed at how much is pouring out of him, and how honored we are to be the recipients. He tells us the Pueblo encourages children to leave and get an education without feeling guilt. But they should come home to the "res" and bring their education with them. Arnold looks at the little kids who play in Mike's yard.

"Sometimes the smallest, humblest ones have the most important prayers!" he says. Mike nods.

Arnold and Mike continue to sing to each other, even though they don't even share a common language: Arnold speaks Keres and Mike speaks Tiwa. This is a strange, strange world that never ceases to amaze, intrigue, and fascinate me.

"I am proud of you," Paul says on the ride home.

"Why? Because I set a new record for eating?"

"No, because you pushed yourself beyond fear. You did things you ordinarily wouldn't have done. It's as though you've made a decision to say 'yes' to life."

I lie in bed, long after Paul has gone to sleep. Somehow, in my contact with Indian life here, I am forced to really examine who I am and what I think and feel. It just strips me naked and pushes me out of the comfort zone!

When we get up in the morning, the first thing I say to Paul is, "We owe them each a watermelon."

He nods agreement.

"They were all very generous and hospitable to us, and the next time we are in the area of Sandia, we'll let them know we appreciated it. We never want to take advantage. We know that we *can* walk into a stranger's house and be received there, but I would never ever do it again. I'd only enter a house if I were invited."

He nods again. That's why I married Paul.

While we are eating breakfast, Filiberto drops by for me to help him with a proposal to get extra money for his documentary about Indian elders and the effects of Columbus on their lives. He doesn't *ask* me if I'll help him. "I was in the neighborhood," he says, "and I thought you'd want to take a look at these pages."

I smile. He smiles.

"I don't have a choice, do I?" I ask.

"Sure you do. But we both know what the choice will be."

When we are almost done, I ask Filiberto why all the elders he wants to film are men, and why there aren't any Indian WOMEN elders in his documentary. He immediately gets very defensive. I feel tension in the room. I can back down and drop the subject, but I decide not to.

"It would be interesting for people to see what the women think."

Filiberto loses his usual aplomb. Without a word, he gets up, his body language jerky and irritable, goes outside for a smoke, and then picks up his papers to leave. I follow him outside, and ask why he is so upset. Dear macho Filiberto, he denies it completely. I begin to have a little silent dialogue with myself.

"Stop it, Judie. This is getting uncomfortable. Leave him alone."

"No."

"He's going to turn on you. In a second he is going to unleash his rage."

"Too bad."

"He's going to hate you. You're intruding in his territory."

"Then he'll hate me."

I surprise myself by forging ahead.

"Filiberto, I know you don't want to hear these words, but it's better for you to hear them from me than from a horde of acerbic women who see your film down the line."

"You don't understand. Women have a different role in Indian life. They aren't the elders. They have their own importance. We respect and cherish them."

When he leaves, still in a huff, I sigh. I hope I have not ruined the friendship.

Later in the day, the phone rings.

"Just wanted to run something by you," Filiberto announces.

"Yes . . ." I say hesitantly.

"I've changed the proposal to read 'We will interview men AND WOMEN elders.' "

Bravo for Filiberto. I guess he heard after all.

I think there is a weird and subtle exchange going on between Filiberto and me. I give him help and he tells me stories. Today he tells me a story about how he and his cousin used to run a shoe-shine stand, and they catered to drunks in Tucson. They only charged a nickel for a shoe shine, and they weren't exactly riding a wave of wealth. His cousin got an idea to ask riddles of the drunks. If they answered correctly, they got a free shoe shine. If they didn't, the shine cost fifty cents. The scheme worked. The drunks played the riddle game, lost, and Filiberto and his cousin started raking in the buckeroos. Things were really going well until the drunks started talking to each other and figured out which riddle was being told and what the answer was. Smart drunks, they broke the bank! Filiberto and his cousin went back to being impoverished shoe-shiners.

In the evening, we go to a dinner party. The hostess, a bright and open woman, is very down on herself. As she speaks self-deprecatingly of herself, Paul keeps whispering to me: "Why is her self-esteem so low?" How do you explain to someone with unassailable self-esteem why people don't like themselves?

The hostess asks me to tell the guests why I am in New Mexico, and about my research with the Indians. After my rap, a journalist from

Why I Owe the Pueblo of Sandia a Watermelon

Albuquerque starts talking to me very intensely. He tells me the "accepted" version of New Mexico history. To make it brief—it is no accident that the Pueblo Indians drove the Spanish out in the revolt of 1680. The Indians are so proud of it, but there was a logical explanation for them being able to accomplish their rebellion. The Spanish were vitiated by then, and there was no real military backup. It was an easy victory.

I grit my teeth, feeling that the Indians are not even allowed to be proud of their own revolution! My interlocutor continues.

"Twelve years later, when the Spanish returned to reconquer this area, it was in the spirit of compromise. They brought sheep and rugs to the Indians. They offered the Indians protection against the marauding Apache and Comanche. There was much intermarriage and commingling. In 1848, after the Mexican-American War, the government put the Indians on reservations, but it was arbitrary. There had been so much cross-breeding, that there was little difference between the Indians and the Spanish. As a matter of fact, the Indians aren't Indians at all, but, rather, mestizos. They care about family and land, and they feel closer to the Hispanics than they do to the Apaches or Navajo, for example."

I don't know why, but this conversation upsets me. The speaker, supposedly an authority on Indians, minimizes totally the unique religion and culture the Indians have. To him, they are the same as the Spanish.

"What do you suppose the truth is?" I ask Paul.

"That depends on whom you are asking," he answers.

In the late morning, we drive to Santa Clara Pueblo for a corn dance. It was originally scheduled for last week, but there was a death at the Pueblo, and the dance was postponed. God knows how anyone finds out the dates of things around here. There must be an underground Indian newsline.

It is a perfectly clear day in Santa Clara. The white clouds look like stage decor, hanging in the sky. The dancers are taking a lunch break when we arrive, and an adorable child with a huge smile and a very open face waves to us and invites us into his adobe house. We follow him in and see a row of the famed black-on-black Santa Clara pottery for sale. As we admire it, the child's parents enter the room. The father is friendly and voluble, and he introduces himself and his wife as Phil and Vicky Ostia. Vicky smiles at us, but doesn't say anything.

Phil speaks to Vicky in Tewa, and I comment about how lovely and beguiling the language is. Suddenly Phil begins to talk about how important language is to him. He is absolutely fanatic about not losing the Tewa language. He and another man developed a bilingual educational system at the Pueblo. We talk and talk, with Vicky standing almost silently at his side. He tells us how he was beaten as a child for using his own language in school. I remark that this is probably why he wants to preserve the language so badly; he confesses that he has never thought of the connection.

Phil and Vicky are quite bright, and their son keeps skipping grades like a game of leap frog. Education is very very important in their household. So is respect. If the kids pass in front of us to go outside, they are instructed to excuse themselves. The house is neat, with all the *schmutz* and chaos reserved for the bathroom. Phil writes children's books, and after a while he volunteers to take us to his office to show them to us.

Phil's office is the bilingual center, and there are posters all over with Tewa letters and sounds. It is very exciting to get a Tewa lesson from the master. One word has several meanings, according to the way it is pronounced or its context in a sentence. Tewa is missing many words that are common to us —for example, giraffe. So the word in Tewa is "animal with long neck." The sounds are made in parts of the mouth and throat that we don't even know we have. As I try to pronounce the Tewa words with Phil, I feel like I am spitting up gum and cleaning my teeth at the same time.

We are taken into the back room and shown Phil's books—illustrated books for children in English and Tewa, or just in Tewa alone. As he shows us the pictures, and I try to guess the stories, he translates. Several of the stories deal with death. It is a normal subject which the adults do not try to hide. The stories are very poetic, even the ones for little kids—for example, "My grandmother sat all day, watching the shadows of people go by."

As soon as I admire the books, Phil gives me one of each as a gift. And then he begins to talk. He tells us how his mother was dragged away in a covered wagon to be educated by force in English. How her name was taken away, and she only had a number.

"Another glorious part of American history," I say.

"It's not history," Phil counters. "It is still going on today. As close as the Navajo reservation."

Then he speaks about his wife Vicky. She was raised very tradi-

90

tionally, and she learned that men always had to enter a house first. A woman followed. Women were only allowed to talk if their husbands gave them permission.

"You probably noticed that she looked to me for a nod every time she wanted to speak," Phil says. "I tell her it's okay to speak, but that's the way she is raised. It's hard for her to change."

Then he tells us stories of history that were told to him by his uncle when he grew up. How the Pueblo Indians made bows with five sinews that could pierce the armor of the Spanish. How the Indians were wily and knew back routes and they basically starved the Spanish out and didn't have to kill them.

"The Indian way is not to kill women and children," he says. "But capturing them and raising them as your own is okay. In fact, the mark of wealth was often how many of these captured children you had."

"Is this version of Indian history well known?" I ask.

Phil smiles. "You're probably the first people who are hearing it this way. All that is usually passed down is the white version."

On the way out of Phil's office, we see buffalo headdresses which the kids use in their ritual dances. I touch the buffalo horn—it is so strong and mysterious to me. A shape I have never felt. Phil watches me silently and then, after a few minutes, he gives me two gifts—a pair of buffalo horns! They were obtained in a trade with Plains Indians.

I feel touched beyond words. All I did was walk into a man's house to look at pottery, and an hour later he is presenting me with buffalo horns.

"Thank you. Thank you. Thank you," I squeak out.

Phil nods. But I can see that his attention is beginning to waver, because he hears the powerful call of the Pueblo drums in the distance. The lunch break must be over.

As we walk outside, rain suddenly bursts through the sun. Rain? There hadn't been any rain clouds in the sky. And yet, miraculously, it is raining as the Santa Clara dancers do the rain dance. I am beginning to believe, like they do, that their prayers cause it.

The dance is very small. Three men and three women. It is like a private performance. For the first time, the movements begin to make sense. I can't say we understand them precisely, but the bending movements seem to be planting, and the rattles and swooping movements of the wands seem to be rain. This is no entertainment, as you can see by the intense concentration and seriousness of the dancers. The dance is done four times, in four small plazas on the Pueblo—four being the holy number. It represents the four directions (north, east, south, west), the four seasons, the four sacred colors, and the four races of mankind—black, white, yellow and red. Once again, the drumbeat comes up through my body and the song is hypnotic. Paul leans over, rain dripping down his face, and whispers that a year ago we would have found this dance boring and monotonous. Now it is mesmerizing. We learn. We learn to look and to listen. And many things, formerly invisible and inaudible, become apparent.

"Look over there!" I say to Paul, pointing toward the drummers. Then I correct myself and point with my lips pursed, the Indian way.

One of the four drummers is Dr. Doug White Wolf, the scholar in everything imaginable who took us to the Puye ruins. He obviously sees us too, because after the dancing, he invites us to his house to eat.

When we arrive at Doug's door, desert ants have appeared out of nowhere and are biting us. Instead of going inside, we stand on the porch, pushing and pulling at our clothes to get rid of the toxic little beasts. One of them clings so fiercely to Paul's shirt he can't get it off. Doug's family comes outside to watch us, and they are concerned about the welts on our arms and legs. They make us promise to put baking soda on the bites when we get home.

Then we step inside and eat—red chili, green chili, turkey, potato salad, posole, lemonade, and a table full of desserts. We note once more the absence of alcohol. We have never been in a Pueblo home where any was served.

I tell Doug about my conversation with the journalist about Indians being Spanish. He just shrugs. I am mad, but he is not.

"We Indians are used to this," he says. "Our history and genealogy are always being determined by outsiders who don't know the truth."

He asks about our adventures and remarks that we aren't laden with Indian jewelry and we don't carry crystals and mini pyramids. We all make fun of New Agers in Santa Fe and wanna-be Indians. Doug makes fun of the non-Indians who claim to be Cherokees. He is not the first Indian we have met who really scorns them!

We retire to the living room, and to the best of my knowledge, this is a neat house. So it does exist. Besides being a scholar, Doug is an educational consultant, a teacher of Indian astronomy, and a jeweler, painter, and sculptor. We admire his paintings. One is inspired by the yarn paintings of the Huichol Indians of Mexico. He has a such a large pool of inspiration to swim in.

Why I Owe the Pueblo of Sandia a Watermelon

Doug complains that his arm is very sore from drumming at the dance. He says they have been rehearsing for three to four hours a day for two weeks. These dances are very very important to his people. They are prayers not only for their clan and for their Pueblo and their people, but for all humanity.

Paul is a very multi-talented man, too. He gets down on the floor and does shiatsu and An-Ma body work on Doug and his wife, Gail. This physical contact certainly breaks the ice, and everybody kicks back a lot. I wish we could relax more and be normal, but to tell you the truth, I no longer know what normal means!

On the ride back to the *casita*, we feel every bump in the road through the tinny chassis of our cheapo rental car.

"Have a good day?" Paul asks.

I purr contentedly. I am full of admiration for these people whose resourcefulness, generosity and intelligence never fail to amaze me. Sometimes it is confusing, sometimes it is exhausting, but I wouldn't trade this experience for a garage full of Mercedes!

"You did well with the ants," Paul says, interrupting my reverie.

"I did?" I ask, surprised.

"Yes. Ordinarily you are terrified of bugs."

"I guess . . . for whatever reason . . . I forgot about that."

93

5

Mid-June, 1991

The weather has gotten very hot. I look up, and it's the middle of June. The season has changed to summer so suddenly, I feel startled. I rub my eyes, squinting in the strong sun. We decide to go into nature today, and to take a few hours off from research, work, and learning about Indian ways. We head for Nambe Falls and Nambe Lake.

Fat chance of putting it behind. A strange thing has occurred. It's somewhat akin to what happens when you look at the sun and then look away—you still see blinding sunspots afterwards. The same phenomenon is true for my Indian learning. Because the Indian way is so powerfully metaphorical, when I turn away from it, I still see metaphors everywhere.

We hike to the Nambe waterfall and stand there looking at it. It flows down from the top of the mountain, pools for a while, and then continues flowing. Suddenly, I feel that I am looking at a paradigm of the human mind. Thoughts rush and gush and flow freely, and then they get "stuck" in a pool for a while. The stagnant thoughts go around and around and you're anxious or depressed or numb or fearful and then suddenly—*whoosh*—the thoughts flow freely again.

As we choose a trail to walk back toward the car, another metaphor pops into my mind. The trails down the mountain are rather labyrinthine. One is dank and Paul observes that there may be snakes. The second trail goes perilously close to the water. The third is rocky and slippery. A fourth leads nowhere. This is just like life, I think. Over and over again, you choose a path and it's wrong for you, or it leads nowhere. You have to try another path and another path and another path until you find your way out. You mustn't get upset if you are lost or it's too hard. Always look for another way. That is the labyrinth of life.

Can everyone see these metaphors in nature? Is the natural world "customized" for each of us, providing us with insight and illumination, if we are just willing to stop, look, and listen? The Indian culture and religion, which are so metaphorical, are clearly inspired by and based upon the natural world. In nature, they receive instruction. In nature, their father the sky and their mother the earth take care of them and provide for them.

After a bit of trial and error, we finally arrive at the car, and I see a lizard. It sounds very strange when I put this down on paper, but here goes: I have a special connection to lizards. I don't understand dogs or cats or birds, but I can communicate with these rapid, watchful animals that stay so close to the ground. Paul shakes his head in disbelief every time it happens. The Nambe lizard is running, and yet, when I ask it to stop, it does, as they always do. Paul just shakes his head. I ask the lizard to please stay there and give me the answer to the question: "How do you overcome fear?" I "hear" the answer: "Stop along the way and listen to friends, just as you are doing now!"

"Are you listening to lizards again?" Paul asks me.

"Yes," I answer firmly. "And they always have plenty to say. You've heard the Indian stories. There was a time when everyone spoke to animals and the animals spoke to them too. People even dialogued with rocks."

Paul picks up a stone and places it to his ear.

"The rock says he's hungry," Paul declares.

We leave the metaphors of Nambe Falls and go on to Nambe Lake. Last night I called my friend Bernie Krause, a musician and well-known expert in sound, who spends his life recording the sounds of nature. I asked him a very uncharacteristic question: "How do I learn to really listen?" He told me to go to a lake, sit there, put on earphones, and listen. I have no earphones, but I take the rest of his response to heart, and have come to a lake. I lie down on a blanket, ignoring the ants and the mosquitoes. I close my eyes. First I hear the rhythmic lapping of the water. It has no human rhythm, but a lazy pace all its own. Then flies, making parabolas of buzzing sounds in the air. In the distance, if I listen very closely, I can hear birds. They fade in and out. Then a gust of wind builds up rapidly and dies down just as fast. Before I know it, thirty minutes have passed. My mind is very quiet. I ask Paul if he has heard a lot too.

"I wasn't listening. I was *looking* instead. For the first time in my life, I watched a cloud form. It was amazing."

"Paul," I muse, "I don't think that looking and listening in nature are a *luxury*, but rather a necessity."

He agrees. I wonder aloud if this ability to look and listen is a large part of the Indian capacity to concentrate, listen, and remember. When you clear out your mind in nature, there is room for new information to come in.

In the afternoon, we go to a trading post at Nambe. I begin to speak to the elderly Indian owner, and it turns out that he is Spanish. (I have no talent whatsoever for discerning race.) His family has been on this land for three hundred years. Once we begin a conversation, he is incredibly talkative. I notice that, as we speak, about fifty white people walk in and out of the shop, and no one even talks to him or his wife. I guess this is a key. If you are friendly, people talk back to you and you learn to see and hear more. If you pass on, they pass on too . . .

The man continues to speak. He says he grew up with Indians. They all learned Spanish, so they could communicate, but they didn't want the Spanish to learn their Indian language. I guess I can understand why. The Indians didn't want to give anything as important and essential as LANGUAGE away to the colonizers.

As this charming man talks, I realize how frequently he mentions his people, or the Indian people. I have been feeling more and more how isolated we all are, and how we need to have some group, organization, community we belong to. I can understand how many of my peers have gone racing back to religion, but that does not seem to be my way. Yet, there must be a way—it is not possible to go through life as though you were a species unto yourself. Meeting so many Indians has only served to bring this home since they have such a keen sense of tribe and community.

When I get home the phone rings and it is Filiberto. He starts to talk about the role of women in Indian life. He says that a woman goes for advice to her husband, the husband goes to his mother (or mother-in-law), his mother goes to her husband, her husband to his mother, etc. I remark that this sounds like a built-in ladder. "Yes, it is," he says. "And when you want advice, why look down if you can look up?" So

I guess a man going to his wife is looking down! Men should go to their mothers and women should go to their husbands when they want counsel.

Filiberto explains that his language is very rich and there is one word that means about a dozen things depending upon how it is spoken. This word, spoken by the husband, indicates to the wife, in any one of a variety of ways, that she has permission to speak. It is a very orderly world. I listen with no judgment, because judgment is not going to get me anywhere, except a place I am already familiar with!

My second talk is with Lenny, who is in town for a day, before going back to clean up his mom's house after her death. I tell him how angry I am with Beaver for leaving us stranded in Oklahoma, and I ask if my reporting her to her boss at the Institute of American Indian Arts is going to cause waves in the Indian community.

"I can tell you how *we* would handle the situation," he offers.

"Shoot," I say.

"No, don't shoot," he quips. "Tell Beaver you want to see her face-to-face. Invite her to bring a witness along. In front of them both, you must tell Beaver exactly what you will be saying to her boss. Let them hear by your tone that you are not doing it out of spite or malice . . . but, rather, just reporting what took place. With a witness, there will be no misunderstanding."

I follow his directions, and call Beaver. I can hear that she is surprised and disarmed by my calling and by the content of my call. She listens to my invitation to bring a witness to my house, and to hear in advance what I will say to her boss. She says it is not necessary to have a witness, as she trusts me. She asks me to tell her on the phone what the content of my conversation with her boss will be. I tell her, and she listens without comment. Funny, when I speak to her directly, my intense anger begins to dissipate.

I realize that through Beaver, I am getting a life lesson in anger and how to deal with it. Beaver begins to call me several times a day, offering to help me with my work and introduce me to Indian people. I know she is trying to win me over. Tomorrow I have an appointment with her boss. Will I denounce her? Let her off the hook? Forgive her? I spend most of the night pondering the alternatives. I wonder if she, in her house, is sleeping soundly or squirming.

In the morning, I feel that I am ready for my talk with Beaver's boss, Garrison Baveur. I decide to deal with the situation the Indian way. I accept the fact that "what goes around will come around," and

I need not tell Garrison anything about Beaver's behavior in Oklahoma. We sit across from each other in a cafe, and Garrison chitchats
about his life, his wife, his past, his future, his plans, his dreams, his
travels, and his feelings. Suddenly, out of the blue, he tells me that he
is going to fire Beaver, and it's been a long time coming. Do I feel relieved? No, I feel guilty. I feel bad that Beaver will be out of a job. Now
my anger is completely transformed to sympathy. This is quite different for me—to sit back and watch emotions work, instead of getting caught up in them. Can I learn to apply this to fear too?

I come back to the present and watch Garrison across the table
from me. Garrison is the executive producer on my television show.
Since the show is about a white man in the Indian world, a decision
was made in Los Angeles to have Anglos and Indians paired up; for
every Anglo hired at a top level, there is an Indian too. This is the first
time such an experiment has been tried, and everyone is anxious to
know if it will work out. Lenny and I are the writers. Garrison is
paired with a white executive producer in L.A. He lobbied me tire-
lessly to get the job, and he lobbied the executive producer in L.A. He
is a real politician.

Garrison takes a forkful of his omelet and begins talking quite openly about how it feels to be a Native American, working with other Native Americans on film and TV projects. "They never got a chance
before. Now they are beginning to get a chance and they just aren't prepared for the professional world. It is very frustrating," he says.

He takes another bite and tells me that he has become very important, and that movie and TV people from all over the country are ap-
proaching him about doing Indian projects. He is both proud of
himself and disbelieving.

"For years I went around talking to people, telling them that this
was going to happen. Now it's happening. Everyone wants a piece of
the action and wants to do an Indian project. I have to pinch myself
to make sure it's true."

Garrison takes a bite of bread and I look at him. He never asks
about my research or writing or anything about the television show,
even though he is in charge of it. Just as I am about to get up from the
table and exit, I tell Garrison that I feel a little weird because I am
meeting people, speaking to people and then writing about it.

"Good," he says. "That's what you should be writing about. You're
the white person encountering the Indian world. The subject of your
writing is your life."

• • •

In the afternoon, Paul and I head out of Santa Fe. It is my job to look around, familiarize myself with the area and do research, so we take the mountain road to Taos. We stop off at Chimayo, and I decide to go back again to the little sanctuary because its holiness made such an impact on me the first time.

"You haven't gone to a synagogue once in twenty years, and you come to Chimayo twice in a month," Paul teases me.

I guess sacredness comes to people in strange places.

An old man addresses me at the door. "Do you know about the cross?" he asks. "It's a miracle. It was found right on this spot, in a field. When they tried to move it to a big, important church, it showed up right here in the same place again. Finally they just built a sanctuary here. That's why pilgrims from all over the world come here to get healed. In the back room, at the very spot where the cross was found, you can get healed too. Take a little bit of earth. Eat it or rub it on yourself. You'll see. Miracles happen."

When I walk inside, the Santuario has the same power as the last time. It is, indeed, a holy place. I decide to go with the experience of the moment, and not be bound by what I learned of religion as a child. I look at what other people are doing, and follow their lead. If there have been so many healings here, they must be doing something right. "I'm covering all my bases," as Lenny would say.

First, I actually kneel in front of all the multi-colored, multi-shaped Jesus figures. They all seem to be looking at me, talking to me, taking care of me. It feels like the safest place on earth. And then I walk into the back, and for a few brief moments, there is no one around the hole where the sacred cross was found. I reach in and take out a bit of earth, rubbing it over my chest and heart, where I feel fear and panic. Then I open my bag and take out a plastic spoon. I reach down and scoop up earth to take home with me, for people I care about now and in the future who need healing.

While I am digging, a blond tourist comes into the chamber. He has a camera. He gets me in focus and photographs me. I can hear the click of the shutter. I am busy meditating and opening my heart, so that gathering the dirt will be a strong experience for me, and for those I give it to.

"What are you doing with the dirt?" the tourist asks.

I mumble something about giving it away to those who need it, and go back to my meditation.

99

"Oh, so you're passing it around," he says. "Do you think it will help? I know people who've gone to other supposedly 'healing' places and nothing much happened. But I guess you're going to give it a try, right?"

At that second I understand how Indians feel when we ask them questions about their religious practices—and for an Indian a religious practice can be breathing in the fresh air or looking at a mountain. It is a totally inappropriate intrusion upon a person in a moment of private faith.

"Do you feel anything when you rub the dirt on?" the tourist asks.

I do not answer him. I do not tell him that I am once again cowed by the holiness of the Santuario, and by the sheer faith and prayer people have brought there. They have invested it with such power.

Outside of the chapel is a little (but locally famous) tortilla stand and we eat there. Dribbling with chili, we also buy a bag of *flavored* tortillas—the latest thing. There are cheese, onion, garlic, jalapeño, etc. I am surprised at how hungry sanctity makes me!

Since we are in such rich Hispanic territory, I decide to use this little trip to get the Spanish side of the story of how and why genocide was practiced against the Indians.

We stop at the home of Pablo, a traditional carver. His wooden statues and *santos* are all hand-carved and painted with natural pigments, and there are so many processes applied to the wood that it takes a year to complete a piece.

Besides being a master carver, Pablo has about five ancillary careers, one of them being donkey raising. It seems he has the largest donkeys in the world. So of course we *have* to see them. Male donkeys are called Jacks and the females are called Jennies.

"*Anda con migo*," Pablo says, as he introduces us to a donkey who is standing by himself in a stall.

"This Jack measures seventeen hands and he's not yet full-grown. He has the distinction of being the stupidest Jack in the world."

"Why?" I ask.

Pablo cackles. "Because it took me and my family hours on end to teach him to screw a Jennie. Each time, he kept forgetting how to do it."

"Pablo," I say very directly, and within earshot of all the donkeys, "you are a very intelligent and informed man. Can you please discuss with me the relationship of the Spanish and the Indians, going way back to the time of the *conquistadores*?"

"Sure, sure. Of course. Come back any time in the future. Just tell me when. Name the day."

In the future. For now, we talk about statues and donkeys.

As we wend our way toward Taos, speaking to people, we start hearing about the *"conversos."* In 1492, the Moors had been defeated in Spain, and the Catholic church held monolithic power. As Columbus set sail for the New World, the Jews of Spain were given a choice: convert to Catholicism or leave the country. Many decided to leave, and those who stayed were converted. Some became devout Catholics, and left Judaism behind forever. Others adopted Christianity on the surface, but kept up secret Jewish practices, at great peril. These were the *"conversos,"* or Crypto-Jews.

The Holy Office of the Inquisition ferreted them out and hounded them, and in some cases the punishment for practicing Judaism in secret was burning at the stake. Frightened for their lives, many found their way across the ocean to Mexico, where they hoped to find peace. But the long arm of the Inquisition reached to Mexico, so a good number volunteered to go to the outer reaches of the New World settlements—New Mexico—seeking freedom from persecution.

In New Mexico, they continued to live an outwardly Christian life, but the secret Jewish customs persisted—lighting Friday night candles or going into the fields to pray on Yom Kippur. Meanwhile, generations and generations passed, and they no longer remembered or knew they were Jewish. They were just Christians with some odd practices like twirling "draydels." And then, someone old would call his son to his deathbed or a father would tell his son in the field that the family was really Jewish and not Christian. The secret would be kept until the next person revealed it to the next incredulous kin. Even today, most *"conversos"* do not know they are Jews or, if they do, they do not admit it openly. Either they are afraid of persecution, or they can't deal with it. What do you do, for example, if you have spent your life as a Catholic learning that "Jews killed Christ" and then you find out you are one? What if you are a Catholic priest?

As we ride in the car, I wonder if the Indians were like the *"conversos"* at the beginning, when the Europeans first arrived and converted them by force. Perhaps on the outside they adopted Christianity, but secretly they continued to practice their own religion, underground in the kivas. Now, centuries later, all they know is that they are Christians. Many of them even spurn or scorn the old Indian religion, or forget that this is where they came from. Just as some Jewish *"conversos"* are now searching for their roots and going back to Judaism, I have met Indians who are looking back to *their* roots and shedding their Christianity. It is a difficult, often painful process because it can be seen by their Christian families as a betrayal. And yet, the need to know who they really are and where they come from is very strong in many descendants of forcibly converted people. It involves their deepest sense of personal identity.

Late in the afternoon, we arrive in Las Trampas, where Paul's friend Jeff, who went to elementary school with him, built his own house with his own hands on his own land in the mountains. As we walk in the door, Jeff's son announces that they've just trapped five mice. I freeze at the threshold and will not enter. It is very embarrassing in front of Jeff's son, who probably thinks I look like a cartoon character, curling my hands and toes in terror at the thought of five little mice. How can I be so helpless when my fears overtake me? I would like to walk right through the fears, waving hello to the little mice, whistling joyously. I would like to but I cannot.

We drive farther and farther north until we pass Taos and arrive at the "secret" hot springs. We park our car, climb down into a spectacular canyon, and there discover, as Paul describes it, the entire original cast of *Hair*. About thirty latter-day hippies tear off their clothes and dive off the rocks into a tiny hot spring bath. Or, alternately, they play Robert Bly and swim across the icy river to the other side. Paul splashes around, having a grand time, and I stand on a rock and watch. I would love to get undressed and dive in. I'd like to be uninhibited, and swim across to the far shore, since I am a good swimmer. But I do not. I cannot. I stand on the quay of life, once again, watching the ships depart.

"What do you think our Indian friends would do in this situation?" I ask Paul as he leaps out of the water in his bathing suit.

"They would either strip and dive in, or not worry about it."

"Well, I'm not Indian and I can neither dive in nor stop blaming myself."

He gently tugs at my arm, thinking he will ease me into the water, but I pull away, and retreat into myself.

On the plus side, Paul is wearing the petroglyph T-shirt I made for him. I have always loved rock paintings, and I painstakingly adorned the white shirt. Every person who comes to swim stops Paul to say how great the shirt is.

102

"I hear there are petroglyphs around Santa Fe," I murmur to Paul. "I sure wish I knew where to find them."

Someone must hear all our wishes around here! Half the people who arrive at the hot springs are self-proclaimed experts on Indian petroglyphs, so we get bombarded with information on where to find ancient Indian markings. Everything we need just falls into our laps.

In the evening, we go to the World's Poetry Heavyweight Championship Bout and the huge turnout and stomping, clapping, howling throngs are testimony to the fact that even with the Inquisition of the last few political regimes, the arts flourish and thrive.

After the bout, I get Amiri Baraka's autograph (in the early days, he was known as Leroi Jones). Amiri helped to raise black consciousness and white consciousness of black arts and artists. As I look at him, I think that being black must be very much like being Indian. Every word you write is a struggle to define and defend yourself against the dominant culture. I wonder why there is no union between Indians and blacks? If the minorities united, they would not be a minority any more.

I also meet a Latino poet. He seems friendly and open, so I ask him if he can help me to understand the Hispanic side of history. Why does no one talk about what really happened to the Indians when the Spanish arrived? Why does everyone whitewash it and make it seem like an amiable, peaceful, friendly sort of conquest? Why do so many Hispanic people continue to look down on Indians today?

The poet smiles broadly, and doesn't hesitate to answer.

"Many Indians died," he said, "but the Spanish didn't actually kill them. What happened is that there was a lot of work to be done and the Spanish settlers worked the Indians very hard. The Indians weren't used to hard work. They worked so hard, they died from it.

"Quite often, Indian women were taken into Spanish homes. Sometimes they had Spanish babies with the men. Their babies got Spanish names, and in many cases the Indian women saw that the Spanish way of life had much to offer and chose to follow it. That's the real story."

At night, we go back to Jeff's house. He swears that the mice are gone, and he is very touching, friendly, and hospitable. I will never forget the image of him in his Thoreau cabin, running around madly, trying to shut off all the fake and real alarm systems he has installed to protect his meager belongings on a mountain in the middle of nowhere!

103

In the morning, we go for a walk with Jeff into the hills, alongside a brook. I have new hiking boots, and feel great in them. I walk across logs suspended over ravines, I climb up rocks.

"Hey, if you lose your grip on the rocks, just let yourself fall and don't worry about it. Know that you'll fall into the water. If you tense, you'll get hurt. Your fall can even be fatal."

I get tense just HEARING about it!

"Don't look back!" Jeff calls. "Just keep going."

Wow! This is great! I let his voice guide me over the rocks. Brava! Brava! I am conquering my fears!

We walk into gorgeous unpopulated canyons. And then we come to a deserted rock next to a running stream of melted ice that descends from the mountains. We all sit down and I decide to listen to the flowing water, as part of my listening exercises. Shrinks say people don't change because they can't listen. I am going to learn to listen by hook or by crook! I close my eyes to meditate on the sound, and suddenly Paul interrupts me. He never does that, so I know it must be important. He tells me to listen to the low voices. The bass sounds. What bass sounds? All I hear is the bubbling of the brook.

I concentrate. I listen. And then . . . my God . . . how can I describe the wonder? I close my eyes and hear a bass instrument playing. *Boom, boom, boom, boom.* The sound is rich, deep, like a bass player in a jazz band. And suddenly I hear the metal whisk of someone playing snare drums. A jazz band has formed within seconds. I keep wondering if I'm really hearing the brook's music, or imagining it? When I open my eyes, Paul has heard it too. If only one person hears the music, it may be imagination; if two people hear it, that's verification.

"Paul," I say, "do you remember what Dr. Doug White Wolf told us the Indian name is for the people of Santa Clara Pueblo?"

"Yes. The people of the singing brook."

"EXACTLY. The same music that we are hearing now. The Santa Clarans heard it too. This is really exciting. We are experiencing the origin of names."

"Hey, maybe you guys can ask the brook to play my favorite song," Jeff quips.

In the evening, we race back to Santa Fe for dinner at the home of Garrison Baveur and his wife, Sonia. Rumor has it that Sonia is Garrison's fifth wife; all of them were Anglo and blond. She is a lovely, gentle woman, whose life revolves completely around Garrison. Garrison himself is half white and half Indian, but he never refers to the former half. His cultural identity is clearly with his Native brothers.

We talk about pristine America and what it must have been like for early Indians, who had such sophisticated knowledge of the natural world. All of that is gone now because the original context is gone. Cities have sprung up and the natural world has been tampered with.

Garrison tells us stories of how he was on an archeological dig and he dug up a Pueblo-style grave with a Plains Indian buried in it. The grave was in a hole in the ground, in the middle of the main room of an ancient house. He insists that many Indians still bury their dead that way. Garrison goes on to describe the cadaver he found. The Indian was buried in his clothes with all of his important possessions around him. He was just laid in the "living room" floor, in a fetal position. As Garrison talks, we begin to feel a little spooky.

"Who do you think is buried under your carpet?" I ask.

Garrison tells us that he grew up like all Indians, never looking a white person in the eyes. Just ten or so years ago, Indians weren't allowed to eat in certain white restaurants.

"That feeling will never go away because it's so deeply ingrained," Garrison insists. "We have gone beyond our parents, who rejected their Indian ties because they caused such pain. Beyond them, yes, but how can we ever recapture all that's been lost?"

We go outside and look up above us. The night is perfect, balmy, completely clear, with a sky full of stars watching over us. Paul says you can see their colors.

"How do you say 'stars that are brightly colored' in your Indian language?" I ask Garrison.

He doesn't know, because he cannot speak his native tongue.

When we get home, Lenny calls. "Whatcha been doing?" he asks.

"I've been doing the work we BOTH should be doing."

He ignores my jibes.

"You're probably asking lots of questions and getting lots of answers. Some may be true, and some may not."

"Well, actually, I've been on a quest to get the Spanish point of view about the *conquistadores* and the Indian genocide."

"Oh, well, forget it," Lenny says matter-of-factly. "You'll never get the truth about that. At least not from Spanish people. Maybe not from Indians either. At my own Pueblo, I've often seen ceremonies that celebrated what the Indians got from the Spanish."

"Really?"

"Sure. We try not to condemn the Spanish people. We don't confuse people with their GOVERNMENTS."

"So are you saying that there has been forgiveness?"

"I'm saying life is a beautiful, complex, and simple matter."

"Like our working relationship?" I joke.

"Exactly. Lots of different levels of reality."

I go to sleep thinking about what Lenny said—that his people try not to confuse people with their governments. This was the very argument my friends and I tried to make during the Vietnam war. Don't confuse us with our government. There are many Americans against the war.

The next morning, I shake Paul awake.

"Get up. Get up. Isn't today the day Belinda James wrote to us about?"

"Hmmm? What is it? I'm still sleeping. I'm dreaming that we're eating chili again."

"It's a prophetic dream. Today is the Feast Day at San Juan, the Pueblo Belinda comes from. San Juan is John the Baptist. There'll be lots of chili."

"Belinda?"

"Belinda. The brilliant Indian ballerina. The one who says toe slippers remind her of deer's hooves. She wrote and told us to go to her grandparents' house to eat."

"Oh, Belinda! Of course!" By now Paul is sitting up and fully awake. "Let's bring two watermelons. Three watermelons. To make up for what we *didn't* bring to Sandia Pueblo out of ignorance."

I telephone Belinda's mother, Povi, and ask her for directions. She tells me, speaking very carefully, that we are BELINDA'S SPECIAL GUESTS for the Feast Day. She also tells me that there had been an awful article in the paper several years ago saying that ANYONE could come and eat at an Indian house on a Feast Day. Could I imagine that? People of such meager means, having to feed strangers! And then, to make matters worse, the strangers really pigged out.

I hold my breath. Does she have any idea that we walked into an Indian home, uninvited, at Sandia Pueblo? Does she know how much chili we ate?

"We're bringing three watermelons, a salad, and a chicken," I say to Paul, covering the phone.

"The feast is now only open to special people," Povi continues. "We don't have much, but we will be happy to have you as special guests.

106

You should feel honored by Belinda's invitation."

We stop off to buy food at the Furr's supermarket in Espanola, en route to San Juan Pueblo. I like this Furr's because, in addition to having a wide choice of foods, in the back and upstairs, it also has the most accessible and cleanest bathroom I have found between Santa Fe and the Pueblos.

We arrive at San Juan and locate the home of Toni and Leandro Cruz, Belinda's grandparents. We are the first ones there. Belinda's very beautiful and spunky mother Povi greets us and drags us inside, urging us to be the first to eat. I feel the poverty immediately. This is no lavish table, and you can tell that the family is being exceedingly generous with extremely sparse means. Imagine our joy at finding plain chicken, for once, among the comestibles. We gratefully bypass the chilis, and settle on a chicken and rice broth that could have come from my grandmother's house. We have a little salad, lemonade, and bread baked in the outdoor *horno*. We are received with great warmth because we are invited guests and because we are Belinda's friends.

Toni and Leandro are the grandparents who raised Belinda, and she speaks of them lovingly in person, on the phone, and in her letters. After the meal, as I sit next to Toni on her threadbare sofa, with her toothless mouth and smooth skin, I feel the softness that I so love in older Indian women, and which I felt from my own grandmother, who is now deceased. Somehow, whether it is true or not, Toni smells of baby powder to me. Even if it is not true, the imagined odor suggests that her gentle and unthreatening presence affects me very deeply, in all of my senses.

We go to see the Comanche dancing on the Plaza and it is very ragged to my eyes. Children are dressed in makeshift capes. Some of the boys carry arrows. Nothing matches. The boys wear heavy face-paint, and one has his face painted with the stripes and stars of the American flag.

"Paul, this looks like a Purim parade to me!" I whisper.

Paul says he is surprised that the Pueblo boys are dressed like Plains Indians, with their roaches (a sort of Mohawk hairdo made of feathers or quills), feather bustles, and facepaint. This is typical of the Pueblo Indian dances . . . they incorporate elements from other tribes and blend them into their own practices. It is part of their flexibility and adaptability. Paul and I both remark that the boys have lots of flamboyant dance moves, and the women just wave their arms and have much more restrained and placid steps.

107

We walk by the stands with vendors selling their wares. Tourists are pouring out of their cars. One carver of *santos* wants $1500 a piece. People are grumbling about the commercialization of the dances. The kids aren't complaining, though, as they slurp their snow cones and ice creams.

After a few rounds of dances, we head back to Toni and Leandro's house. Inside, many relatives arrive and sit at the table to eat. I want to somehow contribute, so I make it my task to take pictures of them all to send to Belinda. At the entrance to the Pueblos, there is almost always a sign warning people not to take pictures, and I hope I am not offending them. Tourists photograph Indians walking, snoozing, shopping, praying, and peeing. It can get pretty insulting.

Some of Belinda's family are flash-shy, some don't want pictures, but I hound them and tease them all until they pose. Leandro is very ill, and I am glad to get a few pictures of him while he is still here. As we hang out with the family and take a few more shots, I find every opportunity possible to sit on the threadbare sofa and snuggle up next to Toni to get some of her grandmotherly warmth.

"You look good today, Toni. You're a real sexpot," I tease her. For on this special Feast Day, she wears the same thing she wears most other days—a shapeless, printed *shmata*.

When the time is right, Toni begins to speak. She says that Povi was unable to raise Belinda and her other children, so she did it. I am praying this isn't awkward for Belinda's lovely mother, who is sitting on the other side of the room, listening. For once, I do not ask any questions. I just let Toni speak.

I have noticed that Toni's house is immaculate, and I soon learn why. Toni raised the kids by cleaning motel rooms, and her husband drove a school bus and then became a janitor. One day she was asked to go into the school kitchen. She didn't dare, because she was dressed so poorly. The school cook insisted, and then, knowing how hard it was for Toni to raise the kids, she asked her if she wanted to be assistant cook.

"How could I accept her offer?" Toni says, wide-eyed. "I didn't know how. I wouldn't be any good at it. I had never cooked for large groups besides my family."

But over her objections, the cook signed her on for the job, and there she remained for many years as the children grew, making pies and cakes until they nauseated her! (Like Toni, most Indian people are modest about themselves and their capabilities.)

Toni's great source of pride is that even if her grandchildren wore patches, they were clean. This reminds me of one of Garrison Baveur's stories. When he worked on a farm as a child, every time he got a fleck of dirt on him his Blackfoot mother made him change his clothes lest people call him "a dirty Indian."

Toni goes on to tell me that she still bakes her own bread, but the outdoor *horno* is broken down, and dirt falls into the bread. So she only uses that bread for herself and her husband.

"I have lived here in San Juan all my life," she tells me. "I got married in that chapel and watched my kids grow there."

"There is a tremendous sense of continuity in your life," I comment. She nods.

"Everyone always knows where to find me, and once a year—today is that special day—all my relatives come to visit for Feast Day."

Throughout our talk, Toni never gets up to greet her relatives who arrive. She just sits on her sofa and watches them come in and sit down. She introduces Paul and me to each one of them as they sit. But then she goes back to telling her story, for she is totally absorbed in the telling.

"Please, see if you can help Belinda," she implores me. "I worry about her. She has such a hard life. All alone there in New York, trying to make her way as a dancer."

"She's a great dancer," I say. "It may be long and difficult, but she'll make it."

"Oh, I hope so," says Toni.

This has been a very successful conversation for me, because I have refrained from asking any questions. But I falter at the last moment. Can I ask one question? A little one? A teeny-tiny one?

"We recently got a gift of two buffalo horns. Where should I put them in our *casita*? Is there a special place for them?"

Toni refuses to answer. Instead she tells me something about the buffalo horns. "You know, buffalo horns are hard to come by. We can't get them like we used to. We use them in our dances. Just take care of them the way you would take care of any valuable possession."

At the end of the talk, she gets up. Her legs have lost circulation, and one of the nephews asks me to rub them. I do so, quite vigorously, until the circulation returns. "You should be an Indian doctor," Toni quips.

"Only two things are missing" I parry, "the Indian and the doctor part!"

Next I sit down with Belinda's mom, who understates her intelligence and drive and apologizes for her audacity as she explains that she has an idea for a business for herself. She wants to teach white doctors a little of the Tewa language and some "cultural necessities," so that their Indian patients can understand them without being scared to death.

"Some of those doctors are a little—I hate to say it—arrogant," she says.

"A LITTLE arrogant!?! You mean those God-impersonating technocrats we kindly call 'doctor'?"

I guess I am a bit less gentle than Povi is.

Paul and I sit at the kitchen table and help Povi put together a proposal that she can take to hospitals and clinics. She doesn't have a clue about how to write it or how to present or "sell" herself. Like many of the Indian people we have met, who are so bright and imaginative, Povi is handicapped in the white world because our ways are so very foreign to her. I doubt that she ever had use for a résumé or proposal when she was growing up.

I think back to a conference of Americans Indians in film, television and video that I attended about eight months ago. I was the only Anglo present, because I was asked to observe and write about it, to filter the experience through white eyes for a white world.

The participants in that conference were fabulous. They came from across the country, and they were vocal, eloquent, talented, and resentful that they were being denied access to the media. But yet, at the end of the conference, when producers from Los Angeles and New York showed up, and sign-up lists were posted for the Native Americans to schedule appointments with them, few actually signed. They left, they went off, they walked away. The whole notion of signing up to hype yourself to someone in order to get a job was totally alien to almost everyone's mentality.

I tried to understand it, as I try to understand Povi. I think that many Indians are deeply affected by their teachings about community spirit and humility. They are taught not to brag and not to stick out. The individual should be part of a group. What do they do, then, when they MUST stand out and "brag" about what their capabilities are? It goes against their grain. It will take time for them to learn how to do it. Perhaps they will be able to do it their own way. To make their talents and qualities known in a way that is not offensive to them.

When we finish talking with Povi, we are urged to eat again.

110

"No, no, no," we protest. "We couldn't possibly." But we are pigs when it comes to Pueblo food. We stop protesting when it is placed in front of us.

"Hey, you guys seem right at home here," says Belinda's cousin.

"Why shouldn't we feel at home?" I joke. "We've got rice and chicken and Grandma."

But on some very serious level, I am not joking. We feel more at home here than we do at dinner parties in Los Angeles. Maybe it's that at the Pueblos, there are no expectations. And no one talks about cars, money, deals, brand names, mortgages, or furniture.

At night, we go to the Santa Fe Opera and sit outside, listening to the music during an invitation-only dress rehearsal. Ordinarily, my eyes would be fixed on the stage, since I come from a theater background. But this night, my eyes drift up, up, over the beams to the sky. Everything seems so perfectly arranged. The moon is draped from the waist down in a gentle cloud. I notice that stars actually twinkle, and the twinkling is choreographed. They seem to do it in turn. A flash of lightning zigzags across the sky, dissolving gracefully. Suddenly I understand why Indians live in a state of awe and reverence for the natural world. It is ineffably beneficent and beautiful.

As we leave the opera, we run into a woman we know.

"I hear you are at the Pueblos a lot," she says. "I've lived here for years, but I never go. Tell me, what kind of food do you eat there?"

Paul describes a diet rich in sugar that gives Native Americans diabetes, and various chili dishes that are no different from a Mexican/New Mexican restaurant. I literally gape at him. I couldn't disagree more about the food. To me it is Indian "soul food," prepared very specially, with love and tradition, a communal effort that makes the table sing. And yet, we have been eating the same things! How can that be?

The only explanation is that Paul experiences the Indian people and the Indian way as "very very interesting," but to me it is all magical. The food, the houses, the bread—it all belongs to another realm, and when I am there, I am entering another dimension in time and space. This is not something good or bad; it just IS. As Paul puts it, it should not be analyzed. As I put it, it is a world where I FEEL things—and feeling that acutely is so rare that I dare not tamper with it by trying to explain it any further.

In the morning, I get up and drive to a meeting with Joe Ost, a very political Indian artist, whose paintings are slashed with stars, stripes,

111

dead buffalo, and broken dreams. We make arrangements to meet at a restaurant next to a movie theater. Within ten minutes I get lost, as I usually do. I start looking for a movie theater. I roll down the window and ask a man who is standing in front of a trailer for directions.

"There's no movie theater around here," he says.

I insist that there *is* one, only I can't find it.

"Hey, look, hang on a minute while I go and check with my wife."

He sticks his head in the trailer, and pulls it out again a moment later.

"The movie theater is right there—around the corner. I knew it all along," he says.

I stare at him in wonderment. "WHAT DO YOU MEAN YOU KNEW IT?!? You just told me it wasn't there!" I am thinking.

As I stare at him, someone is staring at me. "Hi," he says. "I'm Joe Ost."

"Joe," I say, "can we talk?"

"Sure."

"What's with this male syndrome? Do men always have to pretend they know everything? You would rather be lost forever in hell than roll down the window and ask someone how to get somewhere. Can you ever be wrong? Ignorant?"

"Hey, once or twice in my life, I've been told I was wrong," says Joe. "Of course, I was told by women, so they were probably mistaken."

I can see he is laughing at me. I start to laugh at myself. Suddenly, it all makes cultural sense to me.

"WOMEN act DUMB and MEN act SMART. Women get helpless, like they know nothing. And men get inflated, like they are omnipotent. Why do we act this way? Why do we ACT at all?"

"Because we're not content to just be human."

"Meaning?"

"Meaning that it's not enough to be what we are, the way the Creator made us. We try to be what we think we should be."

"You mean we're all coyotes trying to pretend we're buffalos?"

He smiles. I really like Joe Ost.

In the afternoon there is a big meeting, at Garrison Baveur's request, to iron out the problem of Lenny doing absolutely no work on the TV project since I arrived. Garrison rails about Lenny behind his back, but when we all sit in a room, the railing is hardly a whimper. In fact, he takes Lenny's side against me. Is this Indian solidarity, or the fact that Lenny is Garrison's mentor, and responsible for bringing Garrison back to his Indian ways many years ago?

Garrison's argument is that I have to accept the fact that Lenny is busy with other things. I should be thankful that I have had the opportunity to become autonomous in the Indian world. If Lenny had done any work, I never would have been strengthened this way. I should be thrilled that I've been left on my own.

"Wait a minute," I say. "This is unmitigated bullshit. I'm not talking to you about character-building. I'm talking about the fact that Lenny and I were hired as partners, and one of us is doing all the work!"

Garrison turns to Lenny.

"Lenny, no matter how busy you are, you should call Judie once a day. If you're too busy to talk about work, then talk about what it's like outside. There's a lot Judie can learn about the weather."

"I will not be angry, I will not be angry, I will not be angry," I say to myself as I walk home across the field full of prairie dogs that leads to the casita. I step high in the grass, so the prairie dogs will not bite my heels. Usually I am terrified of them, but today I am too upset to be frightened.

"You just cannot be one step ahead of an Indian," I tell Paul when I get home. "They know the road much better than you do!"

"Sounds like you handled yourself very well," Paul compliments me.

"Well, I tried. I turned to both of them and said, 'You know, working with you two is giving me a much less romantic view of Indians.'

" 'I'm glad you no longer romanticize Indians,' Lenny said. 'That's good.'

" 'And it's good that you're learning to see through and confront Indian bullshit,' added Garrison.

" 'Would that this were true, Garrison!' I cried out. 'Sometimes it flies faster than I can catch it.'

"We all laughed then, and it ended the meeting on an upbeat note. But as I was leaving the meeting, I felt very much like a Paleface, and an outsider."

Paul listens to every word.

"I think your self-control is remarkable," he tells me. "I know a lot of other people who would have leapt across the room and strangled them."

In the evening, Povi calls and asks if she can come to the *casita*. I am surprised to hear her voice, but say yes, of course, come. Half an hour later she calls back, says she is lost, and then adds that she thought better of coming and is embarrassed for having bothered us. She wishes us well, and says she'll see us some other time.

We immediately get the sense that the visit is important to her and we take turns speaking into the phone, urging, begging, teasing, and taunting her until she agrees to come. Paul waits patiently in the parking lot until Povi drives up, and he is her personal escort service to make sure she doesn't run away.

Povi says she has come because she needs help. "I need a little boost," she says. "When you came to the San Juan Feast Day, it all made sense to me—about the job proposal and what I should do and how I should write it. But when I got home, I just couldn't do it."

Povi tells us a story. When she was an infant, she wriggled and squirmed in her cradle board. Her grandfather finally agreed to have her grandmother take her out of the cradle board. "That one will never be able to be tied down!" the grandfather proclaimed. And it was prophetic. Povi is a moving spirit. "If I wasn't, where would I be?" she asks. "I'd be stuck on a reservation, with no doors open for me."

It is getting late and we don't have a lot of time, so I take Povi into the second bedroom, which is my office, picking up piles of papers as we go and excusing myself for only having a tasteless muffin and juice to serve her. Worse, I offer her yogurt and apple sauce mixed together. I can't think of what else to give her because she is our honored guest but there is nothing in the house.

When Povi looks at the yogurt and apple sauce mix, she tries to be polite, but she actually winces. Only Paul and my mother know how pitiful my domestic skills are.

I sit down at the computer and have Povi talk through one of her ideas while I put it in proposal form. Then she reads what I write and says, "Well, no, I meant something else." So I rewrite it to her specifications. I hand it to her when I am done and tell her to use this proposal as a prototype for any ideas she has in the future. Then I give her a pep-talk, telling her the truth—that she is beautiful and talented, and she must act as though she believes in herself, even if she doesn't. She must pretend she feels young, even if she feels old. Sooner or later the act will become real to her. She thanks me profusely and leaves. Once again, Paul accompanies her to the parking lot.

An hour later, Paul comes in very quietly. He says he has been with

Povi all that time and she has been sobbing. Years ago, white people had helped her father, offering him their truck when he had none. But she thought there were no more people like that, who were willing to help.

"She kept crying," Paul tells me. "Crying and saying how much it means to her that someone out there cares."

Paul and I sit quietly, thinking that it takes so little to give these people a jump start. And sometimes that is all that is needed.

The next day I continue my research, and when I come home, Laura Fragua knocks at the door. I smile and am thrilled to see her. In L.A., if anyone came to the door unannounced, I would either bite his head off or not answer the door. But here, it is the Indian way. And here, we have learned to consider an unannounced visit as an honor and a pleasure.

The phone rings and it is Lenny, inviting us to a barbecue. I almost never see him, so I am surprised by the call. I think that since we are partners, it would be a good idea to get together once every few blue moons or so.

"I'd love to, Lenny," I say quite honestly, "but I can't. We have a guest here. It's Laura. Can she . . . I mean . . . is it all right if we . . . I mean is there food for . . . ?"

"You bagel brain!" Lenny says, as he bursts out laughing. "Of course she can come."

I had forgotten that when Indians entertain, it's entirely appropriate to bring other people along. It's part of the whole communal spirit.

Lenny made chicken with zucchini and pineapple all wrapped in aluminum foil. We stand outside, watching the orange sun setting and the full moon rising. All seems very right with the world.

After dinner, Laura comes back to the *casita* to show us slides of her art, for she has just been chosen to show her work at the New Mexico State Fair. I expected it to be good, but not *this* good: I am knocked out by her slides and portfolio. She is a fine sculptor, painter, graphic artist. She works in pink alabaster, oil, acrylic, charcoal. She writes poems, too, and we make her perform them for us. She is a student activist and is president of the Alumni Association of the Institute of American Indian Arts. She is a very traditional Pueblo Indian from Jemez, and she comes from a long, proud line. Her grandfather was the last of the Pecos Indians.

I stand there looking at her, smiling. She is probably wondering why

I am grinning. The reason is simple: if Beaver hadn't acted so awfully I never would have retreated into the back of the van, and it was in the back of the van that I got to know Laura.

Before tonight, Laura has been very quiet and guarded, but now she opens up. I am surprised to discover that she is bright and lively with a sharp tongue and warm laugh.

"Did you ever hear of the Mescalero Apaches?" she asks me.

Is she reading my mind? How can she possibly know that I have been fascinated by the Mescaleros ever since I saw one of their frightening, black-hooded masks, capped by a white wooden cross crown, and was shown pictures of their dramatic, primitive dances in a museum? Does she know that I went into the museum bathroom and asked *out loud* to be able to see those dances one day?

"Yes, I have. Why do you ask?" I try to sound casual.

"My husband Steve is a sculptor, and he's also the prosecutor on the Mescalero tribal court. Every year we go to their puberty ceremony. [She pronounces it "pooberty."] It takes place over the July 4th weekend. You can stay at our house and join us this year."

"Wow!" I think. "I really am blessed. Over and over and over."

"The Mountain Gods come out at night and you can see them dance. I think it will be interesting for you."

For a moment, I actually feel a wash of *gratitude* to Beaver. For all the pain she caused, this is the reward.

I lie in bed at night, contemplating what all of this means. Nothing, nothing, nothing is as it seems. I must have no expectations in life, for they will be thwarted and I will get something else—perhaps something better than what I was expecting. I must keep my eyes and ears and especially my heart open. I must help other people and I will be rewarded by the joy it brings. I must continue to say out loud the things I wish for. My voice will be heard and the wishes come true.

"What are you thinking, my little Fearless One?" Paul asks.

"I'll tell you, but you're going to think I've lost my mind."

When I finish telling Paul about my ruminations, he kisses me passionately.

"I don't think you've *lost* your mind. I think you've *found* it."

6

Dancing with the Mountain Gods

Early July, 1991

I'm reading a newspaper, and my eyes linger on the word "Pecos."

"Paul," I ask, "do you know where Pecos is?"

"Nope."

"I'll pay you a dollar if you find it on the map and go there with me. The name sounds pretty exotic."

"If I had a dollar for everything you cajoled me into doing, I'd be a rich man," Paul laughs.

Several hours later we drive to Pecos National Monument. On top of a hill, in the middle of the stones and adobe that mark the site of the old Pecos Indian village, what strikes the eye first is the fabulous ruin of a Spanish church. I try to look away, but the church beckons to me again.

"How can a church be lovely, when it marks the beginning of the Spanish conquest and invasion?" I ask an Indian man who sits among the ruins, kissing his girlfriend. He probably thinks I am nuts for asking.

"It doesn't make sense that beauty and destruction go hand in hand," I tell him.

The Indian man and his blond girlfriend turn to look at me.

"Life is full of contradictions," he says.

Pecos was, in essence, a walled village, with more than two thousand people living there. Amidst the ruins, there are still signs of a thriving Pueblo, where the Plains Indians used to come to trade. By the beginning of the twentieth century, disease, economic hardship, spiritual disaster, and the yoke of the cruel Spanish missionaries had taken their toll. Only seventeen Pecos souls remained! They picked up their meager possessions and moved to Jemez Pueblo, and their descendants remain there today. Laura Fragua is one of them, and her connection to Pecos makes the place come alive for us.

The cactus and desert flowers are in bloom, and the birds are chirping so melodically that it is the first time in my life I can actually hear a bird *song*. The sun shines gold on the ruins, until, suddenly, ominous storm clouds arise and frame the ruins dramatically. "If you don't like the weather around Santa Fe, just wait around five minutes," goes the local saying.

It pours, and then suddenly it is sunny again. It changes that fast. We decide to picnic at this heavenly spot, and suddenly I see Paul doing a very curious thing. The welts from pernicious ant bites at Dr. Doug White Wolf's house are still fresh on his arms and legs, and I watch, incredulous, as he tries to interact with the same desert ants. In fact, he tries to assert his superiority over them.

He leans over and drops a quarter-inch piece of corn chip. "Here, let's see you carry *this!*" he says to an ant, with sarcasm.

Much to our amazement, that tiny ant picks up the chip, which is five times his size, and begins to schlepp it home. We put down our food and watch it on its journey. It must be a hundred feet to the anthill. The equivalent of our walking a thousand miles. It is a very humbling experience. Never once does the ant taste the chip—it just carries it home for the community.

We walk around the ruins some more, and note all the kivas (underground ceremonial spaces—they are easily recognizable because they look like open holes with ladders going down into them). At the time of the Spanish conquest, the first thing the *conquistadores* did as they tried to "civilize" the natives was to try to convert them. When the Pueblos revolted, in 1680, and drove the Spanish away, they increased their religious and kiva life as a sign of rebellion. The Spanish returned to reconquer the area, and they filled the ceremonial kivas with sand. But sand or no sand, reconstructed or not, when you climb down the wooden ladders into the kivas, you feel the power of the earth and the people who once worshipped there. We have heard that to many Indians "breath" is immortal and, at Pecos, you can almost hear the breath of the ancestors that carried prayers to the ear of the Creator.

• • •

Dancing with the Mountain Gods

The next morning we take another trip, this time to Glorieta. Equipped with new hiking boots, which chafe like mad, we hike for three hours up into the mountain forest until we arrive at a ghost town—an abandoned lumber camp. The butterflies are our companions as we cross the mountain meadows and walk beside a running brook. First I get upset as I think about cutting down trees to print tabloids and trashy novels. But then, I begin to wonder and marvel about the fact that logs were transported down from this high and inaccessible spot. How did they do it? Once again, it becomes obvious that people who live very close to nature understand much more about it and its secrets than we do. I grow wistful as I have this thought. There is so much catching up to do, and only a lifetime to do it. I try to take one sense at a time and open it to nature—first comes HEARING, so that I can learn to hear the sounds of the natural world instead of the noise in my own mind. Some people have to go to the Himalayas to get lessons and some have to go to Machu Picchu. I seem to get them at my doorstep in New Mexico.

I get one over the next few days. I begin to feel lousy, the way I used to feel in Los Angeles. Anxious, restless, constantly on the verge of a panic attack. The world seems blurry, and I watch it through a fog. Time hangs. I retreat from human contact. My tongue feels thick. My own voice sounds bizarre when I speak. "Why am I cursed with such messed-up biochemistry and neurochemistry and why does it elude successful and definitive treatment?" I moan.

I begin to blame myself—to feel that somehow it is my fault, and there is something inferior about me as a human being that causes me to have shame and to hide out from the rest of humanity when I am not well. I decide to fight it and walk by myself to the gym. It's about a half-hour walk across a field where there are hundreds of prairie dogs. I am afraid of them. They run back and forth like rats, and I watch my ankles to make sure they are not going to attack me when I walk by their homes—which are ambush holes in the ground.

I step gingerly, lifting my legs like a prancing horse, and I leave the field with great relief. But the moment my feet hit the concrete pavement that leads to the gym, I see something that makes my toes curl. There, in front of my gym shoes, and almost touching them, is the most God-awful creature. It looks like a bee, but about ten times the size of a bee, with a rotund body and a bulbous orange-beige lump for a head. I step back in horror, and look around for another human being. A young, adorable Hispanic kid is walking by and I stop him.

119

"What in hell is that creepy-crawly sucker?" I ask him with disgust.

The kid, unperturbed, looks down. "It's just an insect that lives under the ground."

I make a few more "yech, phooey" sounds. The kid continues.

"It's called Child of the Earth, ma'am," he informs me.

Well, that stops me dead in my gym shoes. What a beautiful name! That hideous thing is a child of the earth, just as we all are!

"It survives by fleeing and tunneling and hiding only," the kid tells me, as he walks away.

That's what I do too! I flee and tunnel and hide in order to survive when I don't feel well. Suddenly a wave of gratitude washes over me. I am filled with a sense of the beauty of the gift of life. Even if we are grotesque insects or a woman with a faulty biochemical balance, no matter *what* is wrong with us, we are all children of the earth.

In the afternoon, refreshed from the gym, I have a long talk with Roland Duvall, a lawyer who represents a lot of the Indian tribes. He is most reluctant to tell me anything, and I have to pass a twenty-minute test which consists of my informing him of my credentials. These have nothing to do with my postgraduate degrees or which awards I have won. Quite the opposite. I have to tell Roland who I know in the Indian world, who I worked with, what my attitudes are toward Indians and Indian affairs. He is most bright and charming.

We speak briefly about the issue of repatriation—that is, returning the bones of Indians to their ancestors and people. For many years now, Indian graves have been bulldozed, looted, and trashed, and the bones are stored in boxes for scientific examination or museum display. I shudder when I hear this, for I imagine how I would feel if my beloved grandmother were dug up and put in labeled drawers in Washington! Or I think of Gramps in a display case at the Smithsonian!

Roland gives me a lot of interesting insight. He says that he must get clearance to tell me specifics from the tribal governments.

"These people must be protected at all cost," he says. "Why, even their bones aren't safe from white people!"

Surprisingly but understandably, Roland says that most of the tribes he works with don't want the bones back.

"There are between 400,000 and 1,000,000 skeletons, and the tribes can't deal with that culturally or fiscally," he explains. "Their dead have been properly mourned and buried already. What they want is for the bones to be reburied, and, whether they do it themselves or the government does it, the white government should pay for it. They can't just dump the bones on these impoverished people and tell them to 'go dig.'

"Furthermore, most of the Indians don't have a problem with bones being used for scientific study, if it is necessary. The best thing would be to take bone slivers and bury the bodies afterwards. The important thing is the dignity and respect afforded to the living and the dead. These bones are currently treated the way Indians are treated. Respect for one would increase respect for the other. Either in unmarked or in marked graves, these bones should be buried again and set to rest!" he says with passion.

We speak more personally, and I am interested in Roland's feelings about a lot of issues I am currently facing.

"I no longer have white guilt over what happened to the Indians," he says. "Of course my preference would be to have these people left alone from 1492 onward. But I have come to realize that if the Spanish didn't do it, someone else would have come to colonize the States. You see, it's a nice place to live."

He laughs. I try to laugh. I realize that I get very serious when this subject comes up. Roland continues.

"My job is to support the Indians in whatever they want for themselves. If they want to reject their religion and go on with modern life, fine. If they want to try to maintain their old ways, fine. I will help them in any way I can. I have made peace with my role with the Indians."

I gulp, embarrassed by what I am going to say, but determined, nonetheless, to deal with the truth. It is abhorrent to me that I am angry with the Hispanics, for it smacks of racism, but I *am*. I appreciate their culture, their humor, their artistry, their music, their dance, but I am enraged over what they did to the Indians.

"I wish I could be tolerant and accepting like you, Roland," I say gently, "but I wish the Hispanics would admit what happened in the past. It makes me very angry with them."

Calm Roland loses it.

"The Hispanics are different!" he cries out. Then he catches himself and moderates his tone.

"All I expect of them is an admission that what happened to the Indians is tragic, but you can't even get that from them."

He pauses a moment. "I shouldn't say that," he admits.

"I know. I feel the same way," I concur.

"I try to understand why the Hispanics behave the way they do," he continues. "The Anglos came and took their land. They were culturally cheated and abused. They are underprivileged. They are treated like second-class citizens. They must contend with dreadful poverty and the erosion of their family support system. They suffer greatly. And now we want to tell them that what they did to the Indians is a terrible thing. I think it's like telling a welfare mother with three kids and no food that she shouldn't have gotten pregnant."

For the rest of the day I chew and think, trying to comprehend why the Anglos, Hispanics, and Indians coexist in New Mexico in peace, but actually have little to do with each other. They are very separate cultures. The whites look down on Hispanics. The Hispanics look down on the Indians. The Indians look down on blacks. The blacks look down on Hispanics. It sounds like a perverse children's song.

In contrast to my very serious phone call with Roland, Filiberto calls in mid-afternoon.

"I'm taking a break," he announces.

"A break from what?" I ask.

"Oh, a break from taking a break," he laughs.

Since he is in a particularly whimsical mood, we invent a game together. I ask him questions, and he comes up with Yaqui-style answers. Question: Why are children small? Yaqui answer: Children aren't small. They're as big as the smallest adults. Question: Why do we tilt our heads back when we drink? Yaqui answer: So we can read the label on the beer bottle.

I tell Filiberto that his mind is incredibly fast and he says his education at the "shoe-shine school" taught him lightning swiftness. He had to speak three languages on the street to talk to the drunks, and if he lost concentration for a minute, he was the brunt of all the jokes.

"You went to the trilingual shoe-shine school of life, and I went to an Ivy League school," I say musingly to Filiberto. "Sure makes you *wonder* about the tens of thou we spend on education."

"Yeah, that's the kind of Wonder bread one can chew on for a long time," Filiberto says.

"You know, I'm going to spend some time with the Mescalero Apaches," I tell Filiberto. "Laura Fragua invited us to stay at her house and attend the Apache puberty rites."

"I'll tell you a little Apache story," he offers, as he begins to recount a tale about his great-grandfather and the famed Apache leader

122

Geronimo. General Crook, who was sort of a reformed Custer, wanted to meet with Geronimo to sign a treaty, but couldn't find him. Geronimo, for good reason, was hiding out. If he weren't hiding out, he'd have been killed, ten times over.

Crook asked around and tracked down the man who knew the most about the countryside and could find Geronimo in those parts—it happened to be Filiberto's great-grandfather. He knew about the area because he went on five-day hunting trips for deer, and became really familiar with the land. Unfortunately, at the time Crook needed him, Filiberto's great-grandfather was busy being hanged for the crime of being an Indian.

Crook literally took Filiberto's great-grandfather off the hanging scaffold to use him as a scout. His great-grandfather refused. He said he would rather be hanged. Instead of hanging him back up there, Crook used Filiberto's great-grandfather as a topographer. In the end, after checking out Crook from up close, Filiberto's great-grandfather did set up the meeting after getting the okay from the fugitive Geronimo. But first he and Geronimo played hide and seek with Crook until he was so disoriented he didn't know left from right.

Today, in the Palace of Governors of Santa Fe is a picture of Geronimo signing the final treaty. In the background is Filiberto's great-grandfather.

"Wow," I say to Filiberto. "Did your great-grandfather tell you that story?" "No," he answers, "my grandfather told it to me. But he told it in the first person, so we felt as though my great-grandfather were telling it."

Apparently, that is the Yaqui way of storytelling. You say you know a good story. You acknowledge who it came from. Then you tell it in the first person. The storyteller literally becomes the story. It makes the tale much more immediate, and draws the listener into direct relationship with the story. It isn't told with the distance of the past; it is brought into the present.

"Pretty sophisticated storytelling technique for a pack of barbarians," Filiberto quips. Then he goes on to talk about contemporary Indians who observe the rigorous ceremonial life of their reservations, year after year.

"Each year as you participate in the ceremonies, you get a chance to do it better. That's how people get wise," he comments.

When he talks about his people, Filiberto always gets gleeful. I encourage him to talk, because I love the tales.

"Let me tell you about invitations," Filiberto offers. "When, for example, my father comes to visit me in Santa Fe, I would never say to him, 'There's a dance in town. Let's go.' That's not our way."

"What is your way?" I ask.

"Well, I tell my father that there is a dance. I say I would like it if he came. My father, in turn, asks me what his responsibilities are in accepting an invitation to the dance. I answer that question. This process goes on and on. Finally, when my father knows what he needs to know about the dance, he accepts the invitation. This is how you show respect to another person. Not by demanding that he come somewhere with you."

"I was going to invite you to go for a walk with me," I tease Filiberto, "but I think I'll forget it. It's too complicated. By the time you accept, it will be too dark."

"Well, enjoy your trip to the Apaches," he says. "I'm sure you'll learn a lot there."

We head south, and after a good many hours which we pass by looking out the window and trying to recall the names of all nineteen of the Rio Grande Pueblos, we notice a sign that says "Three Rivers Petroglyphs," and we immediately turn off the road. I have a positive mania for petroglyphs, ancient drawings etched into rock, which started when I lived in France. I used to trek all over the south of France and the north of Spain, crawling into caves where bats would fear to fly, tracking down Magdalenian cave art (15,000–30,000 years old). Here in America, the mysterious Indian markings interest me even more. Somehow, if one could just penetrate their meaning, one would have a key to the past. I draw them on T-shirts, I paint them on gourds. I don't know what it is that fascinates me. I just can't get them out of my mind.

We pull up at a desolate spot, with a car or two parked in a makeshift lot, and we start climbing up a hill. Paul is ahead of me. I look up, and see no walls, no cliffs, no ruins, so I assume this is all a big nothing. I am about to turn around when Paul cries out, "Look at the rocks right next to you!" I glance over to my right, and it looks like tourists have been amusing themselves by scratching on scattered rocks. I pay scant attention to their scratchings. But as I climb up a bit more, I notice that *all* the stones around us are covered with markings. These aren't tourist scratchings: these are petroglyphs.

I squat down and look closely at the remarkable drawings—bird men, mysterious circles surrounded by dots, rabbits, hands, medicine wheels, shaman-like human figures. Suddenly the banality of daily life slips away and I feel like I am sucked into a magical vortex. The two or three other tourists disappear, Paul climbs up ahead and out of sight, and I am left alone in a world that draws me back a thousand years in time. It is impossible to say HOW I know this, or WHERE this information comes from, but I feel male energy all around me. It's as though the stones can speak and tell their tales. I know that this is no place for women, and all of these amazing petroglyphs were done by men. As I continue to climb, the petroglyphs proliferate. The sheer number draws you out of your everyday world and makes you PAY AT-TENTION. And when you really pay attention in Indian country, you reap rewards. You begin to know things you never knew before. I first have the feeling that I could do a vision quest here. I could leave humanity behind for several days, and come here to pray, meditate, and seek guidance. I feel a tremendous connection to the spot.

As I climb farther up, the petroglyphs continue, and I realize that there are three hills full of these highly evocative drawings. I think it must be a three-day ceremony that drew men here. The air gets thinner from lack of oxygen but thicker with mystery; the faces and bodies of animals run and writhe and gambol on the surfaces of the rocks. I feel all around me the awe and gratitude with which our early brothers regarded nature and recorded it. At long last I know what a "sacred mountain" is, for I am walking on one. I shudder in my bones when I reflect on the developers who want to raze the Indians' sacred mountains to build resorts and condominiums there. It is unthinkable.

I look out. The visibility is almost unlimited across the grassy plains and gentle hills below. White cottony clouds hang overhead. It is a perfect lookout for enemies, and perhaps, too, for friends. Suddenly I hear an Indian voice say, "You'd gladly come up here for three days for God." I look around. An Indian is talking to a few of his friends. When he sees me, he clams up. Aha! So I am right. Three-day ceremonies on the three hills. I am almost ecstatic about having picked this up by myself—by letting the rocks "talk" to me.

I climb up higher still, my bare legs getting scratched by thorns and brambles. I see a lizard, the only animal I can understand. As always, the lizard stops in front of me. "What was here?" I ask it, for I have been taught to ask animals what I need to know. "What WAS here is what IS here" is the answer. I get it immediately: the sacredness, the specialness that the ancestors felt is still around me.

Suddenly I become an acquisitive capitalist. I want to have something from this place. Maybe an object? No, for once I am not searching for something for my collection. This time I want the POWER of the men who were here before me. And I realize in a flash that this power came through prayer. Prayer, something I know nothing about. Prayer, the source of power to Indians now and then. This is a sacred place. A place of prayer. It was then, and it is now. That is the message of the lizard.

Of course it sounds absurd to say that my "professor" at Three Petroglyphs is a lizard, but from talking to my Indian friends I now believe that before we became "civilized" and anesthetized, talking to animals was a common human practice. That is why, in so many of our stories, especially those for children, animals can talk. We teach our children that animals have voices, but we no longer believe it ourselves.

I stop for a moment, feeling the power of the place. Maybe on this spot there was an initiation ceremony into the hunt. Maybe men came here for a vision quest. Certainly, if one is to judge from many of the rocks, they came to tell and to pass on their origination myths, as part of their ceremony. The reflection comes naturally, even though I am used to walking on Wilshire Boulevard and Montana Avenue, and not on sacred mountains.

Maybe the younger boys were allowed on the first hill, the older men climbed up to the second, and the special elders (the leaders) were allowed on the third. There certainly seems to be a difference to the quality and depth of the drawings on the three hills. I look around me. The feeling I have is rapturous. I have always looked UP at petroglyphs, I have always seen them on the walls of cliffs and caves; I have never before been surrounded by them. Thousands of them.

And then, uninvited and unanticipated, FEAR pays me a call. I am totally alone. Paul has disappeared. I have no car keys, no money, and no way out of this isolated place. What if something is wrong with Paul? What if we can't get to help? What if we have to survive on the few animals in the area and the plants that grow around us? This IS a taste of vision quest for me—alone with my spot and my fears.

Suddenly there is a whoop and Paul comes running toward me, seemingly from out of nowhere. Then SIGNS begin to appear, for whenever human beings are in the moment, paying close attention, the universe is full of signs. They appear all around me—it's like I have been blind and deaf until this moment. First a rabbit hops by. Then clumps of white mountain sage appear—this is what the Indians burn for purification. Then a bird begins to circle overhead many times. Next there is a boom of thunder. The bird swoops down—I see white dots on the underside of its wings. Then a rainbow appears at the peak of the mountain opposite us. I am cowed and hushed. Paul feels it too. This is a very special place. A bird somewhere cries out: "Seeeek, seeeek," and I know this is what I must continue to do!

We come down from the hills. As we get into our car, massive storm clouds come in stealthily and quickly. By the time we drive away, the dark clouds cover the mountains behind us and they completely disappear from view—like a sandpainting covered over at the end of a ceremony. The memory of the hills is only inside of us now.

We arrive, bubbling over with excitement, at the home of Laura Fragua and her new husband Steven Wall near Ruidoso. We know Laura a little, but the only time we met Steve was when we awkwardly shook hands with him at their wedding in Jemez Pueblo, soon after we first came to Santa Fe.

We knock on the door and I gasp in horror: an eight-inch, ugly tarantula stares up at me from under my finger. I scream and Laura and Steve come outside to welcome us.

As I inch gingerly across the threshold, eyeing the tarantula, who eyes me back, I present the newlyweds with a gift: a huge bronze hand with the Hebrew word "chai" printed on it. It's a Jewish good luck charm, which they also use in the Arab countries where I lived. It protects the household from the evil eye.

"That's great!" Steve says. "A nice Jewish gift for your Indian friends."

"Let me tell you something spooky," I volunteer. "I gave a 'chai' hand to an Indian woman a few months ago. She hung it on the door of her bedroom in the trailer where she lives. Once day she was gone, and the trailer caught on fire with her husband sleeping inside the bedroom. Within minutes, the whole trailer burned down, and the only room that survived was the one where her husband was sleeping. She attributes this to the fact that the 'chai' hand was hanging there and it was a miracle."

Laura and Steve quickly hang the "chai" charm above their door.

"You can never have too much luck," Steve says.

"This hand gives me the chills," Laura says.

We are thrilled they like it.

The house itself is indescribable. The roof is falling off, half the house is undone raw adobe, and the tarantula has other creepy-crawly friends that play on the walls. In the evening, a cricket jumps into Paul's ear and he can't get it out. While he is slapping and banging his ear, my path is crossed by a mouse! I scream again, making quite a spectacle of myself. The hair stands up on my arms when I think that we are going to be house guests here for the next five days!!

All around the house are paintings, sculpture, decorated plates done by Laura, Steve, or other Indian friends. Of course, I don't know how to appreciate things silently. As I gush from piece to piece, tall, loping Steve pops a film into the VCR about Geronimo, and asks us to watch it. It was aired on PBS, and it recounts the history of the Chiricahua Apache, whom we are to meet. Far from being the bloodthirsty monsters that are traditionally depicted in the white media, they are terribly persecuted people who fought the Spanish and then the gringos for their home and their land. It is another Indian tragedy, another extended pogrom, where the victims are portrayed as the victimizers.

Geronimo, I learn, was not originally a war chief—he was a medicine man to Niche, the hereditary Apache leader. Geronimo's family was massacred, and he would not bow to the white murderers. For years, he and a band of Chiricahua Apaches hid out and attacked to defend their way of life. Many of the other Apaches wanted him to surrender, but he would not. Finally he did, and he and his band were arrested and held prisoner for twenty-seven years in dismal conditions in Florida. They were the longest prisoners of war in U.S. history. Geronimo was finally converted to Christianity, which seems to me to be a Pyrrhic victory for religion, for he was more spiritually potent the way he was!

The government shipped the Chiricahua Apaches to Fort Sill in Oklahoma, in yet another displacement. Those who did not want to go there were welcomed in by the Mescalero Apaches in New Mexico. Today many of the Chiricahua and Mescaleros live together on the Mescalero reservation, close to where we are. As we watch the film, it all seems very immediate. It has the urgency of real life, and not the distance of a documentary. Steve seems to know some if not all of the people interviewed in the film. The descendants of Geronimo and his men.

When the film is over, Paul and I are set up in our "bedroom" in the middle of the living room, and shown the small bathroom we all will

128

share. Laura takes great pains to make us comfortable. It has been a long day, and we all crash out and are soon sleeping.

"What's that?" I sit bolt upright in the middle of the night. The living room sofa sags under me.

"The wind," Paul says in his sleep.

"Fine. Then the wind talks," I say.

The kitchen door opens and Tim Shay and Wilma Mariano walk in. They are going to be our roommates for the next five days.

"Oh, great," I think, "two more people to share the bathroom."

We greet each other warmly and try to catch a few winks. They are very few indeed, for at 5 A.M. Steve bounds in and wakes us all up.

"The puberty rites are beginning. Let's go," he says. He, like many other people here, stubbornly and persistently pronounces it "pooberty" even when they are corrected.

We follow Steve's station wagon and climb high up into the mountains in the chill morning air for the ceremony of a young Apache girl who is celebrating her transition to womanhood.

When we arrive deep in the Mescalero reservation, it is very cold. Our teeth are literally chattering. Steve leads us all to the dusty central Plaza. A row of pine trees about thirty-five to forty feet in height are lying on the ground next to a huge mound of oak branches. A light, murmuring sound drifts toward us. I am learning that in Indian country (as in the rest of life) if you don't stay alert, if you don't listen, you will miss many things that are going on. In this case it is two medicine men, softly chanting. It is so low that if you aren't paying attention, you might miss it. They shake fringed deer hoof rattles, which they kiss after each sequence. For a moment I have to rub my eyes to remind myself that this isn't a bat mitzvah with a rabbi and a cantor, being done outdoors! There is a tremendous similarity to the rabbi and the cantor mumbling prayers and kissing their *talesim*.

Around the medicine men is a small circle of men, and three women in shawls. Periodically, one of the women (the pubescent girl's mother) lifts her hands to her mouth and makes a shrill, wailing cry. It pierces the cold morning air. I can feel it in my bones.

Then, at a signal from the medicine men, the circle of men starts to raise up the pine trees, freshly cut, full of water, and very heavy. First two pines meet, and they are bound on top by a rope. Then four more are lifted. A runner weaves the rope around the top of them. Then, one by one, the other pines are hoisted until twelve of them are in place. Next the oak branches are woven horizontally through the pines. This all happens very fast, and before you know it, you have a tepee!

All around the Plaza are arbors and fires. The women are hidden— they are inside the arbors, cooking for the feast. As I look around me, the young maiden is brought in, lovely, fresh, clean, wearing white buckskin. The medicine men softly bless her and paint her face with corn pollen.

To the Mescalero Apaches, the most potent goddess is the White Painted Lady. Right after a girl begins menstruating, she is considered to be very powerful. During the ceremony, she undergoes a lot of ritual deprivation, prayer, and blessing. She can't touch water for four days—she must even drink through a straw. She dances until she is beyond exhaustion, until she is ready to collapse and drop, in order to become an adult female who can endure—for life is hard and requires great fortitude. On the fourth night she must dance all night. In this process, she incarnates and actually BECOMES the White Painted Lady. She is thought to possess healing powers at this time.

As I stand and watch this little girl turning into a woman, I see the power coming over her. People come before her now. Old and young, healthy and ailing, they stand in long lines, waiting to be blessed by her. The spectacle draws me into myself. I reflect on how different this is from our culture, where menstruation is hidden. Here the whole community is celebrating it! What a wonderful way for a girl to start experiencing the female cycles—openly, proudly, as a source of great power to be tapped!

Following the blessing of her people, the girl is held by her family and lowered onto her stomach on the earth. Older women massage and bless her. Perhaps she is joining with Mother Earth, from whom she has come, and who will give her sustenance throughout her life. I nod at Paul, for he is certified to do massage and body work. This confirms our belief that massage is a very deep and spiritual act if performed correctly.

People are formed in two lines now, watching every move the young girl makes. The lines stay apart, so that they never block her from the rising sun, which shines directly on her. If the earth is her mother, the sun is her father. The young maiden runs toward the sun and circles around a basket full of green herbs and plants four times. Then there is a "giveaway"—gifts are thrown out to all the guests. Candies, fruits, and household items are flying in the air.

I begin to think about what all the stages of the puberty ceremony mean, and I decide not to ask anyone. I am beginning to believe that we have a lot of intuitive knowledge inside of us, and we have to practice learning how to access it. If this rite is as old as I think it is, it came as a deep response to a highly significant passage in a woman's life. I think of my own experience with being female. What is my connection to the earth? Who taught me about womanhood? Who "massaged" me? Where is my "tepee," where I feel safe, honored, and empowered?

Public ceremonies are strange in Indian country. Something fabulous will happen, like the raising of the tepee, and then there is a sort of "milling around" for forty minutes or so until the next event. I used to find these pauses boring. Now they are fascinating. They provide a chance to drink something hot, to look around, to get used to the place, to talk to people. A chance to absorb the rhythm, to slow down from daily life. In this case, it is also a chance to chuckle as I see the local friars standing there in frocks with baseball caps and sneakers. Paul quips that it says "Padres" on their caps. I control myself from thinking that I wish they would get lost. They have wreaked enough havoc on these peoples' lives. They have done away with and still try to do away with thousands of years of culture.

As I stand there, Wilma (who is Navajo) and I whisper about the ceremony. I tell her how it reminds me of my bat mitzvah. She tells me how it is like the Navajo puberty rites. She can understand some of the words being spoken around her. Navajo, like the Apache language, comes from Athabascan roots.

As we are talking, two tourists walk by. One of them pulls her hat low over her face.

"I'm afraid of skin cancer," she says.

"Me, too," says the other. "The noonday sun is pretty torrid now."

Wilma points to her head. "It's all mental," she says. "The mind determines sickness and wellness. It's all in your attitude. It's not from the sun."

The next event that is part of the four-day ceremony is a parade. Far from being an exotic and interesting parade, the theme is Desert Storm. Since it is usually the poor who go to war, it is no surprise that out of this tiny Apache community, seven men were part of that recent overseas incursion. We groan as fake tanks roll by, bearing kids dressed in camouflage and carrying plastic guns. The only Indian thing about the parade is the giveaway—the parade participants throw us buttons and pins and candy as they pass before us, and Lau-

131

ra and Wilma run into the street to catch it all. They are so good, they ought to play third base!

"What's a giveaway?" I ask the Apache woman standing next to me.

"The more you give away, the more you get back," she grins.

Paul and I drive back to Laura and Steve's house in our own car, and we stop off at the Apache crafts center. We meet a Hispanic artist who was a friend of Steve's mother.

"Oh, that's great," I say. "Everyone knows everyone around here."

"Is Steve with you?" she asks.

"No. He and his wife and friends went home."

"Then I will tell you something. Right before his mother's death, she was seeing visions. She would look out the window and see dead relatives. She had visions of what was going to happen to the family house. It freaked me out, and I stayed away from her for a long time. When I came back, she was already gone. People have those visions before they die. I just couldn't handle it."

I take a deep breath, and look at the woman who is telling the tale. She is still shaken as she speaks of it. Superstition, witchcraft, belief in other worlds and other realities are very much a part of life here.

In the evening, we return to Mescalero for the night ceremonies. I have a strange sense that I am destined to be here, for years ago I was beckoned by the simple black hooded masks with eye holes cut in them. I can still see, in my mind's eye, the huge white wooden "crowns" they are attached to.

By the time we arrive at the Plaza, it is dark. In front of the arboreal tepee, there is now a huge bonfire. The logs must be six feet long. Suddenly, out of the black night, the Apache Gan (Mountain God) dancers enter—and they are wearing these masks! They are terrifying. Their bodies are painted black. Under the black hoods, their eyes look absolutely spooky. They carry lightning sticks in their hands, and they move about under their huge white wooden headpieces.

They dance around the Plaza, backlit by the roaring fire, and they look like frightening, supernatural black shadows. I feel like I am being catapulted back into aboriginal America, long before Europeans landed on these shores. Spectators, standing in a circle, surround the dancers. A long line of seated drummers beats rhythmically, repetitively, and hypnotically on the drums in their laps. When each song is done, the words and the rhythm linger in the air. Their breath lives on. The flames lick at the foreboding Gan dancers and they whinny, like rearing horses. They shake their lightning sticks. The experience is ineffable. It is an initiation into the deep, dark mysteries of life. I feel blessed, and fortunate to be alive, witnessing this.

The only interruption of the music is periodic announcements on the loudspeakers about lost kids looking for their parents. They all seem to have the last name Geronimo or Niche. It makes me shiver, and gives a piercing reality to those Apache leaders of long ago. Their seeds are planted in the earth here, and they dance and sing with us here.

The announcements end and all focus is on the dancing and the drums. A circle of women, wearing colorful shawls, surrounds the Gan dancers. They dance in a line, doing a two-step that is coordinated with a swaying motion of their shoulders. They keep the rhythm of the drums perfectly as they advance around the circle. A man next to me begins to talk to me in an Indian language, but I cannot understand a word. I listen with intense concentration, and I realize that he is asking me if I am Navajo or Apache. I laugh and tell him I am belligani—white. But his very question is a sign to me that I do not stick out as an alien.

Suddenly Laura appears and throws a shawl around my shoulders. She shows me how to hold it like the Apache women do.

"Come. Dance," she says.

"Me?" I feel fear shoot through me.

She nods.

"I don't know how. I'll mess up. I've never done this," I protest. I shoot a look at Paul, then at Steve. They are all watching me, to see what I will do. I glance out into the Plaza, scanning every dancer, to see if there are any white people. No. There are none.

"Come," Laura repeats.

And then, before I know it, I am dancing with the Gan dancers! I am with the women, in the inner circle. I am terrified. I am afraid the shawl will slip out of my hands. I am afraid I will not be able to get my shoulders to swoop and swing in sync with the other women. I am afraid I will lose my step or start on the wrong foot, for every time a song stops and a new one begins, the women stop dancing and start anew. They always start together on the same foot, at the same moment.

I move slowly and cautiously. My legs are as stiff as though they are made of wood, for the tension has gone into my muscles. I try to bend my knees a bit, to relax into the dance. A small child is sitting on the ground, right in the line of the dancers. No one asks him to move: he has his place, as the adults have theirs. All of the dancers, absorbed by the dance, bypass him. I TRIP OVER HIM and he makes a face at me. I get flustered, panicky, self-conscious. I feel like a klutz. I try hard to watch the formidable Mountain spirits or the fire, but I can't. I'm too worried about myself and my feet. And then something amazing happens. The circle of women moves around and it is my turn to pass in front of the drummers. It is unlike anything I have ever experienced. The singing gets loud, the beat of the drums is relentless, and then . . . then . . . I feel the drums vibrating inside of me. What is outside is inside. I am completely filled with the sound of the drums. My head turns off. And I realize that this is a form of healing, for when your mind is empty of thought, you are well.

I feel exceedingly well. Better than I have felt in years. I dance on, with the line of women, actually praying that I will pass in front of the drummers again and get another dose of healing. Each time I do, it is the same. My whole being sings the songs. I become the drums. The women in front of me drop away and I am at the beginning of the line. I know the steps well enough to lead. I walk toward the drummers. After that, I remember nothing.

"I almost got killed," Paul says as I join the spectators later on. "I had our camera in my shoulder bag. I snapped a picture of you dancing with the Gan, just to prove to you that you actually did it. I didn't know that it was absolutely *verboten* to take pictures. Everyone around me leapt at me."

As we exit the Plaza for the night, we pass by the tepee. Inside is a fire. The two medicine men are chanting with their rattles. One has deer hooves suspended from it, and it makes a rhythmic click. At the back of the tepee is the maiden, and she is dancing all alone from side to side, her arms held up stiffly with bent elbows, making a windshield-wiper movement in front of her face. This mirrors the heel-and-toe shuffling of her moccasined feet. She looks almost faint, but she holds herself up and keeps on dancing. Her mother and her female sponsor are encouraging her, helping her, but she has to do it alone. Her very womanhood depends upon it. I feel the power of the ceremony for that girl, as she dances on the threshold, simultaneously shedding her childhood and shimmying into the adult world.

• • •

Back at our hosts' house, a whole other scenario is going on. Laura, Steve, Tim, and Wilma are all sculptors. They work in Steve's studio out back, facing the mountains, the arroyos, and the rattlesnakes. They all sculpt in alabaster "without a net"—no sketches, no pencil drawings on the alabaster. They believe that sculpting is simply helping the rock to be what it needs to be, rather than imposing a human will upon it.

Laura is quite extraordinary, and today is a seminal moment in time for her. Tim has brought along a power grinder, and he offers to show her how to use it. I watch her move fearlessly from years and years of hand sculpting to the powerful slicing of the blade. She embraces the technology without flinching. The alabaster dust goes flying; she takes to it like the proverbial bird to the air. She works hour after hour, entranced by the new speed and power, and finishes a remarkable piece: a woman on her knees, holding a corn cob and praying. Her hair is tied back gracefully; she wears a shawl. All is round form and harmony.

Simultaneously, Laura hauls out a faded tombstone and begins carving a second piece. From the used marble, she will make a headstone for the delayed burial of her grandfather, the last of the Pecos Indians.

"It will be presented later this summer at my Pueblo. There will be a ceremony."

I wonder, silently, if I can come.

"I hope you'll come," she says, reading my thoughts.

Later in the day, Wilma is doing the dishes in a plastic tub. Of course I am so domestically inclined that I agree to stand and *watch!* And as she washes, she speaks. We are alone. She tells me stories of her grandmother, who is a "hand trembler"—a Navajo healer. She traveled all over, to Mexico, to Canada, and people came to her from all over too. They paid her in jewelry for her healing.

As a child, Wilma spent her summers tending sheep, like many other Indians I have met. This is where they spent time with their grandparents, and got their life lessons, the foundation upon which they built their adulthoods. Wilma learned to kill and butcher sheep, because her grandma did so. She learned how to remove the intestines. Her mother cleaned the stomach and stuffed it with cornmeal.

"It's my favorite recipe," she grins. "She made it *just so*. It didn't require any refrigeration. It was a real delicacy."

Wilma continues talking. "In the summer, my people, the Navajo,

135

had their 'doings,' " Wilma continues. "Now they are lazier. Much of the language and culture has been lost. My mother was punished for speaking Navajo in school, so she taught me English. This is how our culture was broken apart."

I sigh. It is very painful to listen to.

"I long for a return to the old ways," Wilma says. "I teach my daughter to pray with sweetgrass every morning. I regret that I don't really speak Navajo so well. I understand it and write it, but I wish I could be more fluent with the speaking."

Wilma has another regret. She wanted to be an anthropologist, to dig into the past of her culture, but her people frowned on it. There is a Navajo taboo on the dead, discussion of the dead, and disturbing the spirits. When Laura comes into the kitchen for a moment and makes a joke about a cremation, Wilma bristles.

When Laura exits the room, Wilma resumes talking about her childhood.

"Grandma worked with herbs," she tells me. "Once, when I was ten years old, I went for a walk with my grandma and my cousin. My cousin was always getting acne. Grandma stooped down and picked an herb. She told my cousin to use it so she wouldn't get any more pimples. Well, my cousin put it on her face for two days. She hated the smell and the feel. But she got no more pimples for all her teenage years, and to this day she has gorgeous skin and *never* gets any pimples.

"What mattered to my grandma wasn't just WHICH herbs to pick. It was also WHEN to gather them, and what prayer to say. This knowledge is all gone now. No one 'got the feather' to carry it on. About ten years ago, I asked my grandma to teach me. But Grandma said it was too late. I had to start learning as a child."

Wilma gets terribly sad about the loss of language, ceremonial "doings," and knowledge.

"Now people in the family fight with each other," she says. "The old ways are all dying."

I feel sad too. What have we, who suppressed this culture, come up with to replace it? Cadillacs and CDs? Stealth bombers and fluorescent sneakers? Pity us poor humans for our stupidity and blindness.

The following day, Paul and I let the sculptors sculpt, and we go to Alamogordo, a military town. We go from store to store, looking for Apache art, but can't find anything interesting. It is extremely hot. We stop and drink, but we are still uncomfortable and parched.

We are about to head into the mountains for some cool air when we see a huge iron quonset hut store with a big sign inviting people to come and see rattlesnakes. We stop. Inside, we start talking with the shop owner, and a group of other men materializes. They are all avid members of the NRA. I immediately get on my high horse and tell them I am a pacifist. They look at each other, and smile. Then they laugh uproariously as they fetch their whole arsenal to bait me.

Everywhere I go in the store, someone pulls a gun on me—a pistol, a larger pistol, a rifle, an Uzi. I know they are joking, and do not feel at all frightened. *Frightened* is what I was when I briefly lived in Nigeria under military rule, and machine guns were poked in our faces when we rolled the car windows down. After that, this is child's play.

Paul watches, bemused, as I single-handedly take on the NRA in a discussion on the right to bear arms. They are very bright and their arguments are very cogent. So are mine. I refuse to back down. More men come in and join the NRA clique. One boasts that he is a gun-toting preacher.

"A package deal," I quip. "You can shoot 'em and then administer last rites!"

They laugh at my politics and seem genuinely entertained by my anti-gun diatribe. As a treat for providing them with amusement on a dull afternoon, they give me a balloon, and clip it to the end of a fishing rod. Then they take me to an outdoor pit where fifty rattlesnakes are coiled in the sun beneath us. They tell me to lower the balloon near one of the snakes. I do it nonchalantly. Within seconds, the snake attacks and pops the balloon. The noise, the surprise really gets to me—I scream and jump back about fifteen feet. I didn't even see the snake strike. It was that fast. The men are all howling with laughter.

Our sculptor friends laugh at my story.

"Judie among the rednecks," they say teasingly. "Always getting into trouble."

"Is that bad?" I ask.

"For anyone else," Steve answers, "but *you* always get out again!"

Later that night, they take us to White Sands. It's an incredible expanse of pure, crystalline-white sand dunes, except it's not sand. It's friable gypsum, and it has blown into dune-like formation in the New Mexico wind. As we ride by, it doesn't compute for me. It looks like miles of snow drifts, except how can there be snow drifts in July, in ninety-degree weather? We run out of the car, up into the dunes (they're hard-packed) to romp and stomp. Steve barbecues dinner, and Laura lifts a glass of wine to make a toast.

"Here's to old friends," she says, nodding at Wilma and Tim. And then she looks at us out of the corner of her eyes. "And here's to new friends."

I poke Paul under the dune-side picnic table. He pokes me back. We feel wonderful.

"To be treated like a friend, that is something special," I say. Laura, Steve, Tim, and Wilma nod.

The following day, persistent as ever, I go into Tularosa, which is like a ghost town, still looking for a piece of Apache art. Because there is so little of it to be had, it makes me want it even more. I decide I'd like to find a painting of the Gan dancers to remind me of the night I danced with the gods.

I walk from store to store, finding nothing, and just as I am about to give up (which is how it always seems to happen in Indian country), I wander into a secondhand store and there is a painting of the Mountain Gods on the wall. It isn't terribly well executed, so I want to make sure that it is at least authentic. Steve wrote an article on the exploitation of Indian artists within the art system, and after reading it, I would never buy Indian art made by non-Indians. I ask the old woman proprietor about the painting and she tells me it was done by an Apache painter.

I take the painting off the wall and place it on a shaky old table to look at it. The price is $40, and although it sounds very low, it is too much for such a half-baked work; still, I'll willingly pay it to have an Apache painting. I lift up the painting to buy it. I hold it out to the old woman to tell her to put it in a bag for me, but before I can get the words out of my mouth, a voice behind me says, "DON'T BUY THAT."

I wheel around, and a young Apache woman, who has suddenly materialized, is talking to me.

"That's not the right painting for you. I'll GIVE you one!"

"I can't take a painting from you," I say to the woman, who is obviously impecunious.

"Sure you can," she says, smiling.

Well, I'm learning that when something presents itself to you as an opportunity you don't say no, so I accept Greta's generous offer.

"Follow me," Greta says. "I'm driving with some friends. We'll go back to my trailer."

Dancing with the Mountain Gods

Greta's woman friend is driving, and on the way to Greta's house, she hits a government vehicle in a minor accident. We sit and watch as they call an Apache friend who is a policeman, and he talks to the Indian driver of the government van and convinces him not to pursue the matter. All parties amicably agree to white-out the experience. I suppose no one cares about leaving the tab with the government after all the government took from the Indians!

Greta's friends, who live in the trailer next to Greta, invite us in for a drink. When I walk in the door, their pet wolf jumps on me and licks my socks. It happens so suddenly that I don't have time to freak. "Dances with wolves," says Greta.

"Yeah," I try to smile.

Greta is a tiny bundle of energy and basically, a lovable creature. She is in an abusive relationship with a crazy white man. She tried to throw him out, but he threatened her life and keeps her bound to him by fear. He also prowls around her trailer late at night, acting like a cat, making cat noises, and spying on her. He treats her like she's under permanent house arrest. In the middle of this, Greta invites us into her trailer.

I try to talk to Greta about her situation, and beg her to seek help. She gets teary, and says that she is going to try to move and to change her life. She knows she is stuck. She has had abuse all her life, and this is more of the same. Although she can't seem to mobilize to actually *do* anything, she is at least lucid about her paralysis.

She gets up suddenly and leaves the room. I am afraid that I have offended her. Instead, she comes back, thanks me for my concern, and hands me her painting of Gan dancers, which won first prize for Indian art at her daughter's school. Then she insists on giving Paul a bottle of liquor that has been smuggled across the border from Mexico. And she asks for my address, so she can send me Apache beadwork, done especially for me!

I am floored by her generosity. She has so little, and she is willing to give it away.

In the evening, Steve, Laura, Wilma, and Tim accompany us to the Inn of the Mountain Gods. It is a luxurious hotel high up on a mountain, in a splendid natural setting, completely owned and operated by the Apache tribe. There are Apache treaty rooms, two parking spaces reserved for the tribal chief, and other Indian touches that make this distinct from any resort we have ever visited.

There is gambling at the Inn, and Wilma gets on a winning streak

139

until she changes course and goes on a losing streak. We tease her mercilessly. Teasing is totally kosher here. It is, in fact, a big part of Indian humor.

At night, we go to the Apache reservation again. It's good to be with Steve, because everyone here knows him and treats him like a local celebrity.

"I'm the tribal prosecutor," he explains. "All these people have been brought up on charges before me, or else they are trying to buy good faith for the next time they are!"

Although Steve is not Apache (he is part Seneca and part Chippewa), he is a great admirer of the Apache dances. He says that when a two-year-old kid sees these terrifying Gan dancers for the first time, he understands nothing, but he knows that there is a connection to the supernatural. It stays with him for life. This is how Indian kids are raised—always aware of the connection to supernatural forces, to forces larger than mere man.

As we approach the Plaza, I meet a white couple, ex-professionals and émigrés from California, selling frozen fruit bars from a stand. Something in me envies them. They have opted for a low-stress life. Why can't we do that? What is our attachment that keeps us in the high-pressure fast lane?

The question goes around and around in my mind as I watch the Gan dancers. As yet, I have no answer.

"Things happen when they are supposed to happen," Steve says, as though reading my thoughts.

I get out of my own head, and into the Gan dancers, and the power of the spiritual experience.

The following day I am very unspiritual and very judgmental. Our new friends are TV addicts. It is about a hundred and five degrees in the house and they sit in front of the television set in a dazed stupor.

When the heat dies down to a mere ninety-nine degrees, our friends say they are going out to get marble to sculpt with, and ask if we want to come along. I would gladly go for a swim in a toilet bowl to get away from the TV.

Everyone piles into the back of Steve's old truck, riding Navajo style. That is, everyone except me. I don't feel like bumping along, roasting in the outdoor oven. I am the sole wimp who rides up front in the cabin. I think I had my fill of riding in the back of trucks coming home from Oklahoma.

Dancing with the Mountain Gods

I thought it would be a matter of minutes until we got to the marble shop. Instead, Steve drives into the desert until Alamogordo is a dot in the distance, and after several futile attempts to get the truck to climb a steep, unpaved grade, he parks below a mountain. There it is before us: the marble store of nature. It is an old abandoned quarry, and the smallest block must weigh two hundred pounds. Our friends inform us that they are going to climb up and bring the marble back by hand.

The hike up the mountain is a nightmare with the excruciating desert heat, the hostile cactus, brambles, the huge, craggy rocks we climb over, the altitude, the distance one could fall, the lack of foot-holes in the rocks, the heat exhaustion, and the fact that I want to pull my skin off because I am so uncomfortable.

"Okay," I say to myself, as I begin to panic, "I have two choices here. I can continue this climb, and be miserable beyond belief, or I can wave the white flag of surrender, and crawl back down to the truck. What will it be?"

Fifteen minutes later, a relieved coward, I sit by myself in the truck, waving up at Paul as he disappears over the mountain with the others. I wonder if I will ever see him again.

An hour later, I see seven feet on the mountain: Laura's, Steve's, and the feet of the rusty old wheelbarrow they found up on top. They try to cart large chunks of marble down the mountain, until Steve gets heat exhaustion and can't go on any more. They leave their huge quarry behind, and take a few small pieces in their hands. They come to join me and they, too, wimp out. But the difference between us is that I am embarrassed that I fell by the wayside, and they aren't.

"Boy, I sure hope the people who buy your sculpture appreciate what went into it," I comment, as the dehydrated sculptors guzzle water.

"We just hope they buy," says Steve.

To make up for my passivity during the day, when the sun goes down and the heat lets up, I take a very active role in the evening. Although I am not ordained, and am not religious, I offer to remarry the newlyweds Steve and Laura the Jewish way!

First I drape an Indian shawl over my head and light the candles. (I haven't lit candles since I played with the menorah as a kid.) Then I take their wedding rings in my hand, and make them repeat the sacred and beautiful words after me, with Steve going first . . . "haray, at mekudeshet lee . . . " Then, of course, since this is Orthodox (why

141

not? who is making the rules?), Laura circles around her seated groom seven times. The culmination is Steve stomping on a light bulb wrapped in a dishtowel, while everyone yells "Mazel tov!"

"Two weddings," Laura says. "That really ought to make it last."

This night is a very special night—not only for the newlyweds, but for the puberty maiden at Mescalero. She stays up all night dancing. Between dances, she sits in the tepee with her legs stretched out in front of her, her head lolling against her chest, her eyes fighting to stay open. Once again, the medicine men sing to her, pray with her, and the older women help and encourage her. In the womb of the tepee, she is preparing to be born into the next stage of her life.

The next morning, we get up very early again, for it is the "morning of the taking down of the tepee" at Mescalero. For this occasion, people have a chance to line up and be blessed by the medicine man. I watch carefully, wishing I could be blessed too.

Suddenly, someone calls to me. It is the bright and beautiful Sacheen Littlefeather, the Indian woman who, years ago, got up to accept the Academy Award for Marlon Brando. She comes up to me and tells me to listen carefully. We are standing in the sun, and all I do is ask Paul to pass the sunscreen, and Sacheen gets very impatient. She insists again that I LISTEN. She throws her hand insistently against my heart. "Listen HERE." I realize with a sigh that I still have not learned to listen well enough.

Sacheen tells us that she has just had a healing. She is wonderfully open and very emotional. She starts to cry, for all the pain in her life. So do I. She asks me not to tell anyone what she tells me about her life and her healing, so of course I promise never to divulge any details. Then we hug. The moment she leaves, I am overcome with wanting to get blessed by the medicine man. I am afraid to be the only white person on line, but Paul declines to come with me.

"Okay, Paul, hold my bag. I'll be back." I get in line for the medicine man.

The line moves slowly into the tepee. I watch what all the Indians do, and practice it in my mind so I won't be out of place, and I will be able to receive the blessings. As I stand waiting, and the line moves toward the tepee, I get very sad. I start to weep. This young girl reminds me of some of the unhappiness in my own life, and how, at her age, much of the "damage" had already been done. In my heart, I wish the girl strength, endurance, courage. This tepee is a holy place. The sanctity is palpable. And then it is my turn.

I step in front of the medicine man, and I get flustered. I can't remember what to do. I just stand there, feeling very white, in my sunhat and sunscreen. He barely looks up, but he does me the great favor of treating me just like the others, even though he has to reach up from his seated position to do it, because I forget to bend down. He smears me with sacred mud and corn pollen. On my cheeks. My hands. On my jeans, where the knee is. And then he prays over me. It isn't JUST that he is a medicine man, but that he is a medicine man empowered by days of ceremony and prayer. I stand there, feeling incredibly moved. I never want to wash my face, my hands, my jeans.

The tepee is taken down and suddenly the trees are gone, the branches are gone, everything goes back into the earth. Has it all really happened? It seems like the magic doors were opened, and now they are closed. There is barely a sign of all that has taken place. It's like awakening from a dream.

Sacheen's friend Barney is cleaning up the very last ceremonial remnants, and he calls me over. He scoops up a cupful of the mud, which has been used for days, prayed over, sanctified. It has been used for healing. He hands it to me. He says to use it wherever it is needed. Then he walks away.

I am left, incredulous, holding on to the healing mud, clutching it, knowing that I can use it for people who need it in the future, wondering how it came to me.

I look around me on the emptying Plaza. The women are cleaning up the few remains of feast food. Eight "beef" (whole cows) have been eaten, eight hundred pounds of fry bread and all the trimmings have been consumed. Everyone who came has been fed. And now it is time to go. The ceremony will continue for four days for the maiden, but for the public it is all over.

I step into an arbor, and am introduced to a woman named Roberta. She is a handsome woman with a very direct manner.

"Hi," I say.

She nods at me.

"You worked as a nurse with Dr. Carl Hammerschlag, many years ago, when he was in Indian country. I'm writing a television series loosely based on his work."

"Doctor!" she says, and breaks out into a smile.

"Roberta," I say, "I saw you on the Geronimo tape and I've been trying to meet you ever since I arrived here. Several times I thought I had caught your eye. I asked people to introduce us. But it never happened."

She nods again. I guess that means that we were not supposed to meet until after the public part of the ceremony was over. She was busy cooking. She had no time for me. Now the cooking is over and she has time.

"Come. Follow me to my house," she says warmly.

In the car on the way there, I decide that I don't WANT ANYTHING from her. I am not going to ask her questions about Carl in Indian land. I am not going to try to get a writer's inside track on her life as his nurse. I will just go to her house, and let her talk about whatever she desires. It's the best decision possible. I ask Roberta no questions, so she tells no lies. She just opens up, talks freely, and is quite fabulous to be with.

During our conversation, I try to tell Roberta that Carl speaks highly of her mother, but it is a subject Roberta will not discuss. I suppose that the Apache, like the Navajo, do not speak about the deceased. She does, however, speak about her grandson, who just had all of his foot except his heel amputated from diabetes. She tells us how rampant diabetes is among her people, and speaks about her own diabetes and a recent fall which resulted in hip replacement surgery.

She tells me, with affection and pride, about her grandfather, who was Geronimo's water boy. She talks to me about a trip she made to Fort Sill, where many of the Apaches lived, to try to find out what they died from. Only the white soldiers had their cause of death recorded. The Indians had no reason listed for their death; they weren't important enough. They were treated like animals who could be easily disposed of and forgotten.

She talks to me about going to Florida to see where Geronimo and her relatives had been incarcerated, and how awful and unsanitary it was. She speaks of her recent trip with a band of Apaches to the hideouts of Geronimo and his men. She speaks with anger and resentment. She is a smart, outspoken, very direct Indian elder! "If you ask me about Columbus and his men, they never should have come!!" she says.

She is not at all subtle, quiet, and passive, the way Indian women are portrayed stereotypically. She has very strong feelings which are very close to the surface. She has a paper saying that the descendants of Geronimo are owed twenty thousand dollars apiece from the U.S.

government. The incarcerated Japanese got theirs. "Where is the Indian money?" she asks.

Roberta lives in a gorgeous mountain oasis, which is family land. As she talks, there is life all around her. Her young granddaughters bubble with joyous life. The phone rings. A neighbor arrives at the door. Hummingbirds come in pairs to the window.

Roberta speaks about the puberty ceremony. She says that when you spend all night with the dancing girls during their puberty ceremony, you can tell what kind of woman they will make. If they make it through a dance, if they stand erect and don't slump over, you know they will be strong. She speaks lovingly of the young girls, and she also speaks lovingly of Indian fry bread. It represents the sacred circle of life, and you must never tear a piece of it.

"Always keep it whole," she says. "Eat what you want and discard the rest, but don't break the circle."

She talks about the sun, the east, and how ceremonies start there and that is the direction you enter the tepee. It is the direction of morning. It is a way to give thanks for each new day.

While I am talking with Roberta, her granddaughters drag Paul off into the hills to see their secret sweatlodge. He comes back, laughing and light-footed, obviously having had a ball with these young girls, who will one day dance all night at their puberty rites. Already, Roberta says, they talk about it.

After a prolonged visit with Roberta, during which my watch seems to leap ahead, we jump into the car and head back for Santa Fe. We stop at a restaurant to eat, and there is a salad bar. As I work my way around the salad bar, everyone seems to be staring at Paul, and their looks are hostile and almost punishing.

"Why are they looking at me?" he asks. Then it dawns on him. "They all think I've beaten you," he whispers. "Your face is still smeared with mud from the medicine man. They think you have shiners. Go wash it off."

"Never!" I say. "My face will fall off before I'll remove this mud. It's a blessing. You don't wash a blessing away!"

After dinner, I insist upon calling my Hollywood agent from the roadside. It is the middle of the desert at night, with cars roaring by.

"Hello, Ian! This is Judie! I want to tell you what happened. I just got blessed and smeared with corn pollen and sacred dirt by an Apache medicine man!"

145

"Neat. I've had quite an experience myself. I just came from a screening of *Terminator 2*."

I hang up the phone laughing. I'm reminded that I'm now in a totally different world, as far from Hollywood as Earth is from Jupiter.

"Why don't you call Lenny?" Paul asks. "We're running home so you can begin work with him bright and early tomorrow. Just call and verify."

"I don't need to. I know he'll be there."

"Okay . . . ," Paul says, in such a tentative way that I call Lenny.

The conversation is brief. Lenny tells me that he is still unavailable for work and I blow up and hang up on him.

7

On Baking Bread and Feeding Ants

Mid- to late July, 1991

The deadline has been set for 10 A.M. I have left a message on Lenny's machine, informing him that I am going to begin work, and he had *better be there* because I am tired of being a sucker. Then I spend the night worrying.

"You really ought to live in the present," Paul tells me. "Stop ruminating about the past and fretting about the future."

"Fine. I'll do that if you promise to fold your socks when they come out of the washing machine and to replace the paper in the computer printer every time we run out."

"It's a deal."

The deal lasts for about fifteen minutes. I do a laundry and Paul doesn't fold his socks. My side of the bargain is over when I start worrying about what I will do when Lenny doesn't show up.

Nine o'clock, I start tapping my foot. Nine-forty-five, I'm pacing and mumbling to myself. Five to ten, I am so preoccupied I realize that I have eaten three peaches and just swallowed a pit.

At 10 o'clock sharp I hear a knock. I swing open the door, and Lenny stands there, smiling. I open the door, also smiling, and let him in. And we begin to work. Bing! Zang! Our minds are thrusting all over the place as we finally set to the task of wrestling this TV show to the mat!

I must say that it is quite wonderful to be in that state of mutual challenge that we both know so well, and which is the reason we wanted to work together. We sit over tea inside, we stretch out over mangos on the patio, we come in to Paul's wildly imaginative lunch, then the sofa, then the deck chairs, then a walk, talking, thinking aloud, working. Yippee! We're on our way, and the past lies, not tampered with, not discussed.

As we work, I go into the kitchen and see, to my chagrin, a room full of ants. Paul runs for the natural soap spray and I start flinging boxes of food out of the closet to get rid of the nasty critters. Lenny stands there, looking at me.

"No wonder you're plagued by ants," he says. "It's their revenge because you are constantly offing them."

"Look," I protest. "We aren't spraying chemicals. We're using a soap from the health food store."

"Would YOU like to suffocate from eating that?" Lenny says, scrunching up his face in disgust. "The ants don't know it's supposed to be good for them."

"Okay," I submit, "I can tell you have something in mind by the way you're standing there judgmentally. So tell me what it is."

Lenny smiles, crouches down, and starts following the line of ants from the kitchen to the door.

"First," he says, "you have to find out where the ants are coming from."

I follow Lenny through the *casita,* outside, tracking them to the anthills where the critters emanate from.

"What now?" I ask.

"Now," he replies, "you are going to put some yummy food around the anthills, because these little friends are just hungry, and that's why they come inside your house. You should be flattered. They like your food."

Feeling like a complete idiot, I go back inside, and retrieve a box of graham crackers. I pull out a cracker and prepare to lay it on top of an anthill.

"No, no, no," Lenny says,"you have to feed them *ant*-size pieces."

So I crumble the graham cracker up into tiny particles, and spread them around the anthills where the little beasts are coming from.

"Now sprinkle Ajax outside the door to your house," Lenny instructs me.

"So they can do dishes?" I ask.

"No, just as a gentle reminder not to cross the line."

Now I feel even more ridiculous as I spread cleaning powder in front of the *casita.*

"Am I done?" I ask.

"As soon as you go and talk to the ants."

"What should I say?" I inquire, as though it were a normal thing.

"Tell them that you know they are hungry and you hope they like the food you've brought. Ask them please not to come inside, where you don't like the taste of ants in your food."

I do it. I speak softly to the ants, sending regards to their mothers and fathers, sisters and brothers, and begging them to enjoy all their family meals at their anthouses, not in our *casita*.

"Okay, Lenny. I did it. What now?"

"Now, just be be patient, and feed the anthills every day, for this may take a while."

Lenny leaves, and suddenly it strikes me. A few weeks ago we had had an experience with ants, admiring them and their courage as they carried our corn chips home. How could we have forgotten so soon that we have a relationship with them? Of course it's possible to talk to ants. People talk to plants, don't they? And plants seem to respond. If plants, why not ants?

I go to bed, thinking about ants, reminding myself to always be respectful of all living things.

In the morning, when I enter the kitchen, the ants are gone. I look under the sink, in the cabinets, along the walls, but find nothing.

"Hey, Lenny, it worked. We are ant free!" I exult when he comes to work.

"Good. That's what I like about you. You listen. You're so WILL-ING. Come to a campfire with me tonight."

"What kind of campfire? Where is it? Will it be very dark? Will there be a lot of people? Are there wild animals? Is it outdoors?"

Lenny smiles and says that's where campfires usually take place.

Leading campfires is, apparently, part of what Lenny does for a living. People pay to sit around a fire at night and learn about storytelling.

There are six of us. We drive far out into the country, where rattlesnakes and gnats and Lyme ticks dwell. Then we climb over a hill and come to an open space in the woods. Here, Lenny starts to build a fire. He tells us all to go and get firewood, especially kindling, being careful of snakes under the trees.

"If you find a snake," Lenny instructs us, "just calmly say, 'There's a snake here.'"

"No screaming?" I hiss at Lenny. "Why did you tell me to come here?"

"Because you're ready. I think you could even meet a snake and be calm about it. Of course, the snake might get a fright," he teases.

We disperse and go into the woods to gather our firewood. I tiptoe cautiously, horrified of finding something alive under my feet. Then we congregate around the fire. The gnats are biting like crazy, and we are slapping and swatting ourselves.

"Stand around me in a circle," Lenny instructs us, "and we are going to do integration breathing."

He shows us how to inhale and exhale, circulating the breath of life.

"Now, let the gnats have their way with you if they want to. Just close your eyes, stand there, and not try to swat them away."

I close my eyes, and stop swatting. I hold out as long as I can. When I open my eyes, I see that I have lasted longer than the others, who are all slapping themselves again. Lenny nods approvingly at me.

Then he begins to talk to us about our TONGUES. They are little fellows who always get us into trouble because they can't lie still. They are always moving around, saying the wrong thing, gossiping, carrying tales. But we have to get them to stay still if we want to LISTEN.

He instructs us to gently place our tongues against our palates, and start learning to control them. As soon as everyone is quiet, we are told how to go and find our own "special" rocks to bring back to the fire. Each of us leaves the circle, and heads away, being aware that the fire is our home and we will be coming back there.

I scan the forest floor, passing rock after rock, and suddenly I find a translucent rock that seems to have my name on it. I pick it up and bring it back to the circle. When I arrive, Lenny says, "Welcome home."

As people come back to the fire, they are chattering. They cannot control their tongues. They whisper that it is a very tough thing to do, and they aren't yet capable of doing it. I, however, have remained completely silent. I do it with a glad heart, and am proud of the accomplishment.

Lenny looks around the circle, and asks a very simple question.

"Is there anyone who thinks he or she is beginning to learn how to listen?"

Without thinking, my hand shoots up.

"Repeat the instructions you were given," Lenny says, testing me.

I try to repeat them all, *verbatim*. Lenny says it takes a lot of courage for me to do that. Courage? I don't understand what he means.

"It has to do with humility," he explains. "And with being willing to learn about yourself."

As I ponder what *that* means, Lenny tells us about his childhood, and how he spent the summers with his grandma and grandpa sheepherding. His grandpa told him where to take the sheep and goats, and instructed him to *watch them carefully*. But little Lenny's attention wandered and he forgot his grandpa's words and lost some of the precious goats. When he came back without the goats, although the goats were so important for survival, his grandparents didn't scold him or get upset with him. They just said, matter of factly, "Two goats are missing." Just those words, and the awareness of what he had done, made Lenny sweat all night. He KNEW what he had done wrong. No one had to rub his nose in it or punish him. The next morning, his grandpa told him to go back to the same spot for the sheep to graze, and the goats would show up. Indeed, they did. Lenny had learned the importance of paying attention.

As Lenny tells this story, I think, with sadness, about how I and the people I know were raised. We were punished, berated, even beaten. We learned our lessons, *if* we learned them, through force. There was no dignity.

Lenny speaks about the fire, which is people's "home" out in nature, and how our particular fire is our home for the evening. He tells us how lucky we are if there is someone back in our city home to say, "You're home," when you come home, or "Welcome home." What a blessing that is. We should never take it for granted.

I smile as I realize that Lenny had used those words when I brought my stone back to the fire—"Welcome home," he had said.

Next, since this is a storytelling evening, Lenny tells us two stories. The first is about Pretty Girl and Little Bird. It is sweet and pleasant, but the six of us are a bit restless. Perhaps the others, like me, cannot really follow the nonlinear storytelling. I resign myself to never understanding Indian stories at all, and just at that moment, Lenny begins a story that is mesmerizing and trance-inducing from the very first words. I should learn never to make advance judgments in Indian country!

The story is about BUMBLING BOY, who is always rejected because he is clumsy and maladroit, and how he meets Coyote and learns to hunt deer. We learn, with Bumbling Boy, not to look the deer in the eye, to find the spot where the fur parts and grows in two directions before shooting, to breathe in the deer's last breath and pray with the deer as he dies. We listen raptly as Bumbling Boy brings his deer back to his village, becomes a respected hunter, and lives a happy life.

During the story, Coyote tells Bumbling Boy that one day in the future he will call to him to hunt, and after the hunt, he won't go back to his village anymore. After getting married, having children, and living his life, one day this happens. Coyote calls to Bumbling Boy, and he follows the call and never comes back. Wow! What a death! Just a natural and expected part of his life! I come out of the spell of the story, dazed.

Lenny explains that at night, the stories the Indian people are told get progressively more and more mesmerizing, and perhaps the best stories are told in the wee hours, when most people have fallen asleep. But to understand the stories, you have to learn to *really* listen.

Then he speaks about sharing. How we have shared this time at the campfire, our home, together. He talks about the rocks, our rock friends, whom we have brought to share our home. Now we must give them back. We must always GIVE BACK when we take. We are instructed to go into the dark woods, to our outer limits (of fear), and place the stones back.

I blanch. Luckily it is dark, and no one can see me. I am terrified of what lurks in the woods. I step gingerly, looking all around me, and I freak when I can no longer see the fire or any other human being. I drop my stone, thank it quickly, and go running back to the circle.

On the ride home, I am very quiet. I think about my childhood, and how many wonderful stories I was told from my own cultural tradition. My mother, a terrific *raconteuse,* regaled us with stories in both English and Yiddish. It occurs to me that through contact with the Indian culture, I am connecting more with my own roots, my Jewishness, than I ever have in my life. It doesn't mean I want to go running to a synagogue, but neither am I completely pushing it away from me as I have done most of my life. The continual denial and rootlessness seem immature and inappropriate. You cannot deny what you are.

When I tell this to Lenny, he smiles. "We're gonna write that into the TV series. Whatever you are learning, it's all useful to us!"

When I get home, Elisa Herrera, the Hispanic wife of Arnold, the Indian drum-maker from Cochiti Pueblo, comes to visit. She and

Arnold and their three sons live out near the penitentiary, where there is plenty of space for the boys to hunt rabbits and for Arnold to dry his cow hides and make his drums.

"It must be weird for you to be married to an Indian man," I comment.

"It's even weirder to live near the penitentiary," she says.

"What do you mean?" I ask.

"Well, whenever there is a prison break, the penitentiary's automated voice system calls and leaves a message on our answering machine, telling us to watch out. We get home and find out that some dangerous sociopath is on the loose. They do it as a community service."

"Do they sign off by telling you to have a good night's sleep?" I ask wryly.

Elisa laughs. Then she looks at me and says, "You're so interested in Indian culture. Why don't you come with me at 4 A.M. tomorrow to bake bread for the Cochiti Feast Day on Sunday? I'm going to Arnold's sisters' house."

Four A.M.? I haven't set an alarm clock in ten years. It is one of the few advantages of being a self-employed writer. Although my need for sleep says no, my mouth says yes, honoring my new commitment to say yes, yes, yes whenever someone proposes something here.

So I fall out of bed at 4 A.M. and drive with Elisa to Cochiti Pueblo. When we arrive, we can see the smoke coming up from beehive-shaped, earthen-colored *hornos* in the village.

We enter the home of Bertha Herrera and her sister Jenny. It is so early, my brain is still dormant and everything is a fog. In a corner of the kitchen, in huge laundry tubs, is seventy-five pounds of dough, which was kneaded last night. The women shape the dough into round mounds and set them into tin foil plates. We carry them out to the *horno,* and place them in the clay oven on a long wooden "spatula." The opening of the *horno* is sealed with slabs of wood covered with old jeans, and there the breads cook and turn a delicious brown and are removed with the same spatula forty-five minutes later. Then they are stacked inside the house, standing on their sides in the laundry room, on top of the washer and dryer, until the feast. Yum. Yum. The only caveat is that these breads would never be on sale in a health food store: the ingredients are white flour, yeast, salt, water, and gobs of pure, fatty lard.

"How did you get the *horno* so hot?" I ask Bertha, once the breads are stacked and she has a few minutes to talk. "I didn't see any wood or coals in there."

"Well," she answers, "we do it early in the morning because both the *horno* and the weather get too hot later on. First a wood fire is made inside the *horno*. When the fire dies down and becomes charcoal ashes, it is all swept outside the *horno*. The intense wall heat that remains inside the *horno* is what will bake the bread."

She tells me that this particular *horno* was made by her aunt many years ago. It needs a bit of replastering, but other than that it is just fine. It is much more personal than an oven, for the women know their *horno* and how hot it gets and how to baby it. The building of a *horno* is a complex thing and a specialized craft, and the flooring, thickness of the walls, and content of the walls must be taken into account.

"The point is," Jenny chimes in, "that having the clay and the desire for a *horno* are not enough. You must also spend the time to learn an art. Whatever time it takes."

We go back into the kitchen to make Feast Day cookies with the remaining dough. Most are made with cookie cutters, but one type is shaped by hand. It is an old shape that has been used for many generations.

"It looks pretty easy," I comment, noting that it takes a woman about twenty seconds to make one of the cookies.

Bertha and Jenny and Elisa smile, and invite me to try to make a cookie or two.

I admit to being completely maladroit in a kitchen, and cooking is not my forte, but certainly I should be able to shape a little cookie! However, try as I may, I cannot get the form right. It takes me twenty minutes, and the cookie ends up looking like a crippled crab with five backwards feet. The three women watch me without passing judgment. They tell me it was hard for them the first time too, and they place my impaired cookies on the tray with the rest, to be served at the feast.

When the cookies and breads are finished, Bertha takes me into the living room. There is her darling granddaughter, whose name I cannot pronounce. After I greet her, Bertha shows me a picture of her handsome son Carl. He looks like he is in his early twenties. She tells me he was her only son and he died in an accident. She is now raising his daughter, her granddaughter.

Although the tragic death occurred five years ago, Bertha is so grief-stricken that she speaks about it as though it just happened. It has taken her this long to be able to clean out Carl's closet and it made her nuts—she started flinging things against the wall as she screamed out "Why?????"

I am silent as she talks to me. When it is appropriate we start to talk together, and we both concur that some questions have no answer. You just cannot know WHY. Bertha's whole body slumps when she talks about Carl's death; it is as though she bears the weight of it.

Later in the morning, I hear that Carl was a medicine man, even though Bertha didn't mention it. I learn the following story about Carl, an illustration of his power in life and even in death.

Apparently, last year a young man was in his room, several days before the buffalo dance at Cochiti. He looked up, and the deceased Carl was sitting on his bed. Carl encouraged him to participate in the buffalo dance and told him that he would appear. It was in the month of February. The young man decided to dance, and while he was dancing, a butterfly flew to him. It was extraordinary to see a butterfly in February, and he immediately knew it was Carl.

Back in the kitchen, I sit at the table with the three women, and we are just about to taste the fresh, hot bread, when Arnold shows up in his park ranger uniform, for this is what he does for a living. He is chief ranger at Cochiti Lake. It is his birthday, so we sing for him. He has brought along his boss Russell, who grew up in the black section of Nashville, Tennessee, and treats us to stories about his boyhood. As long as everyone is telling stories, I contribute a few from my childhood and we are all laughing and breaking bread. I glance over at Bertha: she is giggling and cackling, but I am aware of the sadness in her heart, which she has shared with me.

For the occasion, I am wearing a T-shirt that says, "I can't believe it, I forgot to have children." I threw it on at 3 A.M., and now I am embarrassed, for I am sure it is diametrically opposed to the Indian attitude about children, and they are probably shocked or insulted by it. Wrong again. My T-shirt is a big hit. The two Herrera sisters insist they each want one. I laugh to myself as I imagine Jenny and Bertha, these big, solid Pueblo women, wearing my silly T-shirt as they bake bread in their earthen oven. I also smile when I realize that MY sister Patsy gave me the T-shirt, and it is no coincidence that these two sisters want it because, as Elisa says, it "obviously carries sister energy." I decline to tell them that Patsy and I have never baked bread together—we never do anything low-key and normal like that!

Indian Time

It is now late morning, and although I am dog-tired, the family is very congenial and I'm having a wonderful time. When I get up to go, they all insist that I take a bread home. When I say I don't want to take one of their breads, Arnold tells the following Cochiti story to me.

A woman was baking bread, and an old man was sitting next to her. When the breads were done, he asked for one, and she wouldn't give it to him. When she got back to her house, the breads had turned to stone.

"That is why people share bread," Arnold says, and I grab the bread, lest everything in the *casita* turn to stone.

Arnold recounts with obvious delight how, as a kid, he ran around the Plaza at Cochiti with his friends, and when a bread was done, the woman always gave the kids a piece.

"Sharing is at the heart of the Indian way of life," Arnold says. "Hoarding is *really* frowned upon."

As we talk, I understand that baking bread is not just about baking bread, and this is why I was invited. Baking bread is not a casual act. The women do HARD WORK for Feast Days and weddings and ceremonies. They must make incredible quantities of food, and feed everyone who comes. They take their role seriously and are proud of it. Everyone counts on them for food. They do it in the tradition of their mothers and grandmothers. They put spirit into their cooking. Cooking is part of how the Indians, in spite of all the massacres and genocide, have held on to their integrity and culture.

I leave Cochiti with my bread, and Elisa takes me past the Cochiti dam, a huge, enormous, massive undertaking built by Uncle Sam a few decades ago. Cochiti Lake was dammed off for purely recreational purposes, and there was a serious problem with seepage which has been a major headache for the Indians of Cochiti Pueblo nearby. Their fields were flooded, and this changed the life at the Pueblo because a whole generation was unable to plant. Farming is the lifeblood and sustenance of the Pueblo. The dam is an example of another blow struck to the Indians and their lifestyle, even as everyone screams about how things have changed for them.

We go to visit Arnold at his headquarters above Cochiti Lake. He seems pensive and reflective and he begins to talk about the preservation of sacred things. He tells me about the legend of Santiago, who fought in the war against the Moors. He was an officer in the Spanish army who was easy to spot because he rode a white horse, and when the soldiers saw him on the battlefield, it raised their morale tremen-

156

dously, He gained sainthood, and the legend came from Spain to Mexico and traveled north up the Rio Grande. Santiago was adopted by the Pueblos as depicting something special and sacred.

Arnold's brow furrows and he begins to speak about something else that was sacred and special to his people. Before the dam was built at Cochiti Lake, the Indians had a very important shrine there. "It was almost like the center of the universe in the Pueblo world," Arnold says sadly. "The desecration of this shrine affected people as far away as Hopi and Zuni. It looked to us like total disregard. The spiritual significance of the spot remains, but the physical site has been cut right through the middle."

There is a stuffed rattlesnake in the visitors' center and, after I grimace and make a few "yech" sounds, we speak a bit about rattlesnakes. Of course I bring up the famous snake dances at Hopi, where the ceremony includes dancing with live rattlesnakes. Arnold tells me a wonderful Hopi rattlesnake story.

A man from Santo Domingo Pueblo went to the Hopi snake dances, and brought home some corn pollen after the ceremony was over. After he came home, people didn't see him come out of his house, and they learned he was sick. He went to a medicine man, and, in the course of talking, he told the medicine man that he had been to the Hopi snake dances and brought the pollen home. This gave the medicine man an idea. He went to the sick man's home and indeed, just as he thought, he saw rattlesnakes all over the ceiling and walls. They weren't visible to the sick man, but the medicine man could see them clearly, and he knew they were making the man sick! From that day on, the people of Santo Domingo were discouraged from going to the Hopi snake dances. The moral of the story is that these ceremonies are very powerful. You can't just take something away from them. There are snakes attached. They carry the spirit of the ceremonies.

Late in the afternoon, I go to Lenny's apartment and we work. It is exhausting and demanding. I don't know how we will finish our series outline by the deadline, which is three days away, because we are just beginning. We were supposed to be doing this for two months, and now it all has to be crammed in.

This is the first time we have worked at Lenny's apartment, and I must say I am stunned. It is no longer a sty. His Anglo girlfriend, Livia, has put order in his life, and he is very proud of his new image. He asks me please not to go into the second bedroom, although he will not explain why. As soon as he sits down to work, I laughingly run and fling open the door to the second bedroom, overcome with curiosity. There I see an incredible mound of junk that has been gathered from the other rooms. I knew it!!! I tease Lenny mercilessly about hiding his "Indian" room. I guess that each of us, in his own way, hides his "Indian room." There is always a part of us that we can't get in order. We try to make the other parts look as good as possible, so no one will see the "Indian room."

As I walk home across the field full of fearsome prairie dogs, I start to trot so my ankles won't get bitten. And as I trot, I think about my day, about the Feast Day preparations at Cochiti, and about the stories I have heard. I realize that some of the stories my Indian friends tell me are pretty wild, and maybe other people don't believe them. The important thing, however, is not what is true, but WHAT ONE CHOOSES TO BELIEVE IN. Some Indian person or persons believed in those stories, and it helped in their personal healing. My own personal stories and beliefs may be just as bizarre, but if I continue to believe in them, they will help me—no matter what anyone else thinks! As Arnold said to me: "When you go to a doctor, he can only help you if you believe in him and what he's doing." I guess it doesn't matter if it's pills, psychiatry, or witchcraft, as long as people believe in what they are doing and believe it can help them.

As I think about healing and Indian stories, I shift my attention away from my fear of getting bitten by prairie dogs, and I get totally absorbed by my thoughts. I realize that what you pay attention to IS A CHOICE. You don't have to be at the mercy of your mind. Right now, I can pay attention to the fact that it is hot and muggy or that it's a long walk home or that there is nothing in the house to eat for dinner, or that we get older second by second and we're all going to die and probably suffer first OR I can look up at the drama of the clouds and the early pink rays of the sunset that wash across the field and think about the healing power of nature. Which, in the long run, will move me further along in my life journey and really matter?

It makes me recall the words of an Indian man, whom I met when he came outside during the rounds in the sweatlodge ceremony I attended. It was absolutely freezing on the mountaintop, and everyone was dressed, at most, in towels. The participants' bare bodies were shivering and shaking in the night air. My own feet felt like they were going to freeze off. I curled my toes, I spread my toes out, I tried to stand on my heels, but nothing would help my feet. I sidled up to the Indian man, starting to panic about whether I could endure it. "Aren't your feet FREEZING?" I asked him. "Yes," he said, "my feet are freezing." "What do you do about it?" I asked. "Well," he answered, "I choose not to think about it."

In the evening, we go to a benefit to help Leonard Peltier—an Indian who defended his res against illegal FBI incursion. There was a shootout and he was accused of killing two FBI agents. The Indians claim he is innocent, and yet he has spent fifteen years of his life in prison.

Rodney Grant, the Indian actor from *Dances with Wolves,* is one of the speakers. What a surprise! He is funny and self-effacing and very militant in his Indianism. All he ever does in films is sit on a horse and look exotically handsome. The real person is much more interesting, but no one gives him a chance to open his mouth on screen. But the real surprise of the evening is an almost breathtaking lesson in karma.

Beaver is at the benefit. She stands in the lobby, with a captive audience, telling about her recent adventures. I stand in the background, listening. Beaver has just come back from a week in Peru, where she was flown to be a model for an Indian sculpture. After her modeling work was over, she was free to see all of Peru. It was the opportunity of a lifetime for her! Except . . . she was left stranded there with no transportation and no way to get around, so, drowning in frustration, she ended up seeing nothing at all. How quickly the karma wagon has come to roll over her feet! This is just what she did to me! I stand and gape at Beaver as she speaks; I can't believe what I am hearing! What goes around really does come around!

On the ride home, I get very philosophical with Paul.

"I think we are all in Indian country all the time," I tell him. "It happens to be here in Santa Fe that I am beginning to learn how to watch and listen, and to actually experience what is happening to me. I am 'on the trip'—'walking my walk'—paying attention to my life and living it in the blank spaces, between the words, between the lines. My eyes and ears and—gulp—heart are open. But you can be in Indian country wherever you are. Even if you never leave your house. I am sure of that now. Just thought I'd lay it on you."

Paul hesitates a moment. He stops at a red light and stares down at his feet in silence. I imagine he is really pondering my words.

"Do you think we can find a shoemaker in Indian country?" he asks, as the light turns green. "I'd like to walk my walk too, but the heels of my shoes are run down."

I poke him so hard he almost drives off the road.

We wake up Sunday morning and go to the Feast Day at Cochiti. On the Plaza, the dancing is a feast for the eyes. There are two groups of dancers with rattles and spruce branches, and the women wear beautifully painted wooden *tabletas* on their heads. One group of men has their chests painted green and the others wear an orange color. These are the two moieties or societies which make up the Pueblo—the turquoise and the pumpkin. There are zebra-striped clowns, or *koshari,* which I'd often seen as *kachina* dolls, but never in the flesh.

It is good to see so many people dancing—kids, older people, teenagers. As I stand there watching them, a strange thing happens. Maybe it is the effect of the sun in my eyes, or maybe it is the fact that I am tired. But when I look at the dancers, I see the Plaza filled with ears of corn!

"Paul," I whisper. "Do you see corn plants on the Plaza?"

"Nope," he says, looking around. "Do you?"

"Yes. Yes. The whole Plaza is full of them."

He stares at me quizzically.

"I think it means that no matter what genocide is perpetrated against the Indians, they keep growing back like ears of corn. It's obvious that many are coming back to the fold. They're returning from cities, back to the res. As long as there is one Indian who carries the old ways, the songs and dances and prayers, it will never be lost. The single seed will sprout a Plaza full of corn!"

I watch the dancers, and the outside world fades away. Things that bothered me before no longer seem to matter. I am totally focused on the dance. I wonder what they are thinking when they are dancing, for no one ever speaks. Are they praying to the Creator? Listening to the drum? Giving thanks?

Suddenly it occurs to me—these dancers aren't separate from us. They are profoundly linked to us. They are giving their precious time and energy to dance for all of us, for all of humanity, to give thanksgiving and offer prayers for harvest, health, well-being. And we, by watching, are participating in the dance as well.

160

On Baking Bread and Feeding Ants

When there is a break in the dancing, we go into the Herrera house, where dinner is being served. I expect to joke with Bertha and Jenny about the breads I baked, but in Indian country you can't expect anything. There isn't a word spoken about it. It's as though it never happened.

When there is room at the table, I slide in, and eat like a pig. This time there are all the traditional foods—the stews and hominy and succotash—plus corn dogs and chicken McNuggets. After I eat, I teasingly offer my services. Then I split for the living room, making room at my place for another person who is waiting.

Minutes later, Bertha and Jenny come after me and tell me I should come and work in the kitchen. Paul gets all excited and suddenly it washes over me: it was just a month or so ago that I was at Sandia Pueblo for my first Feast Day, watching like an outsider while women bustled around the kitchen and called people to the table when others got up to leave. Now I am invited to participate! I feel so lucky! Being asked to help in the kitchen! My mother would laugh about this ecstasy: I've never lifted a domestic finger, except under duress, in my life. At home, Paul does all the cooking in the kitchen . . . wherever that is!

First I go and get stew from the back room and very seriously and ceremoniously carry it into the living room and set it in a crock pot. This is deadly earnest work. Then I carry dirty plates into the kitchen to be washed, and transport clean ones over to the table. Finally, when I have proved to the others that I am not frivolous, I get to stick my neck into the living room, where people are waiting, and say, "Two more, please," as two more people get up and come into the kitchen to eat. What a treat for me!

When I am ready to go, Elisa Herrera hands me a bread, insisting I take it. By now I know not to refuse bread. Then she reaches into a bag and hands me four cookies to take home. I gasp when I get outside. Of all the cookies in the bag, she accidentally picked mine, the "crippled crab with five backwards feet."

"Do you really think it's an accident?" I ask Paul.

"I don't know what to think any more!" he answers.

After a short night's sleep, Lenny and I get together and work all day. We are late for our deadline, but we finally manage to fax an outline to our producers. Afterwards, we walk to an open field and sit down on a log to chat for a moment so that we can unwind. I absently pick up a twig and begin to play with it in the dirt.

"Those ants are going to keep invading your house," Lenny observes.

I look down. Unconsciously I have been snuffing ants as we speak. When I get home, the kitchen counter is a thick carpet of ants. This time I have learned my lesson. I trace the long trail to outdoor anthills. I go and feed a nice, tasty apple-cinnamon cereal to the ants in their homes. I speak to them and tell them why I don't want them in our house, but I know they need to eat, so I am feeding them. I hope they like my choice of food. Then I line the door with Ajax. Within three hours all the ants are gone, and I haven't offed a single one. I am very proud of this accomplishment until Paul comes home, sees a few straggling ants on the counter, and pulls out the soap spray! When I come out of the shower, I am mortified.

"I am sorry, brother ants," Paul says. "I wasn't thinking. I really apologize for killing you."

"Wow! That's great!" I say to Paul.

"I don't know what's happening to me," Paul grumbles. "Man—the hunter. Ha!"

In the evening, I take my hunter to Lenny's storytelling campfire. There are about fourteen people this time, including a few kids. Lenny is too proud a performer to repeat last week's campfire exactly, and it is good that I am there again because it stimulates him to change. He sends us out, far from the campfire, to get our special rocks. I wander among the trees, focusing on the task, searching everywhere, and finally I find my rock, sitting alone atop a mound of dirt and sparkling in the setting sun. When I pick up the rock, I have an epiphany: the JOURNEY is more important than the stone. The WAY you travel through life is more important than the DESTINATION or what you FIND THERE.

In the morning, we head for the Eight Northern Pueblos Art Show. It's a major art show for Indian artists, perhaps second in importance around here to the world-famous Indian Market. It is at San Juan Pueblo this year, and it is HOT. You can feel the sun entering your body and coming out in liquid form as your clothes begin to stick to you. The food is the usual fare—Indian fry bread and tacos and mutton stew and posole. That does it for me! No more meat and no more grease! From now on, I am bringing along a little picnic in my pocket.

Every hour or so there is a different Indian dance performance on

162

the Plaza, but I really don't pay much attention to them because I only enjoy seeing them in their natural habitat, and not when they are done for display. I know they carry the same prayers, and I know the dancers have the same intentions, but somehow the experience is diluted for me.

The artwork is very varied; some very commercial and some full of integrity and vision. You can buy a pair of silver earrings for $40 or you can plunk down $10,000 for a piece of sculpture. There are hundreds of display booths, and it all begins to be a blur. Nothing is screaming out "BUY ME," so we don't buy anything at all. We know some of the artists now, so it is fun visiting them in their booths.

Lenny's family is all there. His sister and her husband are two of the most famous Indian jewelers in the world. The work they display is in coral, lapis, dinosaur bone, silver, and gold. It is very clean and beautiful and contemporary. All the Smallfeather siblings are very friendly and congenial to us, which makes the meeting most pleasant. It must be hard for them not to have parents any more. I only have one living parent, and I know how important her presence in the world is to me.

The sales for the artists seem to be slow this year, and all of them are trying to sell because they are very dependent upon these shows for income.

When the heat becomes really oppressive, we buy a few fry breads as a gift and go to visit Toni—Belinda's grandmother, the woman who embodies "grandmother energy" for me. She is as bright and spunky as usual, but there is an undertone of sadness. It seems her younger sister has just died, and she is returning from the funeral. What a ghastly thought—losing a sister! Apparently, the sister had diabetes, and had started with a toe amputated, then her foot, then a leg, etc. Diabetes wreaks havoc among the Indians, and no one seems to know why. I also report sadly that I see no modification of the intake of sweets. Our booze and our food are literally killing the Indians! A massive educational program is needed to try to change the way they eat, for clearly many of our foods are not suitable for living beings.

When I get home, Carl Hammerschlag calls. It is wonderful to touch base with the man I am writing the TV series about, and we have become good friends. He shares with me a reverence bordering on awe for the Indian ways. He repeats, in his oratorical tones, that we are doomed unless we understand that we have much to learn from the indigenous peoples we try to kill off. Our own life is without ritual and ceremony. Such a life cannot be healthy or balanced.

As soon as Carl hangs up, the phone rings again and it is Sacheen Littlefeather. She says she is en route to the sacred Sioux sundance in South Dakota, where the dancers pierce and sacrifice their own flesh after intense prayer, fasting, and preparation. She asks if she can stay at our house for a day or two with Barney—the brother of the medicine man of the Mescalero Apaches. I hesitate for a beat, because our place is very small and we hardly have room for ourselves. I would like to say no. But if Sacheen and Barney can lend their support to the sundancers, I can lend my support to Sacheen and Barney. I say yes. I am trying to say yes to whatever comes in my path. "Yes" opens the door to life; "no" closes it.

"We'll be arriving in the late afternoon tomorrow," Sacheen says.

We wait at home all afternoon, and into the evening. At 10 P.M. there is a knock at the door. I go to it, and Laura Fragua and Steven Wall are standing there! We usher them in, and Paul serves his latest invention: macaroni and buffalo meat. As soon as we finish eating, Sacheen and Barney arrive. There is no apology for being late. We say nothing either. We all eat once again.

The conversation eventually gets around to Indians. It has been our experience with our Native American friends that the conversation always turns to that subject. This time it is Barney holding court. He is extremely articulate, lucid, and verbal. First he starts talking about how being with Indians slows down time. This we have found to be true. And it accounts, in part, for our being able to focus on what is happening. Then he talks about the magic of New Mexico, and how hard it is to explain to outsiders. Next, the subject turns to oppression. I say that for the life of me I cannot understand why white people wanted to obliterate Indians. Steve volunteers that when you are afraid of something, you try to destroy it. The talk then wanders to why Indians would want to adopt white ways. This answer is fairly complex.

First, Indians saw that white men had guns and horses, which are very powerful. So they reasoned that the white God and the white religion must be very powerful too. If they converted, they could have part of that. Second, Indians are seduced by those "things" that they see and don't have. "Accept the good change," as our Pueblo friends say. The Indians try to adapt and adopt . . . while maintaining their own identity.

On Baking Bread and Feeding Ants

As we speak, I see Laura getting uncomfortable, and soon she and Steve get up to leave. I'm not sure what it is, but when talk gets around to Indian things, she doesn't seem to want to share that with us.

Sacheen, Barney, Paul, and I stay up talking until very late, and then, when we get up in the morning, it all continues. Barney tells us many things about Apache ways. Traditionally, a woman does not even look her own husband in the eyes. This is a sign of disrespect. A man does not look his mother-in-law in the eyes. When cars first came to the res, traditionalists hung curtain partitions between the front and back seats lest involuntary eye contact take place! This, too, was considered disrespectful.

In Apache society, the mother-in-law rules the roost. It is a matriarchal and matrilineal culture, and the son-in-law will be treated well as long as he is a good warrior and provider. If not, there is trouble. If a woman is dissatisfied with her husband, she simply leaves his saddle and clothes outside of the tepee entrance. He is through there. He must wander until he can find someone else to take him in.

Barney speaks of warfare before the advent of white men. According to him, it was mostly about territory, and if someone trespassed on someone else's declared hunting grounds, there might have been an attack and a killing or two. But battles in which hundreds of people are killed were unknown.

He speaks of friendship—how it takes a long time for someone to shake your hand. When they do, it really means something. You are a friend, a member of the family. That is why many Indians are slow to hug, to show affection, to touch. It is very significant when they do, and implies real acceptance. HOWEVER, here is the caveat: once you are taken in as a friend and family member, if you transgress, you are dismissed as a non-person. You are as good as nonexistent. Forever. In other words, the code of behavior is very well defined. It takes a long time to make someone your friend or family. Everyone knows what is expected in terms of behavior, for you have been observing each other for a long time. If you make a mistake in your actions, you have basically blown it and there is no way back. This rigid code is how moral and social order and law and order are maintained. Everyone knows what is expected of him. If you transgress, you know what the punishment will be. This leaves the human being free CHOICE, and if he chooses to behave improperly, he knows what the consequences will be.

Barney is very articulate and focused when he speaks about med-

165

icine. The medicine man helps you to help yourself heal. He taps into the energy, and he transmits it. When he touches you, this reinforces it. Once he touches you, he has made essential contact, and he can even heal from a distance. This seems to be the Indian attitude toward healing. It takes the collaboration of doctor and patient. Unlike Western medicine, it is not something that is "done to you." You must participate.

Sacheen and Barney both speak about money. Indians don't care about it. They don't accumulate it. They don't hoard it. They are not focused on earning and living to work. Their crafts are not done for money, but to use what is provided by Mother Earth (clay, stones, silver, etc.) and pay homage to her.

As they speak, I wonder how our two cultures can ever really understand each other well enough to get along! Sacheen is a health worker (body work, nutrition), but Barney believes that if you come to food in a good way, no matter what you eat it, won't hurt you. If you ask water to cleanse you, it will do so. If you ask the sun to bless you and shine upon you, it will not give you skin cancer. There is a tremendous belief in the power of the mind and the heart. They both think the white mind is so busy thinking that the white person can't feel, can't know things, has lost touch.

Paul and I both say we feel awkward, because we are always trying to push our Indian friends to market themselves and their arts, to make a living, etc. How can we do it without falling into the white stereotype?

"The answer is that Indians must first trust you before they will take any advice," Sacheen says. "And then, you can give advice in the form of example—by telling stories about things you have tried that worked. This way, if it fails, they can't blame you. You can also ask your Indian friends if they would like help. Criticizing or imposing your way does not go down well with Indians."

Barney says many many more things, about himself, his magic, his dreams and dilemmas, but he asks us to keep it to ourselves, and so we must. I have often wondered what is appropriate to write about.

"When people don't want you to pass something on, they tell you," Barney says. He also says that his Indian language is very unambiguous. You say "I want a tall white stick with three notches and a smooth end." Your words express *exactly* what you want and need and think. Communication is very frank. When Indians speak English, they are often translating from their own language. They can no longer say ex-

166

actly what they mean. It is yet another source of frustration and cultural difference.

The second day of Sacheen and Barney's visit, Paul and I are going stir-crazy inside the *casita,* so while our guests go off to visit Santa Fe, we don our hiking boots and set out into the country. We drive along breathtaking roads, where the panorama is vast and the clouds have very suggestive shapes. We point at them and say, "Look at the mermaid with a bustle" or "Look at Abe Lincoln on a dog." We stop in San Ildefonso, a very picturesque Pueblo, and then drive on to Los Alamos. I expect not to like the place because I am not fond of the nuclear horrors developed there. The streets bear names like "Trinity" and "Oppenheimer," so you can never forget it.

We finally jump out of the car and begin to walk, and once past the suburban streets with no particular personality, we arrive at a path that leads into nature. Ten minutes into the walk, I am stunned by a five-foot-long snake that uncoils in front of me.

"You know," Paul observes to me, as I lean against a tree, trying to stop hyperventilating, "people who are really frightened don't screech the way they do in the movies. When you saw the snake, you gasped, emitted five jerky sounds, and then squeaked out my name. Have you ever seen anyone do that on film?"

Paul reassures me that it is only a harmless rat snake. But he has little credibility in this domain, because he also reassured me that airplanes, spiders, bats, and tarantulas are natural too. Worse, when we saw a cannibal cat, a mother cat who eats her babes, smacking her lips as she crunched their bones, he assured me that this was normal too.

We walk on, and find a most wondrous marriage of a tree and a stone. One has grown around the other in a startling combination, and I stop to photograph it, while looking behind me for more rat snakes.

"You're great!" Paul exclaims as I snap the shutter.

"I am?" I ask incredulously.

"Yes, yes, look at you. The snake didn't scare you off. You continue on the path. Two months ago, you would have been hauled out of here in a straitjacket. And you're taking pictures! You're in the present, watching, responding to what's around you."

"Thank you, " I say quietly, wondering if it will last.

We drive home via Santa Clara Pueblo and realize it has been a while since we last saw Dr. Doug White Wolf and his wife Gail—who comes from Taos Pueblo. We knock on their door, which makes me squirm because although it is the Indian way, I hate arriving at someone's house without calling first. They are most cordial and we tell them we have come to corrupt them and drag them out for a walk. They protest a bit, but give in.

Doug leads us over to the arroyo, and there, I am sorry to say, we are attacked by a swarm of mosquitoes. Doug and Gail show us how to walk while keeping upper body and arms in constant motion and also twisting our backs to keep the mosquitoes off. The swarm gets worse. We are all smacking and slapping and twisting to no avail. Finally Doug suggests we start to run, so we have to run all the way back to his house—about twenty minutes. Our bites are fodder for Paul's humor machine, and soon he and Doug and Gail are cackling like infants as we whip up a paste of baking soda and coat ourselves to stop the itching.

"This is a segment of your four-part initiation," Doug says.

"Very funny," I comment.

"No, I am serious," he says. "The first time you came here it was the attack of the ants. Now it is mosquitoes. We can't wait to see what the next two steps are!"

The following day, Lenny and I meet with our producers, who have arrived from L.A. and are very critical of our work. We try to compromise and satisfy their demands, but we are both chagrined. We know that the series must originate from a place of truth, not plot or commerce.

The meetings go on for two days and are very stressful. Lenny and I do our best to present a united front, even though our relationship has been stormy of late. We have somehow established a very strange communication system. We badger each other and tease each other; I make fun of his Indianness and he makes fun of my Jewishness. This may not be the smoothest form of talking to another human, but the levity and lightness cover over a lot of the intercultural and interpersonal roughness, a lot of the personal pique. To outsiders, it may seem very bizarre, but so far it works for us. It's the best way we know how.

When our last meeting is over and the producers leave, Lenny and I take a long walk outside together. Nothing needs to be said. We bond. We hardly speak about the meetings, or even the TV project. I ask him about the ruins of a Pueblo where his family supposedly migrated from. He tells me how he knew of this ancient home, and what the story of his family is. He tells me how the ancestral connection, the message he got, is to honor and respect all of life—in the form of family, for example. He speaks in that clear, precise, supranatural way

168

he has of talking. Then he talks about his storytelling and how, if nothing else, the participants in his campfire storytelling sessions see a man JOYOUS in telling stories, joyous in his work.

"I don't understand how people do work they hate. Then why do they do it?" he asks. "There is something profoundly wrong. Work should be joy. When I was in Los Angeles, I met all these people who set their jaws and went to work, toughing it out. Why?"

We stand on a newly paved road and I just listen to him. For all the pain and disappointment of working with him, these are wonderful moments, and he gives me a great gift when he opens his heart and talks.

"Thank you," I say to Lenny.

"Thank you, too," he says to me. "I learn a lot from you. You have a lot to say."

I blink, surprised. I frankly didn't think he noticed.

8

Feast Day

"Paul," I say one morning as I sip my herbal tea, "can you remember where we keep our umbrellas in our house in Los Angeles?"

"Nope."

"How about our pile of appliance instruction manuals. Do you know where it is?" I ask.

"Not a clue."

"It seems like we've been gone for years, doesn't it? Our whole life in Los Angeles has no reality."

"Mortgage payments have a certain reality. Car payments too."

"I guess so," I say, "but I am talking about something else. It seems like our whole life has changed. What we knew before is no longer true. We can't take anything for granted or make any advance assumptions. We can no longer have any expectations at all, because they are always flip-flopped by the happenings in real life. "

I finish my tea, and dress for an appointment with Hans Norgen, the New Mexico State Archeologist. "Dressing" means that I put on a freshly laundered pair of gym tights, a T-shirt and sneakers.

"Remember not to have any expectations," Paul says to me, and it's a good thing he reminds me, because Hans turns my notions of an archeologist topsy-turvy.

I set up the appointment to ask Hans about petroglyphs, because I am obsessed with them. When I look at those ancient rock drawings and etchings, it pulls me into the mystery of a life long gone. I come bounding into Hans's office, dressed for a workout, and he matches me in nonchalance.

Hans is a vigorous, robust gentleman with a head full of white hair and a white beard. We sit down, and he puts his hands behind his head, leans back in his bureaucratically appropriate wooden chair, and starts to muse about archeology and his job, giving the official line. Suddenly, something in me revolts. I have no interest in chitchat. No interest in professionally sanctioned information. Not even any remaining interest in professions at all. I simply want to know who Hans is, what he thinks, feels, believes after all these years as a white man working with Indians, and giving the yea or the nay when construction comes too near to their sacred burial sites and bones. I want to know what archeology is, why he is interested in the dead at all, and how he is implicated in all of it as a human being. I lean forward, go into my most intense mode, and began to pin him to the wall. As I am doing it, I am aware of how PERSONAL I am being, but I can't prevent myself. I knew that this is SOCIALLY INAPPROPRIATE BEHAVIOR in the office of a state official, but I can't stop. I'm bored by surface reality, bored with politeness, and I figure he's a grown man and can defend himself. He says I am a nuisance, hems and haws, but is that a twinkle I see in his eyes? And why does he keep me there for three hours and have all his calls held?

Hans keeps throwing the names of books at me, because that is where he is on safe ground. But when he is *not,* he is passionately interesting. He reads the philosophical works of Niels Bohr and *The Tao of Physics.* He writes tomes on archeology, espousing the accepted methodologies and theories, and then he quotes Einstein, undercutting his own observations: "It is the theory which decides what we can observe." He wrote an article on quantum theory and archeology, and reads up on shamanism.

He talks about rock "artists" of antiquity, the people who made those provocative etched pictures on rocks. He knows the petroglyphs were not casually done. There were great consequences for the artist if they weren't done exactly right. According to the Indian belief system, each person on earth must do his job and carry out his duties; if not, the world falls apart as everything is delicately interconnected. The personal consequences are grave indeed for mistakes. People get sick, and their children die. It is *that* serious.

"Do you believe that to be true?" I ask Hans.

"Yes, I suspect it is. Even if it's not that direct. If we dig up sacred sites and mess with the past and have no respect for nature, perhaps a hex is not put on our children directly, but look at the state of the planet they will inherit—the quality of air, of water, of life itself. Look what DOES happen to us, to our health, to our children. Isn't this the evil that the Indians say will come to us?"

Hans muses about his own field and about all of European thought.

"Most of what we think is wrong," he says, "and some is wronger than others. We don't see the universe as a whole. And because we don't, we miss it all."

"Of course!" I think to myself. That is why so much of Western medicine sucks, and why people can go to church on Sunday and screw people on Monday. Everything is compartmentalized and seen as separate from everything else. There is no sense that every action has enormous repercussions.

Hans speculates aloud on the state of science in general, and his own science in particular.

"Things can be right for the current context," he says, "but THINGS CHANGE. Then they are no longer right."

He smiles, admitting that there are no TRUTHS in any science, no absolutes. He does not reject all European thought; in fact, he writes that way and he speaks that way. He is of good, staunch, Norwegian stock. But he is fascinated by ANOTHER WAY too. He talks of Indian prayer.

"They don't pray 'Dear God, please let the rain fall.' No, that is our way. We pray when we are in need. Our prayers are a request or wish. They, on the other hand, think that their actions and the rain are connected. They pray for the whole universe. They are locked into the matrix of all things. They feel great responsibility. Their actions have ramifications. Their actions are tied into the rain, the crops, the welfare of their children. It all depends on how well they 'do their number' in their ceremonial space. We, on the other hand, think it's a dissociated universe. Things are only randomly connected."

He pauses, smiles, and adds, "Maybe we'd better stop and pay attention if these guys are telling us that everything is an interconnected whole! Do we really 'get away with' our lousy behavior? Think about it. I believe not."

After three intense hours with Hans, his wife Dierdre comes into the office. She wrote a big, fat, glossy, well-documented, well-known book on Indian rock art. I expected someone scholarly and stiff, and am completely unprepared for the pleasant surprise of meeting a bubbly, blond, open-hearted woman. She confesses to feeling alienated from white culture, and is drawn to the mysteries of the universe. She admittedly doesn't work much with Indians on her studies of Indian petroglyphs, because it is very hard to get straight or accurate information from them. So she seeks refuge in the speculations of archeology, but her heart is in the right place.

Our meeting comes to an end because Hans and Dierdre have to run off to a wedding. I thank them profusely for being so open and generous with themselves, and when they leave, I think that perhaps Hans is embarrassed about how much he has revealed. I want to tell him to feel good about who he is, because the person that hides behind the title is more exciting and passionate than most people I have met with titles. For some silly reason, I never say the words, and Hans is gone.

As I wander down the corridor, an Indian woman comes along and offers me a free pass to the museum complex, so I have to go to acknowledge her generosity.

I am awed by the new Allan Houser sculptures (he is probably the most famous living Indian sculptor; his work is monumental, humanistic, prayer-ful), and then I HAVE to go into the Indian arts museum, HAVE to see the Turkish exhibit, HAVE to peek into my darling, favorite Folk Art Museum, and HAVE to sit down and watch videotaped interviews with Indian pottery makers. The interviewer simply asks them about pottery, but Indians can't SIMPLY answer anything. One talks about how he feels such joy as he works that he sometimes does a corn dance with a pot as his partner. They all talk about how you can't work when you are angry or upset. The clay doesn't like it and the pots don't come out right. One speaks about going to get clay with her mother. And when she gets there "she knows she has to make a decision about the way she lives her life."

To the Indian potters interviewed, the clay is an offering from the earth, from Mother Nature. They must work WITH the clay. They give to the clay and the clay gives to them. In life, you take and you give. The clay is alive. The goal of work is joy, and working WITH the clay brings them joy. It connects them to their ancestors, who developed these techniques.

One woman potter speaks of the temptation of commercialism, and how she had to turn her back on it. White people want Indian potters to do recognizable Indian art, but she feels that she is Indian and an artist and whatever she does is Indian art. Another talks of how he does one sort of pot to sell, another for ceremony. An older potter speaks lovingly of the thin walls of the pots. And on, and on. Do we feel that way about OUR work, I wonder. This is the joy Lenny speaks of. We don't even associate the two words—JOY and WORK.

Tonight there is the usual late July storm, for this is monsoon season. The sky starts out blue and innocent each day. By late afternoon or early evening the sky is black and ominous and there are flood warnings. The storm rages outside of the *casita*. The miniblinds are clanging and banging against the windows, lightning is dancing around our little abode, rain is lashing against the roof, and Laura Fragua arrives, drenched, with BEAVER in tow! She acts as though nothing ever happened between us, and we behave the same way. Beaver informs me that she has been fired, and asks me if I know of a job for her and will I keep my eyes open! This is beyond irony. One of the reasons she was fired is because her boss, Garrison Baveur, found out about her irresponsible behavior toward me! I look at her in her oblivion. It is neither calculating nor malicious. I am just baffled, baffled, baffled. And the worst part is that if I knew of a job, I would probably tell her!

We sit around until way after midnight, drinking wine and eating whatever I can find to bring to the tiny, round, wooden cocktail table. I serve some hot soup, and Beaver informs me that she met an artist in Peru and wants to bring him here but he needs a hard-to-get visa first, so she has decided to marry him. She pulls out the visa application form and asks me to take a look at it. I ask no questions. I am just baffled, baffled, baffled.

Speaking of things I do not understand, I will probably never comprehend why Lenny behaves the way he does. On the one hand, he is extremely honest about himself and his connection to his culture. He makes it very clear for me, and gives me great insight. But when it comes to personal honesty, he seems not to be capable of it, or, perhaps, unwilling to commit to it. He makes plans to work with me, but I feel like he is a fish, I am grabbing for his tail, and he keeps swimming away. He sets up rules about how we should work and where we should work and when we should work, and then, without explanation, he changes all of the rules he has just made. I am left hanging there, and it makes me nuts!! When I try to discuss the arrangements with him, he gets defensive or evasive.

On the plus side, we have wonderful talks as we work. Today we speak about silence, which is of great interest to me. I do not know how to be silent when I meet someone—I feel you have to make an impression, or else the person you encounter won't even talk to you. I believe you have to show some personality, or there will be no way to connect to people.

"Silence is an Indian book," Lenny tells me. "It's how we learn all we need to know."

"Well, I guess I'll start shutting up and observing," I announce.

Lenny raises a skeptical eyebrow at the idea of me ever being quiet.

After Lenny leaves, I have a most startling telephone conversation with Frederic Marlow, a medical anthropologist with impeccable credentials in the Indian Health Service. He is currently, I think, close to retirement, and a professor at the University of Colorado. He discredits all of Carl Hammerschlag's writings about what he, as a doctor, learned from Indians, and says it is wishful thinking rather than reality. He says "good luck" on the series I am writing, but doesn't believe in it.

"White doctors have absolutely nothing to learn from Indian medicine. In all of my years, I know of only one case where an Indian person was helped by an Indian ceremony. Most illnesses are self-limiting; if you leave them alone they resolve themselves. People say they are helped by ceremonies, but, in fact, the illnesses just go away. In the realm of psychiatry, the Indians are basically useless. Their 'medicine' and 'medicine men' are ineffectual."

Frederic is married to an Indian woman. He has lived on reservations, his children live there, but he remains sadly aloof. He thinks the white way is the good way, and the only really positive thing I hear him say is that Indians stereotype people less than we do. They don't reject all whites or all blacks. They judge a person by his or her own merits.

"Oh, yes," he adds, "there is another good thing about Indians. They are pretty hospitable."

Frederic's objections to all of Indian medicine are based on the fact that there are no statistical studies to prove anything. If you can't measure something and observe it and record it, it is worthless. It just doesn't exist. "Indian medicine is prescientific," Frederic says. "It can't do the job. Modern medicine has the best answers. Lots of Indians even realize that the old ways are no good."

Indian Time

I am nonjudgmental on the phone. I just listen and let him speak. I ask him how he happened to marry an Indian woman.

"If you were living in a world where there was no one else worthwhile, you'd marry one too!" he says.

He believes that Indians should be treated with respect and dignity, and like adult humans. He did a study of "hand-trembling, frenzy witchcraft, and motion madness" among the Navajo and found them all "terrible techniques" for dealing with hysterias and seizures. They are not at all helpful. Frederic has statistics to prove it.

"Hand-trembling is a means of diagnosis," he says. "The tremblers tell a patient, 'you stepped on a coyote track when you were eight years old, and that's why you are sick. You need a ceremony.'"

Frederic groans about how unscientific this is.

"What about the Indians' use of herbs?" I ask.

"There is no dosage control. It can be very dangerous," Frederic says.

"Well," I ask, "can't allopathic medicines be dangerous?"

"Yes, but it's based on science and statistics which doctors can examine."

"But Frederic," I protest, "Western medicine, as we know it, has been around little more than a century yet it even judges five-thousand-year-old Oriental techniques as 'experimental.'"

Frederic believes staunchly in Western medicine, but he does admit that doctors are prejudiced against women. He offers this without my soliciting it. He just thinks that doctors haven't been provoked to think about it.

"How about the WAY Indian medicine men treat patients?" I ask.

"They are no more humanistic than Western doctors," he sneers. "You pay them a fee, they do it for money, and if you don't pay enough or you're late with a payment, they start to grumble."

What, I wonder, does Frederic think of the exorbitant fees charged by white doctors in Rolls-Royces?

I get off the phone wondering who Frederic is. Can he really have gotten so little from so much time spent with Indians? Is he so anchored in Western ways that he only believes in statistics and lab-made medicine? In his world, there is no room for hope, prayer, beliefs, miracles. There is no room for the unknown, for mysteries, for a mind-body connection.

I am neither mad, nor sad, nor glad, just better informed. Frederic

176

is not alone. He represents a way of thinking. Doctors who go against the grain and propose another way of thinking and seeing things run up against people like Frederic. There is no way to beat them because there really is no dialogue possible. Conviction is unassailable, from both sides.

In the evening, Paul and I set out for Pecos, where we have signed up for a full-moon walk through the Indian ruins. There is no moon. There is rain. It is windy and cold. But it is extraordinary. The sunset looks like bright, gold theater floodlights coming up from behind the horizon. The expanse of gold is amazing, almost blinding; it covers half the sky. The other half is divided between silver and purple. It is almost unbelievable, because it is a king to the pawn of other sunsets we have seen in our lives.

The ranger tries to get us out of the rain and chill, so he takes us down into the womb of the earth, into a kiva. There he talks with such respect and sensitivity about the Indians and their beliefs that it is quite surprising. Paul says this ranger is a type of person who has poetry in his soul. He speaks straight from the heart, and even the kids on the tour are totally attentive.

According to the ranger, much of the history of these Indian ruins has been lost, or, at least, it is kept by the Indians and not shared by them. Recently, a descendant of Pecos came forth for the first time with the story that the Pecos Pueblo died when the Comanches poisoned their water system. He tells us another odd bit of information: the Indians at Pecos often buried their dead in the trash heaps, because they are soft and easy to dig, especially during hard winters when the ground is frozen. He speaks, in fact, of many things, including Spanish oppression. He minces no words, and is very frank about it. Of course, he is not Spanish.

"Why are you so set against the Spanish?" Paul whispers to me.

"I'm not set against the Spanish. I think they are warm, hospitable people. I believe they have a rich, wonderful heritage. I think Spain around the time of Columbus was the pinnacle of European culture. But I just want them to ACKNOWLEDGE what went on here."

"You want them to come out and state that they decimated the Indian culture?"

"Yes."

"Why? What will be accomplished?"

"Denial is death. It takes away the reality of the oppressed people. It happens in families. Kids are abused, and the parents deny it happened. It makes the children crazy. They develop screwed-up behavior. Psychologically speaking, they don't know who they are or whether they are coming or going. Only when there is ACKNOWL-EDGMENT of what happened can healing begin. TRUTH is a great medicine."

"You think Indians are abused children in the human family?"

"Yes. They are not the *only* abused children, but they certainly are among the worst-offended. The Spanish started it and then the U.S. government took over. It continues today."

When we finish whispering, I notice that all the other people on the tour are staring at us. I guess we should learn to whisper more quietly.

The next morning, we hurry out of the *casita* at the crack of dawn and head downtown to Spanish Market—a very popular and populated annual event in Santa Fe. Our Hispanic friend Elisa is our cultural guide, and she leads us to the Plaza. Booths are set up, crowds mill about, and there is a lot of expectation in the air, beginning at 8 A.M., when the Spanish crafts and works of art are for sale. Hispanic artists, both traditional and contemporary, come from all over New Mexico and Colorado to sell their wares. They have *retablos* (paintings of saints or religious scenes on wood), *bultos* (*santos* done in three-dimensional carvings), tin work, furniture, inlaid straw art, rugs and weavings, and the occasional stone worker, jewelry maker, or quilter. At first it is a knockout—high colors, tables full of expressive saints, and, most pleasing to my eye, statues where the natural shapes of the wood are used expressively. The figures swoop and bend and sway according to the way the aspen, cedar, or cottonwood grows. Then, a kind of lassitude sets in. The exceptional artists' pieces are already sold, or out of our price range. They all begin to look alike. Vision blurs. It becomes dreamlike. One artist waves a blank check that is given to him. His entire booth is sold out by 8:15 to a high roller. Wisps of conversation float by—the rich, the bored, the pretentious, the ignorant, the traveler. Rows of children are selling their work, and you can't figure out if they are four or forty. You want to buy this and you want to buy that but you end up buying nothing at all. There is a sense that many of these things are made expressly

178

FOR Spanish Market. You can see the FOR SALE sign on the object before the paint is dry. Even the children seem to have churned their work out the night before. Occasionally the lacquer is still wet. Everyone smiles, but something is missing. A bit of soul? It is sad that this wealth of culture is squeezed into the commercial mill. The beautiful, rich Spanish heritage comes out sifted and robbed of its original nutrients.

We leave the Plaza and, on our way to the car, something catches Paul's eye. Away from Spanish Market, standing in front of a blanket with his wares spread before him, is Lalo, a Peruvian musician. He sells absolutely delightful and unpretentious Peruvian clay folk art, and of course we purchase a piece. It is like a breath of fresh air, after the slick Spanish Market.

Today my Los Angeles agent Ian comes to visit, and I thought it would be culture shock to see someone from my city life, but it is fine because he and his wife are very down-to-earth and amenable. We laugh because I want Ian to visit all the Indian ruins and Pueblos, and he is content to do the Beverly Hills thing—that is, browse in the shops of downtown Santa Fe, making his way past the *kachinas,* coyotes, and southwesternalia. He compromises, and after he shops, he goes to visit and climb around an old Indian ruin. He loves it. Every time a person breaks a pattern, there is a reward. I am convinced.

After Ian leaves, I decide to go to a special Spanish mass in St. Francis Church. I open the church door, expecting a trickle of people, and am stunned to see about a thousand people praying, accompanied by a chorus and musicians (guitar players) numbering in the hundreds! Immediately I can feel the holiness of the church. This has only happened to me several times—when I first went to Notre Dame in Paris, and Pierre Cochereau was giving an organ concert. The organ music rolled down through the church, swept me up, and I had to hold myself back from converting to Catholicism! The second time was recently at the tiny Sanctuary of Chimayo, where people come to be healed and the prayers linger in the grotto long after the worshippers are gone. Well, today is the third.

I look around at the Hispanic congregation. No one is overly dressed; no one is on parade. The guitar players are strumming humbly. Children are playing on the bench next to us. The archbishop has the most benign and joyous face imaginable, and his voice caresses the audience. It is an exercise in religious aerobics—the wor-

179

shippers get up, sit down, get up, sit down again. Every time the congregation breaks into song with the Spanish melodies and the guitars strumming, I want to cry. It feels and sounds like ten thousand thousand voices, and suddenly the buttressed ceilings of the church feel like the arches of heaven and the apostles on the stained glass windows beckon me to pray and the paintings of saints on the altar seem to light up and glow and it no longer matters what the words are or in what language—I know it is thanksgiving and prayer. It is full of humility. And I am privileged to be in this "tepee."

I realize that it doesn't matter *where* you pray, and it doesn't matter *how* you pray. As Lenny says, "all of it is noise to get God's attention." So, although I'm not experienced at prayer, I decide to do it in the local fashion, and I kneel long and humbly on the little bench, and when the priest gives out wafers, I am on line taking one. I don't eat it, because that's not my way, but I get to stand in front of the powerful archbishop, and he blesses me. It is like being blessed by the medicine man, and once again I fight back tears. I feel everything here that I didn't feel at Spanish Market. I am in love with the Hispanic culture.

The archbishop speaks about how every person is an artist (the Spanish Market theme), and the tools of the trade are love, compassion, understanding, etc. In other words, your life itself is a work of art.

Then, after the congregation joins hands and everyone wishes everyone else peace (not a bad wish, is it?), suddenly a liturgical dancer floats down the aisle. She is holding flowers, and she dances back and forth, waving the flowers over the congregants and, I suppose, blessing them. Behind her is a chorus of three, and one man has a tenor voice that is clearly a sublime gift. Suddenly the music and prayer and dance all come together in a personally cataclysmic moment.

Just as I think the service is over, the rear doors of the church open and there is a magnificent entrance of heavily costumed Matachine dancers in vivid colors with their faces concealed by black-fringed masks. The woman behind me whispers that "this was taken by the conquistadors from a very old Indian tradition." The woman beside her disagrees: "No, this was taken by the Indians from an old Spanish custom. " I silently shake my head—the blending of cultures in New Mexico is so unexpected and surprising. It wakes you up. It forces you to be watchful and observant all the time.

Feast Day

The archbishop, all in white and leaning on his shepherd's staff, leads a procession out of the church. The Matachine go all the way to the Plaza, where they start to dance, accompanied by fiddlers and with a costumed narrator called an *abuelo,* who clowns and makes lurid gestures, egging on the crowd.

The dancers reenact the story of the bringing of Christianity to the Aztec Montezuma by the Indian mistress of Cortés. The girl playing the mistress can't be more than ten years old. Then the spectators are invited to pin money on the lapel of their favorite dancer. It is all very convivial and joyous. I must say that it has been a long time since I used the word "joyous" to describe my environment. It doesn't leap to the lips in L.A.!

My working relationship with Lenny is not very joyous either. He is being manipulative and deceitful, changing the rules of our collaboration every few hours and then dumping all of the work on me.

I try to joke about it and minimize the difficulties, but the tension is really getting to me. For the first time, I am unable to get into the spirit of the Feast Day at Jemez Pueblo. It is a blazing hot day, and our clothes are sticking to us as we walk out onto the Plaza. There are many dancers, and you can tell by the color their bodies are painted (either tan/orange or light green) whether they belong to the Pumpkin or Turquoise societies. Each group dances separately; when one leaves the Plaza, the other enters. They divide up the Plaza the way they divide up the calendar year; one of them is always in charge. Some of the dancers seem to be wonderfully transported, and they dance magnificently. Others seem only half there; perhaps it is a mirror of my own mood. Beaver is dancing, and it's always exciting to know one of the dancers—it makes the dance very personal.

It occurs to me as I watch the dancers, each very human in his own way, that the dance is perfect, but the dancers are not. This is true of the Jemez Pueblo corn dance, and it is true of life. We are only poor humans and we dance the best we can. I also feel that I now better understand the words of Hans Norgen, the archeologist. Everything in the universe has a reason and a role, even if we do not understand it. We humans are very dependent upon the wind blowing and the trees growing and the rain falling; we need the sun to shine and the corn to grow. Our role is to respect what is and to do our ceremonial tasks. If we dance well, we are part of the universal order which provides for us. If we neglect our tasks, we are part of the chain that leads to our own destruction. This is what you see when you look at an ordinary mortal in beautiful dress, dancing on a sandy Plaza on a very hot summer day.

I turn away from the Plaza for a moment, and there are Sacheen Littlefeather and Barney, back from the sundance in South Dakota, walking toward us. We all hug and say hello and Sacheen tells us she was invited to three different sundances there—I thought there was only one. It's hard to imagine different encampments carrying out that very exacting and intense ceremony . . . the days of dancing and prayer leading to the final sacrifice and piercing of the flesh. Before, I would have concentrated on the drama of the piercing. Now it's the concentrated prayer that astonishes me. Of course Paul brings levity to the meeting by clapping Barney on the back and then quickly retrieving his hand, saying, "Oh, I'm so sorry. I forgot. I hope the wounds have begun to heal."

We all go to eat at Beaver's house at her insistence. It is very interesting to see Sacheen in an Indian mode of behavior, among Indians. She adds "ay" (pronounced as in "way") to the end of every sentence (for example, "this chili is wonderful, ay!"). Barney is slap-happy, and when I ask him to pass me some chicken, he keeps passing me the bones and roaring with laughter. Beaver's family is most hospitable, insisting that we try everything, and making us promise to come back again.

As we are leaving, Beaver introduces me to her aunt, it's a remarkable moment. When I was a small child, I had a nickname for my little sister Patsy. She was very dark-skinned and chubby and she had long, thick braids. I thought she looked like an Indian, and I affectionately called her "Tita Toya Monkaboya." Now Beaver pronounces her aunt's name as I shake her hand: "Tita Toya!" I try to stifle my laugh; her aunt, in fact, looks like a much older version of my sister!

We come home, ready to crash out, and the phone rings.

"This is Laura Fragua. Where are you?"

"I'm . . . uh . . . between the kitchen and the bedroom. Why do you ask?"

"We've been waiting for you all day at Jemez. We thought you'd come and eat with my family. We want to introduce you."

"Well . . . uh . . . I'm really sorry. Can we take a raincheck?"

"Sure," says Laura cheerfully, "you can come back tomorrow. There's 'doings' early in the morning."

182

• • •

We get up at 6 A.M. and head all the way back to Jemez Pueblo again—almost a two-hour drive. In Los Angeles, I consider it a drag to drive half an hour. We arrive at Laura's house for breakfast. Steve is glued to the TV as usual, watching dumb cartoons and looking glazed. I always find it disturbing when people that smart are that stoned on tele-junk. Laura's family is gathered around, eating, talking, facing the day. Her father is quite a character.

"You know what Indians do after they finish breakfast?" he asks.

"No," I answer.

"They go out and slit people's throats."

"Oh."

Then he turns back to his family, and they go on talking. I sit there, taking in the family scene, wondering if I have any right to write about this at all. Out of the blue, Mr. Fragua leans over and says to me: "You want to know what you can write about, don't you?"

"Yes," I say, shaken by his prescience.

There is a long silence. I squirm and fidget as Mr. Fragua looks out the window. I am anxious for his answer, but he takes his time, thinking. Finally he turns and looks at me.

"You can write about anything—*if it's the truth!*" he says.

I do not say anything. I sink into total silence, considering his words very seriously. If I stick to the truth, as I know it, then I am fine. He has given me his blessings.

Things lighten up at the table, and I guess I must be giggling, because Mr. Fragua stares at me and says, "You behave just like an Indian woman—giggling over nothing. But people better not cross you because you have a real temper!"

"No, I don't have much of a temper," I protest, but he doesn't seem to be listening. He has made up his mind that I do.

Laura's father and I retire to the living room for a long chat. He tells me his idea of having older Indian women teach young people about plants, herbs, cooking, and older Indian men teach kids about hunting, planting, and the language. I shake my head at the coincidence—I have just written about that for the TV series!

"I told you you're like an Indian," he says. "You even think like one!"

Then he grows more serious and says that no one is interested in his idea because it isn't a money-making proposition. He seems to be disenchanted with the powers that rule the Pueblo. "We had a lot of problems here," he says, and I squint at him, wondering what he means, but he doesn't explain.

I find out minutes later when Laura's grandma corners me and starts to talk. She is a very strong woman, and she was the plaintiff in a landmark Supreme Court case in the early fifties. She converted to the Protestant faith, and she was hounded for it by the Pueblo cacique and the council. She was actually brought in and whipped! It is fine for Indians to be Catholic, but not Protestant!

The Protestant church took her around and wrote about her and made her a cause célèbre, but she saw little or none of the money they made. Finally the case was taken to court, in the hope that the U.S. government would intercede to forbid this kind of behavior—whipping and ostracizing Indian people for their religious beliefs. The decision was handed down that the U.S. government had no right to interfere in tribal matters on the Indian reservation. This ruling has greatly influenced thought on the matter that persists today.

The family and friends join in the conversation with a litany of grievances against the religious intolerance and bigotry that are rife at the Pueblos and in the Pueblo councils. It strikes me again that the Indian dances are perfect, but the "dancers" are all too human and imperfect.

Laura's brother tells me that, as a child, he was not allowed to play with other kids or go to their houses because he was a Protestant at a Catholic Pueblo. The mail arrived all crumpled up because the church controlled the mail delivery. This is very disturbing information about religious discrimination. As Paul says, everything we brought to the Indians—including the church they now believe in—causes divisiveness! It seems to be true.

I talk to Laura's grandma at length about her past and her present, and she makes a sincere and all-out effort to convert me! She keeps asking if I have Jesus in my heart, and I have to answer honestly that I don't. Grandma is wonderful—strong, outspoken, determined in every way. Her life is ruled by her faith and her adopted religion.

Soon the "doings" begin. The family has planned a dedication of a tombstone to Laura's grandpa, the last of the Pecos Indians. The tribe was decimated by famine, disease, white people, Comanches, Apaches, and whatever else we don't know about. The last remaining seventeen of them left Pecos in 1838. Although it is not recorded anywhere, the truth of those seventeen is that they stopped off in Santo Domingo and Cochiti, where some intermarriage took place and their descendants were given the last name "Pecos." The others moved on to Jemez Pueblo, where the direct descendants live to this day. Laura's grandpa is of that full-blood stock.

"Don't you remember seeing the carving of the old tombstone when you visited us down south?" Laura asks.

She smiles. I smile. I feel a surge of excitement that we were there at the birth of this monument. The very words "last of the Pecos Indians" seem to me to be full of tragedy and the romance of a past that is regrettably gone forever. Laura's husband Steve informs me that he helped Laura with the carving.

I walk over to inspect the tombstone, and joke that Laura and Steve's initials are larger than the lettering! They joke back that their initials will be buried below the earth line. The stone itself is simple. It says "Polito Fragua, 1900–1989" on the front, and it bears a Bible and a cross. On the back, there is a huge corn stalk—that curious blending of Christianity and Indian culture that one sees everywhere at the Pueblos. The top of the stone is stepped, perhaps to represent the Pueblos, or to suggest a cloud.

It is pouring, so a decision is made not to go to the cemetery. Instead, we all gather in Grandma's house. Once again, we eat (we have eaten three meals in three hours), and then the huge family begins to congregate in the living room. Uncle Bill, a self-taught preacher, officiates. He reads from the Bible (Old Testament) about crossing the Red Sea and how each tribe had a stone. He evokes the memory of Grandpa Fragua and how he always spoke of God, telling people about his conversion, wanting to let go in the hospital and be with God. He was a man who cried whenever children cried, was good to people, and lived a life as an important man because of his faith. Then Grandma gets up, crying, and speaks about her husband, reiterating his love of the young ones. She says how important it is to treat the children lovingly—to understand them, and not to hit them. This way they will grow up into happy adults. This is a refrain I hear all the time in Indian country—treat the children well. Don't abuse them. Respect them. Never hit them. Grandma keeps saying how much she loves the children too, all the children, and she begs everyone to be good to them, and to be good to each other as well.

Then Laura gets up and says that each of Grandpa's five children should find a rock, a large rock, and they will use it to prop up the headstone and as a reminder of the family lines. They go off to get stones. The rain lets up a bit, so some of us go to the Protestant cemetery. It is very, very small, an isolated island—an outcast burial place. Grandma tells us that it is her family land, but the tribe is trying to take it away. I guess the beat of religious persecution goes on. We also learn that the Fraguas' cousin, aged thirteen, had recently been buried. A victim of sniffing—glue, aerosol, whatever. This has caused a great wave of sadness to wash over the family. Just hearing about it, I feel sad.

The cousins dig a hole for Grandpa's new stone, and there is joking about their moonlighting and getting arrested. As the rain falls, the children's stones are propped up against the tombstone, and Grandpa Polito is honored well by his descendants. The stone looks dignified and proud in the little cemetery. Future generations will be able to visit the resting place of their ancestor, and pay homage to him.

Afterwards, of course, we eat again and then leave. We drive up into the magnificent Jemez mountains, stopping at the Jemez (hot) springs and getting a tour of the mineral baths that I wouldn't put so much as a toe in. The tub is crumbling and looks like it has been used by fifty people within the last hour. We continue upwards, pausing at rock formations dripping with sulfur, and admire the natural erosion of stones into wondrous shapes. We stop at the "sandal bus" where some hippies, proclaiming that this could be a hemp-based (read: marijuana) economy instead of a petroleum-based economy, are selling rope shoes. As we climb into the entrepreneurial bus, we meet mom, with her shaved head, and see wall-to-wall Grateful Dead stickers and posters. We felt like we are on another psychedelic trip.

We pull up at Jemez Springs, a small town with an inn. The innkeepers are amazingly open and tell us their life story within two minutes. He is a mariner, older but not ancient. They take Indian kids off the Pueblos and put them to work on full-masted schooners with graduates of Ivy League colleges as their shipmates. It gives the kids a sense of worth and self-esteem, gets them off alcohol, and keeps them out of trouble.

"Why are you so involved with Pueblo kids?" I ask.

They shrug and have no answer. It just seems like the most natural thing in the world to them. Kids are kids and these particular kids are having trouble.

Feast Day

The innkeepers tell us how they came here two years ago on motorcycles, bought the inn on an impulse, and ended up at this juncture in life. The inn used to be for hookers, there was a gunfight last year, and people come there to kick back and drink. As we speak, a young guy checks in for the weekend, carrying a case and a half of beer.

When I get home, the phone rings and it's the main producer from L.A. with excellent news. Our TV series has just received additional funding.

"Great!" I exclaim.

There is no joy on the other end of the phone. Rather, it is immediately turned into a problem.

"We've got to come through," she says with utmost gravity. "Everyone is looking to us."

"Well, I'm doing my best."

"We've *really* got to make this good. And we have to deliver fast. We're counting on *you*," she says, and I hang up the phone feeling even more pressure.

Speaking of mounting pressure, there is an interesting article in the local paper today. The Pueblos are trying to create employment, so they can keep the young people there and also implement and sustain social services which the government doesn't provide or has cut back drastically. In addition, the very fact that the Pueblos *have* land makes them a constant target for pressure to develop.

New income-producing sources keep popping up. There is a nouvelle restaurant at Santa Ana Pueblo as well as a golf course. There is a refurbished uranium mine maintenance shop at Laguna, and a sheet metal fabrication operation. But the Indians are wary too. For four hundred years they have kept to their ways, and try to resist Anglo influence. Once you develop land and industry on sacred sites, there is a risk of losing what you have. Development for the Indians is very far from a no-risk proposition, and they gamble with the most precious commodity they have—their Indian ways. Everywhere in the world, when the Anglo-material world enters, things are no longer what they are before.

In the afternoon, we head out to Santo Domingo for their Feast Day. The weather is bizarre as usual—dark, menacing storm clouds, rain, then sudden sun and heat. When we turn off the freeway, we find our-

187

selves in a traffic jam that could rival L.A. It takes us an hour to get to the Pueblo, when it should take ten minutes. It seems as though everyone in the state of New Mexico, every Indian from every other Pueblo, is headed to Santo Domingo too.

The sandy streets of the Pueblo are lined with vendors—we have never seen anything like it. They stretch as far as the eye can see and as deep as the pocket can spend. Since this trip doesn't seem to be about buying, we manage to bypass the Scylla of pottery and the Charybdis of jewelry. I am stunned by the presence of one stand that features a Navajo medicine man. He is selling packages of herbs, plants, and roots with labels like "diabetes," "hair," and "high blood pressure." He is a wonderful, looking old man, with a missing tooth and a wide, welcoming smile. He starts to tell us about cancer, and how nature causes it. He says that lightning emits a lot of radiation, and if you are near it, it enters your body. Doctors cut, but the "sores" (cancer) grow back again.

The medicine man speaks in a low voice. I lean so far forward to catch his words that I almost fall into his lap. I have heard that the Navajo are big on magic, witchcraft, and the belief that many illnesses are caused by natural forces—especially lightning.

A medicine man knows nature well, and he knows that in order to get rid of cancer, you must become a friend to nature, because nature doesn't know you. You need herbs and a ceremony; the medicine man helps you befriend nature, so the cancer can leave your system. He speaks a bit about his wife, who is a tremble-hand healer. No matter what Frederic Marlow from the Indian Health Service says, we take the medicine man's address. You have to cover all your bases in life, don't you?

Beyond the booths of vendors is a huge carnival, and we can see the ferris wheel spinning high above the Pueblo. And then, we enter the Plaza. Nothing in life prepares you for the sight of the earthen kiva, with its ladder pointing to the sky, joining the earth with the heavens. It is the union of the female creative force (the kiva, the womb of Mother Earth) with the power of the sky, the Father.

On the earthen "bench" around the kiva, several corn clowns sit, watching the dancing. They are all so fat that they actually look round. Their bodies are painted white, with black dots. One of them has a leg painted, and another has part of his face painted black. On their heads, they wear the dry corn husks of a hot summer and a fruitful

188

harvest, held erect and pointing toward the sky. I have to blink twice, because the clowns actually look like chunky ears of corn!

The Plaza is very long and very majestic. It is absolutely packed with dancers—if you count both groups, there are probably a thousand of them! The drum echoes everywhere with a regular, rapid beat. The sound of the singers fills the Plaza. It completely overwhelms the senses. On the porch of one of the houses around the Plaza sits Lenny, for his father's family is from the Pueblo. We are grateful to have a bathroom and, best of all, a seat on the porch in the shade.

Then, lucky, lucky us. The singers position themselves right in front of where we are sitting. For me, the day is all about listening with one's whole being. The drum goes directly into my body, especially to my heart. Paul has the same experience. The songs put me into a trance-like state, where I am unaware of time passing. I realize, with great relief, that the singing and drumming are so intense that they fill me completely, wiping out any thoughts, and it is like a sustained state of meditation. I am able to forget the pressure, the TV series, my problems with Lenny. He and I sit on opposite sides of the porch, hardly acknowledging each other. We are each lost in our own experience.

Occasionally I watch the dancers. They have incredible discipline today. Even the teeny tiny ones. Each buried in prayer and thanksgiving, they follow the steps of the person in front of them as though their very lives depended upon it—and, in a sense, they do! On a very deep level, this is a dance of cultural survival.

One of the drummers (there are two groups of singers and dancers) is an old man, thin and worn, yet he drums with a startling vigor and regularity. Another man, carved by age, has one arm, and he dances with absolute joy. Others are bent over, or use walkers to get around—but they all dance as though they are young and carefree, forgetting about their ailing bodies. I just love it. It is everything I aspire to in life. To serve. To be simple. To just BE. There on the Plaza it is hard to be filled with anger, hate, resentment, envy, or whatever feelings humans have. It is just a time and a place of thankfulness and joy. It is a time when it is enough to be human and to be alive. When the corn flag is waved over the singers and we catch the tip of the blessing, or a corn clown dances by and makes a gesture of blessing, we truly feel that we are fortunate to be alive.

The only tense moment is when an older woman comes over to

Lenny and whispers to him. Her face is somber. Lenny's face becomes taut. He bolts from his chair on the porch and strides with
purpose over to the kiva. There, a tourist has been taking pictures of
the dance, despite repeated signs and warnings not to do so. Lenny
is hard and cold with the tourist. The camera is put away. Lenny
grumbles as he walks back to the patio. Non-Indians are guests here,
and they have taken advantage of the Pueblo hospitality once again.
I sigh, remembering that at Hopi, some of the most moving and spectacular dances have been closed to the public for such breach of trust
and respect.

The dances at Santo Domingo go on until 7 P.M., and I never move.
This is no mean feat for a physically restless person. I think of where
these Keresan people came from and how long they have inhabited
the land. I imagine them doing the same dance at Chaco Canyon, and
along their migratory route, and wonder if, when they dance, they feel
themselves surrounded by the presence of their ancestors, who did the
same steps. I think of the gratitude they felt for a good harvest, and
how the cycles of nature sustained them. I look at the symbolism of
their uniform dress, and think that they are draped in prayer. When
they dance before their Creator, there is a great democratic spirit in
the way they present themselves.

At the sound of gunshot signals, it is all over, and we head inside to
eat. Lenny's sister, a world-renowned jeweler, is cooking and serving
and she does both with elegance and grace. I dig into the pot of spicy
lamb and come up dripping. I completely forget that I am supposed to
be a vegetarian. I have just blended with the Pueblo way of eating.
Paul is diving into the chili. Lenny's family keeps refilling the serving dishes as friends and relatives finish eating, get up, and others
take their places at the groaning table. We are grateful for the hospitality and for how delicious the food is.

The sunset at Santo Domingo is no less remarkable than the day.
We walk into the small, mission-style church, with its elegant paintings of pottery and corn on the second-story balcony, and when we
come out, the sky is vermilion and a sheet of rainbow is visible off to
the right. Dark clouds hang in exactly the right spots so that we mere
mortals can appreciate them and be inspired to come back again to
the gallery of Mother Nature.

My city self is cowed and awed again and again by the sheer beauty of what she finds here.

Feast Day

At night I slip under the covers, for once not thinking about the past, worrying about the future, or troubled by any of the vagaries of life on our shaky planet.

"This is the sleep of the fearless," I say to myself, as I feel myself drop into the dark cycle at the end of the day, which I trust, tomorrow, will lead to sunshine and morning.

9

A Grab Day

Mid-August, 1991

Lenny and I are sitting outside of the *casita,* sipping hibiscus coolers and munching bagels. Once again we are negotiating where we will work, and we hit a dead end. I change the subject, just to dilute the tension.

"I can't get the sights and sounds of the Santo Domingo Feast Day out of my mind," I say.

"Sure they're out of your mind. They're in your heart. Where they belong."

I smile. He's right.

"I keep thinking . . . I mean, feeling, the focus and intensity of the dancers. It's very haunting. Tell me, Birdhead, what are those songs about?"

"They're the spoken Word manifesting. They're Indian liturgy."

"And the Pueblo Plaza is the church?" I ask.

"All of the Creator's world is our church," he answers.

This is the first year Lenny has not danced, and he says it is harder to *watch* than to dance. When he dances, he is totally involved in the prayerful act, but when he is observing, he sees what is going on around the dancers. He notices the disrespect of the tourists, who take pictures even though they have been told not to. When they are caught aiming their cameras at the dancers, they lie and claim they are just trying to photograph houses. He feels the intrusion of people talking to him as he sits on his porch and watches. He is so absorbed by the dance and the songs that people around him seem to be speaking a foreign language. He hears their words as they address him, but he can barely understand them.

"When you are dancing, you are absorbed, you are 'in the song.' When you are outside, you have to deal with the life around you," Lenny says sadly. Then he continues explaining to me what the songs and dances mean.

"The dances—and I have to quote the Bible here—are making joyful noise unto the Lord. That's what we are doing. All the little details of the dance add up. They tell the story of where it all comes from. They trace it back . . . back . . . back . . ."

As Lenny says the words "back, back, back," I can feel myself slipping out of the present concerns of my life, into a contemplation of the source of all things, an earlier life, eons and eons ago, when humankind emerged, less duplicitous and twisted, a natural creation. I can feel the power of a human life, lived in prayerful synchronicity with a providential environment.

I don't know WHY this is happening, but it is happening. When Lenny leaves, I walk across the field toward the gym, and I say hello to all the animals—the beetles who looked ugly before, the centipedes, the ants out foraging for food. I am even prepared to greet the prairie dogs, who look like squirrel rats, but I don't see any today. I guess I have come to realize that they all have a right to live; in fact, each one of them is a celebration of life. I can't believe that I, the prototypical urbanite, am having these thoughts. It is staggering to me that I feel connected to, and not afraid of, the four-leggeds.

At night, I need a break from the frustration of work with Lenny, so I suggest that he meet me at a poetry reading by the Indian poet Gerald Garcia. This is a real treat for me. When I was first introduced to Gerald's work, I went berserk! I felt as though I had tumbled upon a major poet, equal in power to any I knew from the Anglo world. I learned that he had a severe drinking problem, and that he gives public performances of his work. Sometimes he is drunk and sometimes sober during those performances. This immediately set my mind aflame, and I created a character for the TV show based on this scanty information. Something about a brilliant philosopher-word-monger who is haunted by a demon of self-destruction makes me cry.

While I was thinking about and reading more of Gerald's poetry, I went with Lenny and his mother to visit Acoma Pueblo, and when we arrived, the Plaza was blooming with potters and their dazzling array of world-famous pots. I wanted to buy a pot for my sister's birthday, since she is an Acomaphile, and she adores the intricacies of those fine-lined black and white patterns. I had no idea of which potter to buy from. And then, something pulled me straight across the Plaza and I ended up in front of a woman in dark glasses. She informed me that she was blind. A blind potter! I told her how impossible it would be for me to execute such pots with both my eyes—how did she do it with none?!? The purchase was made, after my usual indecision, and I asked her to tell me her name. Her last name was Garcia. I paused a moment. "Do you know the poet Gerald Garcia?" She smiled. "He is my brother!"

So, once again, fate put me exactly where I needed and wanted to be. There I was, with a direct, genetic link to Gerald. We spoke about Gerald, his talent, and the awful fact that he was "unwell" and had missed his own mother's death. I continued to be mildly obsessed by Gerald, although I never read any more of his work.

So here I am, waiting to see Gerald Garcia in the flesh. It is an outdoor reading, and we sit in a stone amphitheater. It is cold, my back is uncomfortable, and I start shifting about, waiting for my man to appear. The formal introduction is given, and Gerald comes out. He's about fifty years old, nondescript, and he wears glasses and has a missing lower front tooth. He is very garrulous, and he babbles on, sometimes amusing and sometimes seeming to wrestle with the very words he uses.

Then he begins to read from his latest works. His poetry is totally personal, in that he is the observer of nature and living things, and that the stories he tells are woven through the fabric of his own artistry. But it is totally impersonal, in that the observer has little or no personality beyond his perceptions and his spiritual connection to all living things. I slump in my seat, and feel strangely disappointed. Although the verbal pictures painted of Gerald's life with the Plains Indians are finely etched and possibly indelible portraits, the poetry is too contemplative, too nice, too sure-footed, too academic for my taste. The world seems too orderly and all things have their place— even in terrifying natural occurrences.

"What's wrong?" Paul whispers to me.

"He's too knowledgeable," I whisper back. "He understands too much of the universe."

"Huh?"

"This is poetry to retain and savor. But I miss the rawness and rest-

194

lessness and rage of his earlier poems. All of his untamed emotion seemed to thrash around the page. I like him wilder."

After the reading, I am introduced to Gerald. I want to ask him a hundred questions about the emotional content of his poetry, and whether he is at peace with the world now, or in a period of acceptance, or whether this is maturity. I long to ask him if he still feels angst and restlessness and anger. But when I open my mouth, I babble an incoherent question and get a befuddled and snotty answer.

"I asked the question wrong and the answer came out wrong," I moan to Lenny.

"Maybe you shouldn't ask questions," Lenny says. "Then you'll get more answers. But that's like asking a matzo not to crumble!"

When I get home, I start to read a book about Pueblo life, and one sentence makes me put down the book to think. In old times (and maybe today?) each Pueblo had a sun-watcher, a man whose responsibility it was to watch the progress of the sun, the eclipses, the equinox, in order to determine the correct time for planting. This, in turn, determined when certain ceremonies would take place—linked to growth, rain, fecundity, harvest and thanksgiving. Thus, what the sun-watcher saw in the heavens, and what he reported back, was a matter of life and death to his people.

What we have, in our society, is like a plant with no root. And with no root it cannot be fed and nurtured. We have the SCIENCE of astronomy. We look at the heavens and learn about the celestial bodies. But it is not connected to OUR BODIES, to anything spiritual, to any ceremonies, to anything VITAL to the sustenance and survival of the community. It is just an external body of knowledge. Science is separate from humankind. The same is true of medicine, of anthropology, of history, of math, of ALL OF IT. We learn things that feed our heads, but are cut off from the essence of our existences. What are children learning in their classes? It's separate from their lives. They acquire knowledge and information the way they acquire other material possessions. I feel a sudden revulsion for all the *things* we own and accumulate.

The next day I tell Lenny that I think people should open up their windows and throw away half of what they own. Thus unencumbered, they will be free to really receive what the universe has to offer.

He beams when I say this and then gets a mischievous twinkle in his eyes.

"Tomorrow," he says, "we are going to my village."

We drive for two hours and end up in Paguate, the Laguna village where Lenny's mother lived until her recent death. There is a big barbecue in the backyard for friends and family. I say nothing to anyone, for fear they will think me bizarre, but I can palpably FEEL Mrs. Smallfeather's presence. I can hear her voice and the cadence of her speech.

A few people I recognize from past Pueblo encounters come up to me and ask me about my TV project. They start offering information about Paguate—how it has the highest suicide rate in the nation, and how the Pueblos are now plagued by child abuse and other horrors. Then a woman leans over and whispers to me, "If water is poured on you, don't run away from it. They are praying for rain, and water is a blessing."

I turn around, but the woman is gone. I ponder what her words mean and then, suddenly, the chili and watermelon are whisked off the table and there is a sense of great anticipation and excitement in the air. Lenny, his seventeen-year-old son, his three-year-old daughter, and his sisters and brothers climb onto the roof of the house. A bucket brigade is formed and dozens of plastic containers filled with food, toys, household items, cleaning products, and other goodies are passed along from inside the house to the roof. Then all the guests stand up and gather around the house under the roof; scores of neighbors from Laguna miraculously appear at the right moment. Cousin Ron from Mesita joins the Smallfeathers on the roof, and he greets everyone in Keres. He tells us that this is a Feast Day for everyone in the family named after St. Lorenzo (that means, specifically, Lenny and his son Lorenzo) and that the gifts we are going to get are blessed by the Smallfeather family. When we take them home, the blessings will go with us. He begs us to be good to each other, to treat each other well in life. And then it begins. THE GRAB DAY.

First, the Smallfeathers pour water down onto the crowd. There is some giggling and kids start screaming. When the water falls on me, I do not run away or back off from it. I remember the woman's words, telling me to accept the blessing.

People jockey for positions that are closer to the roof, and they begin to call out the names of the Smallfeather siblings—asking for gifts to be thrown to them. The shouting can be heard halfway across the village: "Lenny—Lenny—Lorenzo—Nancy—Frank—Frank—Howie—Howeeeee!!!" Within moments, the gifts begin to rain down on us (this

196

is called a "grab" or "throwaway"). People politely but insistently push and shove to get the gifts, and is it my imagination or is Lenny really aiming gifts at us where I stand—way at the back?

There are candy bars and rolled-up handkerchiefs with candies inside, toilet paper, sponges, kites, plastic cups, brooms, cans of soda, ramens and raisins, laundry baskets, pencils. Sometimes I wince, afraid I will have my head knocked off or my eye knocked in as people leap for the gifts. Someone whispers to me that, according to the Pueblo people, you give—and the more you give, the more you get back when things come around. Life is always a circle. A nice philosophy. It is obviously a great joy for the Smallfeathers to give. Throwing incessantly, it takes four adults and two children *well over an hour* to throw out the gifts. There must be a thousand dollars worth of gifts on that roof. And they can't throw it out fast enough. The quantity is staggering.

While the throwing is going on, there is a lot of socializing and babbling. Lenny's ex-wife Terry comes to talk to me. She tells me that when she was married to Lenny, he used to bless the water before he took a shower, thanking it for providing for him. When she brought wood into the house for a fire, he would go outside and feed bread to the wood, to thank it for supplying so plentifully! She is a psychologist and has much to say about the dysfunction of Indians in the everyday world, but in the world of ceremony, in the kivas, there is nothing like them! Our life, our hemisphere, is deeply indebted to them for being the spiritual caretakers.

After the Smallfeather grab, the Smallfeathers go to another house in the village, to jump and catch THEIR gifts. And when that grab is over, they all pick up their booty and head for the next grab. All of the houses make sacrifices to supply their guests, but, as they give, they feel that they are receiving. You give, you get. You get, you give.

The next day, I go to an Indian auction and the feelings of revulsion for material acquisition return again. A ballroom full of white people, mostly dealers and collectors, bids outrageous sums of money for Indian artifacts and artwork. There are baskets, rugs, beaded moccasins and vests, pottery, dolls, paintings. The catalogue alone sells for $30. There are absentee bids and bids coming in by phone and items are selling for $10,000 and it begins to look and sound totally ridiculous. Here are Indian people living with the barest of essentials, and gawking, gushing non-Indians are scooping up their remnants after having persecuted them and killed them off! I start a grumbling tirade to Paul.

"I can guarantee you that those cradle boards were not built to be sold at auctions for outrageous sums! They were made to carry babies. The Indians won't glean a dime of profit from this! They will go on eating crap food and wondering where their next meal is coming from while the dealers turn around and double their prices. And you think it's over? No. Of course not. The value of the items will keep escalating. And the remnants of Indian cultures will hang in mansions and estates where no one cares at all about the Indians!"

I look around me. The bidders are curling up their lips, snarling at me. Paul smiles.

"Shhhhh," he says. "But I love you for your passion!"

"I'd go crazy if people were bidding on a *talis* or *yarmulkas* or a *torah*, and then bragging about the great deal they got. Why can't people have that sensitivity to Indians?"

I continue stewing as the auction goes on, and my feelings don't affect the price of the objects one bit. *Au contraire,* the more I rail, the more they seem to escalate.

"Hey, are you so innocent?" Lenny asks me when I tell him my feelings. "You collect that *juju-bawana* stuff too."

"*Juju-bawana*?" I ask.

"Yeah. I heard that word in an old movie. It means ancient stuff with a curse on it."

"I only have little things. I don't pay obscene sums. And I cherish what I have."

"*Juju-bawana,*" he reiterates, snickering. To him, I am probably the same as the other palefaces.

In the afternoon, Dr. Doug White Wolf gives us a special invitation to the Feast Day at his Pueblo, Santa Clara. When we arrive, it is searing outside. The Pueblo is mobbed, and it is so humid we stick to whoever is standing next to us. We end up huddled next to the huge dumpster, grateful for the shade.

At Santa Clara there are three or four small Plazas instead of one big one. There are four dance groups—four being the sacred number (four directions, four seasons, etc.). Doug is singing (and drumming) for a small group, and, to my delight, they are doing the buffalo dance for the first time in a dozen years. It's quite impressive: the men are adorned in full Buffalo regalia, swooping their furry, horned heads just like the Plains beasts. The women wear gaily painted wooden *tabletas* on their heads and beautiful white wool dresses with fancy ornamentation. They all carry sprigs of evergreen and fresh ears of corn. Doug looks particularly handsome with his new knee-high suede boots and his shoulder-length black mane.

I remember, in the past, seeing Indian dances on TV or at special festivals and occasions. They were completely taken out of context, and didn't have the power and meaning they have in their natural environs. When seen live at the Pueblos, they are a moving meditation.

We assume that no photos are allowed, since this is a religious feast, but once again, you can never ASSUME anything in Indian country. Photos are allowed, for a fee of $20 per camera. Gail White Wolf stays with us, next to the dumpster, a lovely hostess. As she fans herself, she tells us that this morning several Hopi singers arrived to participate, because the buffalo dance is like their dances. After the dance is over, Gail shyly goes onto the Plaza and presents the Hopi singers with baskets full of food. Then she walks around the Plaza with big bagfuls of goodies and throws out gifts to the spectators, in the same spirit as the grab. Just as she is about to take her place again amidst the spectators, she presents *us* with a basket—it is full of freshly baked bread, chocolate chip cookies, and assorted candies. I am embarrassed by the generosity.

Suddenly, with no warning, it begins to pour. The craft booths close up, and everyone runs for their cars, but the dancers keep dancing, as they always do, unperturbed. Paul and I smile: every time we go to a rain dance, it rains. Maybe there is something to this prayer thing after all . . .

We go back to Doug's house for the feast. We sit in the kitchen, chatting with Doug's family, eating tamales and turkey and Jell-O and chilis until our bellies bloat up like basketballs. As I leave the room to make space for the next wave of people who have come to eat, I am overcome with wonder that I have grown to feel so at ease in an environment that was entirely unknown to me a few months ago. I think it is *humor*, more than anything else, that closes the cultural gap. Every time someone from the Indian world refers to us as a friend, or every time the phone rings and someone from the Pueblos is seeking out our company, it is a very validating feeling. Whatever we are, imperfect as we are, gauche and maladroit as we are, we are accepted AS IS.

As we leave Santa Clara Pueblo, the clouds are puffs of gray lined with orange, like a hem, on the bottom. I think it would be a very worthwhile enterprise to photograph the sunset here every evening. How could we have lived without sky for so long?

In the morning, I call Lenny with an idea. Since the television series is about a doctor from New York City who comes to work with the Indian Health Service, perhaps it would be better to place him in a small clinic instead of a large hospital. That way, we could emphasize the human part of the story and not have to deal with the complex medical world of doctors, nurses, staff, laboratories, etc. I ask Lenny if he can drive me somewhere in northern New Mexico where I can see such a village clinic.

We head out to El Rito, to a tiny Hispanic clinic, to get an idea of how a small, rural medical facility functions, even if it isn't an Indian clinic. We can fake the particulars of the ethnicity.

It takes us several hours to get there, and it turns out it's near the place Lenny used to live twenty years ago, when he was married to his first wife, had horses, roamed free, and delivered his own baby. The clinic is charming, if a medical facility can have charm. It is part of a whole complex—library, senior citizen center and clinic. As a patient hops onto the table for a Pap smear, she can hear the seniors doing group singing after their noonday meal. Their voices are sweet and lilting.

El Rito clinic has one doctor—in this case, an elderly man from Iowa who is replacing the usual head of the clinic—a nurse practitioner. Dr. Vater speaks so slowly I almost fall asleep, but Lenny keeps saying over and over how much he loves the rhythm of Dr. Vater's speech. This alone is an indication of the differences of the worlds we come from.

Dr. Vater is an old-fashioned, humanistic country doctor. He speaks about how alienated he feels from the big-city high-tech docs, and how many of them should have been MBAs. He says that he depends upon VOICE and TOUCH with his patients. I tell him that I recently spoke on the phone with a doctor from L.A. It took two days to reach him, he could barely spare three minutes, and then charged me $200 for the call. Dr. Vater says nothing, but sadly shakes his head.

The clinic is serviced by one young woman who serves as nurse, receptionist, and dispensing pharmacist. This clinic is actually a model for other clinics in rural areas—it does basic care and refers or farms the rest out. The woman who works there knows all of the local families, so it's a very personal and unthreatening place. The doctor writes prescriptions, but the nurse acknowledges that for certain ailments, the patients take "another kind of medicine." They take garlic for high blood pressure and they pick *cota* weeds from the side of the road when they have urinary tract infections. Sometimes the elderly patients can't communicate with the doctor at all, and when their words are translated literally, it turns out they have "air in the head" or "feel pale" or some other presenting symptom that eludes normal medical diagnosis.

The only machinery they have in the clinic is an EKG monitor, a blood pressure cuff, and the ability to test urine and hematocrits. As Dr. Vater tells us about their medical capabilities, the singing of the seniors goes on in the background, giving the whole experience a certain unreality. I have never before had medical accompaniment. As we talk, Dr. Vater scrutinizes us and checks us out. Lenny is very comfortable with this behavior, because it is the way an Indian would behave.

Only after an hour of talking and giving us the once-over does Dr. Vater say he has read Carl Hammerschlag's book, which the television series is based on.

"You see," Lenny says, as Dr. Vater excuses himself to go off and eat lunch with the seniors, "he didn't volunteer any information until he figured out who we are and what we are really up to."

"I like that he mingles with normal people," I add. "He doesn't act like he's a white-coated deity."

Lenny smiles. He likes it when I'm irreverent.

Because Lenny and I are supposed to be partners, I decide to share with him the most personal part of me—my fears. I tell him very briefly that I have a history of panic attacks and phobias. I want to be open with him, and tell him that I have taken medication, and had lots of unpleasant experiences with doctors. I say a few words, and it's as though I am talking to the shell of a person. Lenny is clearly not there. He has absolutely no interest.

On the trip back to Santa Fe, Lenny and I babble a lot. He points out caves that were used in earlier times—perhaps for Indians fasting or on vision quests. He gestures lovingly to the countryside. There is, for the moment, not too much tension between us, so I take advantage of the opportunity to bring up the subject of our working together. I tell Lenny we will try to find a way that makes both of us comfortable. He doesn't respond.

He takes me to a small restaurant for lunch, and slobbers all over his chili, claiming that this is the best green chili restaurant in the green chili capital of New Mexico. I order a simple salad, which is hard to find around here. I have O.D.'d on grease, fat, and meat. Lenny is openly hostile and scornful because I don't want to eat chili.

When we reach Santa Fe, I casually ask Lenny what work hours he would like to set over the next few days. He just as casually informs me that he is not available for the next five days because it's Indian Market.

I explode. "You just committed yourself, in front of our producers, to be available to work with me. I don't want to do this alone. You made up a timetable. You promised."

He shrugs and says it's just not possible. I take a deep breath, and alight from his car at the *casita*. As I walk away, I look back over my shoulder to see if he exhibits any signs of remorse or guilt. None. He is gone.

Indian Market is the biggest event of the year in Santa Fe, a city of events. It is the time when all of the best Indian artists from across the country are selected through a very rigorous competition, and they come to sell their works to the public. The rules are very stringent about who is allowed to sell, because there are many ripoffs of Indian artists—everything from "made-in-Taiwan" Indian art to outright copies and forgeries. On top of this, there is an attempt at quality control, and all Indian artists can apply for booths at the Indian Market, but only "the best" are supposedly chosen. Whatever "best" means. Maybe it just means those that are lucky. The booths are coveted and hard to get.

The competition for prizes is very intense. The judging goes on for eight hours, and when the winners in each category are announced, the word spreads through the community like a brushfire on a hot summer day. A blue ribbon on a work of art can mean a blue ribbon on the career of an artist. The art increases in value, and the artist gets more credibility and exposure.

I have been dreading Indian Market weekend, because I heard that all of the Santa Fe natives leave town and the place turns into a tourist zoo. But I have learned by now that none of my expectations are met in Indian country.

The weekend starts with a phone call from Carl Hammerschlag, who has come to town to give moral support to the TV project. He knows it is a very difficult undertaking, that the work situation is extremely frustrating, and he wants to "be there" for *moi,* his "biographer." I always laugh when I know Carl is around, for he is about six foot seven and very thin and I am five feet tall when I stand erect. We spell out a lopsided #1o when we walk down the street together.

I meet Carl late at night, and he picks me up and twirls me around as though I had the weight and consistency of a cotton ball. I feel totally manic, and uncontrollably angry about Lenny. Carl behaves like a shrink and tells me that my anger is my problem, and I have to deal with it.

The next evening, there is a call from Jill Stone, a young Navajo woman from Parker, Arizona. She tells me she is in Santa Fe for Indian Market and she wants to meet me. Fifteen minutes later, she arrives at the door and we head, on foot, for the big gallery openings of "the night before Indian Market. " It starts to rain, and I groan as it drips onto my silk shirt.

"Rain is a blessing," says Jill, and she smiles as it pours down on her.

We go to Allan Houser's opening, and I am convinced this elderly Apache sculptor is the Indian Picasso. He has enormous breadth and humanity in his works. I tell Jill I would like to write something about him.

"You know how to write," Jill says, with visible longing. "I wish I could write well."

"You're very bright," I tell her. "I'm sure you write just fine."

She shakes her head no. "Indian education," is all she says.

We weave into and out of gallery after gallery, and I introduce Jill to our local Indian friends. I am surprised that they are not more friendly toward her. Minutes later, an Indian friend introduces me to "another Jewish woman." I feel no kinship whatsoever. What am I supposed to do—discuss our bat mitzvahs? I smile with understanding at the lack of immediate bonding between Jill and the other Native Americans we know here.

After the galleries have poured the last glass of wine and served the last bit of salmon mousse and jalapeño cheese, Jill comes back to the *casita* with me and unloads a tale of extreme woe, involving her background, upbringing, love life, and professional uncertainty. I start to give her counsel, and she comments that I am picking her brain.

"Well then," I ask, "what would you like?" She shrugs. "Do you want me to just listen to you while you talk, instead of giving advice?" She nods. So I do and she does. For a long, long time.

"How come you are talking to me?" I ask her.

She answers very frankly. "I can unload in the white world but not in the Indian world because it would not be tolerated and there is no place for it. In the Indian world, you have to hold it in."

Saturday morning is the actual start of Indian Market. Some of our friends have won ribbons, and we are very excited for them. The Market officially opens at 8 A.M. but the exhibitors start to set up around 6 A.M. The Plaza is a buzz of excitement and activity, and we are there. At 6 A.M. I still can't believe we made it. All around there are tented booths with Indian exhibitors. The smell of coffee permeates the early morning air.

I feel I am going to cry from the sheer honor of being alive and able to walk from booth to booth, seeing such amazing grace, beauty, and dazzling talent. There are pottery, weaving, painting, graphics, clothing, concha belts, sculpture, jewelry, beadwork, pipes, and the fabulous crinkly, wrinkly faces of older Indians, who just sit there, watching the world pass by and remaining impervious to it. There must be one thousand booths, sprawled across the Plaza, down the streets, and spilling over into ancillary spaces around the city. Everyone is very friendly because EVERYONE WANTS TO SELL. A good weekend at Indian Market can support an Indian artist for a year or more.

There is much tension among the sellers. What should they wear, how should they answer dumb questions, smart questions, will they win prizes, will they make money, will Mr. Jones from Dallas come back and make a purchase as he said he would??

The sun is coming up now, the food booths are getting ready, and you can smell anticipation in the air. The artists are not supposed to sell until 8 A.M., but buyers have been waiting up all night, and some of the prize pieces are snatched up the moment they are put out, even if the price is many thousands of dollars.

There is a real problem for Indian artists. White buyers want their work to "look Indian." White people want to buy paintings that depict Indians the way white people think they should look—romanticized, on the Plains, noble savages, dancing with wolves. This discourages experimentation among the artists, and they stick to traditional themes or contemporary portrayals of modern Indian tribal life. Everywhere there are arrows and drums, feathers and medicine shields, Indians having visions, buffalo. Even by very urban Indians. It takes a lot of courage for an Indian artist to break away from this and believe that because he is an Indian, anything he creates will be Indian art. He gets rejected by his buyers and rejected by his people. It takes a lot of courage to be a real artist, period.

By 8 A.M., Indian Market is jammed. We visit the booths of some of our friends—Arnold Herrera, the drummer from Cochiti, Laura and Steve who need to sell sculpture in order to buy a new roof, Roy Telahaftewa, with his brilliant silver concha belt where every buckle is a finely etched *kachina* scene. Roy tells us how he "becomes the *kachina*" as he executes each different one. His mother, Evangeline, is a well-known Hopi basket maker. She is perhaps eighty years old, and she sits there, with her $6000 piece, impervious to the world passing before her. I tease her and tell her that she looks really sexy, and she laughs. She speaks slowly and deliberately, choosing her words very carefully. I admire her ability to be so still and silent. "I talk a lot," she says, as if contradicting my thoughts. "I think I talk too much."

A strange thing happens this morning. As I go by each of our friends' booths, a sale takes place. Maybe I have a lucky presence?

The visitors at Indian Market encompass everything from deadly earnest collectors to gushing Wannabe Indians dripping turquoise and concha belts to pale white tourists pouring out of buses from points east to normal folk, strolling by, looking, fondling, shopping.

"I think this is payback," a woman from Minnesota says to me. "It's an unconscious thing. People in America know what has been done to the Indians. This is our once-a-year day to buy their wares and give back to them."

In the evening, we go to an outdoor performance of Lenny's theater group. Carl comes along, and it is very strange because Lenny is super-friendly to me, but he does not greet Carl. He walks around him, behind him, in front of him, but he does not say hello. Can he possibly not hear me when I tell him that Carl is here? Can he possibly not see Carl, who is two heads taller than anyone else?

Carl tries not to be upset or angry, and even though he denies his feelings, I can see that he is upset and perturbed. He is entrusting his life story to me and Lenny, and it is distressing that he is not even greeted.

"So, my Fein friend, maybe your anger is justified," he says. "Prob-

205

ably most other people would have reacted a lot worse than you. They would go ballistic. Maybe it's even commendable that there hasn't been a Third World War here."

I smile, for Carl is very funny. But it must be very painful for him.

The performance is a collection of Indian stories (that Lenny tells), songs by Lenny's brother Frank, improvised skits by a group of masked coyotes, drumming by Arnold, a personal recital of how one man thought he was Chicano and lived a life of crime and drugs in Los Angeles before finding his path back to Indian ways.

At the end of the show, in true Pueblo fashion, the masked coyotes go through the audience and give out gifts. The idea of sharing *things* goes very deep in Pueblo Indians; it is part of their upbringing and belief system. The more you give, the more you get. I am given the coveted huge zucchini, and I joke with the salacious masked coyote who hands it to me that it is nothing compared to Paul's.

When morning comes, I decide not to feel rancor about my partnership with Lenny. I will cover for him, do my work and his work, and not complain about it. I am quite cheerful as I wander through the annex to Indian Market, admiring the wares. And then a very strange thing happens. I stop in front of a Cherokee artist's work. She tells me about "the little people" in Indian mythology, and says they are everywhere, even though people can't see them. I inch closer to inspect her canvases, and I immediately find many of them hiding among the trees and flowers. I laugh and say that the little people aren't really hiding; they are readily apparent to anyone.

"No," says the artist. "That's not true."

"Of course it is," I counter. "Here, watch this."

I stop people who pass by the booth and ask them if they can see the little people in the paintings. Some laugh, some shake their heads, but all of them stop for a moment to look for the little folk. To my utter amazement, they cannot find them.

"Look," I say, pointing to the sections of canvas where the little people are hiding. But even though I am indicating the exact spots, the tiny folk are not visible.

"You're attuned," says the artist, and she starts to engage me in rather serious and heavy conversation. She mentions that her mother is an Indian dream interpreter, and out of the blue, I laughingly begin to tell her a dream fragment I had during the night. She narrows her eyes and gets very solemn. She begins to talk to me about Red Dog, the Indian version of the devil.

206

A Grab Day

"He is in your life right now," she says. "And he is a terrible threat to you. You must close your circle to protect yourself from him."

"Close my circle?" I ask, bewildered.

"Yes. You must exclude him from your life. You cannot let down your guard or trust him for a moment. He feeds on women, and there is no way you can be close to him and survive. He will drag you and all of those around you down with him."

It is the middle of the afternoon, in the center of a shopping mall, at the height of Indian Market. Objectively, it is light and bright and yet I feel like I am in a dark cave, suffocating. I grow afraid.

"If I'm conscious and aware, nothing bad can happen to me," I tell the Cherokee artist. "You've alerted me, so I'm okay," I say, smiling.

She does not smile back. She is terse and earnest.

"He will subvert you. Get away. Save yourself while you can. You can have NOTHING to do with him. Break off the relationship with him, no matter what you think the cost to you will be!"

Before coming to Indian country, I would have shrugged off the woman's words, and perhaps the woman herself. But, because I am learning how to listen, people and words penetrate me more deeply now. I know that I have been pulled into a different state of consciousness and an altered time zone. I have no idea if we have been talking for minutes or hours.

I am very upset and frightened as I weave out of the shopping mall. I have no idea of what is real or not real. I suppose that I am "attuned," or susceptible, as the artist said. I can see the little people. Perhaps I am an easy victim for Red Dog, if such a thing exists.

At night, I suddenly remember that we have invited four people to a barbecue and nothing is ready. I panic. We race to a store, buy meat to make buffalo burgers, run up and down the aisles grabbing whatever seems to be a good thing to serve. We get home, half an hour before the guests are supposed to arrive, and instead of the expected four, fifteen people show up!

Half the guests are half white, half Indian, and run the gamut from doctors to ex-convicts. Ordinarily, these people would never be at a social gathering together, yet here they are, sharing knives and stories.

"I suppose I should learn something from this experience," I whisper to Paul. "The lesson is *be prepared*."

"No," he whispers back, "that's not the lesson. Look around you."

I glance up from the buffalo meat and see the guests mingling eas-

207

ily. I hear snippets of conversation and ripples of laughter, and know that Paul is right. The lesson is not about preparedness. It's about *moving ahead with life*. If four people show up for a party, fine. If fifteen show up, even better. How many parties have been meticulously worked out in advance and then turn out to be dull, dry, unsuccessful? Life is not something that can be planned. It all works out, one way or another. You don't brace yourself against the unexpected in life; you go with it.

"You're really moving forward," Paul says. "A few months ago, in Los Angeles, you would have been panicked if two people showed up unannounced for dinner."

At the end of the evening, I am standing in the kitchen, washing dishes in yellow plastic gloves, my arms plunged in soapy water up to the elbows, and I overhear some of the Indian guests talking to Tim and Wilma about their upcoming Navajo wedding in a hogan. I sigh, wishing Paul and I were among the chosen, but realizing that it is a private Indian ceremony. Suddenly, Wilma comes up to me. "Tim and I are going to have a traditional Navajo wedding on the reservation. It's a ceremony that's not performed much any more. I don't know how my family will react to having white people, but we'd like you to come. It's a six-hour drive from here, if you're interested."

Interested? I could grab her and kiss her right now, if I weren't so sudsy.

The minute the Indian Market weekend is over and Lenny agrees to work again, our sessions take a different turn. I simply let go of my anger, let go of ANY expectations, and cede to all of his demands. This, in turn, makes Lenny more vulnerable, and he admits he has trouble keeping up. He insists that if we work in an "official place" we will be able to concentrate better. Reluctantly, I leave the *casita* where all my books and notes and computer are. We meet to work at the Institute for American Indian Arts. We try to find an empty room. We work in the hallway. We sit wherever Lenny wants to sit. I am uncomfortable and hot, but I try to let it go.

We talk deeply about Indian culture. We get into heavy conversations about Corn Mother. When the Indians find a perfect ear of corn, with four kernels at the top, they save it and worship it. It is presented to people during healing ceremonies. Then they keep it in their houses, in a special place, a kind of altar. And if, at some time, someone else needs it, they pass it along. This is the Corn Mother. When they walk by it in their houses, it reminds them of who they are, of their spiritual connection, of where they come from. It is beliefs like this that made it easy for Indians to adopt Christian ways, with Mary worship and statues. It was an easy transition from corn to Mary. Corn veneration is also a form of goddess worship, for the corn is female, the corn feeds the people, the corn is the source of all life to Indians.

Although I am nervous because Lenny is oblivious to our work deadlines, I give up, give in, and just talk about whatever comes up. I urge him to let me help him with his new rented computer so we can become computer compatible, but he insists he will do it himself and on his own time. I yield and go home to do the work by myself.

Work now consumes about fifteen hours a day, but I take a break in the evening when Laura and Steve, our sculptor friends, come to visit us in the *casita*. They are in town for a few days before they head back to the scorpions and cannibal cats of Tularosa. It's funny. Somehow, in the course of the evening, our eventual departure from Santa Fe comes up, and I see a weird look cross Laura's face. I wonder if they'll miss us when we leave. I suspect they will. The *casita* has become a little home for them too. They are permanent fixtures here, but we are outsiders, transients, and we will go back to where we came from. It makes me sad. Laura and I look at each other: our faces wear identical expressions.

I speak with Laura about Navajo hogans, and how whole families live, cook, eat, and sleep in one room, because that's how a hogan is built. (Parenthetically, I recall the first time I was welcomed in a hogan. A sheep had just been butchered. Food was all about. People were very friendly and hospitable. Pots and pans lined the walls and a washtub was full of dishes. Family members were sprawled on beds covered with blankets. "How nice," I said. "But where do you *live?*")

Laura's mother was raised that way, although not in a hogan, because she is not Navajo. It is a choice. If you want to live the traditional way, you give up privacy. Once the architecture changes, the way of life changes too. The family becomes nuclear, and not extended. People move into their own rooms, and go their own ways.

We speak about modern Indian dilemmas. For example, a man may have certain tribal responsibilities passed down in his family. Let's say he moves away to the city, gets married, has a city life. At some point, maybe he is twenty-five or thirty-five or fifty-five, someone passes away and he inherits those duties. What is he to do? If he stays in the city, he must bear the responsibility of not performing and fulfilling these functions. It can badly affect both him and the entire tribe. But if he moves back to the res, he loses his city life and a way of living that may be satisfactory to him. To whom can he go for counsel? The tribe will want him back. In the city, no one understands or gives a damn.

"It's enough to drive a person to drink," I comment.

"It does," Laura says, with gravity.

We speak about how suffocating it can be to live in a small Indian community with the envies, the intrigues, the rules, the taboos, the religious demands. But if you move away, life in the white world can be even harder.

"It's enough to drive a person to drink," I comment again.

"It does," Laura repeats, with utmost seriousness.

Steve, too, is particularly talkative tonight. He bemoans the fact that he is in a passive period of his life, and nothing he is doing brings out the fire in him. He is a veritable compendium of information about Indian law—he has studied it, taught it, and he loves it. But he does not exactly know what to *do* with his knowledge.

Steve talks about the debate among Indians on the subject of WHO is an Indian. In order to sell in Indian Market, an Indian must be on a tribal roll. Each tribe in the United States determines what the requirements are. But some Indians contest this, because the tribal government system was set up by the federal government—and, they contend, it is not a true Indian system or a measure of who is an Indian.

The Indian tribes were originally theocracies, and the real governing bodies were the different religious societies which were responsible for every aspect of community life. But with the advent of the white man, those societies were mostly lost. The songs and rituals are gone. When societies remain at all, they are skeletal and totally inadequate for coping with modern needs. Only the Pueblos have remained fairly intact, because they go underground with their religion. And, in keeping it secret from the white man, they are able to preserve it.

So who, then, is an Indian, and who is qualified to determine that? If your mother and father are white, but your grandfather is Indian, are you Indian? Are you Indian if your tribe's government says yes or no? Is personal identity not an issue? Are you an Indian if you don't think like an Indian? If you have blond hair and blue eyes or are black? If you reject the Indian ways?

A Grab Day

It is an important ECONOMIC question, because being an Indian entitles you to medical benefits in the Indian Health Service facilities, certain grants and fellowships, and the ability to make money at—for example—Indian Market. It enables you to capitalize on the times when being an Indian is hot stuff—like now. And where money is concerned, it gets very complicated.

Beyond money, it has passed into a more personal realm. Certain Indians are discriminated against by other Indians because they don't look Indian enough. Maybe they have blond hair and blue eyes. Maybe they are fair skinned, and don't look like Curtis photos. Maybe they'd look silly on a horse.

"It all seemed to work so well before," Steve sighs, obliquely referring to the advent of the Europeans on these shores. "Some people feel they don't give a damn about the Indians any more because it's all so screwed up."

Suddenly something possesses me and I fairly leap off the sofa. I speak with clarity and surety, and I can feel my voice bouncing off the walls and resonating through the *casita* and outside, beyond the *casita*. I feel like the walls are vibrating.

"We *have* to give a damn about the Indians," I say. "It's imperative. Coca-Cola ways are spreading out across the world, invading the rain forests and the former communes in Russia, popping up in Poland and Peru. We're losing a way of life that we may never be able to get back again. Some day, it will be our only means of survival. In our country, the Indians are the only ones who are safeguarding it. We're standing on the threshold of tragedy. The world we created is spiraling out of our control. We'll be lost the day the last Indian is gone."

The *casita* is quiet. We look at each other in silence, but no one speaks.

211

10

Stumbling into
Bear Country

Mid- to late August, 1991

Today, Lenny finally learned how to use his rented Mac, so our computers can relate and "talk" to each other. I suppose it is sort of appropriate that the two writers of the TV series have a "relationship talk" too. Lenny is very frank, and he acknowledges that it has been rough sailing for us. A year ago our relationship was great, but so much has intervened that the ship almost sank.

"We have five hundred years of cultural misunderstanding between us," he tells me. He thinks for a moment, looks me in the eyes, and adds, "I want you to know that this is the first time I am living a bicultural relationship so CONSCIOUSLY. Ordinarily, I'd throw up my hands and be out the door."

He tries to tell me how he thinks and to understand how I think. We are both aware that we are still skating on thin ice, but perhaps the compatibility of our computers is a hopeful metaphor.

"Lenny," I ask very directly, "do you really think it's possible for Anglos and Indians to really get along?"

"I don't know," he answers honestly. "Look at the Feast Day at my Pueblo, Santo Domingo. It is now one day a year that everything is laid out for people from everywhere to come and eat freely. It used to be ALL THE TIME, but now it is reduced to one day only. This is a result of all that is taken from the Indian people. It is their way to still give, but look how reduced it is. They still trust, but look at how hard it is."

When I come home to the *casita,* the idea of "the new Indian" crosses my mind. Indians cannot go back to the way things were five hundred years ago; too much of their religion and culture has been lost. I am in the part of the country where the most cultural integrity has been maintained, but I have had enough contact with other tribes to know how fragmented it has become through systematic oppression. Therefore, an Indian cannot keep defining himself by what *was,* because it is next to impossible to attain in the modern world. He cannot adhere to a set of tribal customs and ceremonies because so many of them have been lost. Many of the chiefs have been replaced by government-ordained tribal councils. Even the buffalo are different, for man has intervened in their breeding to keep them from extinction.

There should, perhaps, be a definition of what a "new Indian" is. How he lives in the world, but maintains a vital connection to a way of thought, a way of being, and a tribe. The "new Indian" may live on a res or in a city, but he maintains cultural ties to a place where his people dwell. In redefining a modern Indian as opposed to always comparing Indians to their past, it may be possible for Indians to have a clearer picture of a way to live, and a freer conscience to do it. It might also remove the burden of white people looking to the past to form stereotypes of what Indians are or should be today. This white stereotyping leads to an impoverishment of the Indians on every level—in the arts (they turn out what white people want based on white images of the past), in self-esteem (the white media define them), in government (they look to a white government for rules and handouts). This is just a thought . . .

After twenty hours of nonstop work, I decide to take a short break because Paul says my eye sockets look like meteor craters. We jump in the car and drive toward Bandelier, a breathtaking national park with Anasazi cliff-dweller ruins. The Anasazi or "Ancient Ones" are pre-Columbian Indians who inhabited the Southwest, built pit-houses dug into the earth, then houses on top of the earth, and oft-times lived dramatically in houses built of stone and mortar that were set in natural caves in the cliffs. The word "Anasazi" means "enemies of our ancestors" in Navajo. Many Pueblo people choose to refer to their beloved ancestors as the "Ancient Ones." Around 1300 they mysteriously "disappeared," abandoning their homes, and no one knows why.

Along the road, I see an open gate leading to some ruins on a mountaintop and ask Paul to stop. What a fortuitous stop it is! The name of the ruins is Tsankawe, and I think they are my favorite ruins to date, because it's a kind of do-it-yourself discovery tour.

The climb to the top of the mountain involves squeezing between huge slabs of volcanic rock, inching up the stone in shallow footholes, walking straight uphill in the path of the ancients. And when you get to the top, there doesn't seem to be much there. There are a few isolated markers, but we don't have an explanatory brochure. Paul wanders off in one direction and I wander off in another.

I find myself in a verdant meadow, with grass knee-high. Rocks are strewn about in odd places. In the middle of the meadow is a very long rectangular space where the grass is much lower. Suddenly it strikes me. This is the central Plaza of Tsankawe! I begin to run around the edges of what I think is the Plaza area. If I am right, then there will be houses, like the houses I have seen at the Pueblos. Right! The stones are piled where the many houses have been. I walk around excitedly, and suddenly my heel sinks deep into the ground. What a sense of discovery! I move my heel a few inches to the left, and it sinks again. A few more inches to the left, and it sinks deeper. I begin to trace my heel along the ground, and everywhere it touches, the earth sinks beneath my feet. Wow! I am standing on the ruins of an old house. If I dug here, I know what I would find.

I run for Paul and bring him back with me. Very quickly, his eyes get accustomed to the "treasures" hidden in the grass. He finds a kiva, and we sit down in it. Suddenly, I am transported back, back, back in time, and I get a vision that this kiva is the navel of the earth—round, centered, protected. I can feel the male Ancient Ones sitting around, praying.

"Stones speak," I whisper to Paul, "if you just listen to them."

Paul listens, but he hears nothing. "Stones speak to *you*," he says cheerfully.

I sit in the kiva for a long time, and I can hear a faint drumbeat. Of course, when I look around me, there is no one there. It is the pulse of another time.

I trace the path from the kiva to the Plaza—it is just the way modern paths are. I can imagine masked dancers tracing the path, and they come from the kiva-womb into the sunlight, to dance. Then I find another kiva, more houses. I have never had a sense of discovery like this!

I would like to spend all day here, but I know I have to get back to work. I start heading down the mountain and encounter my old nemesis: a long, wooden ladder, hanging off the side of the cliff. Paul looks at me and I look at him. Do I dare? I begin to have a dialogue with myself.

"You have two choices now."

"Okay. What are they?"

"You can go down the ladder or not go down the ladder."

"I'll choose the latter. I'll trace my steps all the way back, and walk down the mountain without danger or panic."

"Fine. Go ahead."

I pause. My feet don't move. The dialogue continues.

"Why aren't you going?"

"Because I will hate myself if I back down."

"Then just walk to the ladder, tell yourself you aren't afraid, and climb down."

"What if I fall off the ladder and die?"

"Then you'll join the ancients and become part of the landscape."

Paul stands very still, looking at me. I know what he is thinking: will she or won't she?

In a second I decide that I *will*. Not only do I climb down the ladder, but I actually scamper down the rungs. I am tired of having fear rule my life.

In Indian country, whenever you face a fear, you get a reward, and my recompense is immediate. Although many people must have traveled along this main trail, there are two perfect rattlesnake skins lying there, plunk, right in front of me, in the middle of the path. What a symbol of change! Shedding old skin. Of course I pick them up and take them, because they have been waiting there for me!

I look to the side of me and there, in the rock, is a cocoon . . . the place where the larva decomposes and emerges as a butterfly. I smile at the cocoon, knowing it is me. And then, to top it off, I find a divining rod behind me. Maybe it is my imagination, but when I hold it in my hands, it seems to lead me straight to the ruins of old houses that no one else can see.

In the silence of my grateful mind, I reiterate three lessons that I have learned: (1) When you overcome a difficulty or a fear, there is a reward. (2) The universe is full of signs. You just have to be receptive and they will be made clear to you. (3) There are wonders to be discovered where you are right now. You just have to look. Right there. Not in the past or the future. In the (metaphorical) ordinary-looking grass around you. Wherever YOU are is where IT is. That's why running, running, running makes no sense.

I wander among the cliff dwellings, always preferring the cave-houses that are isolated, set apart, always conjuring up in my mind what ancient life must have been like. And then, at the "magic hour" that filmmakers so love, I come upon some fabulous petroglyphs that stop me dead in my tracks. There are the unmistakable figures of dancers with corn stalks on their heads. Just like I saw at Santo Domingo on Feast Day!

Of course, it all makes sense. Only archeologists talk about a distinct culture called the Anasazi. Why, it's as obvious as the fingers on my hand. These are the ancestors of Pueblo peoples. And they didn't die out mysteriously as scientists say. They just moved on to another place. Their great-great-great-grandchildren continue living in the Pueblos today. No one has to tell me that, and I need no scientific proof. I walk around the ruins, I walk around today's Pueblos, and I know it to be true. I am overcome with awe that I have daily contact with a culture that has existed for perhaps ten, twenty, or thirty thousand years, and I am privileged to see how it has been handed down in its most pure form.

On our way down the mountain, we stop off to visit some "neighbors" in nearby caves, even though they are abandoned now. They are just there in our imaginations. It is impossible for your mind not to run away with you in such a fabulous place. You can almost hear the sound of dogs barking and children playing. You can almost see the men heading down the mountain to tend their fields and go hunting in the plateau below. And all of this materializes at a spot where there seemed to be nothing.

As if this isn't enough for a day, we drive to White Rock Overlook. There, on a mountaintop, you can look down at the snaking, majestic Rio Grande, watching the whitecaps break and roll along. Behind you is a waterfall. You can hear the symphony of the two waters—one vertical and one horizontal. It is mesmerizingly beautiful, with the puff-clouds of the New Mexican sky overhead. You can picture all the Pueblos which are built on the banks of the river, and hear the thunder of the conquistadors who rode in on horseback to inflict the Indians' most awful hours. As we ride back, we get lost, but there are no regrets, because we are in the Jemez Mountains, and the moon is an orange globe peeking out over the tops of forest trees. What can be more breathtaking?

Back in Santa Fe, the bible for the TV series (a narrative telling of the incidents, characters and scenes) is now two days away from being due. The heat is on. Sleeping is difficult, my chest feels tight, I've started losing things in the computer, I only stop for minutes at a time to cram something into my mouth.

"Too bad we have to write the bible," I say to Lenny. "It's all so abbreviated. It would be much better if we could just write the scripts. I hope they understand what we are getting at."

He looks at me and I look at him. Can our producers, sitting at their desks in Los Angeles, hypercritical and very negative, understand what we are trying to do? The only thing Lenny and I have in common these days is our scorn for them.

Lenny and I no longer discuss our method of working or our relationship. I do the writing and he makes minor corrections, adjusting a detail of dress or a turn of phrase. Several times I ask him to do the writing and let me do the corrections, but he doesn't respond. I write page after page, while Lenny goes home to rest or to sleep. We lose half a day because Lenny runs into a glitch in the computer program.

"Why didn't you ask for help?" I inquire, trying not to lose my temper.

"Because some things you just have to figure out yourself."

"Not when the deadline is right here, banging on the door."

Lenny pulls out his mini shaver, and shaves a few hairs on his chin. There is no response from him.

At five o'clock in the afternoon, Lenny says that he has had enough work for the day. He hands me a disk with his latest corrections, claiming that he has been working straight since early morning. When I boot up his disk on my computer, I see that he logged out at noon. He has done no work at all today!

"I will not get angry, I will not get angry," I say, chanting the little mantra of self-control to myself. But I am angry, and I am sure Lenny knows it and feels it. The only words that escape my lips are an honest wish, "Lenny, I wish you would do more of the work and not just dump it all on me."

His nostrils flare. "I knew you thought that!" he explodes. "I figured that sooner or later you'd say that!"

I back off and resume my work. Lenny stomps out of the *casita*.

The only interruption is a visit from Tim, with information about his upcoming Navajo wedding. Wilma's grandmother, a hand-trembler (a traditional diagnostician and healer), is making it at her hogan, deep, deep in Navajo territory, about five or six hours from here. I hear him explaining the directions to Paul in the other room and it sounds like this: "Drive for five hours, turn right at the sheep shearing, then continue toward the mountains and at the ninety-ninth cottonwood tree, turn right again . . . " I smile, eager for the adventure. I hear Tim say that we must be on the road by 6 P.M. or it will get too dark and we won't be able to find our way. We are to camp out on the res, next to the hogan, and the wedding will begin the next day.

As I work, Paul visits all of our friends, borrowing camping gear. I have never camped outside in my life, and, conjuring up pictures of what can eat me, attack me, and leap on me in the middle of the night, I have decided to face my fears and do it. As each piece of equipment plunks down in our living room (which is now so loaded with unanswered letters and bills and things to be taken care of that you can't even find the sofa), the experience gets realer and I get more freaked. Well, I can only freak about one thing at a time, and for the moment it is the bible. The Bible. With the effort we are putting into it, we might as well be creating a universe. And, on the seventh day, Smallfeather rested—again! I work into the night, while Lenny sleeps.

Two hours to go. Lenny is now working, but everything he gives me has to be rewritten and there is no time. I hate handing in work that has not been crafted and polished, but there is no choice. And at 5 P.M., as usual, come hell or high water, Lenny stops working.

Paul waits outside for me to leave for Navajo territory. The car is so loaded down that it looks like fifty-two circus clowns will come piling out of it. It is 6 P.M. and we are not yet on the road. I beg Lenny to fax in the bible, even though he said he was done for the day. He tells me to do it. I tell him, quite frankly, that I have done enough and it's his turn. He refuses. I refuse. Finally I tell him that I am leaving the bible in front of my door, I INSIST that he fax it in, and I slam down the phone.

It is 6:15 P.M. Paul starts up the engine, and I get a toothache. It is Labor Day weekend and every dentist is gone. Paul persists, finally finds one, and after poking and probing and X-raying, the dentist determines that I probably need a "root amputation"—the very words make me tremble in my tennis shoes.

"I guess you're not going to your Navajo wedding," says the dentist.

"Oh yes I am!" I exclaim, startling Paul and the dentist with the vehemence of my insistence.

"I'm terrified of what may happen, I'm mortified of pain, but I will not give in to my fears," I whisper to my husband, whose eyes are bugging out with surprise.

218

Stumbling into Bear Country

The dentist outlines my routine for me. I have to take antibiotics, rinse with salt water three times a day, brush with fluoride two times a day, and do about ten other procedures that would be hard to do in a dentist's office let alone on an abandoned campsite next to a hogan.

It is now too late to think of camping out near the hogan, because we will never find it in the dark. Armed with Tim's hand-drawn map, we spend the night in a cheapo motel in Gallup where I do tooth calisthenics. Then, early in the morning, we set out for the Navajo wedding.

"You know," Paul says, "it's a good thing Beaver behaved selfishly in Oklahoma. If she had behaved well, we'd never be invited to this wedding. Just think about it. When Beaver abandoned us in Oklahoma City, her cousin Laura come to the rescue and got us a ride home in a truck. The truck belonged to Tim and Wilma. This is their wedding. So, thank you, Beaver. Thanks for being selfish."

We both laugh. The strain of the bible has been so great that we have not had our usual dose of laughter in a long time. It feels good to be happy again.

The minute we set wheels on the Navajo nation, the land opens up before us. Vast expanses of uninhabited country lie to the left and right, and dramatic shapes of stone and earth and sand rise up mysteriously and provocatively in front of us. It looks like a mini Monument Valley, unheralded, as most things in Indian country are. And then, suddenly, Indian men galloping on horseback begin to appear, with their colorful head bandannas flying behind them. It feels as though we have dropped back a century or two, and we can see the Old West all around us.

Suddenly the air gets dry, and hogans, the traditional Navajo homes and places of ceremony, begin to dot the landscape. The older ones are a testimony to tradition, and the newer ones, which are just being built, are an indication of the vitality of that tradition.

As we ride along, Paul and I smile at each other as we see tepees in front of houses. We know that these are the prayer houses of the Native American Church; we know it because we sat up all night with Father Peyote, praying in one of those tepees. Now all signs of modern civilization drop from sight, save telephone poles, and then they disappear too.

We trustingly follow Tim's directions even though there are no signposts, and we are now deep onto Navajo land. The little map says to go for eleven miles and luckily Paul is a real scout and he has a sense that we should turn again at eight miles and ignore the map. He is right. We arrive at a wedding encampment. There is a clump of trees, and a large clearing has been cut out. Food is simmering in big covered aluminum pots over an outdoor fire. Relatives sit under impromptu arbors in the shade.

The bride, Wilma, is getting last-minute touch-ups to her traditional woven dress, and she runs around acting very bridey, darting in and out of a family tent, adjusting her hair and turquoise jewelry. The groom, Tim, wears a ribbon shirt—which Indian men wear to all occasions. It's simply a plain cotton shirt, in a bright color, with a multi-colored ribbon sewed across the chest and back. The guests wear shorts or jeans or the long colorful, velvet skirts that Navajo women wear. No one runs out of his/her way to greet us. They just keep going about their business.

After an hour or two of hanging out, the medicine man appears. He is nondescript-looking and very matter-of-fact in manner. He has been making preparations in the hexagonal, wooden hogan. He tersely tells the groom that "his" people should sit on the north side when they file into the hogan. Since Tim is from the Penobscot tribe in Maine and it is too expensive for his family to come, we become his instant family. Of course I cannot tell north from south, so I rely on Paul in front of me and just follow blindly as we line up, single file, with all the guests and relatives.

"I hate being so dependent upon you," I whisper to Paul.

He shoots me a look that makes me instantly stop my worrying.

We file into the hogan in silence. I am very aware that I am being allowed into someone's sacred circle. The hogan is empty except for blankets for guests to sit on that line the walls. It is fairly dark, but the door is kept open throughout the ceremony. Wilma has said that it is all right to take pictures, and I try to be discreet but I have a new camera that practically yips and yaps when I press the button. When I use it, to my horror, everyone turns around. The flash attachment sounds like a creaky door. In addition, I am taping the ceremony for the couple on a portable tape recorder. The metal microphone flashes in the rays of sun. Is this inconspicuous? I wish I could just hang there like a fly on the wall. Every time I make a move, I feel a puff of air as someone snorts out disapproval. Or is it my imagination?

Above our heads, the roof of the hogan has an interlocking weave.

It represents the spider's web of the grandmother Spiderwoman, the female creative spirit that wove all things into existence.

Tim and Wilma sit side-by-side on the floor, facing the hogan entry, which is in the east. All ceremonies which we have experienced seem to have the main participants facing east—where the sun rises. Where life is renewed. The direction Indians face every morning when they thank the sun for another day.

The ceremony begins. It is in Navajo. The medicine man stands and intones, half facing the couple and half facing no one in particular. He is not warm, not personal—at least in our perception. Every once in a while he drops in a few English words like "Mother Earth" or "takes care of us." Wilma understands Navajo, but Tim does not. He sits humbly, understanding the "feeling," as we all do. Then the medicine man gives instructions for the couple to lift the wedding vessel, a ceramic vase with two long necks; each drinks water from it. The symbolism seems very clear: the couple shares (the water) but each remains separate (the individual necks of the vase). This seems like a good prescription for a successful marriage.

Next a wedding plate is brought out. It is a flat plate, woven from plant fiber like a basket, and it is filled with blue cornmeal mush. Tim and Wilma are instructed to scoop it up, eat it with their fingers, and feed it to each other, in a very intimate act of sharing. Then it is passed around and we the guests are invited to dig in. I sink my fingers in the mush.

Next, a huge plate of cut-up steak comes out, and Tim has to eat it all. Wilma helps him. You can see his Adam's apple bobbing in his throat as pieces get stuck. Tim is stressed; it is hard to chow down in that state. And add to it a medicine man and fifty guests staring at every bite!

When the ceremonial eating is finished, different people are invited to speak out and tell the couple how they feel. There is a silence. And then I am surprised to find that Paul is speaking. He addresses Tim, and tells him that he has come to value their friendship. This seems to encourage others to speak. Or maybe they would have spoken anyway in their own time, in Indian time. They make it abundantly clear to Tim that he is a gift to the family, to the Navajo people, and they cherish him. Because he is Indian, even though he is from another tribe, he can now consider himself part of the Navajos, and his people are part of the Navajos. He can visit any time and be welcome. Then things get serious. They tell Tim to take care of Wilma and her children from her previous marriages. The rules are set down very clearly: this is Tim's obligation. If he veers, watch out! Tim looks ashen. As ashen as he can look with his dark skin.

The older people begin to speak. It's mostly in Navajo, but they speak from the heart, and it is easy to understand that language. One whispers, another cries, a third gets up and waves his arms. It is very moving. It is also sad, as many of the children present are educated entirely in English and are unable to understand their elders' speech. I reflect briefly on my own culture: Eastern European Jews are people of the written word, so Yiddish will never be totally lost, but Navajo, even though it is a written language, is—or *was*—predominantly an *oral* culture. When it's gone, it's gone. And it's going. Fast.

The elders in the hogan reiterate the thanks to Tim and the citing of his obligations. They mention over and over how Tim must take care of the children. They all say how important it is that this marriage is being done the traditional way—it is rare nowadays. People have civil weddings, or they just live together and have no wedding at all. Everyone in the hogan is hushed. There is an occasional joke to relieve the tension.

At a signal, we file out of the hogan the way we filed in. Tim and Wilma both feel relief; the ceremony is over. Their life together begins.

We all go outside again and food is set up on long tables. Women relatives serve us, and we eat our fill. The main dish is mutton. Sheep and mutton are food staples to the Navajo, even though as their ways are lost, the sheep disappear too. I retire to a corner to talk to Wilma's dad. He says that he got married here in 1956, but there was no cornmeal mush in his ceremony. His family could only afford a poorer version of the service. A shorter version, without the mush. I find this very odd, but I say nothing, and I don't ask any questions.

I do, however, ask questions of Wilma, Tim, and Wilma's adorable little daughter Tina. I ask them to tell me their feelings, and I tape-record their answers. Wilma and Tim talk about their struggle to be together, and how good they feel about their relationship now. Tina just talks about the food.

Now we begin to feel more accepted. Wilma's family and friends warm up. We ask for directions, and suddenly they all hover around us. I have had this experience before on the Navajo reservation: if you need information about getting somewhere, they all want to help. Maybe they just want to get rid of us?

Paul is now stationed under a tree, giving someone a Shiatsu massage. I am telling jokes. People are beginning to talk to us and laugh with us. Just when it's time to leave.

We drive to Shiprock *and miss it!*—the biggest single geological feature in the state!—and stop off at a tiny Indian swap meet in a sandy backlot. People stare at us because we obviously don't fit in. I strike up a conversation with two wonderful Indian grandmas, and then we just sort of blend in. We meet an herbalist, selling bundles of natural cures. She goes on a violent diatribe about how the Indian Health Service did involuntary sterilization of Indian women. She has no trust in the white medical system. Paul listens and then Paul buys an herbal remedy marked "for high cholesterol." Paul, who is usually so suspicious . . .

It is now getting dark. I have decided to go to a Ute bear dance at White Mesa. I have no idea of where it is, who the Utes are, or what a bear dance is, but I like the way it sounds. Paul agrees. But he agrees less when it is pitch-black, we are completely lost, and we have no idea of how to get anywhere. I get an idea. The sky is a planetarium overhead. I, city thing that I am, don't remember ever having seen skies like this. I ask Paul to pull off the road and turn off the lights so we can see the sky more clearly. When he does so, I freak. It is black. Totally silent. We are lost. A bat floats sonically overhead. A star looks red. Another one looks orange. Stars fall, shoot, the sky is alive. I can hear the pounding of my own heart. I jump back into the car. I'm not ready for so much quiet and isolation.

Near midnight, after driving down mountain roads that twist, turn, and don't lead anywhere, we arrive in Blanding, Utah. I stop at a 7-Eleven and ask how to find White Mesa. The man grins. "Just ask a Ute," he says. "How do I find a Ute, sir?" "Well, when you see someone who is very large around, that's a Ute!" Of course, it is a big, hefty Navajo speaking!

Why, I wonder, do people spend a fortune going to other countries to find weird and exotic adventure?

We spend the night in a motel and, at the first rays of light, start hopping from Indian ruin to Indian ruin. I find myself irritated with the archeologists and with the pamphlets and signs indicating that the Anasazi culture disappeared in the early fourteenth century. Why doesn't anyone ask the Indians?

At one ruin, I pick up a guidebook about petroglyphs and unexpectedly begin to weep. Everyone speculates about what the petroglyphs mean and who executed them and why. I have this flash: the people who did the petroglyphs are writers. Just like I am. And the petroglyphs fulfill all the functions writing does—to record, transcribe, tell stories, retell events, and invent. Unlike writers of today, the petroglyph "writers" were probably important members of the community, and their writings served a cultural and spiritual function. I feel a tremendous link and I cannot stop crying. I pull my hat low over my eyes so I do not make a spectacle of myself.

But someone does see me sobbing. It's an old man, wearing boots, jeans, and a huge slab of turquoise on his wrist. He doesn't intrude, and doesn't ask what is wrong. He simply offers me a bit of information: there's a very interesting road that leads way off the beaten track, but it's all mud. I nod, thanking him.

We go for it. It is very, very hot. We drive through a valley. All around us are red rock cliffs, inhabited by Indians in the old days. The vegetation is like the African savannah. Our imagination works overtime. We imagine people, animals, hunts. This is very evocative landscape.

The road suddenly ends, and dumps us into a paved road. We follow it to the river and there, hardly marked, is a petroglyph panel about two hundred yards long. The pictures are rough, crude, exciting—certainly many come from a very early period. It looks like there are several different eras represented, and they tell the tale of either extended habitation in the area or successive migrations through the area.

On the panel are etched pictures of deer and circles and dancers with crowns. There are bighorn sheep and Kokopelli figures, so common in rock art—Kokopelli, the hump-backed, fertile flute player with the bent legs, rabbit-like ears, and, sometimes, huge, protruding sex organ. What does he have on his back? A burden? A sack of seeds? Gifts? Who is he? What purpose does he serve? Is he a man? A god? Part of each? There is no one to answer the questions. The people who tell of Kokopelli are long, long gone.

Now evening is coming on. We are in Bluff, Utah—a town filled with genuine Old West buildings and terrific, artistic trading posts. I stand in one of these trading posts, in the shadow of the "Navajo Twins," two massive sandstone stelae. As I admire some Indian folk art, a tiny woman, half-hidden under a cowboy hat, approaches me.

"You like Indian thangs?" she asks with a drawl.

I nod.

"Old Indian thangs?"

I nod again.

"Well, there's some pretty special ruins outside of town, across a suspension bridge. No one much knows about them from the outside. But if you're interested, you better head over there fast, because the sun'll be setting and then you wouldn't want to get stuck out there in the dark."

Paul and I leap into the car and follow the woman's directions. The road is unmarked, and we keep getting lost. I look at my watch incessantly, afraid that it is getting late as we race against the setting sun.

"I've never seen people who are as rushed as we are," I tell Paul. "Here we are, in laid-back country, and we are constantly racing against deadlines. It must be our city karma."

We cannot find the path to the ruins, and we are about to turn around when Paul points to a (foot) suspension bridge ahead of us. It is made of crumbling wooden slats, and, in its decrepit state, it spans a river. Every fourth or fifth slat seems to be missing. I have dreadful visions of tumbling down into the chasm and lying there for weeks until someone smells my body and finds what is left over after the vultures have feasted.

"C'mon," Paul calls to me as he trots onto the bridge.

"Forget it. I'm not going."

"But you are the one who wanted to come here," he says, trying to be logical.

"I'm also the one who wants to turn back now."

"Okay," Paul says, "you stay there and I'll go ahead."

I can't believe Paul is doing this! Going off to see the goodies on the other side of the river and leaving me here, alone, on the shore. First I'm resentful, then I'm petulant, and finally I'm envious enough to trek after him. Paul smiles: I think he planned on my reaction, and he sees that he succeeded.

I tiptoe onto the bridge. I try to act calm and I inch forward, but I begin to panic. The bridge sways with every step, and I catch my foot on a broken slat and lose my balance. I start to cry. I have such a primitive fear of heights. I stand in the middle of the bridge, frozen. I cannot move forward and I cannot retreat. I have to do something, so I bend my knees, I stay low, and somehow I waddle across. The motivation to see the special ruins is greater than my fear of tumbling to my death. Before I know it, I am on the other side.

"I made it, but I am not going back that way. You'll have to fly me out of here."

"You're afraid of flying," Paul reminds me.

There are no signposts at all. We walk along a dirt road, hoping it will lead us toward the ruins. And suddenly a bull is running toward us. I think: we are dead meat now. I know you can't reason with a bull or charm him. We are completely vulnerable.

I glance toward Paul, and I see, amazingly, that he seems unafraid. I decide to act unafraid too. I begin to whistle an appropriate song: "Whenever I feel afraid, I hold my head erect, and whistle a happy tune, so no one will suspect . . . I'M AFRAID!!" Surprisingly, the bull comes close to me, takes a colossal dump, and walks on.

Staring at the bull as he retreats, I trip. I reach down to see what I stumbled over and I gasp: it is an ancient bear fetish carved of stone, and painted with red stripes. I pick it up in my hand and it immediately gives me courage. It fits right into my palm, as it must have fit into the palm of the bear hunter when he made it. When did he make it? Hundreds or thousands of years ago? Was it a talisman for him? Did it bring him luck during the hunt? Was he an ancestor of the Hopi, who migrated through this region? Was he a forefather of one of the other Pueblo people? Was he young? Old? Was the bear his animal friend, the source of his power and medicine, and did he use the fetish for hunting something else? I am overwhelmed at my fortune in finding something so rare, so old, so priceless. Perhaps I should leave it lying where it is, half-buried in the dirt as it has been for centuries or millennia, but I take it. I marvel that there is always a reward for overcoming a fear, and I just overcame a handful of them!

We walk for a long time, past cliffs and cornfields, and suddenly I spot it up, up, way up above us—a huge cave with the ruins of former life. The site is gorgeous, and I smile at what my mother always tells us about choosing a place to live: "location, location, location." There is no way to get up into the Indian cave ruin except to scale the cliff— and it is eight stories straight up. I brace myself and go for it, following Paul, who is sliding and inching up the cliff-side. I do not look behind me, because if I slip I am kissing-cousin to an ear of corn. Up, up, higher, and then, suddenly, I am there. I know now that I can overcome terror, suspension bridges, bulls, heights, scaling cliffs when I am motivated. People must have something more important than fear to pull them out of fear. That's the only way.

Paul and I walk around the ruins, visiting the rooms of the prehistoric abodes. We try to guess where the families lived, and where there was storage. Over there—is that where they kept wild turkeys? There are small bones (from a bird?) and a tiny piece of carved shell lying on the dirt floor. On the wall behind the houses is a set of handprints in black. Ruins give you feelings. This one feels young, almost adolescent, sexual. How can a ruin be sexual? It just is. Maybe there were young people in love?

The sun is starting to set as we look out across the cornfields from our temporary "home." We decide to slide down the mountain and start hotfooting it so we can get over the suspension bridge before nightfall. Right? Wrong. Of course, you can never make plans in Indian country. When we get to level land, a couple is standing there. They spotted Paul's white shirt from far away down the canyon and came to see who we were. We begin to talk and there is an immediate connection. Steve is a nice Jewish guy who does survival therapy for a living. He takes *Indians* and white people out into nature, helps them on a four-day fast and vision quest, and then they stay for another six days to process what happens. Steve points to a mountain.

"If you were on a vision quest, that could be your spot," he tells me.

It makes me shiver. The idea of being alone for four days with no shelter turns my stomach. I tell Steve that I am much too fearful to undertake a vision quest. Jessica, his wife, tells me that she has an awful fear too: writing. I guess the thought of facing a blank page with all the world as her judge makes her stomach turn. We have much in common. As a couple, they mirror us. They have similar life experiences and tastes.

It is growing dark. We head back toward the bridge. Paul and Jessica make it over, and I am next. I panic. I bend my knees, keeping low to the slats, heaving with each step. I get about a third of the way and it is an enormous struggle. Steve watches me from behind. I am, once again, immobilized by terror. I feel nauseous and dizzy and—even worse—embarrassed. I have never permitted anyone to see me in my state of phobic paralysis. Now I am exposing myself to strangers.

Steve seems to be studying me from behind, watching my dismay.

"Hey, Judie," he says, but I am too afraid to turn around. "My wife Jessica tells me that when she wants to get across a bridge, she just sees herself in the bushes on the other side."

As soon as he says this, I have a TOOL—something I can do to alleviate the panic. Theory is of no use, but this is very practical. In my mind, I project myself onto the shore on the other side, and I stop con-

227

centrating on myself on the bridge. My feet get lighter, the fear goes, and I practically run across the bridge, fearlessly. Once again, I have escaped OUT OF MYSELF, where all my limitations are.

Steve is open-mouthed. I am more nimble on the bridge than *he* is now! I guess I was ready for the lesson, because when I really needed him, the teacher came along. Paul and Jessica are whooping and hollering. They cannot believe the change in behavior they are witnessing.

We all go to dinner in Bluff and have a gourmet dinner at the Cow Canyon Trading Post. They order what we order. Same main dishes, which they split and share. Same dressing. On the side. It's uncanny. After dinner we go outside to talk, a very intense talk. Steve tells me about how young Navajos with drug and alcohol problems react to the vision quest. Many of them are alienated from the Indian ways. Not only does the vision quest put them in touch with their culture, but it also puts them in touch with themselves. As we talk, bats fly overhead. There is a *huge tarantula* on the wall next to us, and Paul gingerly points it out to me. I look at the tarantula briefly and say, "Oh, that's a nice one." Then I go right on talking.

Paul, Jessica, and Steve howl with laughter.

Once again I see that when my focus is not on the feared object, the fear goes away. I am learning an entire new way to think and to see the world in Indian country. My teachers are everywhere.

Paul and I leave Bluff and head, again in pitch blackness, for the White Mesa Utes. When we get there, it seems like the whole village (there are only about 350 White Mesa Utes left) are sitting under a large ramada. We go up close. Blankets are spread on the ground and some pretty heavy gambling is going on. I can't identify the card game. Although the people very visibly have no money, twenty-dollar bills keep hitting the blankets. They come from men and women, mostly older. They have wonderful age- and weather-chiseled faces.

Next to the card gamblers, there are two rows of chairs and two lines of people who sit facing each other. They are playing the stick game, an Indian guessing/gambling game that pops up all over the country. One person hides two sticks under a bandanna and shuffles them around. The other team has to guess where the sticks are. As the game is played, there is drumming and singing. The drums are single-head drums, tambourines, anything that resounds. The main singer, an older woman, hits her drum with a gourd. It feels unmistakably tribal. We could be anywhere in the world in an indigenous population.

Stumbling into Bear Country

We leave the gambling and wander off to where there are food booths. We begin talking to a Navajo woman, and she is very friendly. She tells us she likes Anglos who are interested in and respect the Indian ways. Then her husband arrives—a tall, heavyset, full-blood Ute. He looks strong, tough, closed. He wears a black hat, braids, his face is set. The energy changes. We stop being so friendly. What is he thinking? Does he hate us for being white? Two dogs start to fight next to us. It looks like they could rip each other apart. The husband goes in and breaks them up. A sign it is time to leave.

When we come back the next time, it is daylight. The gambling continues under the ramada, but we walk off to where there is a huge circle made of planted trees, with saplings woven across horizontally and held by barbed wire. Inside, people sit on plastic chairs and blankets. The bear dance is taking place. There is a tall white flag with a painting of two bears facing each other and perhaps dancing. Below the flag, four men sing and play rasps, which imitate the growling of a bear.

The bear dance is quite possibly the oldest dance known to man. It may be thirty thousand years old. The bear was revered, and it was thought to carry great power, medicine, and magic. Even though it is late summer, the bear dance is a celebration of the bear coming out of hibernation at the end of the winter. It celebrates the beginning of spring, the start of a new growing cycle. It is a celebration of the mating of the bears. To some Indian cultures, the bear is so sacred that they will not kill it. When a bear is skinned, it looks uncannily and spookily like a human being. It's enough to take your appetite away, I guess.

The songs and sawing rasp music sound very ancient and primal, and they fill the whole space as though they were an orchestra. The rasps are made of axe handles that are brightly painted and have serrated notches carved in them. The musicians rub a small piece of metal against the wood to obtain the scraping, growling musical sound. They lean their instruments on a piece of corrugated tin roof which is spread before them, and acts as a resonator.

In the middle of the circle of trees are women in shawls. They choose male partners and dance, as couples, back and forth, forth and back, back and forth, forth and back—perhaps a human imitation of the mating of the bears. It looks almost like a square dance. When someone falls, there is a little ceremony. It is the men against the women, to see who lasts longer. It looks like a tie this day.

229

We got the immediate sense that at one time the bear was central to the survival of these Utes. The bear was sacred here, as the buffalo was to Plains Indians. But bear hunting was outlawed, and the cultural fabric fell apart. It is now reduced to a social dance. And yet, echoes of the past remain. Casual comments are made around us and to us which we would NEVER hear in our own culture.

"Before, people used to talk to the bears," one woman says. Another chimes in: "The White Mesa bear dance comes later than the other Utes. It's too late. The bears are already gone." As in much of Indian country, you have to piece together information from conversational snippets you hear. People say things, but do not explain things.

One gets the sad feeling that this Ute bear culture is dying out, and there is nothing much you can do to preserve it as an outsider. "Record all your stories, gather your elders, don't lose it!" you feel like shouting.

I turn to the Coke-drinking woman next to me, who told me that her people talked to bears. "I talk to lizards and ants," I say quietly. She smiles: "It's all the same!" she says.

I sit there, trying desperately to guess at the meaning of the dance. Was it to thank the bears after the hunt? There is coupling—is it for fertility? Medicine? Is it a dance for the survival of the people, since the bear is part of their survival? Is it a kind of spring rite of rebirth and renewal—symbolized by the bear returning from hibernation?

The dance is obviously open to the public. Anyone can come (if they can ever find it). It is open because these Indians have nothing to hide. Once the bear hunt stopped, the rituals themselves became meaningless. They just serve a bonding, societal function.

Paul and I leave and drive through the Valley of the Gods. For an hour or more, and with no one else around, we drive through incredible natural stone "statues." They rise out of the earth, red and anthropomorphic, towering above us. "That looks like Marat in his tub!" I cry. "There's an Indian mother with a cradle board," Paul says, pointing. The only way to find the Valley is to follow a tiny marker on the main road. Another undiscovered treasure in southeast Utah. No wonder the early Indians stayed here!

We then head for "the *other* Mesa Verde." It is a vast network of ruins that are not reconstructed the way Mesa Verde is. It's on the Ute reservation, near Towaoc, and you can only go with a Ute guide. We show up in time for an all-day tour. The guide, who is a minister and future archeologist and not terribly articulate, takes us off the main trails to back country. We stop at petroglyphs done by the Anasazi and more recently by the Utes and white archeologists. We climb and climb and get to the top of a mountain. I am amazed at how agile I have become! We look down and see cliff dwellings to the right, cliff dwellings to the left, and an entire canyon that was once populated by the Anasazi.

"We're going down there," says the guide.

"How do we get there?" I ask, trying not to sound anxious.

"By ladders, of course," he answers.

Ladders and rock climbing and all the activities from my phobic pantheon. I am able to get down, but I cannot get up: there is one site that is only accessible by scaling a twenty-six-foot ladder, loose and shaking, that hangs over a 1500-foot drop.

"It's okay if you don't go," Paul whispers to me as he heads up the ladder. "You are only human. Forgive yourself. Just look around you."

I look around, and see that four other people do not have the courage to climb. When you have a problem, especially a secret one, you always think you are the only one in the world who has it!

I stand there, forgiving myself, and I see that Paul looks upset when he finally comes down. Apparently, he made an innocent remark to the guide who misinterpreted it completely and launched a long, anti-white harangue.

I don't "feel" much in the way of energy coming from these ruins. Instead, I perceive it as a huge, dead, outdoor museum. It teaches us how the Indians got from place to place, and we actually see the remnants of single-pole ladders and toe and foot holes. We are able to see the wood flooring of a house, and to understand how they made multi-story dwellings. We can piece together information about their daily lives. They ripped the bark off trees and used it for diapers and toilet paper. In the cold winter, they buried their dead in their trash heaps, because the earth was too cold to dig. They traded with southern peoples (Chaco, Kayenta), planted small-eared corn and squash, and fired pottery in kilns. They probably got the idea for building their homes from the way cliff swallows do it—they take mud from the river and use it as mortar, to hold stones together. They used turkey feathers for bedding, so they had something softer than the earth to sleep on.

Our guide is very enthusiastic. He points out petroglyphs of priests with bird shapes on their heads who carried crooks; he shows us how these drawings are possibly related to spherical shapes that could be

231

sundials. This could suggest that the crook-carrying priest announced the right time for planting—which was so essential to the ancients' survival.

As we talk, we arrive at another ladder. "Don't be too careful," our guide tells us. "It's when you are too careful that something bad can happen!"

I repeat his words over and over to myself. They seem to me to be very wise.

The guide points up to a separate cave, where the priest lived—always slightly apart from the others. He tells us these people only lived to be about thirty-five, and they were under five feet in height. He shows us how the Indians used plant roots for food, medicine, survival (they grow under the ground, and they don't get "animal showers"). He shows us how pine sap was used to seal baskets. This is like a cram course in survival! And then the fun. He picks up a little ball of dried mortar. The kids used to make these and, when the balls were still wet, they played a little game where they threw them up against the cliffs and watched them drop off when they dried.

Our guide is a born-again Christian, and we are given hefty doses of his religion and philosophy. Half the time he is lucid, and the other half, we have no idea of what he is saying. He tells us his theory that the people who lived in these cliffs were raided. That is why the Anasazi left the area in 1300, and not the drought that is usually cited. He shows us where the people could have climbed up on their roofs, high in the cliffs, to defend themselves or wait out an attack. It's certainly worth considering. In addition, he tells us that he thinks the Utes, his own people, were the raiders who routed the Anasazi.

The Utes are related to the Aztecs. They come from another language group than the Anasazi—called Uto-Aztecan. They trace their ancestry back across the Bering Strait. So there we are, with the raider, visiting the raidee. Sort of like going on a tour of Vietnam with an American soldier—a thousand years from now!

When we climb up the last ladder to go back to our cars, the guide stays behind to pray. We have "taken" from nature, from the ancestors, from the ruins, and he wants to give back on behalf of us all. He expresses a fear that perhaps he shouldn't tell all that he does. Perhaps he should keep the ruins' secrets.

His prayers are very moving. No matter how secular the context, there is some connection in every Indian we have met that makes him responsive to his responsibilities as a human being inhabiting the earth, and partaking of the treasures of his Mother.

Now we are ready to head for the pièce de résistance of ancient southwestern Indian culture—Chaco Canyon.

I have been thinking about Chaco for years, but I never got there. I know in advance that it will be a very powerful place.

"With your passion for ruins and petroglyphs and early Indian cultures, this is going to be heaven for you," Paul says.

I have come to understand the nature of the fascination. I have a deep longing to know where all of this—all of life—comes from. I have a fascination, too, with the history of my own family. I went to Russia on a bus to track it down. I have an insatiable appetite for minute details from a life now gone. I need to see things contextually. And, I feel, the farther back you go, the closer you get to THE SOURCE. What is sacred about life? What is essential? Why did people decorate items that they used for survival only? What did people worship and pray to? What did they pray for? How did the human imagination use the natural world? What made us what we are today? What made me? I can't understand NOW if I can't understand THEN. Sometimes I actually implore people to speak to their grandparents while the information is still alive. Once the bearers of the information are gone, you can no longer retrieve it. And who you are is directly related to where you come from.

So here we are, staring at Chaco Canyon on a map. It's a three-hour drive away, and it's already 6 P.M. There are no facilities at Chaco, so you have to camp. The access into the canyon is a twenty-nine-mile dirt road that flash floods make impassable. We drive through a "Bound for Glory" dust storm, and now ominous storm clouds hang overhead. It is already raining.

"What do you want to do now?" Paul asks. "Head for Santa Fe and hope we can return another time?"

I hesitate for a fraction of a second. Fear buzzes around me like a fly, and I swat it away. Faced with dark, rain, lightning, storm, and camping for the first time in my life, I decide to forge ahead. Once again, some things are more important than my feelings of trepidation. I HAVE to see Chaco.

When we arrive, the day's light is fading. The canyon is spectacular—massive red rocks, majestic cliffs, powerful rock formations. We ride along, and then the light goes out completely. I decide, once again,

NOT to be afraid. We have to set up a tent in the blackness. One of the sides is missing a peg, and the tent keeps flying away. We make a fire and heat some water for our freeze-dried meal, but we have no light, so we have to eat in the dark, guessing at what we are swallowing. We have one bottle of wine, and we down it. Now nothing bothers us.

"Try to sleep," Paul advises me. "I know it will be difficult for you, but give it a shot."

I immediately fall into a deep sleep while Paul spends the whole night awake, unable to get comfortable. So much for expectations.

After an hour or so, I get up and feel Paul's restlessness. Marriage connects us even in our sleep. We look at the stars through our tent flap, and when I next awake, it is early morning. We get in our car and set off for the different excavated sites.

The first one stops us cold. It's like a city-state. A seat of government. The kivas are enormous. Big gaping holes with mysterious slabs of stone and rectangular boxes inside. The buildings are very long, facing a central Plaza, almost Mexican in look. The beams are still in place. The windows are perfectly square. The corners of the building are worked perfectly. The brickwork is masterful, incredible. There are four different styles and the most proficient is perfectly squared brick veneer over a thick mortar and rock center. All of this was accomplished without the aid of metal tools!

The organization of the village is not haphazard as all the others we have seen seemed to be. It is laid out according to a blueprint. The roads are perfectly straight—all fifty miles of them leading in and out. One cannot help but think of Rome! And, in the Indian world, it calls up images of Hopiland in Arizona—the long, attached buildings, the square kivas. More than that, it suggests the *energy* one feels at Hopi, especially at Walpi. And it reeks of the internal politics and bickering that threaten, even today, to bring Hopi down! Hopi is powerful, but this is majestic! You can almost feel statesmen walking down the paths. It completely takes my breath away. This was the hub of a vast network. It makes me rethink everything I thought before.

In fact, from the moment we set foot here, Chaco turns around everything we thought we knew from visiting all the other ruins. Finally, we believed we had a handle on Anasazi caves, and then along comes Chaco! I guess that's how life is. Just when you think you know how things are is when you learn that you don't. It's nature's way of keeping your mind and heart questioning and alive.

There is much speculation about the fifty miles of roads leading into and out of Chaco Canyon. They are startlingly straight, and about thirty feet wide. There are remnants of shrines along the way, and vestiges of ramps and steps. What were these roads for? Were they the paths of pilgrimages? Did the early Indians reenact their origination myths as they walked along them? Were they trade routes? If so, why were they so large, and so straight? There were no conveyances and no large beasts of burden.

I have a sudden flash, which has no scientific validity whatsoever, but which has a kind of "psychic" ring of truth to me. I wonder if these roads weren't used to haul trees to Chaco Canyon for use in the vast network of buildings? There is ample evidence of extensive employment of wood for beams and floors and ceilings. And, if there were sufficient trees at Chaco, they must have been depleted after a number of years. So was it possible that trees (about thirty feet long or less) were turned on their sides and dragged along these ancient routes? There must have been some early method of hauling, perhaps using slings made of yucca or other fibers, resembling rope. It's just an idea . . .

What is absolutely certain, however, is that these Chacoans were an extremely sophisticated, almost urban people. The jewelry found is lavish and exquisite. We go on to Pueblo Bonito—the most famous of the excavations. There are so many kivas it seems like a vast city. The thousand-year-old buildings are five stories high and as long as modern apartment buildings. The doorways are higher, T-shaped, beamed, beautiful. Behind the Pueblo is a mountain with a protruding rock that looked, to the ancients, as though it were going to fall. (It finally fell in the twentieth century.) The early inhabitants tried to build a rock "dam" to hold the mountain back. They constructed a highly sophisticated irrigation system. The streets have grace and majesty.

I start getting a weird feeling that all of this is very familiar. As we go to the next site, we can see actual stone steps leading to the tops of the mountains. No more tree-poles to slither up! The storage rooms are enormous and testify to rich harvest. The brickwork is impeccable. We can see the stamp of different masons. I make involuntary noises like a five-year-old kid: "Wow! Yow! Wow." This is surely the summit of the Anasazi culture. Was it linked to Mexico? To the Toltecs that mysteriously disappeared around the time that Chaco flowered?

It is time to leave. Paul has a job in Albuquerque, almost four hours away, but we cannot force ourselves to go. Paul insists that we visit the "great kiva," the largest of them all, at another site. As we approach it, I have an "experience" that grabs me and turns me inside out. I have the unmistakable feeling that I have been here before! There is a small cluster of houses nearby, and a pamphlet explains that this is where the first settlers came, and built pit-houses and then standing houses. The energy from the past is palpable. Suddenly I am transported back in time.

I slowly, almost ritualistically, climb the hill leading to the great kiva. I have the impression that people came here from all around, and walking up this hill filled them with expectation. They came maybe once a year, for a huge ceremony, and it was a sort of pilgrimage. No one has to tell me this. I FEEL it. Perhaps this kiva is where the high priest performed his ceremonies, and the village nearby is inhabited by those who served him. It's possible that there were several religions at Chaco, and the one practiced in the great kiva is the oldest of them. Many of the other people did not share a belief in this religion, but they still came to the great kiva to cover their bases!

Inside the kiva, I am breathless with awe and curiosity. What are those large rectangles for? To plant corn and beans and have them grow as part of a ceremony? Yes, it is possible. To offer harvest as a sacrifice? Yes, it is possible. There is an underground passageway that leads to a higher level. Paul heads underground and tells me to follow him. Suddenly, I stop cold.

"I can't walk there, Paul."

"Why not?"

"It's for the priest."

"What are you talking about?"

"The priest. I know it. That was his passageway."

I climb around the passageway and get to the higher level. I start to feel dizzy with excitement. These are the priest's chambers and he is the Sun priest! There are four chambers for the four directions. There is no opening here to the North, as there is elsewhere. The priest looked up to the sky, following the path of the sun. He arrived here in the kiva days before the big ceremony to prepare. He prayed, he cleansed himself. It was an honor for people to come and bring things to him in his elaborate preparation. And then, when the time came, people gathered for the ceremony in the kiva below. He made a dramatic appearance, up from the underworld, through the underground passageway, as his Creation stories taught him that his ancestors first appeared on earth. The "information" comes to me as fast as I can get the words out. It's almost as though it is being channeled through me.

I stop, thinking it is over, but there is more. Suddenly I begin to run around the kiva, pointing out where things took place. Here, at Chaco, there was a council of chiefs. They came on pilgrimages to meet at Chaco. It was a center of learning as well as a spiritual center. My eyes are blazing, my breath is heavy. The information continues to pour through me, from a source I am unaware of. The stones, the walls, the very past speaks to me.

Standing in the middle of the kiva, I feel weak in the knees. It is sacred beyond words. My head is spinning. We stop at the visitors' center where I try to gobble up every "objective" piece of information about Chaco Canyon I can find. I open one book and it speaks about the possible Sun priest. It is too overwhelming. I close the book. And we head for Albuquerque. I am so overcome that for once I do not speak. I need time to process what has just happened.

Back at the *casita,* we crash out at midnight. When I get up in the morning, Paul is off to work, and I still have not spoken a word. As I gaze dreamily into my tea cup, there is a soft knock on the door. I answer it. It is Tim, the groom. He has come to see if we are okay, because they all lost sight of us after the wedding. I appreciate the asking. We sip tea together and talk. I know he would rather see Paul, but he will talk to me.

First, I show him my bear fetish. He says it is definitely the work of human hands. He holds it and says it is very powerful medicine. Then Tim glances at a newspaper and sees an article about racial tension in New York City. He gets reflective and says that Indian prophecy has predicted a lot of what is going on in the world today. The Russia scene seems to be better, but there will be a lot of trouble from that part of the world. In nature, the eruption of Mt. St. Helens was the beginning of a chain of events that will kill many people—through disasters, upheaval, disease, poverty, etc. White people will join the blacks and Indians as the new poor. The earth will take over from man, as opposed to man taking over the earth. Those who are spiritual will have a chance to start again, if they survive. There will be a great purification.

In America, there will be great race wars. The current racial unrest and tension in New York City are the tip of the iceberg. The big cities are not a place to be any longer. The black man and the white man will battle each other. The red man will retreat to the mountains.

I listen with a combination of fascination and apprehension, wondering if there is any truth in prophecy . . .

The weekend comes, and it is the time of Spanish Fiesta. The more I find out about the riches of Indian culture, the more I want someone, anyone, of Spanish origin to come out in public and affirm what happened in the past, so that the healing between the two cultures can begin. I look everywhere, but I cannot find a single human being who is willing to do it. It is a great conspiracy of denial and silence.

I suppose it is naive of me to look for answers at the Zozobra burning, but that is where I do. Although the whole Zozobra ritual is bizarre and exotic, the origins are prosaic and materialistic. It seems that sixty-six years ago, the city fathers of Santa Fe wanted to goose up the annual Spanish Fiesta and attract more tourists. They approached an artist, and he came up with the Zozobra idea. He must have taken a bit from pagan ceremonies he read about or heard about and pasted them together with a personal vision. To the 58,000 people gathered in Marcy Park, the origin of Zozobra doesn't mean beans. They are there for the kill. If, in the hidden past, the Spanish Fiesta was a harvest festival, that past is long hidden and long gone. It is now a culturally insensitive reenactment of the reconquest of Santa Fe and the Indian population by De Vargas and the Spanish.

In 1680, the Pueblos hatched a secret rebellion under the leadership of Popé, and they succeeded in throwing the Spanish out. The Spanish retreated to the El Paso, Texas, area. Twelve years later they returned, and this time they stuck—with their horses and guns and blankets and foods and shovels and hoes and Christianity.

According to the Indian historian Joe Sando, a group of Pueblo men actually *invited* the Spanish back, hoping that with their powerful European horses and weaponry they would be mighty allies against their enemies. As the Spanish cautiously reentered Santa Fe under the leadership of De Vargas, it must have been a tense time indeed, for many of the Indians were opposed to to the Spanish arrival. But acceptable terms were worked out, the Indians capitulated, and a period of (supposed) peaceful coexistence began. In truth, there were further struggles between the Indians and the Spanish as the occupying noose tightened around the indigenous neck. The Indians, harassed into conversion, went underground with their religion and there were further uprisings, but the Spanish were, by then, entrenched for good. The abuse of the Indians was, on the surface, forgiven—but not forgotten.

This complex history of domination, cruelty, rebellion, and the Indian invitation to reconcile has been buried: the Hispanic population wants to remember the reconquest as a victory. They stage parades where people dress up and masquerade as kings and queens and *conquistadores,* reenacting the taking of the city from the natives. The Indians used to participate naively in the celebration, because in government schools they only learned the "official" version of history, from the Anglo point of view. Only recently have they been exposed to the truth of their own history, and the suffering they endured. Now, when Fiesta time comes, they just try to ignore it. It is, indeed, difficult not to notice the Fiesta events. They dominate the city, and make headlines on the news and in the papers.

Perhaps it is because the Spanish themselves were later oppressed by the white population. Perhaps it is because people need an excuse to let go in public. Whatever the reason, Fiesta is a nice excuse for a drunken bacchanal. And the burning of Zozobra is one of the centerpieces of the festivities. It is disturbing that the Spanish Fiesta has thus degenerated, for, at its core, it is a deeply religious celebration. The spirit that hovers over the Fiesta is "Our Lady of the Conquest"— the oldest Madonna in the United States. Her real meaning—peace, brotherhood, and love—recedes to the background as the population gathers to see Zozobra.

As we enter Marcy Park, we are searched for booze and weapons by two good-natured city cops. This is the first time the frisking ritual is enacted, based solely upon the events of past years. Booze is banned, even though as the evening progresses we trip over the empty fifths that lie on the ground, and we smell the sweet pungency of illicit beer that is being chugged in vast quantities.

Paul and I arrive at five, before the crowds. The ground is wet, the mud is slippery, and we sit and freeze and listen to a great mariachi band and some country rock and Dixieland and we watch the huge, forty-foot puppet named Zozobra sway in the breeze on a small hill above a flight of stone steps. A sign in front of us says "Zozobra means Californians." We quickly understand that Zozobra is no Good Guy, since there is a general feeling that Californians are coming to Santa Fe in droves and driving up the price of housing, making things unaffordable for the local population. As the hours pass, more people file in. Zozobra still hangs there, doing nothing. He is an old man, dressed in white with a few bands of black and a bow tie. He has a huge red mouth and enormous, dangling arms. Paul insists Zozobra looks like a white monkey.

By dusk the park is jammed. The band plays the Doors' "Light My Fire" and the crowd likes that. They roar "Viva la Fiesta!" Slowly, teasingly, there are hints that there will be fire and the action will start. We wait. It seems like forever. Finally, children are hoisted onto their parents' shoulders and the weird action begins. We have learned by this time that Zozobra represents Old Man Gloom. And he is going to burn, baby, burn.

The following things happen: a group of young people draped in white sheets surrounds Zozobra; they flap their arms and descend the stairs. They are the Gloomies, the cohorts of Zozobra. Next, some men wave long wooden poles back and forth, and light the tips of them with fire. Then a woman in plumage does a twirling, intense dance on the stairs, up and down, down and up. Now Zozobra starts to speak. He growls and grumps. The crowd goes wild. "He's pissed. He's really pissed," the man next to me says excitedly to his young child. "Let's burn him," says the child's mother. What??? Paul and I look at each other. Now fireworks go off. They have a strobe effect. It is otherwise completely dark. The crowd gets frenzied. They start screaming out, "Burn him! Burn him!" What?? Are they going to burn the Reichstag? Is this a Jew-burning? Will it be monks? Gays? Gypsies? It gets TERRIFYING. Fifty-eight thousand people hissing and pointing and screaming louder and louder, "Burn him! Burn him!" About a puppet! Zozobra's growls get louder. The crowd goes berserk. The fireworks are flashing. We can't see anything ten feet in front of us. People start pushing forward to get close to the action. The strobe is faster. The night is darker. "Burn him! Burn him!" Someone knocks at Zozobra. His eyeball plops out. "Yay! Yay! They got his eyes!" someone calls out. Help! Get me out of here!

Then, when the crowd is apoplectic, one of the pole torches lights the puppet's eyes and they start to burn. Next the head goes up in flames. Zozobra wails. Zozobra groans. Louder. Louder. The crowd jumps up and down with glee. "Burn him! Burn him!" The body is set afire. Zozobra roars. His arms move up and down, his movable mouth chomps down on his words, he is still alive. Suddenly the fireworks form words: Viva la Fiesta. Then a huge cross starts to burn. Zozobra is burning!! The straw is aflame and his torso is a blast of fire. He hangs there, in the middle of the dark night, disintegrating in front of our eyes.

Celebrations come at all decibel levels. This week, Taos Pueblo is quietly celebrating the twentieth anniversary of the reclaiming of Blue Lake from the American government. This was a landmark case, and set a precedent for many Indian tribes to reclaim land that was taken away from them.

When Blue Lake was appropriated by the government in 1906, it wasn't just any old land. All Indian tribes have an Origination Myth, just as we have our Garden of Eden. And, like our Adam and Eve, they have ancestors from whom they sprang. For the people of Taos, Blue Lake is the place their ancestors come from, and it was a sacred place where they worshipped. It is the holy land for the Pueblo today, just as it was for the old Taos Pueblo, which probably goes back to A.D. 700 and which is today only a secluded ruin site.

To get to Blue Lake, it is a two-day trip on foot or a one-day horseback ride. It gives the Indians time to think, to meditate on the past year and on the year ahead, to do inner work as they approach their sacred spot.

One can only imagine how they felt when their Blue Lake was made public land. They could no longer perform their secret ceremonies without fear of discovery or intrusion. And the irony was not lost upon them that the reason most of the ceremonies were secret in the first place was because the non-Indian society systematically set out to destroy them.

So Taos decided not to take the appropriation of their Blue Lake lying down! For almost sixty-five years, they mobilized and fought the issue, and in 1970 Richard Nixon signed a bill returning the land to them! Imagine their joy when they return to Blue Lake now to pray and celebrate once again!

At the celebration, the Taos elders exhort the young people not to forget Blue Lake, for it is both a reality and a symbol of the Indian spirit. This is the first commemoration since 1970, and it is a big event. Indian dignitaries and government officials are flown in—everyone who helped in the fight is honored. Some are still alive, but many are dead and they can only be honored posthumously.

It is strange, but as I sit on the Plaza watching the celebration, I have a feeling that the story of the reclamation of Blue Lake will be told forever at Taos—it will become a legend, just like many other stories from the Indian past. We are watching history that will one day become part of the common mythology.

Once again, we are very fortunate. We were invited to the event by Gail White Wolf, who is from Taos Pueblo. She and I decided to write a magazine article together, so she has arranged for me to interview key religious and tribal leaders to get a feeling for the matter.

This is a very special way to come to Taos on a celebration day, but even without the entree, Taos is a special place. It is probably the most famous and most photographed Pueblo in the Southwest. Around a sandy plaza are five-story rust-colored adobe structures, with their *vigas* (wooden beams) still exposed. It's like an Indian apartment house, and the construction hearkens back to old times, for this is the way structures were built in caves on the sides of cliffs. The multi-family structure is the architectural root of a communal life—people living together and working together. Perhaps because of this communal life which has remained intact, Taos has stuck close to its traditions. The village is arguably one of the longest continually inhabited places in America. The orientation is conservative, which means there is an adherence to Old Ways.

As the festivities proceed, as the speakers get up and reminisce, as the old and young, white and Indians join hands for a two-step circular friendship dance, as the dance group widens and widens and spreads out across the Plaza, an elderly woman sits by herself, a black cloth draped around her head, weeping silently. She is Cesarita "Daisy" Romero. I blink twice, for Daisy looks, in dress, much like the Arab women I lived with in my year and a half in Morocco. And the old men around—am I dreaming? They, too, look like they emerged from the sand in Northern Africa, with cloth draped over their heads and around their chins.

Perhaps this is not an association that exists solely in my imagination. In fact, when the Spanish came as *conquistadores,* there were black people and Moors from North Africa with them. They probably brought their dress customs along with them and taught it to the Taos Indians. It is remarkable how these two cultures, the Spanish and the Indians, who have so little to do with each other today, are so deeply linked. Why can't they come to terms with what happened in the past, so they can go on into the future?

All of this I think about, as I listen, disturbed, to Daisy's soft weeping. And why is she crying? Because she is the wife of (the now-deceased) Querino Romero, the Pueblo governor at the time Taos won the Blue Lake battle. By all accounts, Romero was an extraordinary man—devoted, humble, deeply religious. And he spent much of his adult life trying to win back the sacred lake, the beautiful, pristine blue lake high in the mountains.

I spend much time with Daisy. Her skin is so soft. She holds my hand between hers and she cries warm tears on our blended hands. She begs me to write something that will keep the memory of her husband alive, for he died in 1985 and the memory is still fresh for her.

She speaks of how her husband lay awake at night, worrying, thinking about what he had to do for Blue Lake. She recalls when he went to Washington to meet with the president. He was gone for weeks, and, because she had no phone, there was no communication between them. She remembers how her children had to haul wood and make fires and she had to tend the fields and farm, because her husband was so busy with his office for so many years. As she speaks, her daughter, Crucita, a beautiful Pueblo woman, comes by to help translate and to substantiate her mother's account.

"Every day, every night, it is hard for Daisy, for she misses the man who was by her side since they married at age eighteen," says Crucita.

I cry too, and I tell Daisy I will try to come back and visit her, for she is such a soft, gentle thing.

Next we meet with Thomas Montoya and, at sixty-nine, he is just incredible. He has a dark face, eyes that positively dance, and a big bulbous nose. I start snapping pictures of him and he laughs and tells me his face is in the Tube in London. He is the "poster boy" for the English mail!

Thomas is a joy to interview, because he is a deep, reflective man. He has recently been made a very important religious leader at Taos, and he carries the office and the oath very seriously indeed. He reflects all the time on Creation, on where things come from, on what things mean. He does this so he can, in good faith, answer the questions that are put to him—and not just repeat answers by rote. I think I can say, without exaggeration, that my discussion with Thomas is remarkable. It gives me enormous insight into the man's head and heart. But, an hour later, Gail White Wolf comes to me and says that Thomas asks me NOT to publish his words. He does not think it is a good idea, given his position in the community. I send back a message that his wishes will be respected, and they will be. As much as I would like to pour it all out, I will not. A word of honor must be sacrosanct.

Thomas does tell me something that he allows me to reveal, and it is quite delightful. It has to do with the hoop dance, which is done at Indian powwows and has frequently been performed on TV because it is so spectacular and appealing. The dancer has small "hula-hoop" type rings that he spins simultaneously all over his body as he dodges and ducks and twirls to keep the hoops spinning. Thomas tells me it was his stepfather who invented the dance, and here is how it happened. He was in the woods one day and he took a blueberry branch and bent it. He saw that it made a hoop. He held it up in front of him, like a shield, and invented the swoops and swirls to imitate the motions of an Indian on horseback, ducking and hiding behind his shield in battle. The hoop was twenty-two inches wide, and the dance was done with a single hoop to a special tune. Thomas still sings the tune and dances, but the dance has become elaborate indeed as the hoops multiplied.

My next interviewee is Scott Fields. To look at him, with his light skin and ponytail, you would never know he is Indian—as is the case with many Native Americans. He is a photographer, and he has been photographing Blue Lake all of his life. Here is his Blue Lake story.

When he was young, he was raised by his grandparents. He used to watch them prepare for their journey to Blue Lake, and he would hound them with questions: What is it like? What is up there? What do you do? They promised him that he would get his answers when he was old enough to go himself.

When he was twelve, he went to Blue Lake, and it was breathtaking for him. Now, as a grown man, he continues to go every August. He has gone on horseback, but he prefers to go on foot. It is a hard, demanding journey. It gives him time to reflect on the past, and to evaluate how he can strengthen himself. When he gets to Blue Lake, he experiences serenity. Whatever else happens in the world seems minuscule to him. During the ceremonies, he experiences the whole range of human emotions. It is extremely powerful. It is also an occasion for the whole tribe to live communally once again.

Before he goes to Blue Lake each year, Scott finds that he prepares himself for days in advance, just as his grandparents used to do. He says, like all of the interviewees say, that the presence of Blue Lake is a major factor in keeping people today living at the Pueblo of Taos. He smiles. "Nintendo is here today and gone tomorrow," he says, "but Blue Lake is here to stay."

What does Blue Lake look like? We can see photos of it. But what

244

is it like to be there? I'm afraid we'll never know, since it is forever closed to us.

Another man I meet is Gilbert Suazo. Gilbert, in his silky grass-green ribbon shirt, is running and emceeing the festivities, and I have the good fortune to spend a lot of time with him afterwards. He was the young man who went to Washington twenty years ago to represent the youth of Taos. Accusations had been flying in newspapers that the Taos religion was for old people only, that it was dying away, and that the youth didn't care. Gilbert went to prove the difference. In fact, most of his young years were spent devoted to, perhaps obsessed by, the Blue Lake fight. He formed a Youth Council. He spent all of his evenings and weekends working toward the reclamation. He was employed then, as he is now, at the Los Alamos laboratories. He is currently building a proton linear accelerator. He looks and sounds like anything but a nuclear scientist!

Gilbert describes his childhood, when his father and two grandfathers were esteemed tribal councilmen. They used to speak of Blue Lake all the time, and he listened and he wanted to go to the council meetings and participate, but he was too small. It was only for adults. So strong was his desire that his father snuck him into the council chambers once or twice, and hid him under the table!

On the Plaza, on a table, under glass, for the public to read, is a two-page letter on a yellow legal pad. It was written by Gilbert, twenty years ago, and it is a kind of journal. It speaks of his meeting with Nixon. Gilbert still keeps a journal today. (Gilbert and I exchange a smile, for we both now write while we are driving, with eyes on the road, and one hand stretched onto the passenger seat, scribbling notes as traffic goes by and hoping we won't get killed as our attention wanders.)

I ask Gilbert to talk to me about Nixon. He tells me that he never expected much from him, and yet, when he met him, he became convinced that Nixon had a life-long interest in Indians and really wanted to help them. He did, in fact, sign the bill.

Gilbert has continued to fight for his people, and has learned to draft the legal documents that help in the public domain. He tells me that, as a boy, he learned from his father and grandfathers that there was another way to talk, another vocabulary and tone of voice, when dealing with serious Indian issues. He now uses that tone. I smile. Gilbert sounds like a very serious man. But then he smiles. He laughs a bit. I like him. He tells me that when his grandson was born this year, he realized that THIS was the reason he fought so hard. For future generations. I have heard that so many times from Indian people. We are not the be-all and end-all. We must not be shortsighted. We are part of a never-ending chain of life that exists across time, and what we do in the present determines the course of the future. This sense of purpose gives meaning to life.

I grow quiet, touched by a worldview that gives each human enormous responsibility and yet shrinks him down to an appropriate size in the total scheme of things.

11

Refusing a Jewel

Early to mid-September, 1991

The season is changing. At night it is cooler, it takes longer to warm up during the day, and there is a certain sleepiness to things that wasn't there in the vigorous days of summer. Suddenly the seasons change inside, too. Nagging winter thoughts like "Where am I going?" and "What am I doing with my life?" have taken the place of the carefree thoughts of sun-drenched days, days that seem to have no end. It is good to take stock. To look through the closets, to clean things out, to realize that a transition is taking place.

I feel very lucky to have met a group of Native Americans who are not only making a contribution to my life, but to the life of their communities as well. Steve Wall has been hired to study and undertake an overhaul of the Ute judicial system. It is inefficient, rife with inequities, and the local stakes are high because of the vast mineral wealth of the land. Dr. Doug White Wolf has just been named director of the cultural branch of the Very Special Arts, and he is being made consultant and adviser to every Indian cultural committee you can name. Arnold Herrera is now teaching drum-making to handicapped kids. Laura Fragua is flying to the East Coast in October to show her sculpture, as is Tim Shay. Filiberto is on a long trek, producing a documentary about Indian elders in North and South America. If Indians complain that they are the "invisible Americans," these people are all making the formerly invisible become visible. They are making major contributions to life.

Although it is no contribution to anyone's life but my own, for the first time in a long time, I actually got the chance to read a book! I chose *Songs of the Fluteplayer* by Sharman Apt Russell. It's a collection of essays by a woman who left her city life and came to settle on the (sometimes dry, sometimes flooded) riverbed of the Mimbres River in New Mexico. In a piece about the death of her father, a test pilot, she writes about a safe zone in which a test pilot can fly, called an "envelope of knowledge." I pause when I read that. I think that in my life here, among the Pueblo people, I have gone outside of the secure envelope of knowledge. Unlike her father, who crashed to his death, I am flying. This is a funny metaphor to use for someone like me, who has a horror of planes, but it is true.

I believe that I have really gone off the beaten path and am changing my life. It happens in very small ways. If I ordinarily go into a store to shop, I now go to talk to the shop owner instead, and put my concentration there. If I ordinarily say no to party invitations, I systematically say "yes." If I skip editorial pages in newspapers, I force myself to read them. Instead of always looking at *where* I am going, I am trying to look at the bumps and oddities of the path itself. And, from these small changes in attention and focus, the rest began to change. Beyond the envelope of knowledge. I really like that and feel good about it.

I wish I felt better about the TV project I was sent here to write. What should be a work of joy is complicated by so much pain. It is clear that things are not working out between Lenny and me. It creates incredible tension and I can't imagine continuing to work like this. The producers in L.A. will not discuss the situation with me and they are going through a very aggressive, defensive, power-mad, and obnoxious period. They are insulting to the Indians, perfunctory to me, and they are hovering over "their project" like witches over a brew. They are intimating that I am being difficult when I call to ask how long I will be staying here in New Mexico or I tell them the problems I am encountering here. They growl at me that I will be in New Mexico for another three or four months, and to just "go with the flow." They just got another grant for the project, based upon a treatment I wrote, and yet I do not see any of it. I have to grovel and beg for an office chair. My back is shot from sitting on a kitchen chair and typing ten hours a day. I can tell from my tone that I am angry and resentful, and I have to go inside of myself and find a way to deal with that. The bottom line is that collaborative writing sucks . . .

when it's not with the right partner or the right producers.

"Let's go away," I say to Paul, just as he is closing his eyes.

"Please, not now, I'm exhausted," he mumbles.

"Okay," I concede cheerily, "we'll go tomorrow. Let's head south."

In the morning, we pack up the car, leave northern New Mexico and head for the southwest corner of the state. Several things attract me there. One is that I have just read Sharman Russell's book about the area and it seems fascinating. Two is that the very name "Gila Wilderness" sounds so alluring. And three is that it was the home of the Mimbres Indians.

I know little about that ancient Indian culture except that the Mimbrenos' black-on-white pottery is fantastic. It is startlingly modern, with eye-dazzling abstracts and expressive, charming, varied pictures of bird and animal life. Each animal seems to have a unique personality and to leap off the pot. I know it is uncouth and greedy to want to own that pottery, but I do. I also know it is crass and even illegal to want to dig for old pots, but I do. I know that we should leave what is left of the Mimbres spirit in the earth, but I want to have a piece of it. I have no excuses for these desires, and I guess there is still a materialistic incubus that clings to this flesh and these bones. One day I won't need "pieces" of the Indian culture, but I am not that evolved yet. I hope when we are weighed on the great scale, this is not held too much against me.

We load up our camping gear—since this fearful urbanite can now negotiate slumber in the outdoors—and this time Paul goes a little overboard in the food department. We have five enormous grocery bags full of imported pastas and pâtés, exotic crackers and beans. We have tiny little packets of applesauce and fruit, and huge, bulging bags of granolas and nuts. There are jams and sauces, shrimp and lobster blends. Paul is a gourmet. He does not leave that side of him behind when we head into the wilderness.

"Come on, Paul, " I say, "we don't have to eat like this . . ."

"Fine," he says, with the hurt pride of a great chef, "I'll eat my food and you can graze on found shrubbery!"

As we leave the city, our friends in nature seem to be calling to us for attention. First it is the birds. I think I have never really *paid attention* to birds in my life. This time it is different. As we drive south, there is a small sign for a bird refuge and we turn off the road. We soon find ourselves in marshlands and every few minutes we turn off

249

the engine and just listen. Of course, I am fortunate, for I have now spent some time learning how to listen, and it has become easier. I can actually hear some things. This time, we definitely hear our friends singing to us. Perhaps other people would drive along this same unpaved road, see the swampy goo, feel the mosquitoes, and run in the other direction. But to us, this is Paradise.

We come to a grove of trees where there is actually an ORCHES-TRA of birds. We pull out the tape recorder and tape it, because we can't believe the symphony is so loud and so vibrant. There must be a thousand, thousand birds. Then a pheasant darts out of the under-brush. Ducks pop up in the muck. The birds are singing just for us— or, at least, it feels that way.

Instead of driving on, we spend the night in Socorro so that we can go to the Bosque del Apache reserve in the morning. Other cars drive in and drive out of the bird reserve, spending the time it would take to drop a letter in a mailbox. But we stay for hours, driving along at a very leisurely pace, turning off the engine, photographing a wild daisy or listening to a duck or crane. An old man comes up to me as I am wax-ing enthusiastic about the quack of a duck.

"You all will want to come back here in the winter," he says. "The place is covered with white sandhill and whooping cranes—and they're almost extinct. It looks like the earth is blanketed with snow."

"I will return," I say, and I mean it.

We then head into the mountains and start visiting small-town New Mexico. There still *is* a small-town America. An America where you stop for a cool drink and you can see the whole town from the restau-rant window. Where everyone you meet is a character. Where every-one has a story, and time is slow. Where a nearby town of two hundred is considered the big city.

We camp out the first night, but I picked up an intestinal "bug" and, after nearly wearing out the tent zipper, we pack it in and opt for mo-tels from now on.

"So much for all my planning and shopping," Paul says with good-natured resignation.

"I just want to get this straight between us, Paul," I say. "This is not a failure on my part. The reason I am not camping out has nothing whatsoever to do with fear."

"Agree."

"It's that I am extremely uncomfortable in the nether parts and I need to have a bathroom nearby."

250

"Agree again."

I am coming to accept that I am a human being with limitations. I do not have to back off from life, afraid of nearly everything, nor do I have to push myself needlessly.

Armed with Pepto Bismol, we drive on, and my greedy self is now on the prowl for signs of Mimbres life. Nothing happens. Not a bite. Not a nibble. No one comes up to me and says: "Here. Follow me. I'll give you an inside track." I am getting a little low, thinking that our days have become ordinary, and I'm hooked on the extraordinary. I am appreciative of the birds and the golden flowers, appreciative of the sun and the soft breeze, but I still want *something to happen*. One day passes, two days, we hang out and wander, and I feel disappointed. I have come all this way for nothing.

Finally, we check into a tiny motel in a minuscule village and I decide to stop looking for an adventure. It is night. I am in a small convenience store and a man comes up to me. He speaks with a very strong accent. I think he is Hispanic, but it turns out he is Aztec. He barely says hello and then suddenly he starts to tell me about the Mimbres culture, and secret places I can see petroglyphs. He tells me about a hidden place where I can even see the ruins of an ancient village. He tells me all about the pots he found, and tells me detail after detail about them, cautioning me "not to dig." This is the sign I needed.

In the morning we are up, bright and early. We drive deep into the country, park our car, and start to scale a small mountain. When we have huffed and puffed our way to the top, Paul spots the petroglyphs drawn on high rocks above our heads. Circles and animals and human forms and mysterious shapes that have no translation. Hundreds and hundreds of them. And then Paul spots a baby rattlesnake. I look around me: snakes! There must be hundreds and hundreds of them too. They are in caves, in nooks and crannies.

Ordinarily, I would run screaming from the spot, but something has happened to me and I am not afraid: I simply walk on, undaunted. Paul gapes.

"No sweat," I say. "They're just brother rattlers. I'm feeling very much in balance, and I don't think they'll bother us. The universe is in order today. There is no danger. It's all harmonious."

Paul rubs his eyes, wondering if I am the woman he married, or some masquerader.

I look up, and decide to scale the rocks to get to the mesa on top of the petroglyphs. We find a little niche and up we climb, digging our heels into the rocks for footing. We walk across a grassy plain on the mesa, and there is no sign of any life whatsoever. Not a sound. Not a breeze. Not a plane. Not a human breath. And yet, I become convinced that people lived here once. I have no idea what or who or when, but I know that this mesa was inhabited.

Despite my strong feelings about the place, if there are any ruins or any spirits around, they yield up no clues. Just grass, more grass, and rocks. Paul is getting itchy and he wants to climb down, for I am taking hours just staring at the grass. I agree to leave. And as I am hoisting my leg over the rocks to climb down, just at the moment of giving up, I find a single piece of pottery. Aha! This is it! There were humans on this mesa, hundreds or thousands of years ago!

I trek after Paul, following him down the mountain, and then, in a grassy field full of cows, I just stop. I physically cannot move on. I look down at my feet and there are dozens of pottery sherds. I stoop to touch them, to fondle them, to hold them, to feel them, to feel the life that went into them. I completely lose track of time. I guess I must be taking a long time, because I hear a loud noise and it is Paul, in the distance, literally banging on the hood of the car for me to join him. He is hungry and tired and he has no idea of what I am doing.

"Paul, stop banging!" I yell out to him. I don't want to leave this place. I close my eyes and silently pray for another sign. I have been given so much here, but still I want more. And when I open my eyes, there it is. A perfect, shimmering arrowhead. It may be volcanic glass or quartz, but whatever it is, it is perfection. Delicate. Pointed. Perfectly hewn. Orange-hued. With a hundred facets. It looks like it was carved yesterday. When I run to bring it to Paul, he stops growling and is duly impressed. He tells me to wrap it up carefully and put it in my wallet.

"Are you bored, Paul?" I ask tenderly. "You seem to want to go."

"I want to *go,* in more ways than one. I contracted your intestinal bug!"

As soon as we have attended to Paul's human limitations, I feel a passionate desire, a need, to see more of the ancient Mimbres culture. We drive to where the Aztec man told me I could find ruins. We park the car. We have to slither under low barbed wire to get to the ruins, but after Paul has slithered, I am stuck to the ground, right near our car, unable to move. There, right on the side of the road, half an inch from the asphalt, I become convinced there was an ancient Indian village.

I look down. The earth itself must have spoken to me, yielding up one of her secrets. There are hundreds and hundreds of pottery sherds all around me. Fabulous Mimbres pottery spread around my feet. Designs, pictures. Bits and pieces of a culture that makes my heart beat fast. Why is everyone driving by, oblivious? The sherds line the road, and no one is seeing them. It's something like the experience of pulling over in New Jersey to buy a Tastee Freeze and finding the ruins of an ancient civilization.

"Paul, Paul," I say excitedly. "This is it! The Mimbres people lived here. Tell me, what do you think they were like?"

"Butterfingers," he says.

"Huh?"

"A tribe of butterfingers. If you judge by the number of sherds, they just kept dropping their pottery all the time!"

Paul jokes, and I scour the ground. I find a polishing stone, which was used in the making of pottery. I pick up the broken pieces of a stone slab that was used to mix the paint. I stand on a roadside in a field of pottery. No, I never got to dig and find a pot, but I feel lucky indeed.

"In life, you ask for one thing and sometimes you don't get exactly what you ask for, but you get something else that is equally valuable," Paul says.

On the ride home, the mountains of the Gila Wilderness are splendid. The altitude is high—close to 10,000 feet—and we breathe in the freshest air imaginable. Every time we turn a bend, the panorama changes entirely. Sometimes it is forest and sometimes plains, sometimes hills and sometimes water. What a miracle this state of New Mexico is! And what good taste in real estate the Indian ancestors had!

Why can't I leave well enough alone? Why do I have to find a phone and call my answering machine? One of the calls is from my producers in Los Angeles, informing me that Lenny has finished his hunting trip and is back in Santa Fe. Although they had thought of removing Lenny from the project, they have decided against it. They are going to let Lenny work the way he wants to, at his comfort, in Santa Fe, and are going to ship me home from New Mexico. Lenny and I can collaborate by fax. At this point, I forget the birds and the sherds and the mountains and streams. I lose my balance. I scream at my answering machine, and then call Garrison Baveur. He coolly tells me that Lenny has written a letter to the producers disclaiming much of the work and blaming me for whatever went wrong.

I hear these words, and all my circuits blow. Suddenly the full force of Lenny's behavior hits me. I become absolutely drunk with despair and anger and obsessive thoughts about having to work with him in any capacity again. I am angry at the producers for controlling my life from a distance at their whim. My mind goes wild and I simply cannot help it. I cannot work with Lenny, I cannot collaborate with him, I cannot ever again be in a dysfunctional relationship with another human being. My heart hurts. I have weird physical and psychical symptoms. I panic. I can't enjoy nature. The bird songs fall on deaf ears. I'm blinded to the flowers and fields and trees. The trip home is a disaster.

Back in Santa Fe, I am miserable by day and at night I can't sleep. A question gnaws at me: if I really want to give up any and all collaboration with Lenny, am I also willing to let go of the good stuff— the insights he gives me into Indian culture?

My mind wanders to a Hopi riddle I heard that goes like this: You are walking along and a man approaches you. He offers you a fabulous jewel. The jewel could make you really wealthy. You could cash it in and buy anything you wanted. A jewel. Offered to you like that! Do you take it? Maybe you would ask questions. Where does it come from? How did you get it? Why are you giving it to me? Or maybe you wouldn't ask questions. Maybe you would just take it. Should you take it? The answer is no. You do not ask any questions and you do not take it, because if you take the jewel, it will cost you your life.

Suddenly, I know that I have the answer to my problem with Lenny. His Indian information is the jewel. But I cannot take it, because it will cost me my emotional well-being. The answer is no. No. Definitely no. Whatever I have to do, I will no longer be in a working relationship with Lenny.

I write a letter to Lenny, and fax one to my producers. Whatever happens, happens.

Three agonizing days later, my producers call and tell me I must leave New Mexico IMMEDIATELY. They don't care that our house is occupied in L.A. and we have nowhere to go. They are angry with me everywhere—up our noses, in our clothes. The archbishop and the others at the altar are wincing and shrugging and grimacing all during the service. At one point, before the flies fly toward me, I think that everyone else in the church has a bizarre nervous twitch. (2) There is no air in the tiny Pueblo church. You can breathe in religion and little else. (3) I get stuck in a row where the pew is smack against my feet and there is solid wood under the pew. There is no place to put my feet, so I have to turn them to the side, like a cartoon character. Not wanting to stand out by facing to the side when everyone else is facing the archbishop, I thus have the visible half of my body facing front and the rest facing at a right angle to my own torso. After half an hour, with no air and no feet, I say "excuse me" about twenty times to the people around me, and then I run outside, hyperventilating. I am sad to leave, because it is so gentle, so good, so soothing.

Outside, the sun is now awake and dominating the east. People are lined up on both sides of a long, long, strip of earth that leads far out into the brush beyond where the eye can see. Gail White Wolf is there with her family, and she pulls us into a spot with perfect visibility. She whispers to us that these are the races, and there are two teams, north and south. The north side is all of those who live on the north side of the Taos Pueblo river, and the south side is those who live on the opposite side. Gail's family is from the north, so we decide to root for them. Someone else says that besides Taos, only Picuris Pueblo has races like this, but they are not as good because the racers wear sneakers.

"If the people at Picuris wear sneakers, what do the runners here at Taos wear?" I whisper to Paul.

He shrugs.

We rapidly get the answer when the runners appear. Dressed in breechcloths of many colors and with many patterns, their bodies rubbed in white clay (or corn pollen) and with decorations on their chests and tiny white feathers in their hair and mixed in with the clay or pollen, the men all wear moccasins or go barefoot. A few women solicitously walk onto the dirt path and clear away sharp stones for the men, so they will not cut themselves when they run.

"Do you have a camera?" Gail asks me.

"Why?"

"Because you don't dare take pictures here. It is strictly forbidden."

My eyes become my camera, for I will have no artificial means of

for not biting my lip and putting up with the dysfunction. I calmly tell them that I am staying in Santa Fe until my lease runs out.

I hang up the phone and then I begin to panic. What if the change I've experienced here is ephemeral, and when I move back to L.A. I lose it? Losing it is tantamount to losing my life.

I walk outside the *casita*. I need a break from my own thoughts. I need to enjoy the sight of a bug crawling across my path, or the unusual pattern grass makes in the sunlight.

12

Tribal Stories

Late September to early October, 1991

Now it's getting colder. The trees have changed color, and at the ski lift, they take people up to see the world blanketed in aspen gold. Change is in the air, change is in the wind, change is in the clothes people choose to wear, the foods they eat. Without thinking, the colors get darker, the food gets warmer.

"I get itchy when a week goes by without a festival," I say to Paul. "As long as we're waiting here, let's check out some Indian doings."

"How about we check out some Anglo doings?" he counters.

We compromise and decide to go to both, knowing that they will be worlds apart. Actually, it will be good to compare the fall celebrations of the two cultures.

We start with the Anglo festivities because Paul has been cooking a lot lately, relieving me of the chore of bumbling around incompetently in the kitchen, and I feel I owe him a concession.

We go to the First Annual Chili and Wine Fest, which takes place outdoors at a small shopping mall, with proceeds going to the homeless. Some of the best restaurants in Santa Fe have little booths and serve chili tamales or chili fettuccine or even chili ice cream. For two dollars each, you can get a taste. Then, under a big tent, there is a wine tasting. For ten dollars, you can get soused. Most people we meet have opted for this possibility. The attire is *cas chic,* the racial palette is pale white to dark white, and there is a party atmosphere with lots of chitchat and general good humor.

When we arrive, it is late in the day. We sniff around, sensing immediately that we have missed the party. The food looks tired and

wilted. People are draining their glasses, rather than filling them. And we bump into an acquaintance of ours who is part of the entertainment. "Shhhh," she tells us. "Today I am Margarita. Not Meg. Remember, I am not Meg today." Paul and I rehearse it: she is not Meg. The entertainment begins: a flamenco trio with Meg, draped in dramatic stage-curtain red, singing the accompaniment. She is wonderful—full of life and gusto and with a husky voice and Spanish to die for. Everyone at the fiesta swears she has just flown in from Spain. She smiles at us during the pause between dances and whispers: "Now for us Jews, here comes another tragic song."

We have to smile. Meg from New Jersey is Margarita, Jose Greco hailed from the Bronx, and that's the way our world is. Meg is talented, she is attractive, she can pull it off: so why not? No one knows, no one cares.

When Paul has eaten his fill of chili, and slept off the effects of white wine, he makes good on his side of the bargain and we head for the Indian doings: San Geronimo's (St. Jerome's) Feast Day. It is a very important festival at Taos Pueblo, and we are there at the crack of dawn to experience the whole thing. No wonder Georgia O'Keeffe and all the artists before and after her painted the Taos area. The light is miraculous, and on this chilly morning, as the sun is yawning and stretching and waking up, it is pale yellow, and it flits erratically across the sharp adobe outlines of the Pueblo homes.

The Pueblo of Taos is world-famous for its five-story architecture. Generations ago, many of the other Pueblos probably looked like this, but today most of the houses are single-story. Taos looks like a big, indigenous apartment complex made out of earth and straw. Its sandy color, which blends with the earth and points toward the sky, has been photographed from every conceivable angle, at every season, and at every time of day. Human eyes never tire of the harmonious Indian village.

We go into the adobe church for mass, and Archbishop Sanchez, with whom we have shared mass before, and who is the most joyous, open, infectiously believing shepherd imaginable, is leading it. In the tiny balcony behind us is the chorus, and although there are hulking men and huge women, their blended voices sound as sweet as tiny children. The fresco on the altar is enchanting: a combination of the Indian sun and corn symbols, mixed with pictures of a Spanish friar and the virgin Mary and angels. Everything is perfect except: (1) Every fly in northern New Mexico decides to come for mass. Flies are

257

recording and preserving what I see. The runners of Taos are men of every age, shape and size. The youngest look like they are about four or five, and the oldest are at least octogenarians, if not more. There are a lot of beer bellies or chili bellies, and also a lot of men who are, to put it discreetly, eye candy. The oldest ones do not run, but, rather, give encouragement to the youngest ones.

Behind the men is a huge two-story shrine, with an enormous cross, all covered in golden aspen boughs. The archbishop and his contingent sit inside, presiding over the races. The racers line up in teams, and begin calling shrilly, with quasi-animal or high-pitched undulating cries (like those I've heard in North Africa), to the other half of their teams, who wait at the far end of the dirt track. The other halves of the teams call back. And then, suddenly, the relay race begins.

I have heard before about Indian runners. Runners who, in the past, ran like the wind, and could cover twenty, thirty, fifty miles a day. But reading and seeing are two different things. The men's faces are set in total determination. Their feet rotate under them as though on wheels, and their torsos fly from one end of the track to the other. The tiny entrants, instead of playing with their toy trucks, are out there running for their lives.

As each runner finishes his part of the relay, he comes past us. Some are limping, most are breathing so hard we can see their chests pumping. It is incredibly difficult to run that path barefoot or in moccasins. That's why they say this race exists at only two Pueblos, and this is the best. It is the hardest.

At the end of the race, all the men group together and dance down the dirt path where, moments before, they were running in competition. They sing that deep, low, lilting sort of prayer song that always transports me. A drum accompanies them. Women stand along the route or climb on top of the houses and throw gifts to the men— Cracker Jack boxes, candy, socks. Sometimes the gifts hit the men in the face. A few timid ones actually dance along while shielding their eyes. When the dancers have passed by all the women, they move to the south side of the Pueblo, where they continue their dance and the gifts fly at them. Little kids run after them, picking up the leftover gifts with the speed of vacuum cleaners. We run from north side to south side, across the river, to be with them. The gifts they get are blessings and these runners merit both the blessings and the gifts.

As the runners finish their dancing, I comment to the woman next to me, "Wow. Some of them are really cute." She asks me who I think is cute. I point to a tall man with long, flowing hair. She scrunches up her nose.

"Isn't he cute?" I ask.

"I don't think so," she answers.

"Why? What's wrong with him?" I ask, always the Grand Inquisitor.

"I know him and I don't care for him," she responds.

"What's wrong with him?" I ask. "Is he a drug dealer? A mass murderer?"

"No," she replies. "He's not a full-blooded Taos Indian," she says, pointing to him in dismissal.

I smile, not only at the content, but at the way she points. It is quite different from anything we non-Indians are familiar with. Here at the Pueblos, it is considered very impolite to point with the finger and to make a spectacle of yourself and whatever you are pointing at. The world is seen as harmonious, and things are not supposed to stand out—including your finger and whatever it is pointing at. So Indians point by puckering up their lips and aiming them in the desired direction. Amazingly, this subtlety actually works and I begin to try it. I pucker here and pucker there and point my lips at everything in sight for practice.

After the race, we go back to Gail's mom's house for breakfast—red chili, green chili, vegetable stew, prune/apple pie, bread pudding, turkey—and this is at 10 A.M. During the meal, Paul asks who won the race, north or south? Gail's father very matter-of-factly says, "There is no winner. It wasn't a competition. They are racing for the sun."

I have no idea of how to receive this information. It is said as naturally and casually as though he had said, "Please pass the tea." And since he offers no further explanation, I have to think about it myself. I figure that all of life is a cycle. The rain nourishes the corn, the corn nourishes people, people are made of energy and when they die they become energy again in the form of clouds, clouds give rain, and the cycle of life goes on. Sun is an essential element in this holy rhythm of life. As a matter of fact, without the sun there is no life at all. The sun does its job, and man must do his ceremonial jobs. Man must strengthen himself. Running is one way to do that. By being strong and by running, man is thanking the sun and participating in that life rhythm. He is helping the sun to perform his duties and make his long journey across the sky. That's what I guess it to mean. And that's why I suppose the runners are blessed by the people—because the runners are running FOR the people, for all people, for all of us. To thank the sun for coming up every morning and for shining and giving us life.

Ordinarily, after a pre-dawn wake-up call, we would be exhausted, but we are too interested to be tired. After our long breakfast, we go back to the Pueblo. By now there are many stands selling Indian crafts and food. I must admit that I don't like this commercial aspect to the Feast Days, but I recognize that people need to make money.

The sun is now high in the sky, and the clowns come out. They are called *koshari,* and they are painted with alternating horizontal black and white stripes. They wear dried corn husks in their hair. They are bare-chested and wear long ragtag breech cloths. At first we spot them on the top of the five-story adobe houses, clowning and pretending they are falling or pushing each other off. But it is easy to see, right off the bat, that these are no ordinary clowns. They are priests. They belong to a special society. They represent the profane part of the sacred. They give lessons and teach as they clown around. They carry with them the energy of the ancestors. They are the moral watchdogs of the community.

I must say that my first close contact with the clowns is TERRI-FYING. The clowns run through the Pueblo, exacting tribute. All of the vendors cover up their wares, for if they do not, the clowns will take them. Within moments, cloths are pulled over all the crafts and people offer up candy instead to the *koshari.* Then the *koshari* run wild through the village, and no one has any idea where they will turn up. I turn around, and they are behind me. I am walking or talking and suddenly they are there, yelling in my face. I hold on to Paul's arm.

"I am going to do something completely against my nature," I whisper to him.

"Really?"

"Yeah. I'm going to act like I'm not afraid. Fear can be smelled, and they'll get me."

"Boy, I never thought that clowns would be part of your growth," Paul whispers back to me.

I watch as a woman offers a clown a diet soda. He takes it, shakes it, then opens the can, splashing it all over her clothes. The clowns yell, bully, push people around. They ridicule the Pueblo members, and drag off officials. They make people perform dances and mock-races and do satirical takeoffs on the politics and scandals in the village. They single out the people who have done something wrong or behaved inappropriately during the past year. Supposedly, there is no reprisal, for the clowns have full license to do what they do. Their manner is harsh, demanding. They are rigorous clowns. Holy fools.

And then, for me, the worst part. The clowns start taking small children and dragging them off from their mothers. The children are in a state of mortal terror. They scream, their faces are distorted in horror. The clowns yell at the children and tell them that this is what happens if they do not behave. Then, with no mercy, the clowns dunk the children in the freezing river. I watch, aghast, as two clowns hold a kid of about six years old on a bridge, and then push him off. Some children are doused, dunked, or have their faces washed; there are varying degrees of punishment.

The children chase the clowns all over the Pueblo, frightened and yet fascinated by them. Then the clowns select one of the kids and go after him, as the other children squeal and flee in fear.

I learn, to my surprise, that the Taos parents or grandparents often ASK the clowns to get their children. Perhaps the children have been misbehaving. Perhaps they are too soft and they need toughening up. A dose of the *koshari* will certainly do it! I am sure the little offenders think twice before they act up again!

In our society this would be classified as child abuse. But here it is something else that is soaringly positive. It is part of a miraculous communal life. ALL OF THE NEEDS OF THE PEOPLE are provided for. There are ceremonies for the soul, feasts for the belly, medicine man for the ills, prayers for the crops, learnings for the heart and mind, and punishment for misbehaving that forces you to think about your deeds before you repeat them again. The clowns are the keepers of the moral keys. They go after children and they go after erring adults. There is public acknowledgment of who needs to mend his ways.

As I watch the intricate and very complete lives of the Pueblo people, I have the distinct feeling that humans are meant to live in communities. Our isolation is not healthy. In our communities, it would be impossible for clowns to make fun of specific people, because we don't even know the people around us! I would be hard pressed to recognize the foibles of my neighbor; in fact, I'm not sure I'd even recognize my actual neighbor. It's all so anonymous.

It suddenly gets very cold at Taos Pueblo and it begins to rain, but the clowns keep up their shenanigans all afternoon. They are sometimes very funny, and very bawdy. They are a natural outlet for all repression—they freely pull at their breechcloths, and point at their asses. There is a lot of bathroom humor focused around their dangling members. The more scatological it gets, the more people howl with glee.

For all their clowning, the *koshari* are enacting a myth, but we Anglos have no idea of what the myth is. We just know they are teachers, priests in breechcloths, and we accept that. We know it takes a long preparation period of prayer and planning for clowns to act so playful. I smile as I think of them as a sort of religious Ringling Brothers.

All at once, there is a change of energy at the Pueblo. This happens every time I go to a Pueblo event. Nothing is announced, but everyone suddenly breathes the same breath of anticipation. People begin to gather around for the next part of the activities. Doug and Gail White Wolf lead us up onto a roof—telling us it is a big honor to be there—and by now I run up and down the skimpy, shaky ladders with ease. Paul beams at my progress.

From the rooftop, we have a good view of a huge wooden pole, which must be eighty feet high. On top of it are a dead sheep and huge bags of food. The sheep is bleeding from the mouth from its recent slaughter. All of the clowns are now at their peak of clowning. They mock-marry a couple dragged from the crowd, they "climb" the shadow of the pole as it stretches across the Pueblo on the ground. And then, in an act of daring and skill which I cannot fathom, one of the clowns grabs on to a rope, hoists himself up on it, swings onto the pole, and slithers up it to the top. Then he balances on two pegs on top of the pole and begins to clown some more. The pole is so high that I literally feel sick to my stomach when I look at the *koshari*. It towers above the entire Pueblo, way, way above the houses. But the height doesn't seem to bother the clown. This profane priest is as comfortable on the pole as most people are on the ground. Although I watch every moment of it, I still can't understand how he slithered up there.

It is now freezing at Taos Pueblo. Everyone says it is unseasonably cold. The bare-chested clowns continue clowning, and then, when they are through, the clown on the pole cuts the ropes and releases the dead sheep and the harvest food, spreading bounty over the village. The doings on the Plaza are over. The people will eat and celebrate. Someone asks us if we want a branch of golden aspen from the ramada where the archbishop and the statue of St. Jerome were housed hours before. We take it, and cherish it, because we know it has been blessed.

We run back to Gail's parents' house to beat the cold. Now a fire is roaring in the fireplace, the house is full of people waiting to eat, and we are invited to feast again. We stuff ourselves while saying we really shouldn't, and then they permit me the honor of doing the dishes and setting the table for the next wave of people. That's right, the honor. A Pueblo holiday is the only time in my life I can tolerate being in the kitchen.

"You know," Paul announces at the table, as everyone giggles at his comic delivery, "of all the fears Judie's conquered during this magical journey—heights on a swinging bridge, a cliffside kiva ladder, the discomfort of camping, and insects almost everywhere—overcoming houseworkphobia is her most incredible accomplishment."

I shove him under the table. "Shhh. They don't know I'm phobic," I whisper.

"Of course they do," he insists, and, from their laughter, I am forced to agree.

When we leave, Gail and her mom press packages on us with *horno*-baked bread and pies. It has been a lovely, spiritually satisfying day. An Indian Feast Day.

The following day, when we are going out to dine with Marsha Keegan (a very well-known and inspired Southwestern photographer) and her husband Harmon, we glance into the back of their car and see—a branch of blessed aspen! They, too, were at Taos, where Marsha has been photographing for twenty-five years. I guess you know you've been in Santa Fe too long when you recognize blessed boughs on the rear seats of city cars!

It is good that we are able to forget ourselves at Feast Days and with friends, because on the work front there is nothing to rejoice about. There has been no news from my L.A. producers about the television project or the supposed new writing partner they are finding for me. Is this really a productive way for them to treat their main writer? They are distant and businesslike. They will not reimburse my expenses, which are due to me contractually. I put charges on my credit card and re-bill them but they do not answer my faxes. They are angry at me for staying on in Santa Fe and want me home now. I, on the other hand, cannot just give up my plans and my life and throw people out of our L.A. house at their whim. So here we are, and there they are, brooding and stewing and giving me the cold treatment. Unlike the *koshari*, there is no rhyme or reason to their punishment. Nor is there anything to gain, because they just turn me against them.

I am sorry that the producers do not tell the truth to Lenny—that they are looking for another Indian writer to replace him. They just keep telling him that the project is "on hold." Lenny and his girlfriend Livia are friendly to me, which is as I would like it to be: we cannot work together, but we remain on good terms. We are no longer intimate, but neither are we disrespectful toward each other. I do not like having knots of unresolved anger and hostile relationships in my life!

Paul's parents decide that since we are friendly with many of the Indian artists, they would like a piece of sculpture. They tell us their price range, and we think about it. When Laura Fragua drops in, I propose a commission to her. At the moment she is working in clay, and we come up with an idea: she will do a storyteller doll. Storytellers have become popular with tourists and collectors, because they are among the most "friendly" and accessible pieces of Indian art. Generally, a mother is depicted, surrounded by all the little ones, hanging on to her, crawling over her lap, tucked into her arms, and she tells them stories, passing on the oral tradition. For Paul's parents, however, there will be a twist or two: the mother will be dressed in the Feast Day clothing from Laura's pueblo (Jemez) and the "children" will be different kinds of animals, because Paul's mother loves and supports animal rights.

"Thanks for the commission," Laura says.

"Thanks for the opportunity," I say back. "For several hundred dollars my in-laws can own a fabulous piece of original work. All of you local artists are incredible. You work in clay, stone, alabaster, marble. You sculpt, paint, do bead and quill work. If I were a collector—"

She smiles at me and I smile back. We both know that when I can afford it, I will be a collector, and she will be featured in my collection.

In terms of Indian "doings" we are now coming into the winter season. Some of the Pueblos will have animal dances—deer, antelope, buffalo, elk, eagle, etc. It is hard for us Anglos to understand the Indian connection to the animals they hunt. The foundation of all life—animals, people, objects—is BREATH. It is what all living things share, and what keeps them alive. When a hunter kills an animal, he will use the meat for food, the skin for clothes, he will make a ceremony with the head, he will use parts of the animal for ornamentation. And, most of all, he will take the animal's life, the animal's breath. It is a big deal for an Indian to take breath from something or someone. It is an act that must be done in a sacred way. It is the most intimate form of sharing. It brings the hunter and the hunted very close indeed. I believe, actually, that the Indian hunter BECOMES the animal he is hunting, sharing his thoughts, his feelings, his breath. And when the good dancers dance, they become the animal they portray. They feel the animal's power, strength, grace, life. That is what makes viewing the animal dancers so moving. It is not just a representation. It is inner life.

Speaking of inner life, mine is not doing well the day I set out for Nambe Pueblo to see the elk dance at dawn. We're between two worlds and I'm feeling very unsettled. I have been anxious and worried, obsessive and agitated. After a restless sleep, I fall out of bed, hit my head on the chair, throw on some mismatched clothes, and drive off. When I arrive, there is no one there. I can see the smoke coming out of the kiva, where the men are obviously in prayer. A few Indians arrive from other Pueblos, and, in a leisurely fashion, begin to set up stands to sell their wares. The Pueblo is beautiful. The sun is just rising over the mountains, and everything is tinted in pale gold.

I decide to go for a walk, and I am immediately stopped by a man in a truck who tells me I am not welcome there. Then he drives off, leaving me in the dust of his wheels. I turn around and walk in the opposite direction. A policeman materializes and tells me I am not welcome there either. I use my sweet-timid voice, and ask if there is an elk dance. No. But there is a corn dance in four hours.

I get in my car and drive to the Sanctuary at Chimayo, because it is the holiest place I know, and I need a dose of something besides my own tortuous thoughts. I drive the mountainous roads, watching dawn spread out over the autumnal countryside. When I arrive at Chimayo, there is a little old lady sweeping out the sanctuary, and we say hello to each other. I walk into the sanctuary, where once before I felt the stations of the cross speak to me. Nothing happens. I go into the back room, where there is the pit of healing earth, but it just looks like dirt. A Spanish man comes in, and kneels to pray. I feel I should not stand there and watch him, because he is so full of faith. I leave. I climb into my car in the small parking lot and fall asleep. When I awake, it is about nine o'clock. I decide that I should move my limbs. I begin to walk into the countryside, and then it happens: the magic I am always seeking now.

I look at the red leaves, the apple trees drooping under the weight of ripe apples, the sun darting in and out of the chamiso, and it suddenly seems that the world is bountiful indeed. A small river appears before me and I get the message, as though the river is speaking directly to me: "Keep flowing. Don't be blocked up with thoughts. Don't be STUCK. The magic, the mystery, the wonder is all around you!"

I drive back to Nambe Pueblo and it is time for mass. There is always a mass at the Pueblos before the dancing begins, because, with that curious blend of Catholicism and Indian religion that is found at the Pueblos, the Feast Days are celebrations of specific saints. Archbishop Sanchez is there, and I smile as he tells the same joke he told at Taos. Am I the only Feast Day groupie who has heard it before? Everyone else laughs as though they are hearing it for the first time.

The congregants in the Pueblo church are mostly Hispanic, and I do not see very many Indians. It reminds me of how little mixing there is between the races here. It is the Feast of St. Francis, and I am touched indeed when the sermon is about exactly what I have been contemplating in nature: the connectedness of all things. Humans, animals, objects—each plays an important part in keeping harmony on earth. If you are good to the world, it will be good to you. When the sermon is over, the choir sings—off-key, with a tinny guitar.

I decide to go for the whole experience of the mass, and I follow the procession outside and around the Pueblo. At the head, the leaders are carrying statues of St. Francis, as they do with their patron saints at every Pueblo. Behind me, a woman is talking to her friend, and she sounds very miffed.

"An Indian woman I know told me she doesn't do processions. Well, I'm a cleaning woman, and that's like saying I don't do windows!" she says.

By this time it is late morning, and the Plaza has filled with people. Vendors are trying to sell jewelry, and you can smell Indian fry bread and prune pie. The tourists are getting restless because the dancers are late in starting. I smile to myself. We white people are so impatient! The dancers are praying, but we don't understand that. We want things on time, when we want them. A whole group of tourists leaves. So who is missing out?

Suddenly everyone "feels" that the dances are starting. A group of drummers come out of a low, adobe house, and the dancers follow

267

them. Their headdresses are made of three feathers, they wear love-ly Pueblo clothes, they carry spruce (for long life) and corn (for life, period). It is startling to see how young the dancers are. Some of them are toddlers, wandering after the dancers, trying to do the best they can. I think Nambe Pueblo really had its traditions smashed by the Spanish. According to some sources, there was also a persistent pe-riod of witchcraft and subsequent mysterious deaths followed by ex-ecutions of the witches. This too helped destroy the Pueblo. What I am seeing today is strong evidence of a revival movement. At first I am disappointed, because I feel it isn't "the real thing." But what is the real thing? If people have good hearts and come to it in the right way, it is the real thing.

I am also surprised to see an Indian man I have met several times leading the dance line. His name is Blue. He had no sense of Indian identity when he went to live in L.A. as a young man. He thought he was Hispanic, and he hung out with a really low-life crowd. Cut off from his roots, he fell into crime, drugs, and prison. It was less than a decade ago that he came back to Nambe and found his roots—or his "home," as he puts it. And now, the ex-druggie is leading a dance line. There is room in life for change, for all of us.

I look at the smallest of the children as they dance, and I realize how ridiculous it is for people to "play Indian." You have to be Indi-an to be Indian. It is a worldview that they get with their breast milk, just as we get ours. It is not something they are told once. It is a whole way of viewing and responding to the cosmos. It is a religion. I am glad that with everything that has been taken from Indians, that In-dianness is inviolable!

Several days later, after we finish gawking at the fabulous ascending balloons at the world-famous Albuquerque Balloon Festival, we cross the city to find Laura Fragua and Steve Wall at a big Indian arts show. They have a prime booth, their sculpture looks terrific, but they say there have only been about thirty people at the show all day, and no one is buying. I guess the depression is hitting home, and they are very upset because they live hand-to-mouth anyway, and now they can't even fill the hand.

I leave their booth to take a quick look at all the other booths, and I find something I really want to buy. Although I have seen thousands of gorgeous Indian crafts, I have bought virtually nothing since we left L.A. over five months ago. Paul has left his work in L.A. and our salaries are too low and unstable. The things we like are wildly expensive. But there is a pair of suspenders decorated with Indian beadwork that is not at all costly, and when Paul tries them on, he looks like a cross between a wrestler and a king. I try not to haggle about prices with Indians, and I am just getting ready to write a check when Laura and Steve grab me and pull me away. They glare at me and tell me NOT to buy the suspenders.

In our world, this would be acceptable and normal behavior, but our Indian friends are completely non-invasive, and it is out of character for them to tell us what to do. They have to feel pretty strongly about something. It turns out the vendor/artist is a man who pretends to be Indian, but is white. One day he says he's from Jemez, and the next day from Isleta. He is capitalizing on Indianness to make money, and he is not entitled to call himself Indian. (Many Indians look white, so it is sometimes hard to tell.) The Indians are very resentful of non-Indians who do this. They have a meager enough income, and it is siphoned off by con artists.

Here I am, dying to buy the suspenders for Paul, but I don't want to offend our friends. So I take a deep breath, control my impulse, and say I will forgo the suspenders even though I have never seen another beaded pair and I really want them. I know deep in my heart that if I give up something important in life, I will get something better as a reward.

This proves to be completely true. Virtually as soon as I arrive home, I get a call with a dinner invitation from Veronica Orr. She and her husband, Jerry Ingram, are world-class beaders. I tell the story to Veronica, she knows the man in question, and she immediately agrees to make Paul a pair of beaded suspenders herself! Much better! I'm learning all my lessons!

The next morning, we set out on a Jewish tradition, because we have been neglecting our own tribe for quite a while. Jim Terr called and invited us to a cemetery weeding. Ordinarily, I would ask a thousand questions about such a bizarre invitation, but in Indian country I have learned that when something comes in your path, say yes.

We set out for Las Vegas, New Mexico, home of the largest and oldest Jewish cemetery in the Southwest. We arrive at the burial grounds and look around us: Jews from all over have come to pull up weeds and clean the cemetery. It was vandalized a while ago, and this is an effort to take control back and make the home of the vanished ancestors look nice.

269

"Are Jews really concerned with their ancestors?" I ask a pretty, blond woman.

"Of course," she answers. "We are always looking backwards, as far as the forefathers, for advice and inspiration."

"Just like the Indians," I muse, but I don't think she hears me.

Paul immediately observes, and correctly so, that when Jews get together they discuss ailments, death, and food. As I wander from stone to stone, everyone is "kvetching," discussing the upcoming lunch, or musing on someone's demise. Paul starts digging and weeding with a frenzy, as though it were forced labor in a prison. I never pluck a weed. I start talking to a wonderful man named Marvin who is trailing an oxygen tube, and he takes me to visit a headstone he erected for himself.

"Excuse me for prying," I say, "but why would someone build his own monument?"

"I have no family left, so there is no one else to build it for me."

Everyone at the cemetery is open and chatty and smart and a character; it is all so communal that for a moment I forget I am with my tribe and think I am still with the Indians.

Then, suddenly, it is food time. Everyone puts down rakes and hoes, grabs a sandwich and chips, and blithely sits down on the tombstones to eat. It seems oddly natural for Jews to combine all of their obsessions at once!

I meet a woman named Greta, who seems to know an incredible amount about Judaism, and it turns out she is Gentile. She observes Judaism but will not convert because she believes in Jesus. I question her a bit, one thing leads to another, and she invites me to take a walk with her to the perimeter of the old ghettoized cemetery. When we arrive there, out of earshot of everyone else, she proceeds to tell me about two cosmic experiences of revelation she had—the first at the tender age of four when the sky opened up for her and the second, eight years ago, when she saw a vision of Jesus. If this came from the mouth of a blubberbrain I would laugh, but it comes from the lips of a scholarly thinker. We sit on a hillside and discuss God. Before coming to Santa Fe, I would never have entertained such a discussion, but now the hills, the sky, the cemetery itself seem to be invested with something larger than all of us, something holy and beyond words.

I quietly walk back to join the others among the tombstones. The cemetery around me is fascinating. I naively thought there were no Jews in the United States before the time my grandparents came, at the beginning of the century. But here are Jews who settled as pioneers in the Old West. Las Vegas was a railroad town, and the Jews traded and sold *shmatas* or whatever goods they had. They were buried in the nineteenth century, and their dates, down to the months and days, are recorded on their stones. One headstone is shaped like a tree, another has two hands with the outstretched fingers—the gesture Leonard Nimoy borrowed for his Mr. Spock "Star Trek" character, and which, to the non-Jewish world, now means "Live long and prosper." The chiseled names on the headstones are decidedly out of fashion—Aaron, Fanny, Moshe, Isidor. Isidor! That was my grandfather's name!

When we leave Las Vegas, there are buffalo grazing along the roadside, and we head south for the home of the well-known bead-workers Veronica Orr and Jerry Ingram. They live in a vast mobile home that is impossible to find and, much to our embarrassment, Jerry has to ride to the main road to meet us.

When we arrive in the trailer, we are stunned by the beauty of the objects inside. It is covered, wall-to-wall, with Veronica's batiks, beadwork, medicine wheels, medicine pouches, paintings, poems, Jerry's award-winning paintings and decorative quillwork. Jerry puts the porcupine quills in his mouth to soften them, chews them flat, and then applies them to hides. He makes knife and gun sheaths, shirts, horse masks, rattles, and ceremonial objects. He is a quiet and unassuming man, with tan skin and long black hair. He stands proudly next to his work as we look at it. When we compliment him profusely, he smiles.

The dinner is buffalo roast, and I am a bit reluctant to eat it because we just saw its brother on the roadside. But I close my eyes and dig in, so Veronica and Jerry are not offended. To my surprise, the buffalo is scrumptious. Although I no longer eat red meat, I scarf the buffalo down, serving after serving.

The other guests in the trailer are a blue-eyed, tawny-haired Indian man who makes moccasins, an Indian storyteller named Sashie, a black woman who has a reggae band, her Rastafarian husband, and assorted children. They all swap minority stories. Every word is interesting to me, because they are all outspoken, smart, and survivors.

"Quite a cry from a Hollywood party!" I whisper to Paul.

"Yeah, at a Hollywood party, you can't order moccasins!"

We all waddle into Veronica's room, stuffed from buffalo, and look at her bead collection. Paul and I choose a few colors for Paul's suspenders. I can't wait to see them! As we leave, everyone thanks us for coming. I realize, during the ride home, that many of our Anglo friends in Santa Fe, although they are smart and curious and friendly, have no particular interest in the Indians who live around them. I, on the other hand, wouldn't miss a visit with a Native American for anything in the world! It's like going to school without all the attendant unpleasantness.

The next day, I am sitting in a cafe with an Indian painter named Yellowtail, and I ask him why so many Indians broke with tradition and hid the fact that they were Indians.

"Survival," he says, as he sips his espresso. "Our ancestors were treated pretty brutally. So our parents didn't want us to suffer the way they did. They tried to assimilate, so no one would know they were Indian. It was just too hard."

"So how did you get back to being Indian?"

"There's something deep inside of you that's always Indian," he says. "One day, it just speaks to you."

Once again, I find a parallel between the history of the Indians in New Mexico and the history of my own tribe here. There are estimates that range from the hundreds to the thousands to the tens of thousands about how many *conversos* Jews there are in New Mexico. Even though it seems relatively safe to be a Jew here today, many of the *conversos* have not come out of hiding, and their families do not know the truth of their background. Some people think that New Mexico is dominated by them and that, in fact, many of the Hispanic people here can trace their heritage to the Jewish population of Spain.

"We think we know who we are, but life is really full of surprises," I say to Yellowtail.

"Yup," he agrees, as he chows down on a croissant.

"A lot of Jews weren't told they were Jews," I tell him, and he looks at me curiously.

"The truth comes out in the end," he says, and I concur.

In the evening, Bernie Krause, a world-famous specialist in sound, arrives in town. He was just granted the right to release the music of the Nez Perce Indians, and I start to question him about Indian drum sounds. Bernie believes that if you want to understand Indian culture, the best way to access it is through their music. It contains their history, their cosmography, their relationships to each other and the world. Although Native American music sounds repetitive and droning to the untrained Western ear, Bernie says it is full of subtle changes in rhythm, tone, intensity, and density.

To Bernie, all of music comes from nature. People who are directly connected to the earth, like the Indians, pay tribute to nature and thank nature through their music. Nature provides for them, and they make flutes to embody the sounds of reeds, gourds for the sounds of rain, and drums to capture the heartbeat of all living things.

When Bernie leaves, I languidly play back the messages on the answering machine. Suddenly I get very attentive, because there is a message to call my new friend Topgyal, a Tibetan lama I met when he was chanting in Santa Fe. I dial the number and get him on the phone fresh on the heels of a chanting concert in northern California. I am very happy to hear his voice and he is ostensibly also happy to hear mine. He is tired, and his English is even more halting, but he is obviously trying to tell me something.

"I Topgyal," he says.

"Yes," I concur, "you are Topgyal."

"And you are Judie Fein," he says, syllable by syllable.

Again, I agree.

"I take new name," he says.

"What new name?" I ask, thinking that this must be some Buddhist ritual.

"Now, I call myself Topgyal Fein!" he exults, and I can feel him beaming on the other end of the phone.

WHAAAAT?!? How lucky can I get? A lama from Tibet wants to share my name!

Lest I should be too excited, I get a dose of cold water in my face the next morning when my producers call from L.A. They inform me that they are still looking for a new writing partner for me and that they plan to move ahead with the project, but their tone is robotic and remote and very businesslike. I wonder why in the world these producers ever chose to do such a humanistic story when they don't seem to like or trust people very much.

When I hang up the phone, I feel good that I did not engage in conflict with them, and did not personalize their negativity. I feel that I am beginning to employ the "tools" I discovered here. As a friend of mine puts it, before you go on a healing journey or have therapy, you are stumbling around in the dark, bumping into furniture. After the healing process, you still bump into furniture, but the lights are on. I like that.

Another thing I like is the richness of the palette of autumn in New Mexico. Paul and I set out early in the morning for the Santa Fe ski basin, where the aspens have changed color. On this page, the experience only consumes four words—"the aspens are gold." But the experience is far, far beyond hundreds and thousands of words; it transcends normal language and goes to the language of feeling.

We drive up the mountain, and suddenly there is a burst of color, and everywhere we look, the slopes and byways are gilded. Maybe the most spectacular part is not the gold itself, but the gold *next to* whatever is contiguous. The green trees provide for comparison. Seeing a fir tree with only the top daubed in gold allows us to appreciate the way the gold crowns the tree. It makes me think: if everything is gold, there is no way to estimate its value. But if there is gold among the ordinary, it really stands out. This is the way it is in life, of course. Joy, ecstasy, bliss, peace are born of the contrast of all that is not.

When we return to the *casita*, I glance at my calendar, and realize that in less than three weeks, our house will be vacant and I will be back in Los Angeles. It's all going so quickly now that I seem to be on a countdown treadmill, and I can't stop it. The "teachings" I am receiving here are so constant and powerful that I am afraid of what will happen when they cease.

"I'll be eaten alive by fear and phobias back in L.A.," I tell Paul. "I'll have panic attacks. I'll run out of supermarkets and hyperventilate when I can't get the aisle seat at the movies."

"How about concentrating on RIGHT NOW? We're invited to a wedding at the Ghost Ranch."

I got so caught up in anticipatory anxiety that I almost forgot it.

The bride and groom are Steve and Joy LeBeouff. Steve, a Blackfeet Indian, is a potter and radio personality. As for the locus of the wedding, any respectable Georgia O'Keeffe fan knows about Ghost Ranch, where she painted and lived.

Ghost Ranch has a long "spiritual" history, to Indians, Spanish, and Anglos alike. There are myths in these hills—about red demons appearing, and a thirty-foot-long snake named Vivaron. There is even a story about a flying cow. The area is peaceful and secluded, and people come there to get in touch with nature, themselves, and the Creator. When Georgia O'Keeffe lived there, the Ghost Ranch owners protected her privacy with a large sign for tourists: "Please Do Not Ask Us About Georgia O'Keeffe."

When we arrive at the Ghost Ranch, Steve drags me over to meet Sid and Flo, so we can "talk Jewish stuff."

"I guess it's only fair," I say to Steve with a sigh as I approach Sid and Flo. "I've introduced Indians to each other about a hundred times."

It turns out that Sid and Flo are pretty knowledgeable, and Sid is a cantor of sorts. They are bubbling over with what they think are more than coincidental similarities between Indians and Jews. According to Sid, both have agrarian roots, ceremonies for the seasons and cycles of nature, prohibitions pertaining to women during menses, sweats or sacred baths.

"We'll talk after the ceremony," Sid says. "I bet we'll see even more similarities there."

We gather in a field under a tree and the wedding begins. A reverend performs the ceremony the white way, since Joy is Anglo, and then there is a Navajo elder, who gives the couple the Indian touch.

"Many Indians believe that if you get married the white way and the Indian way it will last twice as long," the Indian man next to me whispers.

It is the gray-haired Navajo elder who captivates me much more than the gentle reverend. The elder stands in the shadows of the trees and hills, waving his fan of prayer feathers over the couple. He blesses the four sacred directions and uses the four elements. A pan is brought in with hot coals (fire), cedar is thrown on the coals (earth), the smoke is fanned over the couple (air), and there is a pitcher of water that is sprinkled on the future husband and wife (water). Always, always, the sacred number four. Then a woven blanket is presented, to represent the way the man and woman must weave their life together. An elk horn is blown to the four directions, to announce and bless the marriage. The prayer feathers are waved over the guests, so that they are blessed in their good thoughts for Steve and Joy. And, as a side benefit, the guests are blessed as well. I breathe in deeply and close my eyes, for when an elder blesses you with prayer feathers as he stands in a sacred way in his sacred space, you feel lucky indeed. As the smoke wafts over the couple for purification, I can feel my own negative thoughts and emotions drifting away. And I begin to pray silently because a very holy and worshipful climate is created and I feel in tune with the universe. I hope the prayer feathers will carry my prayers too—up, up, on the wings of birds, to a place where they can be listened to. I feel myself crying, because I have never really prayed before, and the strength of the feeling overwhelms me.

After the service, in a most secular and charming way, the bride and groom ride off to the reception in a golf cart. The Navajo elder waves to them.

Before the reception, Dr. Doug White Wolf takes us for a canyon walk and shows us where to pick strong sage, which is used for ceremonial purification. Then Gail White Wolf presents Paul and me with ribbon shirts she sewed by herself! Paul's is aqua and mine is a small blue floral pattern. We have both wanted Indian ribbon shirts since we got here! And these are the real McCoy.

At the reception, Sid and Flo come running up, all excited.

"Did you see it?" Sid asks excitedly.

"See what?"

"The ceremony. How Jewish it was!"

I laugh, charmed by Flo and Sid. Sid is bubbling over.

"When the Indian elder waved his long feathers in the four directions, then up and down, it was just like what we do with the *lulav* for the holiday of *Succoth*. They carry evergreen branches—which is what our succoth are made of! And the elk whistle—it's like the ram's horn that we blow—you know, the *shofar*!"

I have to nod, for I agree. The similarities are many and very enticing to contemplate. The shawls that the men wear around their shoulders and heads at Taos Pueblo look like *talesim*— Jewish prayer shawls. Indians, like Jews, plant for six years, and on the seventh year they let their land lie fallow. An Indian elder recently told me that at his Pueblo, the secret name for God is the same as ours—Yahweh. Were we once connected and did we belong to the same tribal pool before we swam off in other directions? Are there just commonalities because we are both desert peoples with agrarian roots? All of this goes through my mind, as it goes through Sid's and Flo's minds. We have questions, but no answers.

Since we are already an hour and a half from Santa Fe, we decide to take an impulsive trip. We head north to fulfill one of Paul's boyish dreams. He wanted to ride the Cumbres-Toltec narrow-gauge steam train that leaves from Chama.

Chama is a lovely little town in northern New Mexico that is built around the railroad yard. It is kept up as a homage to railroad days gone by, and as I look at all the woods and metals and the puffs of steam and the boiling water and the water towers, I go dancing back in my mind to a simpler, slower past. The engineer cries "all aboard," and soon we are riding in a closed-in cattle car with the *click-clack* of the wheels and the long stream of white and black smoke from the engine as our traveling companions.

The highlight of the train trip is the fall colors—the golds and ambers of the countryside. And now that the gold leaves have started to fall, the earth, too, is blanketed in gold. Gold above us in the trees, gold beneath our feet, gold all around us as the penny-shaped leaves pirouette in the wind. I remember vaguely the East Coast colors of my childhood, but I never remember striking gold this way! I had never seen the earth painted this shimmering hue before I came to the Southwest.

After the train, we head north to Ignacio and the southern Ute reservation. It is odd to be in Indian country on Columbus Day. If there had been no Columbus, there would be no reservations at all. The Indians would travel the whole country lightly and freely, as they always did.

We meet a few Ute people down near a stream where we are indulging in a canned picnic. They are very helpful with information about what to see and where to go, but it gets a bit embarrassing when they suddenly turn and ask us for money.

As we pull up at a gas station, a hefty man named Cy notices my T-shirt from the bear dance of the northern Utes, which we went to a while ago. Cy has been indulging pretty heavily in beer, but he's lucid and articulate when he talks about the southern Ute bear dance. "It's kinda like a new year celebration," he says. "The bear's been hibernating all winter and now he comes back. The old patterns are left behind and now new ones are begun. Anything is possible. It's a chance for a new start."

I ask Cy about the origins of the rasp and the resonator, the haunting, primitive instrumentation of the bear dance. He smiles and tells me that the instruments imitate the growl of the bear. I smile at the homage humans pay to the animal world. Cy continues talking.

"The bear dance used to be four days and one night long, 'cause that's the amount of time it takes a bear to get used to things after hibernation—you know, he's got to shake himself off, find a mate, and get some food. Now the dance happens later in the year, but it used to be in March, 'cause that's when the bear emerged."

"What does the bear mean to the Utes?" I ask, thinking that this is one of the most intense conversations I have ever had in a gas station.

"Everything," Cy answers. "He's one of the wisest and bravest of the animals, and he carries powerful magic. The bear dance cements our friendship with the bear, and the bear will help us with our healing magic."

When he finishes talking, Cy gets in his pickup and drives off, weaving slightly down the road. In my mind, I thank him for being so open with me, and for giving me such beautiful insight into his people and their vital connection to the natural world. I think that is why people are swarming bookstores, workshops, following gurus. They are trying by any means possible to get back the vital connection that has been lost. They want to get close to anyone who has it, or a bit of it. I guess this is why I follow the Indian trail, from Apache to Chippewa, from Pueblo to Ute—looking, always looking for the connection.

We leave the southern Utes the next day and drive through countryside in Colorado that makes us gasp—the mountains of Ouray with its mineral springs, the Alpine beauty of Telluride—and it is a distinct downer when we spot the famed Shiprock in the distance and drive into Farmington, a pool of pollution and smog. "I wouldn't stay here for the world," I tell Paul, so, of course, that is where we end up. And that is where we have our next adventure.

It starts innocently enough. We are looking for the Bisti Badlands, and we drive onto some private property where we see a trailer to ask directions. The Indian man who draws us a map of the area has a fine, sure hand, and, upon questioning, we find out that he is an artist. One subject leads to another, and soon we are walking past the ubiquitous barking dogs and heading into the trailer, looking at Little River Simpson's sandpaintings. Although Navajo sandpaintings are part of healing ceremonies, and are executed on the earth by highly trained medicine men, who "erase" them when the ceremonies are over, secular versions are now executed and permanently preserved by artists. Colorful and linear, they are big favorites with tourists in gift shops.

Little River, a handsome, appealing man, sits with about thirty plastic pots of colored sand spread around him, and he makes rapid, fine lines of glue on particle board, and sprinkles sand to fill in the color. Then he blows off the excess sand and sprays fixative to hold the sand and bring out the color. Next to Little River is a pair of binoculars, and he uses them to scour the countryside to find new colors of sand.

278

He jokes that he *really* uses them to spot women in distress, so he can go and save them.

In his black felt hat with its wide brim and his even wider grin, Little River is an interesting character. When he was fourteen, he saw a man making sandpaintings at a country fair, and he spent all day watching him. He immediately started making them on his own, and he decided not to be ripped off by dealers. He found two white women who do his merchandising, and he is doing a booming business through mail orders. His paintings fetch about $600, and he quickly informs us that they sell "like water in the desert." He makes intricate sandpaintings of old men and white buffalos, and people order them from Europe and California, the South and the East. He is very tough-minded and will only pay 5 to 15 percent commission to people who hawk his works. He knows the value of his work and stands firm, refusing to be exploited by middlemen. He is his own industry, and he is proud of it. He reminds us twice that he sends blessings to that sandpainter he first learned from, although he doesn't know if he's still alive.

As we speak, his brother Clifford enters the trailer. He has just won an award for a pastel painting, and posters have been made of his work. He takes me to his trailer to see how he uses the techniques of his mother's blanket weaving to get patterns on the page. He sharpens a #2 pencil for his pencil drawings so that it is almost a weapon. The pencil drawings serve as sketches for his charcoal works. His textures are amazing. Unlike Little River, who can turn out a sandpainting in hours, Clifford's take him months. He renders the textures and tones of still-lifes, with an occasional human figure contemplating the beauties of the natural and man-made world. His female subjects come from his imagination, or from magazines. I smile inwardly as I think of these two brothers, living and working side-by-side. "I was just wasting my time, hanging out," Clifford says. "Then my brother told me to make something of my life, so I did."

We come back to Little River's trailer, and he looks out the window and laughs aloud as he works. "If I weren't selling art to white folks, I'd be out there painting on rocks," he says. It's true. I can close my eyes and imagine him painting petroglyphs.

Another brother appears (there are eight Simpson brothers), and he has a woman friend with him. Her husband has just died, and she's trying to keep her sanity by making sandpaintings on little plaster jewelry boxes. When she finishes them, she takes them into Farmington to sell them. We start to talk. We tell her we recently went to the Tim Shay–Wilma Mariano Navajo wedding and show her the photos. It turns out she knows the family, and is a relative. This makes for intimacy, so now the conversation gets a notch deeper. Little River shows us a favorite pot of sand. He says it comes from the Reverend's parking space. The Reverend doesn't approve of Little River's Indian art, and calls it voodoo. But Little River gets the last laugh by using the Reverend's sand to produce the scorned art.

Out of the blue, we start talking about healing ceremonies. The woman friend says she saw a cripple cured by a medicine man. The medicine man made a sandpainting, and the ill man sat in it. He was cured in body, mind, and spirit. It took one and a half years after the ceremony for the healing to be complete, for healing is a process. The ceremony was very costly, paid for by the crippled man's family and relatives. "Healing works faster for white people," the woman friend muses. "I don't know why. It just works that way." Little River laughs and makes a joke about the speedy white rhythm.

After many hours, we have to leave. We spend a few minutes looking at a sandpainting of a fire dancer. The woman tells us a bit about the fire dance—it is part of healing ceremonies, and is performed around a huge bonfire at night. Little River gives me a gift of a stone with a gorgeous vein of turquoise running through it. He signs it and hands it to me, giving, giving, like all our Indian friends. Then he smiles his toothy grin at us: "Hey, if you guys ever get lost again anywhere, just send me a smoke signal and I'll help you out. Of course, if I'm sleeping or there's a lot of pollution in the air, I won't be much help at all!" He laughs again. Laughs and works, very aware that he must keep up with his mail orders.

We head for the Bisti Badlands, where exotic, suggestive, multi-toned formations (called hoodoos) made of shale, sandstone, and coal rise out of the earth. We wander around inside these forms, finding gorgeous autumn-toned stones and petrified wood. There is no one else around. It's a lunar landscape, and we expect a spaceship to land at any moment.

After Bisti, we decide to check out the gallery where Little River and Clifford show in Farmington. The gallery owner is new to the business and he tells us that the older dealers, who rip off the Indians, are trying to run him out of town for being fair. Little River coincidentally walks in and we have a little reunion. We only spent several hours with him and his family in his trailer, but we are already like old friends.

"You guys passed the sniff test," Little River comments.

It is getting late now, and we head for the Aztec Indian ruins. We are amazed at the personality of each ruin, and how different they all are. This is a ruin in the Chaco style, but with the later additions of the Mesa Verde people. Many of the rooms are intact, and the ceilings are surprisingly high—maybe twelve to fifteen feet. There is a well-preserved reed-blind on one of the windows, as well-made and durable as our mini-blinds and Venetians. We can still see the T-shaped doorways, and the room that is a refuse heap. It is late in the day and the light is perfect, magical. When we stand in the doorway of a room, we can see all the rooms line up in front of us. They seem to extend to infinity.

Aztec is the only ruin in North America that has a fully restored and reconstructed grand kiva. The size is stupendous. The shape is round. Inside, there is a long plaster bench all around the circumference. In the center of the circle, there are huge columns and big square plaster vats on the ground. When I press a button, soft, subtle drumming fills the space. There is a row of ceremonial or waiting chambers between the outer and inner walls. For a moment it seems that we are in the ancient civilizations of Mexico—the size and shapes and scale suggest that more than most Indian ruins.

It is almost sunset. On the way out of the town of Aztec, which is largely a polluted pit, there is a shop that draws me. Bruce is the very polite and knowledgeable white owner. He never goes to Indian ceremonies unless urged and invited, but he knows a lot about Navajo culture. The store is like a museum of one-of-a-kind objects. Bruce is extremely respectful. When I tell him about finding a bear fetish, he immediately presents me with a gift—two small hide medicine pouches from medicine men to house the bear. I open the medicine bundles carefully, slowly untying the hide ties. Inside is the powdered hematite that Indian men use to paint themselves during ceremonies. I can't believe it! I just keep getting gifts that are overwhelming.

Bruce looks me in the eyes and tells me that there is a reason all of this is happening to me in Indian country. I am meant to be here; it is here that I am in tune. He tells me a story of his own. A few years ago he had the best retail day of his life. He was glowing. An Indian man came into his store with some jewelry to pawn, and Bruce was attracted to and purchased a silver bracelet with a square piece of

281

turquoise on it. He paid $50 for the bracelet, and the Indian man collected his money and left. When Bruce was alone, he slipped the bracelet on his own arm. As he did so, he noticed a signature on the back. Upon inspection, he realized that the signature was his own father's! His dad was a trader in the 1930s and this was the very bracelet he chose to wear.

"Yeah," says Bruce, "when you're on the path, interesting things happen to you."

"And . . . you think I'm really on the path?" I ask. "How do you know for sure?"

Bruce just laughs. To him it seems so obvious.

Just as we are getting ready to leave Bruce's shop, I notice a set of dancers' wands from a Navajo fire dance and I have never seen anything like them in a store before. Bruce holds out the long wands with (multi-colored) painted geometric shapes, decorated with flowing ribbons and topped by a bird. They must be about four feet long. He tells me that they could use a good home, that they can't be "contained," they must be hung facing east, and I must honor them by feeding them arrowheads. It has taken me this long to begin to understand how to feed my other objects with cornmeal, but I have no idea how to feed the wands arrowheads! I tell Bruce I only found one arrowhead, a notched beauty. He smiles, tells me it's a female arrowhead, and says it will do. I no longer question what people tell me. I just listen. Somehow I will figure out what it means to "feed" arrowheads to dance wands.

When I pay and ask Bruce to package the wands for me, he clucks his head disapprovingly. These wands cannot be wrapped in anything, and he refuses to let me carry them in newspaper. Ceremonial objects are invested with power and prayers, and they must be treated the right way if they are to retain those properties. If anything, a Navajo blanket or natural-fiber wrap will do as a wrap for wands. I shrug. I have nothing. I carry the delicate wands in my hands. I muse that I know nothing about the fire dance, but I smile at the coincidence. I was just shown my first picture of a fire dancer a few hours ago, in Little River's trailer. I guess I am meant to own these wands. And time will reveal more to me about the ceremony. Whatever I need to know.

Why do I keep getting gifts? And why do I have wonderful experiences in places like Farmington and Aztec, which I would ordinarily avoid? "Look beyond the ordinary, and don't judge what seems worthless at first." These are my learnings in Indian country. Wonderful adventures are all around us, with people who are right under our noses! We don't have to go searching and we don't have to go to Indian country or any other country; we just have to shift our attention, to pay attention to what is already there.

We head toward Santa Fe, and drive for several hours. Dusk is setting, and the pollution provides a red/orange sunset glow. Many hours ago, we asked the Farmington gallery owner where to gather sage, and he told us about a place just south of a trading post. Miraculously, we are now at the spot. There is barely enough light to see, but just enough to reveal the sage, exactly where the gallery owner said it would be. We pluck the sage, and then, as we take the last sprig, the light fails. It is a miracle of timing.

13

Under the Gun

Mid- to late October, 1991

It's three o'clock in the afternoon, and I am feeling anxious. I have not heard a word from my producers, I have given up all other work opportunities to write this TV show and now I have no source of income, we are moving back to L.A., there are a thousand moving arrangements, and all of this keeps going around and around in my head, driving me nuts.

I forgot what an formidable adversary fear is. I thought I was past these prolonged spasms of angst and worry.

"Why don't you use your bear fetish?" Paul asks me. "It helps with healing."

I draw a hot bath, and sink into it, taking my bear fetish with me. I clutch it to my body, and try to draw strength from it. I know that, in the distant past, it helped the Indian who carved it, and I hope it will now help me.

Pretty soon, I stop projecting into the future, and start thinking about the bear fetish and healing. I find it strange that all of the other cultures I encounter have provisions for healing, and the magic of healing is a basic need and desire. Our culture puts its emphasis on all the material accomplishments, but the soothing of the soul is never sought, never mentioned, and, worse, those who seek it are ridiculed and pushed into the margins. I guess that is why I have always been drawn to marginal people. We seem to share common concerns. We all, as humans, have a choice of where to put our attention; I, as an individual human, fall into step with others who put growth and wholeness ahead of all other gains. I am attracted to ceremonies and rituals that enact the healing magic. As I sit in the tub, I realize that I am performing a kind of ritual bath, and I begin to feel better.

As I step out of the bath, Jim Kee comes to the house. He is a Cherokee Indian, and his past is strewn with broken marriages and abandoned children. He has been on a drunk for weeks, and he is trying to hide it. He tells me about all his other friends who are drinking. He avoids looking me in the eyes, because he knows I know he is lying.

We are both relieved when he changes the subject and begins to talk about his spiritual life. He has tried Buddhist meditation, yoga, the church, lucid dreaming, prayer, long walks alone in the desert. He says he tries to keep his life in line with the Creator. I look at Jim Kee with his sunken, pained eyes and realize it is not coincidental that the people who have suffered the most are often the true seekers. It is as though life sets these vulnerable people on a path out of their pain, and this path often leads to discovery. I mention this reflection to Jim.

"Yeah," he says, "there is real learning in hardship. Sometimes if you wait out the pain, you get something unexpected and pretty spectacular."

"How do you wait out pain?" I ask.

"You just look at it from the outside. You watch yourself suffering, as though you were at the movies."

"Every Native American I've met is a philosopher!" I exclaim, delighted at Jim's lucidity, even through a haze of alcohol.

"Maybe every philosopher is a Native American," he quips. Or is he serious?

The following day, I have a chance to test out Jim's ideas about pain. I am at the gym, and I lift a big, pancake-shaped 25-pound weight to place it on a machine. Somehow the weight slips through my fingers and falls on my toes, crushing them. Maybe they are broken, maybe the bones are only bruised. I immediately distance myself from the pain, and observe it happening. I see myself crumpled up on the floor of the gym, and I watch as someone brings me an ice-pack. I watch my foot elevating and look at myself in pain. I try hard to be objective, and Jim's words ring in my ears.

"I admire your courage," a man at the gym says to me.

Me courageous? The biggest coward in the world!

"When you are inside of subjective pain, it is unbearable. When you step out of it, it can be borne," I say.

The man looks at me, having no idea of what I am talking about. I guess part of being a good philosopher is knowing who you are talking to.

At night, Paul comes back from Albuquerque and says he has a few voice-over jobs lined up there.

"Well," I muse, "you'd better hurry and finish them all up before we leave for L.A."

Paul grins. "Maybe we should just stay here in Santa Fe through the New Year."

"WHAAAAT?" I bellow. "The rent in Santa Fe is no longer being paid by my dear producers and ditto for our car rental. We have to be out of our *casita* in a week and we have nowhere to live. Plus we would have to pay rent here and a mortgage in Los Angeles and we can't do that. I thought we were renting a van to drive home. I'm ready to send out change-of-address notices to the post office and to all of our subscriptions."

Paul just smiles enigmatically. "Let's trust things. Whatever is supposed to happen will happen. If we are supposed to go, we will go. If we are supposed to stay, we will stay." I sigh, balk, and then agree. Here we are, a week away from a major move, and we have no idea if we are coming or going, quite literally. This is totally unlike anything we have ever done—we usually decide, plan, and execute. Now we are just suspended in limboland.

"Whether we go or stay, we should make the most of every second we have here," I muse aloud.

"Great idea!" Paul exults. "That's real progress in your thinking and I love you for it!"

"Let's go to La Cieneguilla," I suggest. "I've heard there are lots of unexplored Indian petroglyphs there."

"Do you have any idea of where, exactly, the petroglyphs are?" Paul asks.

"No, but I'll find them," I announce with absolute certainty.

We head out into the countryside, about ten minutes from Santa Fe. I find a dry river bed and and begin to apply my guesswork routine. It goes like this: this river bed once had plentiful drinking water. It was probably also a watering hole for animals, and if there were animals, the hunting was plentiful. There are hills, for visibility and protection against invasion. Now, if I were an Indian, hundreds or thousands of years ago, where would I have lived and drawn petroglyphs? This simplistic reasoning, which seems so rudimentary, actually works.

I pick a spot that looks just right, we get out of the car, and I think

286

Under the Gun

I see some rock drawings from the road. When people are searching for petroglyphs, their eyes often deceive them, because reflections and odd natural markings can look like rock art from a distance. But I decide to trust my hunch.

We find a place where we can easily cross the river bed and we end up in front of a very forbidding barbed-wire fence. This does not stop us so, tucking my injured toes under me, we slide under the fence. By this time I am covered with cactus thorns and about a thousand burrs, and I laugh when I think of how the old Judie would have recoiled in horror.

We climb up the hills and there, wonder of wonders, is an entire world of petroglyphs carved into the rocks.

"You were right!" Paul declares, amazed.

"Of course I was right. I was just being logical!"

I have never before seen so many petroglyphs in an unmarked area . . . and they all look so familiar from our treks and wanderings! First, there are recognizable shapes of humans dancing with *tabletas* and corn husks on their heads, and carrying branches in their arms. They look just like the Pueblo dancers we see today, so there is no doubt that they are ancestors. Then there are many, many Kokopelli figures—the hump-backed flute player, half-man and half-God, trickster and fertility symbol, that is so omnipresent in rock art. There are deer and elk and spirals and river serpents and saw-tooth designs and enigmatic dancing figures and one fish! It is very exciting to be alone in the hills of La Cieneguilla and have this sense of discovery. It is awesome to think that we have seen the very same markings as far away as Utah and Colorado and to know that these are the same people.

We climb over the rocks (me being mildly skittish about snakes, and particularly rattlesnakes) and come to the top of the mesa. It is completely uninhabited but as my heels sink into the earth I have no doubt whatsoever that there are buried pit houses or stone houses beneath our feet. We look around us. In the distance we can see the houses of La Cieneguilla, which look like pieces on a Monopoly board. To the right of us the mountains rise, with that curious New Mexican "shadow" quality. It is as though one ridge of mountains is real and then there is another shadowy ridge behind it and it becomes hard to tell which is real or if all are real or if they are transparent mountains. It is mysterious and disorienting.

We climb down from the mesa top and continue our petroglyph

search. We follow an old Indian trail, and it is extremely exciting to walk the walk that the old petroglyph-makers walked. Everywhere around us are these drawings, large, small, ultimately unknowable. When we speak, it is only to speculate on why the drawings were done and by whom. Were they done casually? Part of ceremonies? Did elders do them? Kids? Do they tell stories? Do they retell the intricate paths of early migrations? Are they clan markings? Do they depict scenes from the lives of the Indian ancestors—like ceremonies and dances and animals they hunted? If so, what do the symbolic forms mean? Is it a coincidence that they are facing east?

After several hours of walking and looking and pondering, we start to climb down from the hills.

"Uh-oh," Paul says under his breath. Then he points with his lips, as our Indian friends do, and I look in the direction he is indicating. A truck has pulled up at the bottom of the hill, and a young Hispanic man is standing there. Behind his back, I can see that he is holding a gun. My blood congeals.

"Hello," the man calls up to us, "having fun?"

"Paul, we are trespassing on private land! He's going to kill us!" I whisper.

"Act dumb. Just act like a ditz," he tells me.

I try to remember how a ditz acts. I don't know any. I've only seen them in movies and on television.

"Uh . . . hi!" I say, with a silly grin. "We were just out walking."

"See anything?" the Hispanic man asks me.

"Oh, yes," I coo. "There are all these rock pictures up in the hills."

"Reeeeallly?" the man drawls. "Isn't that interesting!"

We wait. He waits. We stare at each other.

"Do you folks think I might be from this area?" he asks.

We shrug innocently.

"Do you think people might be watching you as you trespass in these hills?"

We shrug again.

"Well," the man says, "for your information, the whole town knows you are here. There is a telephone relay and every person who saw you climbing up in the hills made a call and that's how I knew you are here."

Paul and I exchange nervous sidelong glances.

"We keep a close watch on these petroglyphs because this is OUR

LAND," he says, and the veins on his forehead are standing out.

I start making my will in my head. Who will I leave my books to? My *shmatas?*

The man swoops down and picks up a handful of dirt, speaking in Spanish.

"Leave the land in peace. *Deja la tierra en paz.* This is our land. My ancestors lived here. We don't want people trashing these petroglyphs. And we don't want developers here. There's a white man who is trying to build 350 tract homes right in front of these petroglyphs. He doesn't know who he is dealing with when he provokes us!"

He suddenly brandishes a 12-gauge shotgun which he has been concealing. He grabs it close to his heart and says that if push comes to shove, this is how he will defend his land, the ruins, and the petroglyphs from encroachment. "This is my land, my land," he tells us vehemently.

His voice bellows and resonates. I am about to turn, run, and hotfoot it out of there, when it strikes me: This man isn't a lunatic. He isn't violent. He is concerned, passionate.

"What's your name?" I ask him.

"Joseph Villegas," he answers proudly. "My Spanish name is Jose."

"Joseph, you're Hispanic. Why are you so concerned about saving the Indian petroglyphs from destruction?"

"Por los niños," he answers with no hesitation. "It is for the children, for future generations. When this goes, it goes forever."

Of course I lose no time in asking Joseph about Hispanic accountability for what happened to the Indians, but he skirts the issue. He speaks about his heritage, and how the Spanish have lived here since the 1600s. He wants to preserve old Indian and Spanish sites.

"But didn't the Spanish drive out the Indians and then settle on their land?"

Joseph is spared the task of answering me because his wife Casita (Cathy) drives up with two beautiful children. She, too, has been watching, and she knew her husband was with gringos (or the local variant "gringadas," which Joseph translates as the equivalent of "yuppie"). He was gone for a long time, and she became nervous that he might have been hurt. We end up talking and hugging (Joseph initiates this) and reassuring them that we are not out to harm them. They reciprocate by inviting us back to their home for dinner.

Their home is an adobe that they built themselves. For years they lived in a living room/kitchen while they built it, but now they have two bedrooms and a beautifully beamed house that took five men to hoist the timber. Cathy's brother is a mason, so the wall of the family room is a gorgeous arrangement of adobes surrounded by *nichos* and a swooping arch.

In the middle of the living room is a mass of files and papers—seven unheralded years of Joseph's life that he has devoted to the petroglyphs. He has documented 4500 of them! They are catalogued, photographed, mapped. He has letters from the Museum of Natural History in New York, explaining all the relics that were taken from early (circa 1915) excavations near the site. He has correspondence from the government, stacks of letters he wrote to them in his efforts to preserve the land and declare it a national historical monument. And he has become a self-taught archeologist, digging, interviewing.

"Come," he says. "I will show you a secret."

He takes us to an unknown Indian ruin site, where the oldest Pueblo in the area once was. He tells us that when the Indians revolted against the Spanish in 1680, there was much bloodshed at this site, and the Indians never returned. They went to live in Laguna—the very Pueblo that Lenny is from! And, trusting us, he shows us photos and documents that no one has seen, because he is afraid they will all be taken out of his hands.

"This is our land, my land," Joseph repeats, shaking with vehemence.

Over dinner, we discuss how strongly Hispanic people feel about their ties to the land. This ancient Latino bonding with the earth has been corrupted into the modern barrio "turf wars."

Paul and Joseph and Cathy and their kids (Joe-Joe and Candy) are talking and eating and I look around me and decide then and there that I have to help Joseph and his local organization to preserve the petroglyphs from development and encroachment. Is this, I wonder, the reason that I have been SO DRAWN to petroglyphs? Am I supposed to help out? The last time I became obsessed with something, it is was my grandmother's natal village in Russia. I went there by bus, I interviewed every survivor I could find, and after ten years of chasing it down, I met Paul and found out that his ancestors come from the same village! Something was pulling me toward that village, as something is pulling me now.

I wonder what I can do to help.

"Joseph," I ask, "do you know any Indians?"

"No," he answers.

"Do any Indians know what you are doing to preserve their heritage?"

"No," he answers again, shaking his head from left to right. "That's just the way it is."

In New Mexico, the "way it is" means that the Hispanic, Anglo and Indian cultures co-exist, but have little to do with each other. Joseph has written letters to the head of the all-Pueblo council, but got no response. I am sure his letters were the proverbial farts in the blizzard of issues and matters to be dealt with.

"Joseph, I have an idea."

"Sure, shoot."

"How about we plan an event where Indians and Hispanic people will come together for a common cause—to save the petroglyphs? Not only will it bridge the separation between your peoples, but it will raise public consciousness about the plight of the petroglyphs."

Joseph squints and looks at me like I'm crazy.

"You have to understand something, Joseph. I have been walking around here with a terrible anti-Spanish bias because of what was done to the Indians and the fact that everyone denies it. But it's time to heal and to get the two cultures together. If these petroglyphs fall under the bulldozer, you *all* stand to lose—your culture, your history, a way of life . . . and your land."

Joseph thinks for about two seconds and then beams. "Let's go for it!" he says.

I pick up the phone and call up Doug White Wolf, because he is influential in the Indian community and can be of help. I talk to him for a few minutes and then tell him I am going to put a Hispanic man from La Cieneguilla on the phone. Joseph's eyes grow wide with apprehension. He takes the phone, and his tone becomes stiff and formal.

"Hello, sir. My name is Joseph Villegas. Pleased to hear your voice, sir."

They talk for a few moments and then Joseph hangs up.

"Is that the first time you've ever had a conversation with an Indian?" I ask him.

He nods.

"Okay, dude, now loosen up. Indians are funny and crazy and wild, just like you are!"

Joseph grins. I call Arnold Herrera, the Cochiti composer and drummer, and put him on the phone with Joseph.

"Uh . . . hi, there," Joseph says, trying to relax and be natural.

The vision of what we should do is clear, and I do not hesitate for a moment. I tell Joseph that we should spend our time mobilizing Indian and Hispanic entertainers—and this should be a party. A petroglyph party. Paul will cover the event for the newspaper.

Joseph's eyes bulge with excitement.

"This will be the first time Indians and Hispanics have gotten together like this," he says.

"Yup," I concur.

"Let's go for it!" we both exclaim, laughing.

We both know that this is going to be difficult. There is much hostility in the air of Santa Fe. The Indians resent the Spaniards because of their colonial murders and takeovers, and the Hispanics look down on the Indians. As a matter of fact, the direct descendant of Christopher Columbus is in Santa Fe these days, and most of the Indians won't even acknowledge him.

"Discover us?!" they say scornfully. "We were here for centuries when that Columbus guy came! The Europeans were invaders!"

I watch Joseph as he continues to talk on the phone to our Indian friends. Ordinarily, in my city life, I would never have the opportunity to be in the home of someone like Joseph—our circles are just too different. He is an ex-Marine, a SWAT-team cop, a man who grew up in the *barrio* in Arizona. He has an incredibly agile mind, and when he is exposed to a new idea, he embraces it immediately.

Joseph has now warmed up, and he cradles the phone against his shoulder, waxing eloquent with great passion and fervor about the two cultures and their sites that need to be respected. He tells our Indian friends that he, like them, wants people to "leave their land in peace!"

Joseph must be striking a responsive chord when he speaks of this and "God's will in bringing us all together," because our Indian friends on the other end of the line are quite receptive and say they will help. Arnold, sight unseen, volunteers to hand-walk a letter into the Cochiti Pueblo council. Aha! It is working! The next plan is to get Joseph together with our Indian friends in person, so Indians and Hispanics can see each other face to face and form a coalition that will benefit all and protect these wonderful petroglyphs. We begin to dream and brainstorm about the public event, and how the Indian and Spanish cultures will intertwine.

Suddenly, Joseph turns to me and Paul and says, "My family and I are overwhelmed. You are like angels, sent to help us."

I gulp, flattered and touched by Joseph's words.

"I'm just sorry we'll be back in Los Angeles, and I won't be here to participate in the doings."

"Don't you get the message, girl?" Joseph coos. "You are supposed to stay in Santa Fe!"

I gulp again. Is this any way to plan a life?

After a humble and delicious dinner of potato and meat stew in a coffee sauce, green beans, and white bread, Paul gives Joseph and Cathy a little Shiatsu massage, I taunt Joseph about his 12-gauge "Betsy," and we start to leave.

"Hey," Joseph calls after us, "don't misjudge my Betsy. That's how strongly I feel about protecting my land."

We leave the Villegas house and there is a light rain that lasts about five minutes. Our Indian friends would say this rain is a blessing. We are hushed on the way home, overwhelmed ourselves by this new adventure. A few hours ago I was just saying I wanted to see the petroglyphs. A few days ago I expressed a wish to meet interesting Hispanic people, and see the hidden Indian ruins I had heard about. We got it all!

When we get home, I miraculously find a newspaper article about La Cieneguilla I had clipped out moons ago. It is wrinkled and folded, but when I open it, it is all about Joseph Villegas! This is very spooky, and it's happening just in time for the upcoming Halloween.

There is a knock on the door. It's Ronn Spencer, a friend of ours who left L.A. and has settled in Arizona.

"Here in the Southwest, you can have adventures all the time," Ronn says. "It happens when you pursue people and events and places that others would find inconsequential."

I nod, knowing exactly what he is talking about.

"Why don't you stay here a while longer?" Ronn asks.

"Because it's expensive. Because we have to go back to L.A. to find work."

"Oh . . . bullshit," Ronn says. "Here you can find a life."

We have exactly six days more at the *casita,* so it's really down to the wire. Do we stay or go? Do we choose what we already know in L.A., or hang around for more uncertainty?

I walk through the streets of Santa Fe, trying to figure out what to do, and I stop in one of the most expensive galleries of Indian art and artifacts. I hear the owner talking about stone animal fetishes. I listen closely, because I am interested, since I have my bear fetish that I found near a prehistoric cave in Utah.

"We have a small one here, and it sells for $1200," the gallery own-
er says. "These prehistoric fetishes are very rare. In all of our years
in business, we have only come across a few of these. Of course we
have no idea where they are from, and of course they are more valuable if you know the exact origin."

I do not tell them that my fetish is the real thing— rare, prehistoric,
from a known place, mine. I also do not tell them that there is no
amount of money in the world for which I would ever sell it.

I come back to the *casita,* and there are three excited messages
from Joseph Villegas. He's got his first commitments from entertainers. He asks me to help him plan the party. I return his call, reminding him again that when the party takes place, I will not be here. He
smiles.

"You just don't want to read the Divine signs," he says.

In the evening, Steve Wall, the prosecuting attorney for the Apaches, comes here with Laura Fragua, his wife. As far as they are concerned, it's a done deal. We are staying here.

"This is where everything is happening for you," Steve says. "This
is where your hearts are open."

When our guests are gone, I sit down in a big, uncomfortable chair
in the living room to think. If I had a daisy in my hand, I would be
picking petals—we stay, we don't stay, we stay, we don't stay.

Paul looks up from an article he is writing, wipes a hand across his
brow and says, "Okay, we're staying."

"But the rent is so high here. And we have to pay for a rental car.
And, and, and . . ."

He wipes his hand across his brow in the opposite direction. "Okay,
we're not staying."

"But, Paul, I want to be here to make the petroglyph party. I really
think it will make a difference."

"Okay," he says. "We'll find a way. WE ARE STAYING."

A decision is made! Voilà! Now we have to leave the *casita* and find
a cheaper place to move.

In the meantime, we are invited to see the home-under-construc-
tion of a fabulously wealthy Anglo couple from New York. The house
(called a compound and christened "Soaring Eagle" by the wife) is
built on sixty-five acres, and it is designed to combine Inca, Egyptian,
and all of the wife's past life readings. I make a crack, "What, no altar?" and she answers with a straight face, "Of course we have an altar!" A few more yards of trekking through the mud, and there it is:

a crouching jaguar Inca altar carved in stone. Every stone in the house is hand-picked and has prehistoric fossils in it. There were stones left over from the building, so they had their gardener build their own Indian ruin! The wall of the bathroom is designed with arrowheads and a reproduction petroglyph, and there is a tepee and a sweatlodge for the woman of the house. Each section of the house has a name, and the house itself is in the shape of an eagle—with two windows for the eyes. There is a terrace to watch the sunsets (with a view of three different mountain ranges) and if it is cold, there is an indoor room to watch the sunsets. There is a separate "mud room" where you take off your ski boots and coats. The headboard of the bed is designed to copy the shape of the mountain range you can see from the bedroom. Of course they hired a geomancer and a shaman has been consulted every step of the way.

The house is very "Indian," but when I tell my Indian friends about it, they turn up their noses.

"We are poor. We make our own adobe. It sounds like rich people who buy imitation everything and then lock themselves behind security gates. Money doesn't buy you Spirit."

Late at night, we sit talking with Steve Wall and Doug White Wolf about the upcoming petroglyph party.

"It makes sense for the two cultures to get together. They share an awful lot of blood," Steve says, and Doug concurs.

"Huh?" I ask, for the history and culture of New Mexico are endlessly complex and fascinating.

Both Doug and Steve think that virtually all of the Indians and Hispanics in New Mexico are mestizos. When the Spanish conquistadors came, there were no women with them. And men do what they do. They mated with the Indian women—by forced rape or complicity. There was so much mixing and matching that there is almost no pure blood left. The first women did not arrive until 1598, at the earliest, and even then, there were far fewer women than men. So the commingling continued. Most probably, the only thing that now separates the Indians from the Hispanics is which culture they identify with. Of course the Indians won't concede that this is true, because if they are part Hispanic they lose their claim to being special, to being full-blood Indians, to government benefits. And the Spanish have adopted the white attitude of looking down on Indians, so certainly they won't acknowledge it. The two cultures are very, very separate, but it's interesting to contemplate their common origins.

295

On the more mundane side, I've been pounding the pavement every day and I finally found a place to live—chez Uncle Alfie. He is seventy years old, a sometimes musician (he goes to the church, sits there and teaches himself the viola), and he has trouble with any excitement in his life. After he met us, he had to take a break from the stimulation. He couldn't even produce a lease the first day because it was too much activity after showing us around. When we met him, he was screaming into the phone receiver at a deaf friend. When we sat to chat, he squatted on the floor and rocked back and forth. He just bought his wife a Moroccan *djellabah* (robe) at a yard sale. It is old and stained with urine. He paid a dollar for it. But now he is reluctant to give it to his wife, and wants to keep it for himself, because he likes it. He drives a VW bug with no seats and sits on a milk crate behind the steering wheel to save money—"Who needs seats anyway?" He built barstools for his house out of bits of wood, and the fact that you can't sit on them doesn't bother him. He collects odds and ends and builds "things"—but he has no idea of what they are.

"Okay," I say to Paul, when we have finished looking at Uncle Alfie's strange two-bedroom house. "We'll take it."

"Fine," Paul says. "When they dig up our bodies from the basement the Eyewitness News neighbor bites will all say . . . 'Well, until that smell, we just thought Uncle Alfie was a little eccentric!' "

There is no furniture in Uncle Alfie's house. I cringe at the idea that guests will not sit, but will LIE on a mattress on the living room floor.

"Hey," Paul says cheerfully, "this is the way *most* of our fellow Americans live and who do we need to impress?—our friends accept us."

It's a long way from our life in Santa Monica.

We sign the lease with Uncle Alfie, and then we quickly shower and run off to a historic event. We have asked some of our Indian friends to come to La Cieneguilla to meet the Hispanic people there. It is the first time such a meeting has taken place. At the eleventh hour, most of the Indians cancel or are taken sick. Only Arnold Herrera and his family show up.

Joseph has called me five times this morning. He is very nervous, but he rises to the occasion.

"You have to understand," he whispers to me. "This is the FIRST TIME I ever had close contact with an Indian or had an Indian in my house."

Arnold's wife Elisa comes late, and when she opens the door to the

Villegas house she breaks into a big smile because she worked with Cathy at Sears!

For most of the day, Arnold addresses himself to me, because he knows me and it is awkward for him to address Joseph. I keep saying to myself: "My God! Five hundred years of ice are being broken here. I'm so fortunate to be witnessing it!"

At first the conversation is very political, since Joseph is a real activist. He gives Arnold a rundown on the history of hundreds of years of payoffs and scams in Santa Fe, and gets into issues of water rights and land rights and petroglyphs and all the ways the indigenous people are being ripped off. He is sure to include Arnold's Pueblo, Cochiti, where he feels the government looks the other way while hospital waste is being dumped into the river and ends up in the Pueblo drinking reservoir.

Arnold nods, listens, volunteers to show Joseph how to conduct fecal bacterial tests to prove his theories. Then Joseph takes Arnold outside and introduces him to Cathy's father. I start snapping away with my camera, because Joseph's father is picking beans in a field of desert shrubbery, and he has long flowing white hair and a beautiful, chiseled, weatherbeaten face. The two men begin to talk about beans and growing. I have to stop myself from crying. There is no talk of past hatreds and grievances. Just two men, tenderly fingering beans.

Cathy's father and Arnold give us bean pods—I have never seen this type of bean—it has almost a lima bean shape. They show us how to crack the beans in our teeth and eat the insides. I almost crack my crowns so I give up, and they gently hand me a young green bean. It is so touching, watching them bond over the beans and a common manner of eating desert food.

Next, we climb into the hills. Arnold is really amazed at the number and complexity of the petroglyphs. His eyes are very keen, and he points out to us that some are drawn upside down and some have crosses—which means they were done after the incursion of the Spanish, who brought Christianity. He points out a vague one, which I think is a mass of lines, but he shows me that it is the outline of a buffalo.

Then we climb onto the top of the mesa, and Arnold spots cholla cactus. He says this area was probably once inhabited because when humans leave houses, the vermin come and they defecate all over the place, which is a good fertilizer for cholla.

"So when you see cholla," Arnold says, "you can pretty much assume ancient peoples lived there."

Indian Time

Joseph listens wide-eyed to everything Arnold says. After another rock-climbing foray to see more petroglyphs, Joseph takes us to the tiny, unknown church on La Cieneguilla land—the *capilla* de San Antonio. He plays a tape recording of a man who used to live on the land, explaining that many years ago when he was a child, the bones of Indians used to wash down the arroyo whenever it rained. He says these bones are from a great massacre of Indians that took place here during the Pueblo Revolt of 1680. And, startlingly, he says that the Spanish *capilla* was built to commemorate those Indian deaths.

Arnold is moved. He takes off his cap as we stand in the church. The bones of his ancestors were spiritual mortar for this sanctuary! Joseph gets down on his knees for a moment in front of the altar. Arnold and Joseph share a few words about the Catholic church, and how it is a money-making business. This is why the archdiocese does not recognize this little church in La Cieneguilla; it doesn't bring in any revenue.

We go back to Joseph's house, and we are all given little packets of piñon nuts as gifts. How much like an Indian home this is—the hospitality, the gifts, the emphasis on food! Joseph's seven-year-old daughter Candy draws a picture "to honor the Indians and welcome them back to the petroglyphs."

Arnold and Joseph look at each other. They each say that they feel comfortable in the other's presence, and the dialogue should continue in the future. Aha! A success!

In a moment of silence, Arnold inquires where he can spit out his piñon nut shells. Surprisingly, Joseph holds out his hand, and insists upon taking Arnold's shells. When Arnold is gone, Joseph looks at me. His voice resonates with awe.

"I took Arnold's shells in my hand. I took his saliva and held it. It is as though we shared blood!"

Joseph and Cathy unwind after the tension of this first meeting. Then we all sit down at the table, munching on tortillas, and start to plan, in earnest, a public event with Indians and Hispanics providing joint entertainment. We are a little chagrined that we don't have enough Native American entertainers.

When I return home to Uncle Alfie's house, Tim Shay and Wilma Mariano come to visit and Tim says he will round out the show. In fact, he volunteers to open the event by making a fire and giving an Indian greeting. When you need something, it just seems to materialize!

Under the Gun

Tim leaves the house, and I feel badly because he is so smart and talented and in such dire need of money. No sooner is the door closed than a friend of mine calls from L.A. to ask if I can find him a beautiful piece of sculpture. He describes what he would like, and tells me his price. Within an hour, Tim is back at the house with a stunning piece of translucent alabaster sculpture that fits the description. His price is double what my friend wants to spend, but because he needs money, he agrees to let it go. So everyone is happy. The universe just continues to provide!

These are hectic days of getting ready to move. We get up one morning and suddenly it is snowing. While we were busy making plans, winter snuck up on us. Paul runs around outside like a kid, pointing out every snowflake, because he has been in California most of his life. Ordinarily I would bitch from the first snowflake, but I actually find the cold kind of invigorating at first blush too. I race out and buy boots and gloves and hats for us and we look like snowmen. All that is missing is the corn-cob pipes.

Soon the novelty of the snow wears off. We drive to Albuquerque and get caught in a blizzard. The freeway has turned to ice, and there is almost no visibility through the frozen windshield. Cars are stalled and abandoned all over the freeway, and a truck skids, turns around, and heads straight for us.

"Oh, my God," I think, "what have we done? Do I really want to stay here?"

Paul stops skidding long enough to read my thoughts.

"Hey, Jude, when there are so many things for us to worry about, the best course of action is not to worry at all!"

The car slides off the road and I laugh. I try to put things into perspective so they look small instead of looming large. I try to learn from my stay here to look at the BIG PICTURE and not focus on the scary details. Once again, it's all a question of where you put your focus.

I have one little disappointment as October comes to an end. The Indian people celebrate All Souls' Day, but it is a very private thing and I know I will not be invited to go. I am reluctant to miss anything, but I have to accept the fact that many things in Indian religion take place behind closed doors. Just when I have resigned myself to the non-invite, I get a call from Lenny Smallfeather's girlfriend Livia inviting us to their house.

Indian Time

Lenny Smallfeather. I have not seen my ex-partner since the last day we worked together, at the end of August. I think he is transforming All Souls' Day into a "public" celebration, because he has invited some people to his house.

"Boy," I say to Paul. "Who ever thought Lenny would invite us to All Soul's Day? It's the same old refrain. In Indian country, you never know what is going to happen. Ask for something and you get it, although not always in the form you imagined."

We celebrate an Anglo Halloween at Rita and John Goodman's house before heading out to Lenny's. One of the guests is a rabbi, and he reveals to us the precise details of how he sleeps with a T-shirt over his head so his cat will not find and sleep on his head. While we are all laughing, I sort of slip outside of myself and watch: Is this the same person who went for months and months on end without seeing anyone in L.A.? What is going on here? Who am I now? This really is a new life.

We drive out of Santa Fe to Tesuque to visit Lenny and Livia in their new home. There is snow on the ground, and we stomp around the house until we find the entrance. Then I lift my mittened hand and knock on the glass pane on the door of the kitchen. It is very awkward seeing Lenny at first— this man, who was like my brother, is now estranged from me, as I am from him. Lenny and Livia welcome us in. They had planned a party, but we are the only guests there. Us, and the dead, who are also in attendance.

Lenny and Livia have spent the whole day cooking for the dead and putting out the favorite foods of their departed ancestors and loved ones. Some of the bowls and plates have food that is half-eaten, for the living have shared their food with the dead. Earlier in the day, Lenny took a bowl of food out to the arroyo, to offer it to the spirits of the animals, who could not come in to partake. Livia says she is exhausted, as though she really has a house full of company! She says they are really crowded, and she can feel the spirits all around her.

As they speak, I can feel my own ancestors hovering around, and I am sorry that I didn't have such a Feast Day to welcome them in. How wonderful the Indian cosmology is! The dead are never really gone. And there is a special day for them, when the living party with them, and make them their favorite foods. But even on ordinary days, the Indians are always aware of their ancestors, and those who have crossed to the other side. It makes death an ordinary part of life, and

300

reassures the living that when they are gone, someone will be cooking up a storm for them too!

As time passes, so does the extreme awkwardness. The food is wonderful, and a full and happy belly tends to soften the soul. We speak vaguely about what Lenny is doing, Paul entertains, and when we leave, Lenny and Livia say over and over again how happy they are to see us. I guess this is a day for the dead, and for people who have been absent from your life, too.

I decide not to stay too long, because the atmosphere is thick with past feelings. When I sleep, my dreams are full of rich, swirling images of Indian land. In the morning, as we prepare to move, I make the mistake of calling my producers in L.A. because we have to deal with final business arrangements as I vacate the *casita*. The day goes by, and they never even call me back. Every negative thing I heard about them is true. They have a wonderful way of treating all the people who work with them! I decide not to focus on my producers, but to focus instead on all of the good things in my life. I love the fact that my mind has finally developed the flexibility to choose what it will dwell on. I think that before, events overwhelmed my mind. I am licking the lollipop of freedom for the first time.

I guess that when we leave the *casita,* a chapter in our lives will come to an end—"introduction to Santa Fe." When we move into Uncle Alfie's it will be a new season, a new set of circumstances, and a new adventure. A healing between two cultures is on the horizon.

I anxiously await it.

14

The Origins of Things

Early to mid-November, 1991

Here we are in Uncle Alfie's weird little house with the mismatched curtains and a stack of mattresses in the middle of the living room for a sofa. On each side of the small bed we sleep in, there is a strip of carpet to keep our tootsies warm; one strip is blue and one is gold. It sort of fits in with the general theme of "anything goes." The door knocker is a meat mallet hanging on a string. The walls are lined with white acoustical tile. Uncle Alfie is trying to refurbish a battered black suitcase to make it into a mailbox. It is truly hideous. Still, it has become our new home.

My producers are taking an incomprehensibly long time to find me a new writing partner, and I rarely speak to them because it's not a pleasant experience. They shoot down every Indian writer, applying standards that no Anglo writer could meet!

"Racists!" I hiss under my breath as I hang up the phone. The phone rings again. This time I hear Garrison Baveur's voice on the other end—the Indian co-executive producer of my TV show.

"Hi, Garrison," I say cheerfully. "How are you?"

"Everyone wants to work with me, and I have offers flying at me like golf balls," Garrison gushes.

"That's nice," I comment. "Glad you're so popular. But can you tell me what's happening with our project?"

He doesn't seem to hear me.

"Our project," I repeat. "You know, the one I wrote the bible for. The project you and my L.A. producers are in charge of."

Garrison clears his throat.

"Yeah," he says. "That's the reason I'm calling you. I want to tell you that I've been trying to get you thrown off."

I think he is kidding, but his sickening silence slams home the ugly truth.

"Are you nuts? The whole series was my idea, I'm the one who found the book, Carl Hammerschlag is my friend, the project was funded on the basis of my treatment, and, may I remind you that I lobbied like crazy to get YOU taken on. The producers in L.A. never wanted you in the first place!"

"Well," Garrison says, "I figured you and Lenny didn't work out as a team, and since they got rid of him, they may as well dump both of you."

"Dump me?"

"Yeah. Get another writer. There are lots of them."

"Who do you think you are!?" I explode. "You really think you're so important don't you?"

"Maybe I made a mistake," Garrison concedes. "Maybe I was a little hasty. In fact, I think you're a very good writer. But I figured, if the team of writers doesn't pan out, let's just move on."

I hang up the phone, stunned. While I am still reeling, the phone rings again, and this time it is the head of business affairs at my producers' office, calling to hassle me about reimbursing my expenses.

"I have some year-end greetings for my producers," I say in a sweet voice.

"Really?" asks the man in business affairs. "What are they?"

He's probably sorry he asked, because I calmly, coolly tell them all, in *two very clear words,* what they can do to themselves. I simply have no desire to speak to them or work with them any more.

After I have said it, I hang up the phone, depressed at the amount of energy expended on the project and the mess it has become.

I decide not to dwell on this, but to focus my thoughts on the Hispanic/Indian celebration to save the petroglyphs from desecration and encroaching development. Joseph comes to Uncle Alfie's house every morning, and we plan the party. There will be Indian entertainers and Hispanic entertainers, and food and speakers and formal blessings bestowed by both sides. At the end of the day, I'd like to have a friendship dance that everyone does together.

"We were wise to decide to stay here," Paul announces, when I tell him about the friendship dance. "I think this is very important."

We are sitting over breakfast when Tim Shay arrives. He sits down to join us and tells us that he has gotten into one more in a string of freak automobile accidents. This time, someone hit his truck. I jokingly ask, "Why don't you go to a medicine man to get rid of the curse?" He *un*jokingly replies that he and his wife Wilma are doing exactly that. In the Indian worldview, they believe that someone is envious of them and trying to impede them.

"Indians will do that to you if you try to pull ahead of them," Tim explains.

"I wonder who is trying to hurt you two?" I muse.

"They'll show themselves after the ceremony," Tim offers. "They may even dance around us during the ceremony. We'll find out who they are."

To Tim, if a person even has bad thoughts about you, it can seriously affect your well-being. But beware having these thoughts, because there is a price for them—they will ricochet back to hurt you and your family.

We hear a knock of the meat mallet banging against our door. When we open it, Wilma walks in. She offers her interpretation of all of the accidents. "I think it's someone who doesn't approve of our marriage," she says.

I just smile and shake my head. What a wonderful, complex, multi-layered way of seeing life!

As soon as they leave the phone rings, and it is Povi.

"Hi, drifter!" I say. "You keep drifting into and out of our lives. Where are you? We miss you!"

"I've been . . . busy."

"Oh?" I say, hoping that "busy" means she has found work.

No such luck. Povi is caught in a Pueblo administrative hassle; she had to leave her old apartment and she currently lives in a mobile home with no heat, electricity, or running water. She has to go and fetch water, and she stays under the covers most of the time to stay warm.

"It's a transition," she says, trying to sound optimistic. "It must be a transition for you too. What will you two do for jobs and money?"

It is difficult for all of us. Sometimes I have bouts of anxiety and attacks of panic, and all I want to do is get back into bed, pull the covers over my head, stick my feet up in the air like a dead parakeet and lie there. But I fight against it. Today, for example, my heart is palpitating weirdly in my chest. I decide to fight the symptom by going to the most healing source I know: nature.

As an Indian friend named John Crown said to me a while ago, "If you can get out of your head and pay attention to the sky, the clouds, the details on a pine cone, or the sound of rushing water, it will put you back in alignment."

So I decide that because I don't feel well, I will climb a mountain.

We drive to the Randall Davey Audubon Center and start up a trail. I can't concentrate on my external environment at all. I ruminate, I worry about the past, the future, and everything else I can conjure up. I haven't even made the effort to change out of tights and thin gym sneakers, and it is pretty hairy climbing. The earth is wet and muddy and rocky, my feet ache from the thinness of my soles, and I fall about five times, once tearing my tights. The altitude increases and the climb gets steeper, and soon we have lost the trail completely. I want to stop and turn around, but Paul keeps egging me onward: "C'mon, we're almost at the top."

I try to hold on to my newfound belief system that when you push through a difficulty, you get a reward. As we climb higher and I master the breathlessness, the view gets splendid, and we can see a long green valley beneath us and mountains all around. But the greatest reward is that I finally get out of my head, and I am able to enjoy myself, which was unthinkable hours before. I come back laughing and feeling in sync again, just like John Crown told me I would.

Back in Santa Fe, I am feeling very chipper as Louis Begay comes to call. He is Navajo, he has worked in the prison system, and he makes brilliant black-and-white pencil drawings. They are detailed and intricate beyond belief. He does not consider himself an artist although he is one.

He tells me that he has fallen in love with a white woman, but his family is adamantly opposed to the union because she is not "Dineh," not one of them.

"You know, when I grew up, there was a Yiddish term—'unserer.' It means that someone is Jewish, or one of us," I say.

Louis looks at me, understanding.

"Why do ethnic or religious groups need to feel that they are superior to everyone else?" I ask him.

He shrugs. "Many Indian tribes refer to themselves, in their own language, as 'the People.' Maybe it's not about superiority. Maybe it's just that they feel they were the first ones here."

"Or they think they are the Chosen Ones, just like Muslims and Catholics, Jews and New Agers," I add.

"I think we are all chosen," Louis says simply. " 'Chosen' means we have a special relationship to the Creator."

Louis falls silent for a moment, and I continue his thought.

"You mean that when a one-on-one relationship to Creation becomes apparent or is revealed to you, it makes you feel very special?"

"Yes," Louis agrees. "But it can also be a trap. Spirituality should open up your heart to others, not close others out. It connects you to every living thing with which you share breath, and it doesn't separate you or make you superior. "

"Then we are all 'the people'?" I ask.

"I hope my parents don't hear me . . . but the answer is *yes,*" Louis says.

We both fall silent. I am able to sustain the silence for a good minute or two before I get edgy and start to babble about food, the weather, and anything else that comes to mind.

Louis smiles. "You're okay for an Anglo," he says.

"And you're okay for a Dineh."

In the evening, Paul and I go to see a hot air balloon "glow" for the first time. It is at the Santa Fe Downs race track, where we have never been, and even though it is cold, people sit outside the clubhouse, drinking coffee, and waiting. Inside the clubhouse, it is strange indeed. Although there are no races, gamblers with folded newspapers marked with scrawled writing line up under video monitors, watching and betting on races that are far away. The atmosphere is thick with smoke, and there is a seriousness in the air, more serious, I think, than anywhere in Santa Fe. I feel that rising sadness I always feel when I know people are stuck, and I hope these gamblers find some other place to put their attention and some other way to pass their nights and days.

It takes a long time for the huge balloons to fill with air and Paul and I decide to go for a trot around the race track, pretending we are horses. I think the fact that Indians do deer, buffalo, elk, antelope, eagle, and multiple other animal dances has opened up our minds to what is possible. We are the only ones there, and we have no idea *why* we want to go around the track, but it just seems appropriate. We start to run, and the farther we get from the clubhouse, the more we can smell the odor of other horses who have run here before and the more we feel the tension and the excitement of the straightway, the far turn, the near turn, and then the home stretch. The night is dark, and the moon is a sliver above us. In the distance, we can see the yellow and blue lights of the city, and the cheer of the crowd goes up as the balloons light up the sky when they are fired up with propane. The lights in the clubhouse go off, and all we can see are the billowy shapes and colors of the balloons that never leave the ground, but just sit and glow, sometimes all at once, sometimes in sequence.

Paul and I, the horses, retire from the race, and we are pleased that once again we have seen something from another perspective, which always makes it that much more special and meaningful for us. We have, for a short moment in time, become horses. We have done it without self-consciousness, which is something we would never, ever have done before.

"Hey," cracks Tim Shay when we tell him about our equine adventures, "remind me to step out of the way when you two become buffalo!"

The next morning, we decide that it is time to have a party, and to introduce our friends to each other. We know full well that Anglos, Indians, and Hispanic people don't usually mix here, and that is exactly why we decide to do it. Aren't we all "the people" after all?

We call everyone up and tell them that we are turning our weird abode into a beatnik coffee house. Everyone is required to dress in black, and the women can load on as much dark eye makeup as they please. People have to bring their own cushions or pillows, so they can sit on the floor. And one more thing—everyone has to write an original poem.

We plaster the house with home-made poems and cartoons and food is served in paper bags, under the light of candles. Signs call for "Allen Ginsberg for President," or remind the guests that they are cool cats. We spend a good deal of time explaining to some of our friends what beatniks are, and who Allen Ginsberg is. As one of our friends comments, in the outside world, the challenge is to stay in touch with the spiritual. In Santa Fe, the challenge is to stay in touch with the outside world.

The guests arrive. One brings an electronic keyboard and another comes with a guitar. Arnold Herrera has a drum. Sometimes the singing is in Spanish, sometimes in the Indian Keres dialect, and sometimes in English. After the initial awkwardness wears off, there is much mixing and mingling. The guests all gather in the living room, sprawled on the floor or standing, and we instruct them not to clap, but to snap their fingers . . . hip and cool.

One by one, I call people to come up and, in the dim light of an old lamp, read their poems. Most people have some form of stage fright, but they all hide it very well and only a few hand-held pages tremble. I expected the "roses are red" variety of poem, but no no no. Not in Santa Fe. One woman does a performance art piece, and another writes about her clitoral potted plant. Some of the men open up and pour out their guts and one English man recites an abstruse multi-page poem about the twelfth-century Children's Crusade. Tim Shay reminisces about fire, and Arnold Herrera sings an original drum song. John Goodman, taking his courage in his hands, reads his poem with wit and grace even though he is verbally incapacitated by a stroke. There are poems in four languages (English, Spanish, Portuguese, and Keres), odes, and rhyming ditties. It is an amazing show of creativity and open-heartedness.

As I walk around the house, serving food and drinks, I see that there is a lot of mingling between the guests of different cultures. They seem to be listening to each other and really talking. For a few Spanish people, it is the first time they have talked to Indians. For a few Anglos, it is the first time they have socialized with Hispanics or Native Americans.

"This is foreplay for the petroglyph party," Joseph whispers to me. He is dressed like a terrorist, for even though I tried to explain it to him, he cannot understand what a beatnik is!

Toward the end of the evening, there is a lovely private moment for me when Arnold Herrera tells me that during the day he took his sons hunting at Cochiti Pueblo. Last night, before the hunt, he taught them old Pueblo hunting songs, and one of them is particularly beautiful. The hunter sings to the deer: "You are so old now. Instead of falling over the cliff, which can happen to you, let me take you home with me. Let me take you home." There is no talk of death and killing, but a gentle invitation to the deer spirit to "come home" with the hunter.

"If the deer could sing back, I wonder what he would say to that!" my sister Lonnie muses when I tell her about it.

Tim Shay stays until 3 A.M. His eyes are sunken in his head and his voice is hollow and distant.

"How come Wilma didn't come to our party?" I ask.

His answer is totally unexpected. He says he has been on an extended drunken binge, which culminated in his throwing a vacuum cleaner across the house at Wilma and breaking the wall. In fact, he trashed the place, then went to a bar, and got thrown out when he had a showdown with some bikers.

"And Wilma?"

"I don't know where she is. But when I last saw her, she had a look in her eyes like she was really afraid of me. That hurt bad."

I share a long breath of pain with Tim. His feelings are all bottled up and they explode in a drunken rage.

"I come from generations of alcoholics," Tim says. "Sometimes the pressure gets too much and I just break."

"You mean 'break down'?"

"No. I break. I just withdraw into inebriation, into my own world, and I get away from it all."

"What's the pressure you feel?"

"We're raised a certain way—with tradition and spirituality. We try to keep to those ways, but the real world makes us act another way and have a different set of values. Man, there's nothing less spiritual than the mighty dollar. So we try to walk in both worlds, keeping one foot in each, but sometimes it's too much. Me, I break."

I look at Tim. He's had a life of pain, abandonment, incarceration, and struggle.

"You have a heavy past to overcome," I say. "It is a horror story that is echoed on every reservation in this country."

"Yeah," he says. "It's always with me. We Indians had a real number done on us. If it wasn't the Spanish, it was the Anglo politicians. If it wasn't the Anglo politicians, it was the priests."

I feel the anger well up in me again. How could we have taken these people, so close to nature and to the spiritual light of life, and crushed their culture, their land, their food source, their religion, and their dignity, leaving them impoverished, alcoholic, self-loathing, and at the bottom of the social ladder?

"I've seen Indians living out of dumpsters, rolling in the streets. I saw one like that in California in the late sixties, and then I saw him again twenty years later. That's a miracle of survival. Something just lets him hang on."

I take a deep breath, as I realize that Tim identifies with the disenfranchised, the poor, the people who hang on by their fingertips.

"The Indian will rise again," Tim says.

"It is already happening," I agree, "but it takes such effort, almost like mountains rising up in a volcanic blast and exploding into existence."

He nods.

Tim starts talking about the petroglyph party, and he is going to make a fire with a bow-drill. He is a hunter/trapper/survivalist, and he has a whole procedure whereby he makes fire from rubbing wood. He says it is rigorous, like lifting a two-hundred-pound weight, and it necessitates serious training because it requires great upper-body strength. He shows me his hands, and they are completely calloused. Tim rhapsodizes about fire, and it seems to be his preferred element. Where there is fire there is warmth, heat, food, life.

Suddenly, as Tim speaks, I begin to laugh.

"What's so funny?" he asks.

"I can't help it," I say. "I was thinking about my life in L.A. and how never in a million years would I be sitting there in the middle of the night discussing someone's preferred element."

"Certainly not with a drunk," he says, laughing a hollow laugh. Then he grows serious again, and he starts talking to me about the sacred run he went on in Europe, and, specifically, his experiences at Auschwitz.

"I went there as an Indian runner, and I had a revelation that Indians do not have a lock on suffering."

"Meaning?"

"Other people, in fact most people, have suffered and been the victims of extermination campaigns. Going to Auschwitz was a very humbling and bonding experience for me."

My Indian friends see all of mankind as related ("to all my relations," they say in the sweatlodge), and Auschwitz gave Tim a direct experience of feeling this relatedness—through suffering.

Tim is obsessed with early cultures, and he believes that the Vikings had extensive early trade routes in the Americas. He figures the Chippewa, who are so big, "almost like giants," and the subcategory of blond-haired, blue-eyed Sioux, are descendants of those Vikings who mixed with the natives.

I laugh again. This time Tim catches my eye and smiles. He understands that for me it is an enormous change to be with people who talk about origins and elements and things other than deals and Hollywood gossip!

The Origins of Things

The talking seems to have a salutary effect on Tim too. It draws him out of his self-loathing about his drunkenness, and his guilt about what he has done to his wife and his life.

As soon as we finish cleaning up from the party, we look at the calendar and realize it is November 12th—the annual San Diego Feast Day at Jemez Pueblo. It is a one-and-a-half-hour ride, and ordinarily we would leave early in the morning, but winter makes us get up later and drag, rather than bound, out of the house. The day is gorgeous, and the sun is thin and strange with a diffuse wintery light. There is mystery in the air, mystery on the mountaintops, mystery on the desert floor as we head south.

For months I have been looking for giant gourds, because I like to decorate them with colorful painterly designs, and at Jemez we strike gold. Vendors are lined up along the road leading to the Plaza, and two men have a beaten-up old truck with huge, thin-necked gourds with bloated bellies hanging from strings. After getting careful instructions on how to dry them, I purchase the whole lot, and I also buy a cow-bone rattle with an old bell and a strange brown necklace made of unidentifiable flat brown beads. As Paul heads off to put the gourds in the car, I overhear the two vendors say, "Wow, what a happy couple! They have a really good marriage." It makes me feel very special.

I walk down the dusty road to the Plaza, and every other vendor is selling piñon nuts, which have been picked by the roadside by either shaking trees or gathering the tiny brown nuts on the ground, beating the rodents to it! I remember a story Wilma told me about being admonished for shaking the trees. She was told that people must respect the time frame of the piñon tree and wait for the nuts to fall. Shaking the tree to feed an impatient human body was considered disrespectful in the Navajo world.

The piñon nuts have a crunchy, addictive taste, and although most people spit out the shells to get to the tender pine nuts, I usually blow off the middle step and eat the nuts whole. A month ago you couldn't drive fifty feet along the road outside of town without seeing people, mostly Hispanic, diving under the trees for the tasty nuts. Now they are sold in shops and in villages like Jemez.

At the Plaza, there is a very intense thump of a drumbeat, and hundreds of dancers, their eyes vague with their inward focus, weave

311

around the space. Ordinarily, the women have one shoulder bare under their black sleeveless dresses called *mantas,* but because of the chilly weather they wear blouses underneath. As usual, they carry evergreen branches in both arms, and do their hip-hop-back-and-forth step while the men progress in a more straightforward fashion. The women wear turquoise-colored *tabletas* on their heads, and many have a T-shape cut into them, the shape of the doorways in the ancient Anasazi ruins. The men are bare-chested, with fox tails and evergreens, shells and rattles draping their bodies and paint on their faces.

As soon as I see the dancers, my mind begins a dialogue with itself. "If each of these people is praying to the Creator, can the Creator really pay attention to each one individually?"

"What happens when one prays," comes the answer, "is that it puts one in an energy field that is the same as the energy field of the Creative force. Thus, it makes you glow with the energy of Oneness, and the concerns of the flesh don't matter to you. You go into an altered time/space mode, where solutions come rapidly to problems, and miracles seem to occur. Life becomes a fluid thing."

It is hard to watch the Pueblo dances without being transported, without wondering and asking yourself questions about the order of things.

I go back, in memory, to the first time we saw a Pueblo dance. It seemed exotic but repetitive, and we had no idea of what we were looking at. Now every dance teaches us more, and brings us closer to the spirit of the dancers. Each dance is part of an annual calendar of observances, and it is also part of humankind holding up its responsibility on earth. Rain falls, crops grow, and people pray and dance. On the pragmatic level of social organization, dancing keeps people responsible, aware, and aligned. When Indians are dancing in the sacred space of the Plaza, they are like gods. They can do no wrong. They are all bonded, and they move as one to the great drum heartbeat. Their attention is focused on the Creator, and their hearts are full of prayer and thanksgiving. It is only when they leave the Plaza and return to the temptations and problems of everyday life that they become wayward. So the idea is to keep them in the ceremonial mode as often as possible.

As the afternoon wears on, we get hungry, and we drop into Beaver's house, which is right on the Plaza. There, we sit in the comfortable indoor heat and watch the dancers. There is a great hustle and bustle in the kitchen, and the house keeps filling up with people, from the back door and the Plaza-side door as well. But for some reason, no one ever asks us to come in and eat. Beaver is dancing, and we can't find anyone we know from her family. We know we can just meander into the kitchen when there are two vacant places at the table, but our own sense of propriety prevents us from doing so. We laugh. Never take anything for granted in Indian country.

We decide to head toward Laura Fragua's house, which is at some distance from the Plaza, but something on the Plaza arrests my attention. The dancing has stopped, but none of the dancers moves. They stand in two long, long lines, facing the altar, which is rimmed with the heads of deer and antelopes. It is cold now, but even the littlest children stand uncomplaining, the boys with their bare chests painted turquoise or pumpkin, for the two society colors. Suddenly, down the center of the two lines comes a group of men, beating rapidly on small hand-held drums with sticks. All of them are dressed in black-face, and they wear strange berets with corn husks popping out of the top of them. One of the men is a priest. They intone strange songs and chants, and all the dancers stand still, and watch them pass. The black-faced men come to the altar, and I think they bless the drummers, and then they turn around, and head back to the end of the line of dancers again. When they reach the end, they turn around and march back, again intoning and chanting and beating on their drums. Back and forth they march, over and over and over again. It seems to take forever.

A few of the white people on the Plaza grow restless, since they are watching the same thing again and again. They leave, but I feel like imploring them to stay, for the repetition induces a kind of hypnotic trance, where things become clear, and where the mind drifts naturally into a deep and spiritual mode.

As I watch the black-faced men in the dance, I assume that they are probably clowns, who, as I have learned by now, are very priestly beings. They often take on disguises, and here they are impersonating black men. The berets are meant to imitate kinky black hair. I believe they are imitating Estebanico, the black man who first came, accompanied by a Spanish priest, to Zuni Pueblo. Little is known of Estebanico, but he was probably a Moroccan slave who came to the New World. There was a Zuni prophecy that made the Zuni people open their arms, their houses, and their hearts to the black slave, but he betrayed them in every way—he probably got drunk with illicit power. Ever since and even until this day, black people and Spanish people

313

are unwelcome at the Zuni Pueblo. This display at Jemez seems to be a reenactment of the arrival of the Bible-toting black colonial. Perhaps the story has been tempered by time, and now it represents some kind of half-serious joke.

"I think Estebanico is like Haman, the object of taunts by Jews at Purim time," I whisper to Paul.

We leave the Plaza before the very end of the dance, because it is getting dark, and Paul is afraid he will not be able to spot Laura's house. It takes a lot of meandering to find it, and when we walk in there is a warm welcome by Laura, who is doing the cooking and serving, and her husband Steve Wall. We immediately sit down and are served turkey and yams and chili stew and fried ham and Kentucky Fried Chicken and cottage cheese mixed with Jell-O and endless sweets. We eat hungrily, and then we begin to talk. Across from me are two Indian women from the Northeast. One of them says her tribe is Cayuga, and I smile. I went to Cornell University, I tell her, and Cornell is on Lake Cayuga.

There is a silence. The woman grows very serious. She says that all of Cornell is on Indian lands, and the Indians are suing to get them back. Lake Cayuga is the sacred ancestral lake of the Cayuga tribe, and it has been given away in land sales. Now it is the domain of people who want it to be a preserve for ducks, so they can shoot them unimpeded. "We are making progress," she tells me. "Cornell has to reckon with us. Already the courts have said we must reach some kind of settlement and they want out."

I say I am ashamed, but when I went to Cornell I had no knowledge of Indians in the region. "Of course! That's the way they want it! They want to keep us invisible!" says the Cayuga woman. I ask her if the Cayuga tribe is alive and well, despite what has been done to it. She says that there are only about four hundred Cayuga left, but there are chiefs and the traditions and customs are maintained and are very strong.

The two women are very political, and I like that. One is preparing a show of corn-husk dolls for the Smithsonian, and the other is a jewelry-maker. They devote their life to Indian crafts and Indian perpetuity.

"It's not enough to bemoan what was done to Indians in the past," says the Cayuga woman. "It is still going on today. We have to stop complaining, and fight it. In the court system, in the press, any way we can!"

The Origins of Things

After the meal, Paul begins to give freebie Shiatsu massages, and I hear giggles as each person massaged howls with the pain of cramped muscles and blocked channels. In the meantime, Laura's dad Geronimo (Jerry) comes up to me and starts to talk. I tell him that he helped me in the past. First he told me not to write about anything Indian. Then he recanted and informed me, "You can write anything, as long as it's the truth." I tell him that I am writing everything I have in my heart as I reside here in Indian land. He listens carefully, then nods and says it is okay. "Is it even okay if I quote you in my writing?" I ask.

He nods again. And then, for some reason which Paul calls my witchiness, he begins to open up his own heart. He tells me that he was given away at birth to be raised by his grandmother, who lived at the Plaza. His own mother and father and siblings lived farther away. He says that until he was an adult, he called his mother and father "sister and brother," and would not recognize them as his parents because they had done nothing to raise him. In fact, he did not recognize them until, a grown man, he went off to fight in World War II.

It was very hard for Jerry, and he says his whole life involved "seeing things from both sides." His grandma was a traditional medicine woman, and his mother was one of the first Protestants, scorned and rejected by the largely Catholic Pueblo of Jemez. On Feast Days, his mother was locked up and banned from the doings. He used to sneak away to see her, and then he would get into trouble on his grandmother's side. But if he didn't go, he felt guilt and responsibility.

"The same was true of food," Jerry says. "We were all poor, but if my grandmother provided a good meal for me, I could not eat it in peace unless my brothers and sisters were invited, from my mother's house, to share it."

His voice gets very quiet. He says he was constantly torn in two—between his parents and siblings, with whom he did not live, and his grandmother. He kept it all buried, crying to himself inside, and only now does he dare express it. He has never faced his parents and asked why he was given up at birth. There has never been such a discussion. But it has affected everything in his life.

The discussion with Jerry is not straightforward. He tells me his story in a very indirect and elliptical fashion, and I try to listen as hard as I can and piece it all together. Occasionally I have to ask a question to clarify what is being talked about. Mainly, I just try to pay attention.

Jerry looks around the room, and his eyes rest on his young grand-

315

sons. He tells me how he has just taken them hunting, for the first time. He taught them how to distinguish the footprints of rabbits and squirrels, skunk and deer. He told them how to build a bluebird trap, even though he didn't at the moment have the equipment to build one. He taught them to observe before shooting, and how to come to the animals in a good way.

He thinks for a moment, and then says, "My grandsons must learn English and math. Those are the important things." Jerry only got to finish the eighth grade, to his regret. He spoke only his Tanoan language, and was first exposed to English in the military. Unfortunately, all he learned was how to curse, and he was ashamed to speak that kind of English when he got home. Thus, he determined that learning English correctly was important, because it enabled Indians to communicate with the outside world, and with Indians from other tribes who didn't speak the same language. As for math, Jerry thinks it is essential because all things in life are measured. How much should you eat before you get sick, how far do you have to walk to someone's house, what time must you leave in order to be somewhere on time? It's all mathematics.

Jerry takes a deep breath. He sees I am interested, so he goes on. He talks to me about the Feast Day. It is no accident that it happens AFTER the harvest. It is an invitation to everyone to come and share in the crops, and the Jemez people will dance and entertain them. They get all dressed up in their traditional garb, but "we don't worship the foxtails and the feathers, the bells and the rattles. They are the trappings. We worship the Creator." He tells me that we are all the messengers of God, and we must be good people to carry that message. It is something we must pay attention to every second of every day. When we meet people, we must really be interested in them, and try to help them and care for them—not just be satisfied with superficial contacts. If we are creative people, we must create from the heart, and when we talk to people about our work we must explain the background and what went into it. "This is being religious, in the true sense," Jerry says. I smile, and I feel good, for I believe that Paul and I are trying to live "religious" lives, by Jerry's own definition.

Jerry continues. Now he is talking about the Indian calendar year. I do not ask one question, but he continues to give me information. He says that the Indian way is not to divide the year into months, but, rather, seasons. There is the planting season, then the harvest season, then when the ground grows cold and when Indians must prepare their

316

tools and fields and ceremonies again for the planting season. It is all about cycles, things that are predictable and that repeat themselves each year and give order to the world. There is also the sun: Jerry says you must watch it each day, and where it is in the sky in the morning. You must follow its progression and see how it makes a certain, predictable path, and then it repeats that path again.

"Order. Tuning in to the order in the universe. That's what's important," Jerry says.

Now he is really warmed up. He leans forward and tells me that on a Feast Day, you can bring a piece of jewelry and ask an Indian dancer to wear it. The piece of jewelry will receive all of the blessings on the Plaza, and at the end of the day, when it is given back to you, you get all the blessings. I make a mental note.

I listen to Jerry talk, and I ask why he has never been on the Pueblo council. He scrunches up his face and says he is too outspoken. He is not politic in his speech, and people don't like how direct he is. I smile. I like it. I tell him what a good time I have had at the Feast Day, and I tell him I bought gourds. He starts bubbling over with ideas of what I should do with the gourds. I could make dippers and decorative items, I could cut them and use them to make brooches and earrings. He gets excited about how lightweight and versatile the gourd material is. I ask why he doesn't do art. "I don't do it," he says. "I just like to talk about it."

After our visit to Jemez, the weather turns cold again, and it snows. Paul and I now trek around in boots and hats and scarves and big, fat ski gloves and we're a step away from buying face-masks; luckily we are able to pay attention to the novelty rather than the temperatures.

Joseph Villegas calls, and he sounds very excited. The coming together of the Indians and Hispanics is progressing faster than I ever dreamed. Joseph is now in touch with the Pueblo leaders, and both parties keep discovering how much they have in common—after centuries of being apart. Our big day of entertainment for the public is slated for December 14th, and I love being part of history!

History is everywhere around us in New Mexico. As much as L.A. is cut off from the past, New Mexico is entrenched in it. There is a lecture given about Columbus and his putative Jewishness, and I go. According to the speaker, Spain has a history of cyclical anti-Semitism, when Jews were forced to leave or convert. But this was interspersed with a long spell of peace, when Christians, Jews, and

317

Moslems dwelled in peace and Spain was a center of European learning. It was all the more cruel, then, when the Christianization of Spain resumed with a frenzy known as the Inquisition. Many Jews were terrorized into conversion, and Christopher Columbus's ancestors were among those. Although Columbus lived as a Christian, there are many indications that he maintained a link to the Jewish faith. He dated one of his letters with the Jewish year and the Christian year, he referred to King David as an ancestor, he had the physical characteristics of Mallorca Jews, his family seems to have fled to Italy during a wave of persecution. Well, I sure wish the Jews would claim a more noble historical figure, because Columbus engendered the decimation of the Indians on this continent!

It is extremely disturbing to me to think about Jews as *conquistadors*. They were trying to get out of Spain to escape being killed. Many converted to Catholicism, but secretly kept up their Jewish faith. They joined expeditions to come to the New World, where they continued to be hounded and persecuted. They volunteered to go to New Mexico, the farthest outpost, to escape the senseless fury of anti-Semitism that pursued them. So how could these same people participate in the slaughter of Indians, an innocent people? Some things I do not understand . . .

I guess there are many things I do not understand, like how I ended up as a champion of Hispanic culture? I was so angry with the Spanish for their behavior toward the Indians and subsequent denial of that behavior, but I have come to learn that, in Indian country, whatever you fear or resent or avoid will eventually end up directly in your face. I guess I really shouldn't be surprised that I have ended up being extremely friendly with Joseph Villegas and his family, and falling in love with them. The more I learn about Hispanic culture, the richer, deeper, and more interesting I find it. Just one little apology, and I would probably embrace it all wholeheartedly!

Poor Joseph. He has to bear the brunt of my conviction that three little words need to be spoken by a Hispanic person—"I am sorry." He walks into my house, sits down, and immediately I confront him with Spanish guilt and responsibility.

"There is blood on Spanish hands, and if you hold the blood up and look at it, it will wash away."

Joseph squirms, as all the Hispanic people we have met squirm, when I ask: "Has there been an apology made to the Indians for what was done to them?" He keeps squirming and I keep asking, and then finally I get very personal and very direct.

"Joseph, I am imploring you, on December 14th, in front of all of those Indians and Spanish people, beg the Indians for forgiveness for what your people have done."

Joseph grows very silent. I think his skin turns white. But I will not let him off the hook.

"Okay," he agrees, "I'll acknowledge that something happened. I'll say 'Let the past be the past.' "

"No," I say firmly, "that is not enough. This is a case of extreme abuse and denial. Joseph, you have to acknowledge WHAT was done."

He thinks and thinks and I wonder if he wants to strangle me and then finally he says, "I'll do it. I'll say I know we killed off the Indians and destroyed their culture and I will ask for forgiveness."

I leap across the table and hug him. Finally, finally, someone who really will do it!

I ask him if there will be repercussions. He says that his own people will attack him because it is a macho culture that never begs. And certainly not for forgiveness.

"Can you take the heat?" I ask.

"Yes, I can," he says.

"Joseph," I say with real respect and admiration for him, "there will be an incredible healing on December 14th." He nods. He is going to do it. Publicly. In his own name. The first apology ever.

"This is monumental, amigo," I say to him.

"Yes," he echoes, "it is."

The following day I receive a small package from my monk brother, Topgyal Fein. The gift has the most viscous wrapping I've ever felt. It is like trying to open solidified ooze. I finally realize it is a Hefty garbage bag, glued shut. Inside the garbage bag is a treasure. A set of Tibetan prayer beads and a prayer shawl and a book on the Tibetan initiation ceremony. I am incredibly moved. How fortunate I am to get the tools of prayer selected and blessed and sent by my brother, the lama!

At night, Laura Fragua shows up from her home in southern New Mexico and she asks to sleep here because her sculpture studio in Santa Fe is too cold. After we have chatted a bit, I tell her in strict confidence what Joseph is planning to do on December 14th in the way of

319

apology to the Indians. I have never seen such a strong reaction from Laura, who is very controlled. Finally she explodes: "It's about time!!!" She urges me to have it recorded on videotape, and says that it will be like the explosion of a big bomb. She recognizes that Joseph is going to take great flack from his own people. "What do we have to apologize for?" is the basic attitude. As I think of Joseph's courage, it makes me love him even more than I do. And as I look at Laura, I realize how much our friends here enrich our lives!

After some sleep, breakfast, and more talking, Laura and I set off the next day to a storytelling session with Joseph Geronimo, the direct descendant of the famed Chiricahua Apache medicine man and warrior. There is no way to look at Joe without thinking of Geronimo, and imagining him the way he looked in pictures—intense, remote, mysterious. Joseph sits there with his nephew Abraham, both dark-skinned men under dark brown wide-brim hats, both wearing jeans, and Joe wears dark shades over his eyes, so I never see them. A little toddler plays with him and runs around throughout Joe's storytelling session, but Joe never rebukes her or does anything other than reach out his hands for her. Next to Joseph and Abraham, a fire roars in the fireplace, and it seems to be timed so that when the fire burns down, the stories are over.

Being a spectator at an Indian event is something that takes adjusting to. The storytelling is not necessarily flamboyant and theatrical the way Anglo drama is. Joe is quiet and intense. The stories sometimes get lost in details, and sometimes wander—they are not linear in form. It's hard to tell when a story is over, because it flows into the next story and suddenly you are there, following the characters. But the stories are held together by the truth of what they are about, and the storyteller shares that truth with his audience. It is a very bonding and deep experience that requires concentration and internalization.

Before he begins, Joseph asks that no one tape-record his stories. Why? Because it is very important to respect the time of year when stories are told, and they mustn't be disseminated without paying attention to this. Stories should be told after the last thunderstorm of the year, to announce to the animals that it's winter. And they continue only until the first thunderstorm of spring, when their cessation tells the animals that summer has come.

The stories are not only entertaining, but they are instructional for kids. Joe learned from his grandma that Apaches don't beat or yell at or abuse children. They don't give them lessons. They just tell their children Coyote stories, and the children learn life lessons from them and remember them always.

Joe tells us that next to stories, there are a few other things that are important to remember for an Apache. One is that you don't kill rattlesnakes. You talk to them. You say to a snake, "I'm sparing your life now, so when you come upon a member of my tribe, please spare his life too."

Joe then begins his stories in a very low-key, almost droning voice. His nephew occasionally gets up and does a small, subtle dance near the fire or beats on a hand-drum. The first tale is about a gambling game, where the forces of dark (monsters, snakes, and beasts) are vying for control of the world with the forces of light (small animals and birds). Each side buries a bone, and a member of the opposite side has to guess where it is. Each side is given four sticks, and if they lose a round of guessing they lose a stick, or if they win a round they win a stick. Whoever has the eight sticks wins.

In the telling of the story, whenever it is time for an animal to guess, Abraham gets up and does a little dance while Joe sings that animal's song. These songs have been passed down for thousands of years and they are accompanied by delightful details like "the bear shook his big rump and then sang." As I listen, I go into a trance and am sucked back in time. I realize that I am participating in the oral tradition as these songs and stories get passed on.

Near the end of the story, the forces of light are about to lose, when Turkey turns it all around. "That's how we got daylight, and that's how we get the seasons," Joe explains. "In the winter, when there is a sudden warm and sunny day, it means the forces of light are triumphing. And in the summer when there is a cold day, it means the predators have the upper hand."

I realize in a flash that these stories contain not only life instructions, but a cosmology as well, a way of looking at and understanding the forces in the natural world through metaphor.

The next story is about a blind person and a crippled person and how they meet the Gan (he pronounces it "gynas") dancers. As he speaks, it is very vital and alive for me because I went with Laura to the home of the Mescalero Apaches for the puberty rites and I danced with the awesome Gan gods around the fire at night.

As Joe tells the story, Abraham beats on the drum and Joe sings the Gan songs. Laura turns and winks at me, and then gives me a poke with her elbow. "Yes," I whisper, "of course . . . I remember." She is asking me if I remember the Gan songs and the masked gods and our dancing around the fire. How could I ever forget the night I first became filled with the sound of drums? I smile back. My experience makes the stories so much richer and realer.

In the story, the Gan mountain gods always say, "Follow us and believe in us and you will be okay." Joe holds up a Gan *kachina* doll to show the audience what a Gan mountain spirit looks like. When the blind man and the crippled man follow the Gan, they get past mountain lions and rattlesnakes and crashing rocks. They learn to resist temptation when they are offered three sets of gorgeous and expensive buckskin clothes, and they are instructed to choose a fourth set that is well made but more like what other people have and not set apart. And they are healed of their afflictions.

Built into this deeply religious story is a great taboo about people revealing the names of masked Gan dancers they recognize. A little girl points to one of the Gan and identifies him and she is thrown up into the air and cut into pieces by all the other dancers. I guess kids would be terrified to disobey after hearing that!

"The Gan are the most powerful thing we know," says Joseph. "They can cure anything. But there is a heavy penalty if people transgress the law." He translates this moral for the audience, but it is already quite clear, as it has been clear to Apaches for millennia.

Joe then slides into a story about Coyote, who looks up in the sky and sees something that resembles an arrowhead. He realizes it is a goose, and it is followed by other geese that fly with incredible precision. Immediately, Coyote wants to be like the geese and fly. They show him how, but warn him not to look down. On earth, the villagers see Coyote flying above them and they tempt him: "Look down, Coyote, and we will show you something incredibly beautiful that you have never seen before." Coyote looks down, and he goes crashing to earth. "That's how we teach our kids to be comfortable and happy with who they are. If you're a coyote, don't try to be a goose," Joe says.

On the tail of this story is another one, about how Coyote sneaks into a tepee, opens the owner's bundle, and gets stung by a bee. "That's how we teach our people not to go into others' belongings. You never know what you will find there. It may hurt you."

As Joe explains the moral of each tale, I feel the raw force of these stories. I never realized before what strong instructional tools they are. I wonder if they come from the same source as Aesop's fables, and if that source is cultural or the earth itself?

Soon Coyote is watching a big male whale, and noticing that his little baby whales follow him in a straight line. Coyote tells the whale that he has kids and they don't obey him. He asks the whale to show him how to keep his children in line. The whale obliges and tells Coyote that he makes a hole through the neck of each kid and puts them all on a string. Coyote does this to his kids, but when he tries to have them follow him, all of them have died. Joe comments, "This teaches how to be comfortable with who you are and not to try to be like other people." It seems to be a teaching that occurs in many of the stories, and if self-acceptance is the lesson, it is a potent one indeed.

I look around me at the mesmerized faces. I find myself delighted by the seemingly innocent but very sophisticated and direct method of imparting information and behavioral norms. I stare into the dying embers of the fire. I hear Joe's hypnotic voice telling us that he learned all of these stories from his infancy to his teens and they were all told by his grandma. He never even found out her real name. All his life he just called her "Grandma." The last time he saw her, she revealed to him that all of the Apache stories have a purpose, and that is to teach right from wrong, and to hand down a moral system. "Just tell the stories," she exhorted him, and he obeys.

Joseph looks at us through his sunglasses and tells us bits and pieces about the Apache way. For example, there is a cardinal rule about taking the life of anything, no matter how small it is. "You only kill to eat or to protect yourself. If it's not one of these two reasons, don't kill."

Joe continues talking about what it's like to be Apache. "We talk to animals and rocks," he says. "I talked to gila monsters as a kid. To this day I swear they talk back to me."

Someone in the audience whispers that Joe Geronimo is a fraud—he is not really descended from Geronimo, but just capitalizes on it. Is he a direct descendant of Geronimo? Is he opportunistic? The bottom line is that he is a good storyteller, and I let it go at that.

I have to pause and take a breath after meeting Joe Geronimo, because the experience is strong and I want it to linger. Laura and I go to a new cafe/bookstore/performance space in town (the Old Santa Fe Trail Bookstore), and Beaver is working there. Once, I was shaken to the core with anger at the mention of Beaver's name. Now I am happy to see her and we hug and exchange stories. From my relationship with Beaver, I have learned a lesson in patience. I rode out the strong emotions, and they passed.

In the afternoon, I give a two-hour talk on playwriting, and I notice how influenced I have been by everything I've encountered here. I talk a lot about fear, overcoming it, facing it, dealing with it, coming out the other side. It applies to writing obstacles as it applies to life obstacles. I smile at how much I am changing!

In the evening, Paul and I race out to Camel Rock. The night is bitterly cold, and we have to curl our toes under our feet to cushion our soles from the deep chill of the earth. Camel Rock is a famous eponymous local site: it is a rock that looks like a camel. Across from it, our friends Lalo and Rose have just opened up a huge Peruvian gift shop. There is no heat, but other than that, it has the warmth that we love in the ethnic communities. Everyone at the party is from South America, and Spanish is the language of choice although English is the language of communication. Our friend Consuelo Luz shows up, and she sings in Spanish, accompanied by Lalo on keyboards. There is a drummer, someone plays shells, and everyone picks up something or other to join in the percussive ensemble. It goes on till the wee hours. I spend a lot of time talking to a woman named Cristela who channels spirits when she dances, and she gives me a solo singing recital of a sun salutation in Nahautl, an ancient Aztec dialect. She also dances around the room by herself, oblivious to the noise in the room, doing an improvised ballet. She is descended from the Toltecs, she tells me. Paul says she looks like Frida Kahlo. I approach Cristela when she is done dancing.

"Cristela, how would you like to perform at a petroglyph party?"

She blinks at me, not understanding. I tell her about our plans for December 14th.

"Si, si, si," she says. "I will dance."

"Will you help to open up the program? Will you do a sun salutation in Nahautl?"

"Si, si, of course."

When we leave the party, I am jumping up and down in the car seat with excitement.

"This petroglyph party is going to be amazing! Sun salutations, bow-drill fires . . . and this is just the beginning!"

Paul stares at me.

"What are you staring at?"

324

The Origins of Things

"How will we ever go home to L.A.?" he whispers.

"I know," I whisper back. "We are obviously so much more connected here, and there is the fluidity of moving from one ethnic community to the other. No one talks about deals and fame and amassing money, and everyone we meet is full of passion and devoid of pretension."

"The problem with Santa Fe is that you can't earn a living here," Paul says. "Architects work as waiters. Lawyers have part-time jobs selling ads for papers. It is probably the richest state in terms of culture, and one of the poorest in terms of per capita income. The very thing that keeps this place great—urban sophistication in a countrified setting—is also the reason you can't find work—lack of industry."

We look at each other, and fall quiet. We know we will have to go back to L.A. in order to earn a living.

At night, I try to sleep but the wind rattles the windows and my tootsies flip around like fish trying to get comfy in the icy sheets. Somehow I start thinking about the Hopi Indians. The Hopi are known for their prophecies, which have predicted everything from Hiroshima to the breakup of Russia. The Hopi have said that they would give four warnings, and if the world did not heed their warnings, life would end for humankind as we know it. They have recently given their fourth. They revealed stone tablets, which are their prophetic instruments, and they say the earth will be engulfed in famine, disease, earthquakes, and natural catastrophes if humankind does not opt for peace and start saving the planet. "Has anyone out there heard the prophecies?" I wonder as I fall into an exhausted sleep.

In the morning, my mind turns to a more pleasant and less menacing subject—Tent Rocks, at the Jemez Pueblo, where I have been wanting to go for ages. It is a perfect day for hiking, sunny and crisp, and we step into our hiking boots and head out of town. As soon as we leave Santa Fe, I am swept up in the magic of the countryside, and my daily cares slip away as nature takes over.

Tent Rocks rises out of nowhere. We travel about five miles on a dirt road near Jemez, and suddenly we see rocks that are shaped like tepees all around us. We walk into the arroyo, and our only company is a circling crow and a magpie. Slowly the shapes of the rocks change, and they become anthropomorphic—here are three Corn Maidens, and over there is a grandmother with a basket on her head. Soon there are animals—a lion, a bird of prey, a mouse holding a football. Paul and I always have fun naming rocks.

I find a marvelous red, dramatic rock that looks like it is dripping with blood. Paul bounds around, marveling at the sight of snow on the tips of rocks, rendering all of the shapes more stark and beautiful. We trek around for a few hours, and I actually start to bless the Creator out loud for the beauty of the natural world. I really start to understand why Indians worship the earth, and why nature is their church.

Then we go to visit Joseph Villegas's wife Cathy where she works at Sears. We find her behind a cash register. As she checks out ski outfits and shimmering sweaters, she tells us that Joseph has been going through an identity crisis since he met us. Until now, Joseph has always proudly proclaimed that he was Spanish, because he could trace the family name "Villegas" to the *conquistadores*. He knew that his mother was "Mexicana," but he never thought about what that meant. Now he is beginning to wonder how he can really be "Spanish" if his mother is Mexicana. And when he thinks about what Mexicana means, it's the mix of indigenous Indians with the Spanish. So, in fact, Joseph is part Indian. How can he apologize to the Indians when he is also part Indian?

"It's easy," Paul suggests. "You stand up and ask for forgiveness and then you can also accept the offer."

Cathy is very relieved that she knows who she is—pure Hispanic. "Not so fast," we taunt her. "The *conquistadores* did not come with women. So who did your ancestors mate with if not Indians?" She blanches and says, "Oh, my God, this is too much. It's mind-boggling."

We call Joseph on the phone. He is speaking fast, and he says that his mind is racing, day and night. He is realizing that his knowledge of the past is built on lies, and he affirms his desire to stand up in public on December 14th and start to deal with the truth. He WILL apologize to the Indians, he WILL claim who he is, he WILL start the healing process.

"I am just beginning to find out my real identity," he says.

It's fascinating, to say the least, to see Joseph and Cathy wrestle with who they are. I think that a combination of pride and wanting to spare children from discrimination has led Spanish-speaking people to tell their children they are Spanish. But then, there is also the truth. Are they Spanish or part Indian? Are they Mexicano, and, if so, doesn't that mean they are part Indian? Who is who? All of this is happening so fast that each day brings a new awareness and level of consciousness.

Watching Joseph and Cathy come to terms with this is like seeing *converso* Jews find out they aren't Catholic but are really Jewish. Do any of us know for certain who we really are, or do we just believe what we are told? As we unravel the mystery of our own pasts, it seems to link us to more and more groups of people. Are we all just part of the same family?

The days fly by and we brew here, like tea bags in a cup, getting richer by the moment. Of course this is the richness that you cannot take to the bank because it's only a human investment.

"Pretty soon Thanksgiving is coming," Paul says to me when I kick off my furry slippers and hop into bed at the end of a long day.

"We have so much to be thankful for," I muse. "Life has been good to us, and it will be nice to take one day out of the year to really say 'thank you' and to enumerate all of our blessings, large and small."

"Let's not wait," Paul whispers.

So we lie there in bed, holding hands, and expressing aloud our thanks for everything we are learning and for all that life is giving us.

15

A Healing
of the Heart

Mid-November to mid-December, 1991

I am speechless. I gave Joseph Lenny Smallfeather's phone number, and today they met over tea. Joseph looked Lenny in the eyes and apologized to Lenny for what his culture did to Lenny's culture. Lenny began to cry. Joseph began to cry. They walked out to their cars, took each other's hands, and then fell into an embrace.

As Lenny drove away, someone called to Joseph, and he turned around. It was the head of the Cruzados, an organization of Catholic Spanish men. "What are you doing hugging that Indian man?" the Cruzado asked Joseph in a critical voice. Joseph swallowed his nervousness and answered, "He is my brother. This is about healing." And he went on to tell the man what we are doing on December 14th. The man thought for a while, and absorbed it. Then he said, "Joseph, can I be part of it?"

THIS IS THE TIME FOR HEALING. This is as important as anything I have done in my life . . . and I am determined to stay completely behind the scenes and invisible. That is the way it must be.

I am flopping around the house in my slippers when the doorbell rings. It is Elisa Herrera, the Spanish wife of Cochiti Pueblo drummer Arnold Herrera. She is barely in the door when I accost her: "Elisa! You are the only Spanish woman I know who is married to an Indian man, and you have had a wonderful but rough time of it. I want you to get up on December 14th and speak to the public. Enough hiding behind Arnold and being Mrs. Wife. I want you to speak from the heart and go public about it. Tell what it has been like and continues to be like."

She sits down, drinks tea, eats bread, turns green then red, like a traffic light. Finally she says, "I don't know if I can do it."

"What are you waiting for?"

"I don't know. I just can't decide this fast."

I look at Elisa, or rather, I look *through* Elisa. Here is a smart, competent, imaginative woman who is dragging herself through life, functioning as a second-class citizen, doing other people's chores and laundry.

"Elisa, it's time for you to have your moment in the sun. Get up and share with people your inner vision—because it is clear you have one. You keep all of your feelings bottled up. Let them out."

She sets her jaw. She avoids my eyes. I wonder if she is angry with me for pushing her.

Two minutes go by. Three. Four. Then Elisa looks me in the eyes and nods.

"I'll do it. It will be difficult, but it will be healing."

I hug her. She has just taken a major step forward in her life.

Joseph and I have discussed this petroglyph party from every angle. Although we want the public to learn about the petroglyphs and the impending development that threatens them, we have decided not to make this an informational event. We want this to be a celebration of people, and a time for healing. We must heal ailing personal and cultural relationships and get in touch with our hearts. Joseph and I agree that we have never felt clearer about anything in our lives. We settle upon the Unitarian church as the locus.

Tim Shay drops in shortly after Joseph leaves. If possible, he looks worse than before. He has been going through a terrible period in his life, but he wants to reassure us that he will participate on December 14th, and he thinks it will be healing for him. Suddenly, out of the blue, the word "healing" is on everyone's lips.

"I am going to build a fire for the audience," Tim says. "I'll do it on a slab of slate or concrete so I don't burn the church down."

He asks me to find the concrete or slate for him, because he'll be leaving town a week before the party.

"Where are you going?" I ask.

"Rehab center," he says. "This time I'm serious. My drinking is ruining my marriage to Wilma and destroying my life. I've got to straighten out. But don't worry. I'll get a leave to come and participate in the petroglyph party. I'll be there in time to go onstage."

I blanch. No rehearsal. No preparation. And this is the opening act!

329

Will I just get a piece of stone and trust Tim? I'm afraid of everything that can go wrong. But I look Tim in the eyes and do not give in to my fears and worries.

"So be it, Tim. Good luck to you. That's the way we'll do it."

Tim leaves and there is a loud knock on the door. It is Wes Studi, the Indian actor, en route home to Oklahoma for Thanksgiving. He has about twenty huge envelopes full of pictures from *The Last of the Mohicans,* which he just finished shooting. He plays the villain Magua, and he has a haircut and makeup that are pretty terrifying.

"Wes, how would you like to be master of ceremonies?"

"For what?"

"Oh . . . a petroglyph party?"

"I can't. I'm going back to L.A."

"Fly here from L.A. There's no money involved, but you don't have to audition either. I think you'll be great. If you want the job, you have it."

"A petroglyph party?"

"Yes. A celebration of the breath of the ancestors, chiseled into the rocks."

Wes smiles, and says he'll do it!

"It's dangerous to walk in this door," Paul says. "No sooner does a person cross the threshold than he's roped into performing."

In the evening, I see an article in a local paper that really gets my attention. It says that there is a rumor among the Indians that the direct descendant of Christopher Columbus, who just passed through Santa Fe, is going to apologize to the Indians. The writer calls this a stupid, deluded idea that will never happen. Little does he know that it is going to happen, and soon. On December 14th!

On the work front, I get a call from my producers. They say they are sorry for the way they behaved and they still want me on the television project. I do not even comment. I just listen, make polite chitchat, and then get off the phone. I do not have to tell them how I feel about them. They have betrayed my trust and broken the magic spell; I can never have that intense an involvement with them again. My mind, my eyes, my life are now geared toward healing. Nothing else matters.

"You're so calm," Paul says as I get off the phone.

I do not even tell him who was on the phone. I just wax philosophical. "The universe will keep us afloat," I say elliptically. "It often seems like we're sinking, but there's always a life raft and it's life it-self."

It is almost the end of November, and my sister Patsy arrives for Thanksgiving. This is the first guest from real life that we have "al-lowed" to come, because our life here is very intense, our place is small, and it is hard for us to entertain. There is a saying about San-ta Fe that either you fit right in or it will "chew you up and spit you out," and we have no idea of what will happen with my sister.

She steps off the airport shuttle in Santa Fe and we whisk her to Arnold and Elisa Herrera's house for Thanksgiving dinner. It is a cel-ebration of the Herreras' first Thanksgiving in their "new" home, for they have just expanded their place enormously. Before they were all crowded into a tiny, messy space, and now they have bright *vigas* and white-washed walls and much room to enjoy and to grow.

While Patsy is in the bathroom, Arnold brings out one of the drums he made and begins to serenade her. When Patsy emerges, Arnold sings a lilting Pueblo song for her—much to her delight. We all sit at the table, with the kids running around and being very funny and crazy, and Arnold makes a long blessing in Keres. Then he takes bits of food and drink and disappears outside. He explains that they be-lieve in spirits. They call the spirits in and ask for protection, and they feed the spirits to thank them for coming.

Patsy begins to slide into a mellow Indian mood as Arnold speaks. He shows us gifts that were recently given to him by the *kachinas* at Sandia Pueblo to thank him for his contributions to their dances. He is very moved by the acknowledgment of his singing and drumming for other Pueblos. The gifts are blessed corn ears and a beautiful ar-row with a red flint arrowhead.

Arnold's children have been brought up off the Pueblo. They don't seem to pay much attention to the blessings or the Indian parapher-nalia, but the eldest is off in his room *making* an arrow when we ar-rive. Somehow, without Arnold ever shoving the Indian ways down his children's throats, it permeates.

After dinner, a most surprising thing happens. The kids and Arnold and Elisa take us out to secret ruins they have on their property. I nev-er knew they were there. Arnold's maternal ancestors came from Pecos, and he was most excited to find potsherds at this private ruin, and to discover that the sherds were in the Pecos style and came from the migration of his predecessors!

"I guess it's no coincidence we live here," he says. "We're right on the path from Pecos!"

As Arnold speaks, the kids are running around. They have brought along their air rifles; they are looking to bag a rabbit, so they will have sinews to complete and bind their home-made arrows.

"You see?" Arnold whispers proudly. "They are learning." He feels validated in his Indian belief that you can teach kids by example, and not by force.

As the sun goes down, we all appreciate the natural beauty of the land, dressed up for a true Thanksgiving.

We then race to Rita and John Goodman's for Thanksgiving II. As usual, the Goodman spread is lavish in their art deco home, and they have told us to bring along our friends.

"Are you sure it's okay?" I ask.

"Yes," Rita answers. "Your friends are our friends."

"What if I invite Indian friends and Hispanic friends and it's the first time they are ever getting together socially?"

"My pleasure," says Rita. "We'll have a historic Thanksgiving."

I invite Joseph Villegas and arrange for him to meet Laura Fragua and Steve Wall. Joseph is chomping at the bit to meet Indian people now, but even though the setting is social, it is very tense. Laura, like many Indian people, only recently found out the truth of what the Spanish did to the Indians, and she is angry indeed. She and Steve are extremely aloof as Joseph gets more and more anxious and tries to tell them how much he cares for them and their culture and is trying to preserve the petroglyphs. Sometimes, as Joseph speaks, Laura walks away.

I wonder who, at this Thanksgiving party, knows what is going on? My sister Patsy looks over toward me, and I know she is attuned to what is happening. As Joseph's little daughter Candy blithely demonstrates her ballet, as guests laugh and chat, a five-hundred-year-old drama is unfolding. And it doesn't get any smoother or easier. In fact, Joseph gets stiffer and more insistent, and Steve and Laura retreat to the other side of the room. Just as Joseph is about to leave for his night job at the police department, he turns to Laura and apologizes to her for what his people have done to hers. She just stands there and listens. Then Joseph goes to shake her hand goodbye, and suddenly they fall into each other's arms and stay there for a long time, with tears in their eyes. I watch, my jaw hanging open. I have no idea how it happens, but suddenly I run toward them and put my arms around both of them, thanking them over and over. Patsy stands a few feet away, and there are tears in her eyes. She knows, as I know, that we are witnessing history.

When Joseph and his family leave, the party gets ribald and crazy and none of our Indian friends speaks a word about what happened. Not even a syllable. Some things just have to be experienced and not commented upon. For half the people at the party, the exchange took place so quietly that they never knew anything was going on.

The next morning we leave for Taos, which Patsy has never seen. It is snowing, the roads are supposed to be slippery, but the sun comes out and we have the joy of clear routes and the beauty of the countryside air-brushed in snow. We ride north for an hour and a half, through the mountains and alongside the Rio Grande. We see bright red chile ristras against the white snow and we all feel lucky indeed.

We arrive in Taos and I can't bear to take the tourist route because even at this off-season time I know there will be many visitors. So we stop instead to visit Gail White Wolf's parents. I can only surmise that my sister's presence acts as a catalyst, because I have never seen Gail's very traditional dad so open and talkative. We sit in the living room, with feather bustles from dances on the wall, pots and wooden animal pieces on the windowsills, and a soap opera blaring on the television, and Gail's dad tells us how he trains the deer dancers for their dances. He says he goes into the kiva on December 20th and teaches the deer dancers until they emerge for their Christmas dances. He explains how the *koshari* clowns cannot touch him and he cannot touch them when he is working with the dancers. He is "safe" or off-limits for their clowning. Gail's mother chimes in and tells us that she was a female deer dancer two years ago—every year only two women are picked, and her husband trains them.

"What an honor to train the deer dancers," I comment.

"Honor?" Gail's father bleats. "It's a lot of hard work and responsibility."

At one point Gail's dad asks us if we see a vase across the room. We all say we do. He crosses the room and points to the root of the plant in the vase. He says that Taos is like the root of all the other Pueblos. Religious leaders from the other Pueblos come there to learn. He says that he has worked with Apache and Ute children as a counselor, but the values of the Taos people are the strongest. I look sideways at Patsy and can see her eyes widening with interest as she takes it all in.

Then Gail's father speaks to us of the drums he makes, and he hands me a small drum, the size of a Christmas ornament. I thank him profusely, and he bluntly informs me that it is for my sister Patsy but he will give me one too, which he does. I am thrilled when Gail's mother tells me that she has enlarged a photo I took of her, and I offer to take a photo of her husband too. Although he protests, he finally agrees and he leads us into his private quarters where he makes drums. The huge drums are beautiful, made with elk and cow and deer and horse hides. He beats on each one to demonstrate, and says the thinnest hides (deer) give the best sounds.

We take a few photos of him with his drums, and then Patsy and I get into the pictures. He says he feels awkward about smelling from his hides, so we laugh and take photos of us sniffing him. Patsy rapidly sees the wonderful sense of humor of all the Indians we know. It is very bonding. Most people do not see it, because they talk to the Indians as though they come from another universe.

At one point, Gail's brother sticks his head in the room and barely grunts a hello to us. "He's a real Indian," Gail's father tells us. "He won't talk to you because he doesn't think you have anything important to say." That is a very honest way of reminding us that we are white.

We then hug Gail's family goodbye and head for the Pueblo. As we leave, Gail's mother comes after us and gives us slices of her delicious fruit pies to take with us.

Predictably, there are tourists at Taos Pueblo, even with the cold and snow. We walk into the adobe church and Patsy smiles when she see the murals—Indian and Christian motifs mixed. Corn and Jesus. She photographs the gorgeous five-story Pueblo in the snow, and we are fortunate to have the sun come out. It really is very dramatic. The tips of the *vigas* are white and the famous outline of the Pueblo is radiant with the snow drippings.

We go into a shop in one of the Pueblo houses, and as other tourists wander in and wander out, we stay to chat. We comment on the thickness of the adobe walls, and how much insulation they provide on a cold day. Bobby, the seller, waxes eloquent about adobe and about Taos as well. He tells us that the first settlement at Taos was 10,000 years ago and dated from the time of Noah. (!) The survivors of the flood came and established the Pueblo of Taos. The present structure was built 1300 years ago. He says it is similar in construction to the houses of Mesa Verde or other cliff dwellings, but instead of stone, the early Indian settlers used the rich clay earth to make adobe by mixing it with straw.

I am startled at how open people are—telling us about their history and their holidays and their oral tradition. It is a tribute to Patsy, who is busy buying a wonderful necklace that hangs from the wall. She is so open and interested that she gets back a very heartfelt response.

It is now late afternoon, the snow is falling again, and we do not have snow tires. The safe thing for us to do is to hot-foot it back to Santa Fe, but we decide to drive instead to the Hispanic mountain village (Las Trampas) where Jeff Klein and Consuelo Luz have a country home. Jeff, a white man from Los Angeles, built the house back in the sixties in his hippie days, and it is a staggering feat. He used no power tools, so every piece of exposed wood in the ceiling had to be cut and hauled and scraped by hand. The huge beams were dragged by horses across icy snow, which made the pulling easier but the builder colder. The 4500 adobe bricks were all made by hand. Even now, two decades later, Jeff is very proud of it.

The kids are playing Nintendo. A mat with footprints is spread on the floor and they bounce noisily up and down on it until the *vigas* shake, as "runners" on a TV screen respond to the movement of their feet. "We were deprived kids," Patsy jokes. "No video games."

Then Patsy and I grow serious, and we reflect about the deprivation that Indian children have grown up with. On their reservations, they have among the highest rate of alcoholism, fetal alcohol syndrome, and suicide in the nation.

"They had a society that provided for their needs," Patsy comments. "Now we have imposed our way, and everything is messed up for them. They are caught between two worlds, two conflicting value systems, and it drives them nuts."

"You're catching on fast," I say.

The next morning, there is a knock of our door-front mallet. When I open the door, Tim and Wilma come in with Wilma's daughter Tina. I am relieved to see Tim and Wilma together, but disturbed to see how pale and gaunt Tim is. And his eyes are wide and terrified, as though he has come face-to-face with the devil. He holds his hand up for us

335

to see—it is bandaged up so thickly it looks like a bear paw. It seems that he was practicing fire-starting for the December 14th event, and he slashed some tendons with a knife.

"I guess you won't be doing a fire ceremony," I tell Tim sadly.

"Yes I will," he says. "I don't care if I'm in rehab. I don't care if my hand is busted. I am going to find a way to do it with one hand."

Patsy walks in the room and, when there is a pause in the conversation, she tells Wilma that she saw medicine bags for sale and wonders what people put in them. The next thing I know, Wilma is offering to make one for Patsy, and to come to the house to do it so that Patsy can observe the process and it will have more meaning for her. She tells Patsy to put her blood, sweat, and tears inside, and I tell Patsy she will have to think about what that means. We all go out to eat, and Wilma is talking a bit of Navajo, Tim is doing a sentence or two in Penobscot, and Patsy tells a Yiddish joke. No one has any trouble understanding.

The next morning, as promised, Wilma arrives. She sits down at the kitchen table with little Tina at her side, and she pulls out pieces of hide from her purse. She and Patsy pick the softest buckskin, which is almost creamy in consistency, and Wilma spends the next five hours cutting and sewing the pouch for Patsy. And as she makes the pouch, we all talk. About life and men and marriage. We joke. We speak of Hanukkah and little Tina tries to write Hebrew letters. Patsy is completely entranced. When the medicine bag is done, she offers to pay Wilma, but Wilma refuses. She says she will make medicine pouches for other people for a minimal sum, but this time she will not take money. Patsy ceremoniously slips the medicine pouch around her neck, and says she will be hard-pressed to ever take it off. She immediately feels that it is healing. We put some sage in it, and then she says she is going to find out what "blood, sweat, and tears" means, and add that too.

While we are sitting around, Doug and Gail White Wolf stop in, and Paul and I look at each other and agree that this is a good way to spend our sixth wedding anniversary—sharing warm drinks and talk with our friends. Doug tells us that he has heard a lot about our December 14th event. Wilma and Tim chime in that it is a people's movement, and there is no institute, no grant money, no formality behind it. The interest generated by our petroglyph party just grows and expands daily.

A Healing of the Heart

When everyone leaves, Patsy says she is very sorry that she will not be here for the event, so Paul and I decide to take her out to the petroglyphs at La Cieneguilla. The weather is freezing—in the teens, I think—and our toes and noses and hands have a hard time of it. We climb through barbed wire and up the slippery snow-covered rocks until we come to the top of the mesa. And there Patsy sees the spirals and animals and people and snakes that we love so much, chiseled dramatically into the stone. They are offset by the snow, and it really is spectacular as enduring testimony to early Pueblo culture.

As we climb down from the hills, Joseph Villegas comes to meet us in his truck and to check on us to make sure we are okay. How different from the first time he met us in these hills with his loaded Betsy! He insists that we come back to his house, and there his kids present Patsy with a framed picture of the petroglyphs and a picture of them, inscribed on the back. By now Patsy is in tears. She cannot believe the generosity and warmth that are being bestowed upon her and upon us.

I speak to Patsy by phone after she gets back to San Diego and she tells me a wonderful story. She was wearing her medicine bag and an Indian woman commented on it at the Phoenix airport where Patsy was changing planes. Patsy told the woman how she got the medicine bag and the woman handed her a card, invited her to visit her in April and go to see the *kachina* dances. Patsy was blown away by the openness, the warmth, the generosity. If human connection is healing, then the medicine bag has already proved to Patsy its unique healing properties!

I get another negative and disturbing call from my producers. I try to focus my attention on the complexities of the Hispanic and Indian world instead of the Sturm und Drang of Hollywood. Today Joseph Villegas takes me to a private meeting. It is chaired by Christina Rodriguez, a very powerful (Hispanic) lady here who is the queen of land grant claims. Christina comes from the very old and very strong Lovato family, and most of Santa Fe, right up to the Pueblo of Tesuque, is on an old land grant made to the Lovato family by the king of Spain before New Mexico was part of the United States. New Mexico did not join the States until 1912, and this land was given to the family in the late 1700s. Christina is a real firebrand with a rebellious spirit, and she wants to take Santa Fe back and give it to the indigenous peoples who rightfully own it according to land grants. Needless to say, this is a political hot potato.

Christina says she is half Indian and actually refers to herself as an Indian. She teaches New Mexican history and says everything we are told about it is lies. She has a close affiliation with the Hopis, and says they consider Santa Fe to be a sister Pueblo. Now all of this sounds fantastic and amazing, and Christina is going for sovereignty—that is, she wants Santa Fe to revert to Pueblo status, and it should belong to the natives. In this case, it means the land owners, and the original land owners are the owners of the Spanish land grants. Part of the manifesto she reads involves getting rid of the Indian school here, because Christina claims that it is a thing of the past and the Indians do not want to be educated separately as Indians. They want to go to public schools.

Now here lies the problem. I think the Indians very much want to be Indians and want to know about their own culture. Christina speaks up for Cherokees and Hopis and Utes and everyone else, but she pooh-poohs the Pueblo Indians and I have to find out why. Is it because these Pueblo Indians are the original inhabitants of Santa Fe, before there were land grants? Christina's manifesto claims there are no indigenous Indians in Santa Fe; there are just indigenous peoples. But what does that mean? Weren't there Indians here before, even if their Pueblo at Santa Fe was not formally occupied when the Spanish arrived? Is this a new twist to the old conflict between the Spanish and the Indians?

It is likely that the movement Christina leads, or another movement like it, is going to set the pace for the rest of the Southwest. There are going to be major land grant claims because the people who own the land also own the water rights, and water rights are going to be the big issue of the future. Whoever owns the water owns the wealth. This is all overwhelming to me, and of course I am the only Anglo at the meeting, while they all sit and denigrate Anglos.

Christina tells story after story of how younger Hispanic people are manipulating land and homes out of their elders—telling them they have Alzheimer's, getting powers of attorney; basically stealing land. She then confesses that it is happening in her own family, and her siblings have thrown her off her family land and forced her mother to exclude her from her land inheritance. Everyone at the meeting is part of the Lovato family, and I am just gawking at all of this, trying to take it in. I have never been exposed to such intense cultural issues that are not my own culture. I feel deeply privileged to be witnessing all of this!

I would give Christina my support right away, but the problem of the Indians —and what their rights are—gets in the way for me. I try to discuss it with her, but she keeps claiming that there are no native Indians in Santa Fe, and that there are only indigenous peoples. I want to know what happened to the Indians who were here when the Spanish came, and why they are being excluded from this. I do not get a satisfactory answer.

At the meeting I pipe up and say I want Joseph to run for public office. Christina looks at me and says I should be his campaign manager, and they will all back him for county commissioner.

"Well, will you do it?" she asks.

"That's the big time," I say to Christina. "I have to make sure I really comprehend all the issues because they are amazingly complex here."

"Yes," she says, "and as for your questions about the Indians—well, we'll keep talking!"

The next morning, Joseph goes jogging along his beloved Santa Fe River, and suddenly something possesses him to jog to the source of the water that comes down from the Sangre de Cristo mountains. He is very surprised to find that at some point the river bifurcates, and half of it, the part that goes to the Sangre de Cristo mountains, is dry. The "wet" part, which everyone thinks is the Santa Fe River, is runoff from a sewage treatment plant. In other words, what is thought to be the Santa Fe River comes straight from the toilet bowls of Santa Fe. Joseph immediately calls the Environmental Protection Agency, where they know him by name, and files a complaint. It is the first complaint ever filed. He is like a shotgun now, and his targets are everywhere. Every day he uncovers another lie, another sellout, another cover-up. A lot of it has to do with precious water rights. I keep teasing him that he's doing *Chinatown,* but he's never heard of the movie. Joseph and his wife Cathy are terrific people, who come from a very different world from mine. "Is Jewish the same as Buddhist?" Cathy once asked. There is a huge gap, but what binds us is a set of values, and that is much more important than the differences.

The local newspaper assigns Paul the task of writing the advance story on the petroglyph party, so Paul goes out to La Cieneguilla to take a photo of Joseph. He takes Tim Shay and Wilma with him because Tim is part of the December 14th event and he has never seen the petroglyphs. When they get out there, Tim crouches down, and

339

with a hand-made wooden bow-drill, he makes a fire from the fric-
tion caused by rubbing wood together. The process takes about two
minutes—even though Tim can only use one hand. Joseph is practically gasping from being so moved. "It really touches my heart," he
later says. He tells Tim that this is probably the first time in hundreds
and hundreds of years that the Indian petroglyphs have again seen a
fire made like that.

Tim looks around, and he says the petroglyph site is a sacred space.
He notes that it is protected by rattlesnakes. Joseph says that the rat-
tlesnakes never bothered him, and Tim says it's because they know
Joseph's intentions are good.

Wilma is very moved too. She once went to the petroglyphs a year
ago, by invitation, and she was suffering a lot that day because she and
Tim had broken up. Now she is back at the petroglyphs with him, and
he wants to heal and she feels it is good and right. They have only
been married a few months, and it has been a nightmare, but maybe
now they can set things right. She looks around gratefully at the hope
and inspiration she gets from the ancient stone markings.

In the middle of all of this petroglyph activity, Paul and I decide to
make the most of the time we have left in New Mexico. We borrow
every stitch of warm clothing we can find, jump in our car, and head
south.

We go to Socorro, and then to the Bosque del Apache bird reserve.
We were there during the summer, and I vowed to go back in winter-
time because the locals say it's supposed to be quite a spectacle. The
weather is gorgeous, and as we drive onto the huge reserve, we see
only brown shrubbery, and so we think all the raving is probably much
ado about nothing.

Wrong. We should know by now how expectations are reversed in
Indian land. Within minutes after our arrival, Paul stops the car,
points to a side road, and says, "What is that?" I get out of the car to
look, because I see a huge patch of snow on the ground. When I get a
bit closer, I realize it isn't snow at all. The earth is carpeted with snow
geese! There are thousands and thousands of them. As I walk closer,
I probably scare them, because there is a great "thwapping" of wings,
and the birds scatter and soar up to the sky. The sound is deafening,
as they call to each other and to the sun—"awh—awh-awh-awh." It
goes on for about ten minutes. Paul pulls out the tiny tape recorder,

and he is bug-eyed as he walks under the cloud cover of geese, recording them. I, on the other hand, am mesmerized as I look up at the sky. The white geese fly in air force formation, sometimes silhouetted and back-lit against the sky, sometimes with sun glimmering on their wings. It is an overwhelmingly direct contact with the beauty and social organization of the natural world and our brother birds. There is no question that they are every bit as alive as we are.

We drive around the Bosque after that, and Paul plays his newly recorded tape to the sandhill cranes and snow geese that strut and fly everywhere. It is his way of talking to them. Sometimes they answer back. The weeds now turn to reeds and they are red, ablaze, fiery against the afternoon sky. The mountains are reflected in the water, and we can see doubles of everything. Suddenly a shadow is cast across the visual field, and when we look up, a swarm of black birds flies overhead. Then we look out into the distance, and the geese are covering the land like snow again.

We fall asleep in a Socorro motel, our heads full of visions of birds and wings and streaming sunlight. When we awake, we stock up with food and head for the Zuni reservation and the present Zuni village of Halona:wa.

All of the Pueblo Indians have emergent creation stories, and the Zuni are no exception. According to their legend, they emerged into the fourth world near the Grand Canyon, and they traveled east according to instructions from the Creator on where to live. They were looking for the "Middle Place" and they found it at Halona:wa, where they now live.

According to archeologists, the Zuni valleys were probably inhabited from about 8000 B.C. on. For thousands of years, the early hunter-gatherers lived under dome shelters built atop pits. In roughly A.D. 300–400 farming began, corn was introduced from Mexico, and an agrarian lifestyle developed. Houses became less transitory and people began to congregate and live in villages in pit houses. The staples were corn, beans, and squash, and the early inhabitants required storage space and proximity to water. This is probably why villages sprang up along the Zuni River.

In approximately A.D. 1000, significant changes took place in these villages. Although no roads have yet been found, there was contact and trade with the people who lived at Chaco Canyon. The influence

341

of the Chacoans is seen in the way the buildings changed, and the fact that kivas were introduced. There was also the introduction of "dry farming," and this gave versatility to the locus of villages and allowed people to live away from water. It is estimated that about 7000 people lived in the Zuni area. (From what I can recall, ancient Athens, at the height of its glory, had fewer than 25,000 people, so the Zuni-area Anasazi weren't doing too badly!)

In the mid to late thirteenth century, this whole area of the Southwest suffered from a prolonged and terrible drought. People moved from the valleys to higher elevations, to take advantage of increased rainfall. Villages combined and became larger. Walls were built for protection, possibly against raids. By 1350, many of the people from these villages had moved to the Rio Grande, or to Hopi or present-day Zuni (Halona:wa). When Coronado arrived in 1540, there were six villages occupied, and Halona:wa was one of them.

The Spanish arrived with their usual greedy goal: to find gold. Zuni is in the area where the Spanish were seeking the famed Seven Cities of Cibola, but the Indians used their habitual and clever ploy of telling the Spanish that the gold was farther on, just beyond them. The Spanish were deflected, but they finally returned to meet fierce armed opposition from the Zunis. The Indians fought with rocks and arrows, and although they fought mightily, they were eventually subdued by the superior force of guns and small cannons.

The Spanish never found gold at Zuni, but they pursued their other mission of conversion. The Zunis did not fully accept Catholicism, like many of the other Pueblos finally did, so it is possible to see the purity of old traditions, untainted by and not mixed with Christian ways. The high point of their year is the Shalako celebration, and this is why we go to Zuni, in hopes of seeing it.

Many people, both Indian and Anglo, warned us about Zuni. It is supposed to be freezing, and it requires tremendous endurance to participate in the festival. Everyone would love to go, but most stay away because of the physical hardship. No longer paralyzed by my fear of things, we decide to brave it.

At the entrance to the Zuni village are craft shops, and many are owned and run by non-Indians. The prices, marked 50 percent off, seem extremely high and I wonder how much of the money goes to the crafts-people. The Zunis are world renowned for their detailed, colorful, mosaic-like inlay work. They also make fetishes in the form of animals that are carved out of stone, alabaster, and antler. Most important to us, as we arrive in town, is the fact that the stores have maps which indicate where the Shalako houses are.

Every year, six houses are chosen as Shalako houses, and it is an enormous responsibility. It takes the better part of a year to build special rooms and to decorate for the event. Without the maps, visitors would be hard-pressed to find the houses. Even *with* the maps . . . we realize that it is going to be hard to try finding unmarked houses on unlit night roads!

We cannot find any published information about Shalako, so we have to keep our ears open and learn whatever we can. We overhear someone saying that you can see the Shalako in the afternoon, but no one mentions the place or time. When we ask anyone, including a cop, the time of any event in Indian country, the answer is always the same: "Who knows? It's on Indian time."

We have the name of one woman to look up, named Rebecca, and we decide to try to track her down. At an Indian village, you just ask around, and you can pretty easily track down any inhabitant. Someone points to a cluster of houses in the distance, and we head that way. Within seconds, we are wading in mud. It has snowed, and when the snow melted, the earth turned to soft, red mush. We can hear a squishing sound as we walk, and our shoes are soon buried. We can't find Rebecca, but we meet her sister Charm, and she is charming and friendly. She tells us right off the bat that she isn't going to Shalako, and she tells us why. Some years ago her eleven-year-old son went out to play with his friend. It had been raining, and they both drowned in the river. Ever since then, she stopped going to the dances and ceremonies. Her sisters warn her that she will die alone, off somewhere, if she doesn't go to dances. But with great humor Charm says she will not die alone—she will be with all the other people who don't go to dances!

Charm comes to Zuni all the time, but she moved her family away to a village where they are the only inhabitants. I guess small-village life gets to her, for there is no privacy. She tries to keep her other children away from the river, but it's a hopeless cause. They keep going there to play, driving her wild with anxiety.

We leave Charm, feeling very saddened by her tale, and a small girl appears out of nowhere and guides us through drier patches of earth. Suddenly the little girl points at the distant mountains and says, "The

Shalako are coming down from their cave. Look. Over there. It looks small, but it is very big." We look. We see a whitish patch in the striated mountains, and we are awed: that is where the gods come from.

The Shalako is a very powerful god; I think it is the most powerful being in the Zuni pantheon. It gave original instructions to the people about how to celebrate Shalako. The men who impersonate the Shalako each year go into rigorous training—they fast and pray. When the day comes, they are transformed. They are more than men, but less than Shalako; I guess you could say they are like angels. Their bodies are present during the Shalako ceremonies, but they are somewhere else, in the Shalako energy.

We walk to the north side of the village and stand waiting, with other people who have gathered. The Shalako are supposed to come down from the cave and cross the river and the bridge. We stand and watch the bridge. It gets colder. The sky turns dark. Still no Shalako. We hear people talking about picture-taking, and how violently they oppose it. In past years, people tried to take photos and touch the Shalakos. I think one year they actually banned Anglos for their unspeakable behavior. We are warned that cameras can be confiscated. This is very sacred, and we are not to record it for our amusement.

Suddenly a child calls out: "There they are!" It is hard to see in any detail, but we can vaguely make out the shapes of six huge figures (twelve to fifteen feet tall), surrounded by adult attendants. These are the six Shalako; one will visit and bless each of the six houses. In addition, there are two other houses: Longhorn and Mudhead.

Hours go by. People line the streets, looking toward the river and the bridge, waiting for the Shalako to cross. Ordinarily, we have no patience for standing and waiting, but in Indian country it is a way of life at ceremony times. It puts you in the mood. It unites you with the other people waiting. It gives you a chance to meditate on your life.

It also gives you a chance to freeze. I am wearing leather sneakers, and have not yet put on my warm gear because it was pleasant in the afternoon. But now, as night falls, something happens to my feet. It may be the wet mud that penetrated, or it may just be the cold. Whatever the case, my toes freeze, then my soles freeze, and I soon lose all feeling in my feet.

I get a little panicky, because I cannot get the circulation back. I rub my toes, I dance around, I jog in place, I massage under my socks, but nothing helps. The numbness spreads. In the meantime, the Shalako have come to the bridge. They are getting closer to us, but who knows

344

when they will pass by us? It is getting darker. We can barely discern their white forms now, and all we can hear is a strange wooden "clapping" sound. We later realize it is the Shalakos' beaks.

Men wearing bells, colorful Zuni headbands tied off to the side, and equally colorful Pendleton blankets cross to the bridge to attend the Shalako. I try to stand there, but I feel that at any moment I am going to start crying from how frozen my feet are and how little mobility I have in my shoes.

At this moment, just as the tears are forming, an Indian woman next to me, with two tots dragging at her arms, asks if there is something wrong. Not being shy, I tell her. She asks where I am from, and I answer that I hail from southern California. She is very sympathetic, and offers to take me back to her house and put my feet in hot water. She informs me that her feet once froze, and a woman from California saved her, so it is right and good that she return the favor. "What goes around comes around," she says.

We leave Paul there, and go back to the woman's house. I feel terrible that she has to leave the Shalako site, but she says it is okay. Her tots, who turn out to be twins, are cold anyway. The woman's name is Delight. And she really is a delight in my life!

Delight is not a native of Zuni. She comes from Acoma Pueblo, and she had these twins late in life. She is a special education math teacher, and her husband does maintenance work at the Public Health Service hospital in Gallup, about forty miles away.

As soon as we get to Delight's house, with the kids screaming, she begins to heat water and to fill a plastic tub for my feet. She apologizes for the smell of the water, which is highly sulfurized. She keeps pouring warm water into the tub, but my feet will not unfreeze. She calls the hospital and they tell her to bring me in if my feet are still frozen in half an hour—"Her toes may fall off," they tell Delight.

Finally my circulation begins to return and Delight gives me fresh socks and we go to get Paul. He has been sitting in our car, after the Shalako crossed, and he is turning blue from the cold. Delight drives us by the Shalako houses for a sort of "dry run" so we will know where they are later on, and then she takes us back to her house. She feeds us, I contribute matzo to the general welfare, and we all sit around munching on the unleavened bread. Delight says it tastes like a thick version of traditional Indian piki bread, and she also informs us that there is a Catholic holiday where they eat unleavened bread too. She says that next year she'll eat matzo!

345

The adorable twin boys are a constant, relentless demand on De-light, but she never loses her cool. At one point they are screaming and fighting and hacking and spitting up into the garbage can, but she remains completely calm. She says she was raised by a calm grand-mother, and when she has trouble with the kids she prays to her dead grandma to help her and teach her to stay calm.

Delight talks with great joy about her childhood at Acoma—the Sky City perched high on a mesa top. All she remembers is playing down the hill. She muses that she probably never went back up the hill for lunch because she was too busy playing. Did she ever eat lunch? She can't remember. She recalls that there was no paved road up the mesa and the kids rode on a sled. She loved it. To this day there is no elec-tricity at Acoma. Things have changed, but not that much.

Delight talks about the time she froze. It was snowing and she had been playing in the snow. Her Indian friend told her that she froze be-cause Indians are not supposed to frolic in snow. You should talk to snow. Snow shouldn't be played with.

Delight turns on the TV and there is a loud basketball game which remains on and blasting for the rest of our visit. I hate watching sports, but Paul, who is a TV addict and would watch static if that was the only thing on, begins to watch. The kids curl up in front of the TV. Delight has spared us from the cold and we sit with her until half past midnight, at which point the Shalako are supposed to dance.

"Go now," Delight says.

"Delight," I say, "if my feet hadn't frozen we wouldn't have met you. And if we hadn't met you and been taken in like this, I can guarantee you we would not have stayed. The cold is just too piercing. So I guess, in the long run, I'm glad my feet froze."

"Yes," says Delight. "There is a reason for everything."

This time we load on all the clothes we have. We each wear three layers of pants, I wear three sweaters, we have ski gloves and hats and scarves and lined boots, but still we are cold. We go to the first Sha-lako house. There are few people inside when we arrive. One room is reserved for Zunis only (and their guests) and it is a huge space with large windows. The walls are decorated with brightly colored shawls and rugs and woven belts and deer heads. A bunch of red gourds hangs near the rear, and there is a brightly painted altar on the ground with birds perched atop all the spires. There are prayer offerings in front of the altar. Hanging from the ceiling are Shalako dolls. There are bridge chairs lined up, and people sit in them. Some of the older people are dozing off. In front of the bridge chairs is a long canal dug into the ground—it is the length and shape of a lap-pool. Cornmeal is spread along it in a line that sometimes crisscrosses.

But by far the most arresting thing in the room is the Shalako figure. The headdress is made of white feathers with black tips. The body is mostly white, and ornamented with feathers, silver, and turquoise. The head is birdlike, with a long cylindrical wooden beak, and there are also horns. The face is collared by a thick wreath of black feathers. And the Shalako has long, long black hair flowing down its back. There are also painted designs, a printed textile body, and silver and turquoise jewelry ornamentation. The shoulders and arms are draped in animal skins. The Shalako sits absolutely immobile. Not a flicker of movement for hours. You know the person inside is in a heightened state of meditation, and out of his body, or he could not hold that still.

We stay there for about an hour, with nothing happening. In a back room, people are eating, and there are chili and bread and coffee on the table for us if we choose to eat. People start piling in, but because we are early we have good viewing spots. There is a group of older Anglos, and they are really obnoxious. The most vocal woman is draped in Indian jewelry, and they converse loudly about what Anglos can and cannot do. They exchange rumors and information they have heard about Shalako and its meaning. And they do this within earshot of the Zunis. We cringe with embarrassment.

Suddenly a bunch of men take down the gourd rattles from the wall and start drumming and singing in a corner. Still, many in the room sleep on. Others smoke, and it looks irreverent, but I guess it is sacred smoking, for tobacco is sacred to Indians. Others are drinking sodas, but I guess people have to drink if they are thirsty.

Then a group of young men gathers around the seated Shalako and drapes rugs around him so we cannot see. After about five minutes, but it could be ten or fifteen, the Shalako arises to his full height. Paul says the Shalako looks like Big Bird, and he does not mean to be irreverent, but it is so unusual that one feels the need to compare it to something. The Shalako is about twice the height of a man, and it is awesome and very ancient. Maybe it is 10,000 years old. It is utterly mysterious.

The Shalako begins to dance up and down the "lap-lane," back and forth over the cornmeal, blessing the house. Because the room has a bare dirt floor, this sunken "lane" allows the super-tall figure to stand erect. Every once in a while he opens and closes his long beak, making a clacking sound accompanied by a shrill ricochet-like cry. Then a man, wearing a white beanie with a short handle (shaped like the top of an acorn), dances down the lane, alternating with the Shalako but never looking straight at him. One senses that the man is dancing for his life. He is sweating. He is "gone," lost in prayers and meditations. In his hand, he carries a long green stalk. It looks like the shaft of a sunflower, or a "lulav" that is used in the Jewish religion at Succoth time.

We begin to understand the reason for the many windows—people are gathered outside, looking in. Unless you are well situated, as we are, it is hard to see all the doings in the room with the Shalako. Going outside and peering in the windows gives you a better vantage point.

It is very hard to describe how foreign and mysterious the Shalako is. There is nothing in our lives to relate it to. Every element of the costume, decor, and ritual has symbolic overlay, and it is breathtaking when we think about how all of this evolved. We are watching the human imagination in relation to the divine, and how that imagination translates the supernatural into accessible terms. This is what it must have been like to be alive thousands of years ago, before cynicism in the form of industry, economy, and the media set in. It is at once literal and poetic; it is the presentation and representation of the deepest human beliefs.

I have heard much about Shalako, but I have no way of checking the accuracy, as I wouldn't dare ask a question of anyone in such a holy setting. The coming of the Shalako each year represents the rebirth of the whole Zuni nation, and it has the passion of being reborn in the Christian faith—multiplied by a thousand! It keeps happening again and again every year, and it is not an individual but a communal happening. The coming of the Shalako is so sacred to the people that for a month afterwards they cover their heads and extinguish their fires. They go into a prayerful retreat.

The Shalako are the bearers of all seeds that humans eat; this means they bring the seeds of all that sustains people. They take human beings from the Mudhead stage and elevate them to spiritual rebirth. Year after year.

A Healing of the Heart

The Shalako are gods. They live in the mountains. They teach the men who impersonate them each year and follow their instructions. The men are elevated to a god-like state in the execution of the Shalako rites. It is an extraordinary commitment on the part of the dancers, and even the visitors. It is physically and spiritually very demanding. The Shalako impersonators probably can't work or keep up their workaday world life. The preparation is too demanding.

The Shalako dance directly on the earth, so they touch earth and bring their seeds. Visitors like us are called "rain-clouds" in the Zuni language. We bring the blessing of rain and we get the blessing of the Shalakos in return. After the Shalakos bring the seeds, the earth goes to sleep with the seeds in it. This is a winter solstice celebration in preparation for the next spring.

Many people come to Shalako and they can't take it. They leave. And leaving is very bad for them. The Shalako is too powerful and overwhelms them.

The dancing of the Shalako is an awesome responsibility, as it carries the hopes and prayers of the Zuni nation. If a Shalako falls down, the heart of the people falls. It means they will have a bad year. This happened back in the 1970s and the people suffered greatly.

After we watch the Shalako for a while, we head outside to our car to drive to the next house. On the way, we see *kachina* dancers, their faces ringed in black feathers, on their way in. They strip off their clothes and stand bare-chested in the freezing cold. We look in the window, and see them dancing down the earthen lane with the Shalako.

We go, then, from house to house. The decor varies a bit. Cars line the road, and when we see a clump of cars we know it is a Shalako house, for it is much too dark outside to see street signs. Sometimes we go in and sometimes we look through the window. It is freezing, below freezing, below below freezing. And we hear that it usually gets worse. You cannot cover every part of you, and a nose or a finger freezes. Paul starts to get sick—he is coughing and has a sore throat. This is not easy, but I will not back down.

We go to one more house—the Longhorn house, where there is no Shalako. The *kachinas* are dancing, and one of them looks just like a petroglyph at La Cieneguilla! He has a turquoise head, and big eyes. There is a stuffed bear in the room. We watch through the window. The groups sponsoring the dances have wonderfully evocative names

349

like "manure kiva" and "mudheads" and "brain kiva." Every detail adds to a more enlightened enjoyment of the whole.

Toward morning, we go into a small cafe for tea, and once we are inside we can't bear to go out again. We drive forty miles to Gallup, and check into a motel at 5 A.M. We crash out till late morning, and then ride back to Zuni again.

It is now time for the races. We are told they are going to start at 10 A.M., but they do not start till around 3 P.M. They take place near the river and bridge again. People are lining the streets, and everyone is very friendly. We all wait together. Most people are hacking, coughing, snot drips from their noses, and they sneeze from the cold and from colds. Paul is among them.

Finally we see a line of men coming down the road. All of the Anglos are tapped on the shoulder and asked to cross to the north side of the street, where there is limited visibility. The south side is for Indians only. Paul is asked to cross. Amazingly, no one taps me on the shoulder. I am so short I just blend in. Plus, there is an albino Indian next to me, so my fair hair is not so shocking or noticeable.

I am allowed to stay, and it is to garner a reward. I have a bird's-eye view of the doings that overwhelm me with their power. There is a line of men that walks in front of me. The first man in line is older, and he carries long prayer sticks with feathers. He has a pottery bowl full of cornmeal. The Indians come up to him and bless him with cornmeal. He walks on, covered with meal, carrying everyone's blessings. He is followed by *kachinas,* and they, too, carry prayer feathers. The people cover them in cornmeal too, to bless them.

The men group at the bridge and wait. In the distance, on the far side of the river, the six Shalakos have appeared with their attendants. Lines of people come up to the *kachinas* and offer cornmeal to them, and then the *kachinas* cross to the Shalakos. Suddenly, I am pulled back 10,000 years in time! Everyone around is Indian, and I can imagine that it must have been just like this in Anasazi days. The *kachinas* seem to carry all the prayers and blessings, and they begin to run back and forth, one at a time and then all together, in front of the Shalakos and their attendants. The Shalakos are clacking their beaks and the attendants are singing, and the dancing is very powerful. I have the feeling the *kachinas* are dancing for the whole Zuni nation, for all people, for the world. They are offering prayers and thanksgiving. They are getting blessed for all the people.

A Healing of the Heart

The final part is the most remarkable, and it touches me the most.
The Shalakos now begin to run back and forth. They lean forward, almost like chickens running across a barnyard. Their little legs stick
out from the bottom of their huge dress. They run back and forth, back
and forth, blessing all of those who see them for the coming year.
They run with intensity, wisdom, total concentration. It builds and
builds until finally they stop. I feel I have witnessed one of the great
miracles and secrets of the world, and that I am blessed, among the
Anglos present, to have seen it!

We leave the area slowly, and I feel obliged to stop a family, at random, in the street, and thank them for letting us outsiders witness this.
They reiterate that we have just seen blessings and thanksgiving for
the coming year, and they tell us how awful it is if a Shalako falls. We
ask them where we can buy fetishes, because my sister has asked me
to buy one, and they tell us to go knocking on doors, so we do so.

Actually, we pick a door at random and I knock. A woman answers,
and I tell her I am looking for a bear fetish. She tells her four-year-
old child to take me to a neighbor's house, and exhorts me to please
return her little daughter intact. I am stunned at her trust of a stranger.
I follow the little girl through the mud and we arrive at another house
after about ten minutes. There is no bear fetish, but the woman drags
out an elk antler sculpture of an eagle that just won first prize at a museum contest. I tell her I'm not looking for elk, so she gives me her
address and tells me I can order anything I want and she will make it.
In her hands, she holds out to me some of her wonderful fetishes—a
rhinoceros and a fabulous, delicate bat.

When we leave Zuni, I turn and wave goodbye, as though I am taking leave of a person.

We come back to Santa Fe tired, but not too tired for me to go to see
Our Lady of Guadalupe. The story behind the painting is well known
here and throughout the Americas, and she is the patron saint of Mexico. The Virgin of Guadalupe made a miraculous appearance in the
1500s to Juan Diego, a poor Indian boy, in Mexico. She gave him roses in the midst of winter and, in reporting the vision to the local archbishop, the boy opened the poncho he put the roses in, and there,
inside, was a painting of the blessed virgin. She became the patron
saint of Mexico and she has been honored and revered ever since. A
photographic copy of that painting is circulating through the United

States. All of the faithful are invited to come and see it. I go along for a look.

The large Catholic audience is gathered in a nearby church. When I walk in, the painting is up front, on the pulpit, and everyone is standing and reaching out to Our Lady with open, extended arms. The priest is singing to Mary about how she was there until the end with Jesus and what a good mother she was. Then the congregants are asked to come up and pray to Our Mother, and to ask her for anything. There is a great outpouring of faith and belief and prayers. People file by and touch Mary's praying hands, her face, her heart. They touch her with rosary beads, asking for the fulfillment of prayers and healing.

And then it comes. The religious manipulation that makes me nuts. It is announced that Our Lady is the mother of the unborn, and everyone is told that in the name of Our Mother they have to oppose abortion. It is their obligation. This is the message of Mary. I am shocked. The real message of the Lady of Guadalupe was that she was The Mother, and that she would safely nestle her children in the crook of her arm. This is such blatant distortion, and such abuse of praying people in a vulnerable state, that I can barely control myself. There is praise for pro-lifers and disdain for those who perform abortions or get them.

The next morning, our house turns into petroglyph support central. Belinda James, the fabulous Native American ballerina from New York, whom I saw in performance when I first came here, arrives in town. She is roped into performing on December 14th. Joseph drops in, and when he sees Belinda he gets right to the heart of the matter: he apologizes to Belinda for what the Spanish did to the Indians, and then they get along just fine. We listen to Belinda tell us about her plans to choreograph a ballet about the Pueblo Revolt of 1680.

"I will be dancing the eagle," she says. "Popé, who led the revolt, had a vision in a kiva, when he was told he would be leading the revolution. I will bring him that vision."

As Belinda talks, her tough exterior melts away, and she is soft, gentle, poetic. Joseph's daughter Candy wants to be a ballerina, and he can see her in Belinda. He is smitten with the beauty of what Belinda represents: an indigenous New Mexican woman who follows her heart and devotes herself to dancing the story of her people. When Belinda explains that she wanted to be a dancer because toe shoes reminded her of deer hooves, Joseph gets out a pen and writes her words down.

"A few weeks ago," he whispers to me, "I had never even spoken to an Indian!"

In the other room is Elisa Herrera, composing her speech. Every once in a while we all meet in the kitchen and have a glass of wine. It is a very nurturing, supportive environment.

When Paul comes home he bursts out laughing. "Here you all are, in spiritual nirvana, and I have been in Albuquerque doing a voiceover for spray-on car polish!"

Over the next few days, the petroglyph party preparations continue, with only one hitch. December 14th is only a few days away, and we have not yet found someone to do the opening blessing. The question keeps coming up: "Who is going to say the blessing?" And I keep answering, "Wait and the person will materialize."

One night Wilma is here, and she is talking about her friend C.R. She speaks about her so highly that I finally ask, "Is she a medicine woman?" "She's a grandmother!" Wilma answers, with great respect. Going on blind instinct, I ask Wilma if she would ask C.R. to say the blessing. Wilma gets very protective of C.R. and says it isn't a great idea to ask her. So I let it drop.

The next morning, Wilma shows up at the door with C.R. She is some grandmother! She is clan sister to Russell Means, and she went on his sacred run through Europe. She has a young Swedish boyfriend, she is extremely outspoken, and she "carries medicine"—which means she has power.

During the course of conversation, she picks up our phone and says, "The Indian prophecies warn us about the snake. THIS is the snake." She speaks a lot about walking the Red Road (following the Native American way), carrying the pipe (which is sacred to many Indians, including the Sioux), and how sweatlodges release toxins. She talks about her childhood in Minnesota, and says there is no doubt the Vikings came there in A.D. 36.

"How do you know that?" I ask.

"How do you know where you come from?" she shoots back.

She speaks about her sense of responsibility, and how she works for "all the children" and not just her own.

"I guess that's why you agreed to come here. Because we're preserving the petroglyphs *por los niños,* for the children," I say.

C.R. is a very complex lady, and I think she has walked a path that is common to many Indian women. She watches out to be sure that

men do not misuse their "medicine," she preaches sisterhood to other women, and she lives in poverty and poor health. I think it is appropriate to have her give the blessing on December 14th because she is very human, both perfect and very fallible, and because it is right for the benediction to come from a woman, instead of a man.

After C.R. leaves the house, I am soaking in the tub when I hear a knock of the meat mallet. I throw on a robe and when, dripping, I open the door, Lenny Smallfeather is standing there! This is the first time he has crossed the threshold of my house since the breakup of our partnership. He is accompanied by a mutual friend from out-of-town who wanted to visit.

The friend is very talkative, and Lenny just sits there, quiet, smiley, and observant. I wonder what is going on in that active brain of his. I would love, one day, to really talk about what happened between us, but Lenny is not prone to intimate relationship talk. He leaves, cheerful and inscrutable, and I thank him for coming, because I know it is awkward for him too.

The mallet now bangs against the door day and night, and there is a steady stream of visitors to Uncle Alfie's house. Paul is sick with a cold he brought back from Shalako, we are both exhausted, and we need a break. So of course we go out exploring in Indian land.

First we treat ourselves to lunch at the Prairie Star in Bernalillo, and we eat fishy delicacies as we look out over the golf course and lakes to the mountains. The waitress, instead of discussing the daily specials, talks to us about the color of the glow on the mountains at various seasons. I think there is not a person here who is insensitive to the beauty of the natural world.

Then we drive to Jemez Pueblo for the dance of the Matachines. It is a cold day, and we are heavily bundled up with scarves tied tightly around our necks so that we look like two fat sausages. The small gathering of people at the Pueblo is predominantly Indian, and we like it better that way because there is a quietness about intimate Pueblo dances that is very special to us.

The story behind the dance, which was probably brought to Mexico by the Spanish, is very confusing. On a literal level, it is about the Aztec Indian princess who served as an interpreter to Hernando Cortés, and whom he took as a concubine. According to legend, she converted the Aztec leader Montezuma to Christianity. On a metaphorical level, it is a celebration of the (forced) coming of Chris-

tianity to the Indians. The little princess is the Virgin Mary. It is about the triumph of light (Christianity) over darkness (paganism).

In Mexico, the Aztec princess (named Malintsin but later baptized Malinche by the Spanish) is considered to be a traitor. But there is no sense of anger or resentment here at Jemez or elsewhere in New Mexico. In fact, Malinche is celebrated as the first New World convert to Christianity. The Matachine dance is very open-hearted and joyous, celebrating the Christian spirit. Why do Indians dance the dance of their own conquest and the obliteration of their native religion? Beats me. I can only guess that it is a celebration of Christianity during the Christmas season, and that includes telling stories of their own conversion. Also, it is an oral culture, and dances are a way of preserving their history and keeping it alive for all the generations. A more psychological interpretation might be the internalization of oppression, or identification with the aggressor.

The role of Montezuma is danced by a figure known as El Monarca. The Malinche is danced by a young virgin who is between six and twelve years old. It is a very beautiful and complex dance.

When we first look out across the Plaza, the colors are blinding. The twelve male dancers who depict Monarca's subjects are dressed in colorful women's cape scarves and high, ornate headdresses suggestive of bishop's miters. Some of them wear lace leggings over their trousers. On their feet they wear fur-lined moccasins. They all carry glittery tridents which vaguely represent the cross. In their right hands, they carry multi-colored gourd rattles. The Monarca looks pretty much the same as the other men, with the addition of a suggested crown. The Malinche wears a black, one-shouldered Pueblo *manta,* and she is young and lovely. There is also a boy who dances El Toro, the bull (a symbol of evil or temptation). He wears a cow-skin, sports horns, and leans on two sticks which double for an extra set of animal legs. He cavorts with a few horned and masked clown figures who wear chaps, carry whips, and look like Spanish cowboys. He tries to prevent the conversion from taking place. The whole dance is performed by the Pumpkin society, and is done to the beat of a drum.

The dance takes place in sections. It is hard to follow the story in a linear way, but I guess it goes something like this: the Malinche meets with Montezuma, she brings Christianity to Montezuma and his subjects, she fights off evil, the Aztecs embrace Christianity, and all is okay.

When the Pumpkin group is done, the Turquoise society comes onto the Plaza, and the dance begins again. Now, instead of the drum, there is a fiddler and a guitarist. The second little Malinche, a tiny girl with long hair who wears glasses, is dressed like a bride, in traditional white, and with a veil. The dance steps are now jig-like. The whole feeling is softer, quieter, and more hypnotic. The spectacle is mesmerizing. Each step is precise. It is very ritualistic. Once again, it draws me back in time, and Paul whispers that this dance is certainly older than the coming of the Spanish to America. It probably incorporates other, earlier traditions, although we have no way of knowing for sure.

Suddenly Beaver comes up behind me, puts an arm around me, says hello, and informs us that the tradition of the Matachine dance is Moorish. She never explains anything about the dance, but just watches with us and makes comments like: "The tridents used to have flowing ribbons instead of glitter, and I liked that better." Or, she tells us this is her favorite dance, and she thinks the Monarca is a wonderful dancer.

Sometimes I get so absorbed in the dances that I think I will lose my daily mind. I will just float off in contemplation of impossible questions, like where things come from and what they mean and how human beings pass on passion and belief and keep it alive. My mind will twist and turn about why Indians are so internal, and why the same dance done by the Spanish looks and feels so different when it is done at a Pueblo. I get completely caught up in the meditations of the moment, and only some jarring physical sensation like the fact that my toes are freezing brings me back to the present.

Beaver, too, is freezing. The moment the dances are over, she takes us to a friend's house to eat. We open the door, and there is an immediate welcome and an invitation to sit at the feast table. There is posole and chicken, pumpkin pie, chili stews, and a few healthy things which no one but us touches. We eat ourselves sick and drink a mixture of lemonade and Seven-Up until we feel we will burst. Beaver has brought along a friend who is an upstate—New York Indian. He is extremely nonverbal. I used to think that people who didn't speak well weren't bright, but being in Indian country has made me do an about-face on that one! Beaver's friend is a painter, potter, and graphic artist, for starters. When he speaks at all, he refers cryptically to the fact that the Mohawks fought last year against the expansion of a golf course over their sacred burial grounds. There are rumblings of discontent everywhere across America. The Indians are not taking their

356

obliteration lying down any more. I think this will be a period of great and continuing activism.

As we pig out, there is a calm acceptance of who we are and whatever we talk about by the women who feed us. The food is great and we keep complimenting them and they love that. Suddenly the door opens and one of the Matachine dancers comes in. When we turn around, we find that the headdresses and gourds have been placed on a little floor altar in the living room. We did not see anyone put them there. We ask no questions, but just eat and joke. Then we leave, and they tell us to come again and ask our names.

How many times a year can these poor people, who have nothing, open their homes to us? All we can do in return is open our hearts to them. And we try to do this. On a daily basis.

We come home, and *bang, bang, bang,* the mallet is going again. Elisa Herrera comes in, dressed like Little Red Riding Hood, and it is obvious that her life is changing. She tells us that she feels completely alive for the first time in years. She reads us the beginning of her speech for December 14th, and it is fabulous. She is going to talk about her kids being half-Spanish and half-Indian, and how they are ashamed of the Spanish side because of what the Spanish did to the Indians. She is going to say the unspeakable: that those who call themselves Hispanic are often mestizos, who mated with Mexican Indians when they came to the New World. She will call for a bonding of the cultures, and it's all quite personal and very well written. Up until a few days ago, Elisa was the retiring wife of a Pueblo man, who thought she had nothing to say.

Joseph parades around the house saying he can FEEL other people for the first time in his life. Now he wants to give up his gun, his Betsy, which has been his macho symbol all of his life. Wes Studi comes driving in from L.A. for the event, and Joseph meets him, hugs him, and again begs for forgiveness for what his culture has done.

The only sadness hovering over the event is that Tim Shay is gone from the scene. He has checked into an alcohol treatment center since he feels that he is in need of emergency help, and there is no way to reach him. I do not tell anyone where he is, but I just keep making excuses for him, saying that he's not feeling well. Then the word comes that he will get a special release from the facility to participate in the event!

Elisa seems to be transforming by the hour. She is wearing pastel colors. Her complexion is pink. People tell her that she looks beautiful and radiant. The healing just sweeps over all of us, carrying us along in a great wash of compassion and love.

The night before the big event, I can hardly sleep. We all keep calling each other, whispering about how tomorrow, the Native Americans and Native Hispanics will get together!

December 14th arrives. The party begins at noon, and goes nonstop for five hours. Hundreds of people come. Joseph is positively numb, and Paul has begun calling me "Sol Hurok," after the late impresario who had a lock on virtually all ethnic performers on the American stage. There are about a hundred performers, and it is all a tight-rope act of blind faith. We are performing without a net because there was no rehearsal, no budget, an unknown space, and no quality control. Some of the performers are people I just met somewhere and roped in. Some are working together, but never met until today. The entertainers were just told what time to show up. There is incredible nervousness in the air.

The Native Americans are the first ones to enter the large room at the Unitarian church. They immediately set about rearranging the chairs so that people can sit in a sacred circle. Life is a circle to them, a continuous cycle without beginning or end, and that is how they want this to go down.

The women of La Cieneguilla go into a second room and set up their frito pies and drinks. Then, before we know it, the audience starts arriving. They sit in a circle and we give Wes Studi the signal that it is time to begin. He starts talking, completely winging it. He welcomes everyone, ad-libs, and sets a congenial tone.

The first "act" is Tim Shay making a fire with a bow-drill and wood. The audience is very hushed, and we pray the smoke alarm won't go off and make the church people frantic. Tim looks like a cadaver from his alcoholic binge and the treatment center. He has lost a lot of weight and his skin is pale. He sweats onto the wood, working with all his force, but he can't get the darn fire lit. Joseph and I turn to each other and begin to panic. What an auspicious beginning: the fire that won't start!

But Tim, trapped onstage, has a lot more aplomb than we do. He looks up from his fire-making, faces the audience, and asks, "Anyone got a match?"

The audience roars. Tim proceeds to light the fire with a match, and to talk about the importance of fire. He doesn't miss a beat. Arnold

A Healing of the Heart

Herrera spontaneously jumps up on stage and starts drumming, creating a very mysterious and powerful atmosphere, both saving the day and giving it a heartbeat.

Once the fire is burning, and the smoke alarms are trembling, C.R. gets up. She is dressed deliciously in blue, with feathers and pendants, facepaint, and she has all her medicine accoutrements. She closes her eyes, finds the center of her power, and she starts talking in her native tongue and burning sage, blessing us all and railing against the misuse of Mother Earth. Once she gets wound up, there is no stopping her. She goes on for about twenty minutes. She calls up Wilma and her daughter Tina and makes a blessing for the four directions. She refers to little Tina as "the grandmother," for one day she will carry the tradition.

When C.R. finishes, Cristela Cano-Romero gets up. She is cloaked in a shawl, and she sings an ancient Nahuatl chant—part Aztec and part Toltec. Then she plays a Spanish song about the land, and she begins to dance around the room. When she moves, she is no longer earth-bound. She is there with us in the room, but she is not there.

By this time, the audience gets the idea that this is not your average afternoon's entertainment. Joseph, breathing rapidly and with his heart beating insanely, gets up and gives his speech. Even though he has practiced on our friends, nothing could have prepared him for this thoroughly public gesture. When he apologizes to the Indians and begs for their forgiveness, it is HEAVY. He keeps saying that history books taught the Hispanics lies. Their relationship to Indians was violent and not peaceful. He says that the Spanish kids are messed up because the adults are messed up. They don't even know who they are. "I am Joseph Lorenzo Villegas," he says, and *"Yo soy Mexicano."* It is the first time he has ever spoken these words, identifying himself as Mexican, and he cracks. He starts to sob, and he can't speak. His three-year-old son leaps out of his chair, runs across the room, and joins Joseph on the podium, holding on to him, giving him love and support. When Joseph finishes his talk, the audience rises en masse and gives him a standing ovation. Joseph, blinded by tears, doesn't seem to notice.

Moments later, Arnold Herrera spontaneously grabs the mike and starts to talk about how moved he is and how right Joseph's words are. Then he begins to drum and sing his soulful and meditative songs, and his two sons dance Pueblo dances in the middle of the room.

Indians and Spanish rarely mix their cultures here, but as soon as Arnold has finished, Angie Miller comes on with her Baile Español.

359

Indian Time

There are about fifty Hispanic kids, in full costumes, doing Spanish dances. Some of them are only two or three years old. Their poise and concentration are impeccable.

The audience is really spellbound when Andy Garcia arrives with his San Juan drum group to do the buffalo dance. The smallest buffalo dancer is also about two or three years old, and he follows the intricate steps and movements precisely. Watching the dancers with their horned buffalo headdresses, we are all pulled out of the church, out of Santa Fe, to another place and another time. No one coughs or sneezes. No one even moves.

Afterward, a Hopi (normally a close-to-the-vest tribe) spontaneously takes the mike, blesses the proceedings, and promises his personal ongoing support. We are all stirred by the fact that the Spanish children and the Indian children are dancing and watching each other dance with admiration. These are the future generations, dancing together, for the first time, under the same roof. It is all, truly, *por los niños*. They are the hope.

Next come Los Crusados, a Spanish Catholic men's choral group, and then Consuelo Luz plays guitar and sings in Spanish with much gusto and flair. The audience loves her. While they are applauding, Joseph's kids circulate in the room, giving all the spectators free packs of corn to plant, as Wes speaks about the petroglyphs and why we are trying to save them.

I am scrambling to make program changes, because everything is out of order, running long, and we have to make it seem smooth. I look across the room and see Elisa Herrera, who has been bumped from her position about five times. Even though she is very even-tempered and low-key by nature, I can see that she is nervous and I decide to put her on next. I have no idea of what her talk will be like, because when I left her at midnight last night, I told her very honestly that I thought her written speech sounded too flat and "planned." I exhorted her to open up, get very personal, and speak from the heart.

She climbs onto the stage, and I feel anxious for her in the pit of my stomach. Will she stick to her written words, or really take a chance? Elisa puts down her speech and goes for it! She looks out at the audience, and speaks from the gut. She tells what it is like to be a Spanish woman married to an Indian man. She lays out her pain at her children's minimization of their Spanish part, and she begs people to be proud of their heritage. She makes the people in the audience turn around and talk to each other, breaking the barriers of strangeness

360

and separation between their cultures. She is fabulous! The audience thinks she is extremely brave to say all that she says, and they give her the day's second standing ovation. Fifteen minutes after she gets down from the stage, this first-time speaker already has another engagement to speak—someone in the audience approaches her.

We are now running way behind schedule, and we have to clear the church. We give Wes the signal, and he asks everyone to come together in an Indian friendship dance. We all join hands—all the cultures—Anglos, Hispanic, and Indian—and dance in a circle to Arnold's drumbeat. Lenny Smallfeather grabs another drum and joins Arnold in singing in Keres.

And then it is over.

I go off into the church bathroom by myself for a few minutes. I try to absorb what happened. A Hopi medicine man spontaneously got up and pledged to stand behind Joseph and what he is doing. Indians and Spanish people have called each other "brother." Suddenly the disenfranchised indigenous people are bonding, just as we had wished. The children have come together to celebrate, and we watched them in their joyful discovery of each other. Anglos in the audience also vowed to help: everything from fellow archeo-ecological preservation groups to vested government organizations like the BLM!

Paul is sick and has lost his voice entirely and we want to go home, but Wes and his girlfriend Maura insist that we go out for drinks. They comment that Joseph is a very spiritual man, but he never had a place to express it. You can't exactly radiate light in the Marines or on a SWAT team. Wes says he had a ball, and gave out lots of autographed photos. He and Maura declare the day a huge success.

I think I can honestly and pridefully say that we accomplished everything we wanted to. Real healing has taken place. Why, then, aren't I excited? When we get home, there are phone calls congratulating us, but I hardly react. Maybe I was so wound up before, and we were working so intensely, that I am bound to feel a slump and a release. Perhaps it's the haunting question, "What now?" since this has been occupying so much of our lives.

I sit quietly and think about all I have learned about healing, and about trusting the feelings in my heart. I have changed very much since I came to Santa Fe. I have gotten into alignment. It makes me feel quiet and awed. Our party is on the ten o'clock news tonight, and the Sunday paper has a big color photo of our event on the first page. I need no public credit or acknowledgment or validation for my part in it. I know in my heart that one person *can* make a difference. And one person working with other people for a common goal can make a *big* difference. It makes me keenly aware of how I should always live my life.

The holiday season is upon us. I think of this huge, vast, wonderful universe that I am part of, and I send out feelings of joy, healing, and love.

16

*The End
of a Cycle*

Mid-December, 1991 to mid-January, 1992

The Christmas season is upon us, and the nation is in a dreadful slump. I am glad we do not have a television, because it's unhealthy to be bombarded with doom and gloom, especially on the news at night before you go to sleep. I used to think that something awful would happen if I didn't follow the news. Now I think that something awful will happen if I do.

A rather startling piece of feedback comes my way as the year draws to a close. Wilma is sitting in the kitchen, eating a spoonful of soup, and talking about Tim's restlessness in the alcohol rehab center. Suddenly she looks up and says: "Tim says you are very adventurous." This stops me in my tracks, because Tim is a survivalist, a true adventurer, and I consider myself the Queen of Fear.

"He says he first knew you were a real risk-taker when he saw you dance with the Mescalero Apache women during the puberty rites. He says you are someone who is not afraid to take chances and do something new." This pleases me very much, and it is an image I would like to have of myself, even though I don't really believe it.

I decide to ask Wilma what she thinks.

"I think you're a warrior," she says.

I burst out laughing. The image of myself on a battlefield seems hysterical.

"A warrior isn't someone who goes to war. It's a person who is really out there, who sees what is wrong and then goes about fixing it," Wilma says.

When Wilma leaves, I can't get this off my mind. Who am I? I see myself as someone who shrinks in fear from life. How can other people possibly think of me as being brave and adventuresome?

I call my sister, and ask her. She says she thinks of me as the most intellectually fearless person she knows. I ask Paul when he comes home. He says I do many, many things that he would be afraid of doing, and I just hang out there, on the edge, taking chances. I ask Carl Hammerschlag, and he says that he sees himself as an observer and me as a doer—someone who is unafraid to plunge right in.

I am overwhelmed by this. Have I come to Indian land to get a completely new perspective on myself?

Another person who is not afraid of taking chances and doing new things is Joseph Villegas. Our petroglyph party lit a match under him, and he is burning brightly. He is now hooked up with another Hispanic man, and they are going to try to inject some self-esteem into the Spanish culture. They are proposing the "cornification" of New Mexico, and they want their people to plant corn everywhere, as a connection to life and a revitalization of the land. Joseph is hot and heavy on the trail of water rights for his people, and today he got up at a town meeting and said he is going to block development of a huge country club by invoking the land grant treaty whereby his ancestors were given land that was later stolen by the Anglos. In other words, he is claiming that the land that is being sold for development isn't legally allowed to be sold. This land grant issue is a can of worms in the Southwest, because before there were present-day cities, the land was deeded to the Hispanic people in perpetuity, and then taken away from them by ruse, guile, abuse and their own naïveté or poverty. Now, militant Hispanics are going to be fighting to get that land back. Joseph will be among them.

Joseph and I sit down in the quiet of dusk and exchange our vision of the future. I tell him the way I see it.

"There is going to be an indigenous revival in this country. Around the world, dictators and dictatorships have fallen and people have laid claim to their own freedom and dignity. This is often accompanied by chaos and violence, like children who take over the house from abusive parents and then start fighting with each other because they don't know how to run it. I think we are going to see big doings in America. The dictatorship of money and power has wreaked havoc with the ethnic minorities. The 'have-nots' are probably more numerous than the 'haves' by now. They have retreated into drugs, crime, random violence, gang-banging, graffiti, and other negative modes of asserting themselves in a culture that squeezes them out of the mainstream. And, mostly, they are separate from each other, each retreating into their own scenario of loss and pain.

"But somehow, out of the graveyard of racial rejection, the dead and near-dead are rising. They realize that the revitalization of their culture and laying claim to what is rightfully theirs is the path to self-esteem and feelings of worth and belonging. Treaties have been broken with the Indians and with the Hispanics. Development has plowed their fields and stolen their land and water rights. Drunk and drugged and bleeding in their ghettos, they destroy themselves with anger and powerlessness, and they roll over and watch the murder of their people by Progress and Success.

"Little voices are beginning to squeak out the truth: Our culture is beautiful, don't lose it. Our cultures are all beautiful: let's learn to know one another. Here and there people listen. Soon the nation will be listening as the dogs begin to bark and the souped-up cars backfire louder and louder. We can no longer keep these people down. They have access to books and education. They are learning their way around our legal system. They will try to beat the Dominant Culture in the streets and in the courts. They are learning our language, and language is power.

"The obscene celebration of the conquest of America that began in 1492 is backfiring. All of the attention being paid to the beginnings of European culture on our soil is making indigenous people sit up and take notice too. They are learning who they are and where they come from. They are taking advantage of the spotlight to speak their piece. We are just seeing the beginning of it. The domination of America by white Anglo culture is finished. Non-European cultures are making their mark. The melting pot is boiling over. Maybe the cultural soup will be more hopeful than the mess we have now!"

When I get off my soapbox, Joseph applauds. Paul, who has apparently been listening from the next room, makes an appearance and begins to speak.

"I'm more pessimistic," he says. "Until the recent pinch on the collective wallet, there seemed to be no end to what the American people would take or what they'd believe from their leaders. We've remained an isolated, untouched, and willfully oblivious nation. What would any other country in today's world do if large segments of its populace were living under police state conditions yet were constantly subjected to physically and fiscally dangerous crime, were economically disenfranchised, lived under deteriorating conditions in a stressed environment, and had indifferent politicians tell them blatant lies?"

Joseph nods. Living here in the Southwest brings out the passion in us. In Los Angeles, so much of our energy goes into the enervating politics of earning a living. Here, we have been introduced to the politics of survival.

When Joseph leaves, there is a hardy knock of the mallet and when I open the door, Belinda James strides in. She continues to work on her ballet about the Pueblo Indian revolt of 1680, and she has come home to see her people and do research. I love talking to her because she is completely outspoken and provocative. She thinks the Indians should chuck Christianity and go back to their old ways. She believes that modern Indian culture is completely dysfunctional because of the colonization and influence of the outside world. She was not allowed to take part in the masked night dances at her Pueblo last night because she does not own a skirt. She is outraged! Indians used to run around with hardly any clothes on, and now they ban their own from the kiva because of Western clothes?! Belinda stomps around in her life and in her mind, oblivious to the niceties of dress and speech, totally true to her feelings and speaking what she feels. Life is very hard on her in return, but no one, no one can accuse Belinda of selling out or being a hypocrite!

It is, indeed, hard to relate to the Indian marriage to Christianity. We rationalize it by saying that the Indians incorporate it into their own beliefs and rituals, but, in fact, it is Christianity that broke their continuity and much of their spirit. Belinda is cut off from her own mother because Povi is a born-again Christian and Belinda cannot relate to that.

Christianity is pervasive at all times of year, but especially now, during the Christmas season. Santa Fe glows with *luminarias* and *farolitos*: candles in paper bags that stand on ledges and roofs, illuminating buildings and lighting the night. Originally, only candles were used, but now they have been largely replaced with light bulbs. We are trying to see and understand as much of the indigenous Christmas celebration as possible.

One of the big traditions here is "La Posada." It is a reenactment of the story of Mary and Joseph trying to get lodging in Bethlehem, and being turned away, so that the birth of Jesus eventually had to take place in a manger. It is, symbolically, the fist of evil (the innkeepers) flexed against the good (Joseph and Mary).

In the Spanish villages, Los Posadas are performed every night during the week preceding Christmas. In the cities, it is generally done only once, officially, but other versions crop up in unofficial places.

We go to our first version of La Posada at a museum, and it is done in Spanish to the accompaniment of guitars. It makes for delightful "indigenous" theater, with people from all walks of life becoming actors for a day. The performance lacks sophistication and polish, and every once in a while someone freezes under the glaring lights and can't retrieve a prepared speech, but the audience howls with glee at the lazy shepherd and the devil whose sword falls apart at the high dramatic moment when he is supposed to do battle with the angel.

The scenario is a little hard for us to follow, but we understand that it is a battle of good vs. evil, and that there is recognition of baby Jesus at the end and much adoration. We love the guitar and the tinny voices of Spanish singers that is so hypnotic and moving. Paul remarks that he would much rather see the Christ story on a tiny stage in Spanish with local amateur actors than spread out garishly in the Crystal Cathedral in California and costing millions of dollars.

Our second Posada is part of Flamenco Navidad, the brainchild of Meg Savlov. Meg, who is a nice Jewish girl from the East Coast, has a passion for flamenco. She put together a Christmas story done through multi-cultural dance. It includes Moorish, Spanish, Indian, Middle-Eastern, and Jewish influences. Since the Christ story took place in the Middle East, there is a logic to the belly dancers and beggars, the poor and the sinners of the Holy Land. Some of it is symbolic, as the immaculate conception, where a lone Mary dances with a scarf that radiates light and fills her with the Holy Spirit. Some of it is highly emotional, as when Joseph finds out that Mary is already pregnant, and he has to decide if he wants her anyway. La Posada ends with the climactic moment when the birth of Jesus takes place, and the holy parents are enveloped by an angel who has been hovering over the whole production. Pretty impressive! It's "professionalism meets La Posada."

Our third Posada is a chilly affair, because it is outside at the Plaza. I go with Rita Goodman—two Jewish women venturing out to celebrate the birth of Jesus! I am bundled up in so many layers of clothes I can hardly walk. I bought a pair of Sorel mountain boots that are

367

mustard-brown and black and they are so clunky and ugly and rigid that I look like a poorly designed robot when I move.

There is a young couple dressed up as the holy parents. Mary wears a simple dress and Joseph carries a shepherd's crook. They are accompanied by singers who carry candles to light the way. There are many, many onlookers as the duo walks by, and people join in the singing. Every few hundred yards Joseph and Mary stop in front of a restaurant or hotel. They sing in Spanish, asking for lodgings. Suddenly there is a spotlight on the balcony, and the devil appears, garbed in red, and sings back to them that there is no room, and tells them to get lost. They move on in the cold night, spurned and rejected.

I don't know how it happens, but in trying to get a better look, I end up in front of Mary and Joseph with the newspaper photographers. The throng sort of disappears just long enough for me to look into the couple's eyes. I wonder if Joseph and Mary are using Method acting, and if they feel "as if" they are the original pair. Or is it just an acting gig to them? Who knows?

The whole affair is very communal as we sing and follow Joseph and Mary and boo the devils loudly and wrap our coats tighter around our necks and finally arrive at the Palace of the Governors. There, fires are lit along the ground, and we cough as we pass by and inhale the smoke. Then we are given songbooks and we follow Mary and Joseph to the back of the courtyard into a "manger." Everyone gathers around to sing Christmas carols in Spanish, and Rita whispers stories to me about when she was growing up and refused to sing Christmas songs in school because she was Jewish. The kids in her class, advocates of the first conspiracy theory, taunted her and said, "You killed our Lord." It's kind of chilling.

Paul and I spend our days caught up in the holiday spirit—something we have never done before. We decide to celebrate Christmas Eve in the best way we know how—which means going to Taos for the famous evening bonfires at the Pueblo. We arrive early in the day and drive to the Taos ski basin. There we are, dressed in makeshift layers like two schlepps, puffed up like matzo balls from all the clothes, watching all the high-tech skiers whiz by in their neon outfits. It gets very cold very fast, and so we ride back to Taos village and hop around in the stores, biding our time until the bonfires.

When we get in our car at the end of the day, we notice that there are hundreds of cars coming down from Taos Pueblo, and we wonder why. It looks like the last scene of *Field of Dreams*. WHY? Because while we were wandering through the stores, we MISSED Christmas Eve. The cars are driving down from the Pueblo because it is all over. By the time we arrive at the Plaza, there are tiny fires with embers, and the spectacle is a memory. There are young guys, gathered around the cinders, drinking and telling jokes. Billows of smoke float over the adobe walls and rooftops.

We have dinner with Gail White Wolf's family, and they explain that they celebrate Indian Christmas, which means that they are too impatient to wait until after midnight to open the gifts. I have never seen such an array of presents. Hundreds of boxes lined up and distributed—there are even gifts for us. I confess that this is the first time I have ever really celebrated Christmas, and they can't believe it. There is a groaning feast table with ham and turkey and chilis and pies and bread pudding and posole. Gail's father goes to bed very early because he has to be up at dawn to marshal the deer dancers he's trained.

The following day we make sure to be at Taos Pueblo early. We don't want to miss the doings two days in a row. It is very hurtful when Gail tells me publicly and firmly: "Don't ask any questions during the dances. Don't even ask other spectators." I know I am inquisitive, but of course I mean no harm. Everything in Indian country is so fascinating to me that I want to know more about it. In white culture, asking questions is a sign of interest; in Native American culture, it is considered poor etiquette. Thus, the public warning. You can bet I won't ask anyone for the time of day!

It is cold at the Pueblo. We stand next to Gail's mother and grandmother. Her tiny grandma holds a blanket wrapped up around her head, so that only her forehead and nose show. I jokingly tell her that she looks like a tepee, and then I'm afraid she may be mad but she jokes right back, "The only thing missing is a fire coming out the top of my head!"

People are gathering to watch the famous deer dancers, and our Indian friends comment that all the tourists around the Plaza are white. The Native Americans stand on top of the houses watching. We are invited up on the roofs, and we gladly accept because we want to see everything.

My new boots are even more hideously ugly than the last pair, but they are guaranteed to function down to minus twenty-five degrees. My feet are still freezing. We stand on the rooftop and watch the corn dance first. Gail White Wolf is dancing, and she, like the other women, has one bare shoulder. The men are half naked, as they shake their gourd rattles and hop from foot to foot, celebrating the growth of seeds and rain and praying for the well-being of all people. The *kosharis* are making fun of the public and running around imitating the dancers and the drummers. Then they build a huge fire, and they take tires and go sledding over the snow. Everyone laughs good-naturedly and chats.

Then, suddenly, there is a change of mood. A hushed expectation comes over the Plaza. It always happens at the dances. Sometimes there is a drumbeat and sometimes there is no sound at all, but there is a palpable change of energy and you know something is going to happen.

From off in the distance, a line of deer dancers enters the Plaza. First there are two men smeared with white clay and bearing white antlers on their heads. They look like ghost deer. Following behind them, in the most mysterious of spectacles, is a line of many, many men dressed like deer. Each has the head of a deer on his human head. Some of them look like they have just been killed. Their tongues loll or there is congealed blood or their eyes are buggy. Some deer look meek and tiny. Others are huge, brazen. There are a few elk and even buffalo. The men wear animal skins down their backs, and the rest of them is just naked flesh, bared to the freezing winter winds. Each of the dead animals has a large sprig of evergreen in his mouth—it is as though the animals are still alive and eating. Every once in a while, a *koshari* runs and grabs a deer dancer, slings him over his back, and carries him off—just like a hunter carrying home a real deer. It is the most ancient ritual imaginable. The hunter and the hunted join in an ecstatic sacrificial bond.

We stand on the roof and we watch the antlers bobbing. Some point straight up, some point forward. Reality gets blurred, and we aren't sure if we are watching deer or men dressed as deer. There is such respect for the deer that the dancers actually "become" them. They move like deer, breathe like deer, probably think like deer. I suppose this is part of a very old ritual where the hunter "becomes" the animal to understand it. There is a blending between the hunter and the hunted. And there is a profound complicity. The Indian knows that the deer makes a sacrifice of its life so that humans can eat. And the Indian blesses and thanks the deer for the sacrifice. The "blending" with the animal is part respect and, probably, part trying to feel what the animal feels so that the hunter has more knowledge of and power over the hunted.

Doug White Wolf stands close to us, and he tells his son to go and wash his face. At first I think his son's face is dirty, but I realize that it is part of a ritual. The boys wash their faces in the village river so that they are clean for the new year, leaving undesirable thoughts and acts behind them.

We meet a Taos man we know on the Plaza, and he says it is his first time seeing the deer dance. We think he is teasing us, but he isn't. He has made a choice not to participate in the dances, but he will not show his face either. He does not want to be embarrassed by having the other men, who are dancing, see him. It is part of the heavy communal responsibility Pueblo Indians feel. It is very touching.

Once again, I feel the mystery of being at a Pueblo and participating, if only with my eyes, in an old and sacred ceremony. I understand that these people are freezing, but yet they choose to dance half-naked as they choose to live without running water or electricity. It keeps them in touch with the old ways. It makes them tough, able to withstand hardship. I marvel at traditions so pure that genocide, Christianity, the lures of money, nothing, nothing in the world can erode them. What these Taos men are dancing today, their ancestors danced a thousand years ago. And when a man today dances, he is with those men, back then, connected through the elements of costume, dance steps, songs, drumbeats, words, to all the ancestors and to the earth in a primal and magical way. It all makes sense to him in the ceremonial space. He must do his part—dancing, and the deer does his part, sacrificing so that the human species may survive.

We come back to Santa Fe in time to run to a party at the Herreras. The children amuse themselves by zinging put-downs at the adults, and Arnold and Elisa are generous and model Christmas hosts. Arnold is telling us that the Catholic church is under the jurisdiction of the Pueblo where it is situated. Once they threw out a priest who was a drunk. I always thought it was the other way around—that the Pueblo is under the thumb of the church. I am relieved that somewhere there is a hierarchy where the Indians are not at the bottom.

The next day, with a caravan of friends, we head out to San Juan Pueblo for the turtle dance. We drive onto the Pueblo and stop first at the home of a friend of a friend. Five of us walk in, four of whom are

371

strangers, and they welcome us like family. It is a fabulous meal—red chili and green chili and turkey and banana pudding and prune pie and salads and prepared so tastefully that we all overeat and feel like falling on the floor. We are bloated, and then we are also bloated-looking from wearing so many layers of clothing. It is hard to ma-neuver our way out of the house. No matter how many times I go to a feast, I can never get over the incredible generosity and hospitality. The women spend half their lives cooking and it is a love science. The food comes to the table and you can feel the spirit behind it. The women are prepared to feed anyone who shows up, and whoever walks in the door is welcomed. It is a monumental feat. I freak if two peo-ple show up for dinner—announced! I just fling open the refrigerator door and say, "Help yourself." These Pueblo women are totally at ease about their skills of shopping, preparing, cooking, and serving.

After feasting, we go out to the Plaza for the turtle dance. It is star-tlingly different from the other dances we have seen because there is no drum group and no accompanying choir. The chorus of men sing as they dance. They wear a headdress that looks like a horizontal ar-row. It is made of eagle and parrot feathers, and on the end is a gaily painted half gourd. They wear turtle shells on their calves and have bells around their waist and calves. They are daubed in gray/green clay, and their chests are bare in the winter cold. They wear colored scarves around their necks, and the only way you can tell the winter society from the summer society is that one wears white boots (snow) and one wears yellow boots (sun). I can only guess what is going on.

According to Indian lore, the world is an island carried on the back of a turtle. The turtle is like the mother, the earth, and everything that is needed to sustain life is transported with her. The dance is a celebra-tion of all of life, of everything that is provided. It is a blessing and a prayer for fecundity, replete with rain gods. The dancers move from one space to another on the Plaza, and the visitors run after them, tracking their movement as they face the four sacred directions. The dancers are in a trance, their eyes focused somewhere else, in a place of prayer, tran-quillity, meditation. There are two foreboding figures who wear hairy masks and carry whips—which they crack intermittently. The white face is from the winter society (white = snow) and the black face is from the summer society (the sun burns your face in the summer). They leer at the public through two red slits which are eyes. As I watch, I try to con-nect empathically to the dancers, and to feel what they feel. Maybe they are counting their blessings or thinking about their connectedness to all things. Perhaps they are just focused on the steps, the direction they should face, the words of the songs.

I have heard that there are two striped clowns at San Juan—called *k'osa*. I look around during a lull in the dancing, but do not see them. It seems that if a *k'osa* has a drinking problem or any other serious behavioral disorder, he does not perform. I wonder if there are problems this year . . . I hope not . . .

As we stand waiting for the dances to resume, I reflect on the awesome way one gets to be a clown. While the *k'osa* perform their antics, a huge circle is drawn around them in the dirt. Children are warned not to cross the line, and adults know to stay behind it. If anyone disobeys and enters the circle, he becomes a clown, a member of the society of *k'osa* for life, and all of the ceremonial responsibilities fall to him forever.

After the dances, we go to visit Belinda James in her grandmother's humble Pueblo home. Grandma Toni isn't feeling well, and Paul massages her ankle. Grandpa Leandro is in bed, with oxygen in his nose. Once he was the war chief at San Juan, mighty and powerful, but now the poor soul is reduced to fighting for his life. The family, of course, invites us to eat, but we wouldn't dare take the little they have. It is enough of a gift just to be there, sharing their Feast Day, praying for Grandpa's welfare. In their house, there is a reminder of the poverty and hardship most Indians endure. There is no Hollywood there.

I am stunned at how different this holiday season is from the way we spend the holidays in L.A. There, I go months without seeing a person, and here we are bombarded daily, almost hourly. Our friends give us gifts and tell us how much they care about us and don't want us to leave. When we go to a party, THE HOSTS call US to thank us for coming. We only hope we can carry this spirit with us when we go home. We are overdosing, so we have enough left in our systems when we leave!

"It's not anchored to physical place," Paul insists. "If you haven't changed in your heart—and if you can't take that change with you—then you've missed the point."

Boy, Paul sure is waxing philosophical these days!

One morning, some friends of ours from Colorado come to visit at Uncle Alfie's house and they tell us about a freak car accident they recently had. They were in a Bronco and it suddenly flipped over and they found themselves upside down in their car, unable to get out. I ask them about the accident, and they say they observed every second of it as time slowed down.

"What does that mean?" I ask. "How can time slow down?"

"Well," they answer, "we knew that every detail mattered, so we really paid attention."

I think about this when we go to our next Pueblo dances. Why do we keep going to dances, when most other Anglos would have dropped out a long time ago, or gone to just a few? I think it is because, at the Pueblos, we really pay attention and time slows down for us. We notice the most minute details of costume and dance, and we get infused with the drumbeat, which is the heartbeat of the world. We go into a trance state where we become NOT absent, but, on the contrary, extremely mindful. We are not caught up in the hectic pace of life, and so we pay attention to what really matters.

It is frightening to think that an entire life can go by, and all one hears is the noise of traffic, the sound of TV and the whining of an unsatisfied world, groaning with greed. When it all slows down, you pay attention to the sounds that fill silence, and you are able to think and feel clearly, unobstructed by the obstacles that keep you from yourself.

We drive to Santo Domingo, where the Plaza is filled with hundreds of male and female dancers doing the corn dance. It is very different from the summer corn dance. There are few spectators, and most of them are Indian. There are no clowns. The women spectators hide in their colorful blankets, protecting themselves against the cold. They wrap the blankets around themselves, grip the edges with their hands, and all you can see of them is their eyes, which never look into your eyes. It is as though you are a tourist in a world of secrecy, and all the secrets are hidden under those blankets.

The male choir is enormous, and the men sing their hypnotic, repetitive songs to the beat of a drum. The women carry evergreen in both hands, and as they move the branches up and down in a balancing motion, they do a toe-heel step forward. The men, more vigorous but equally prayerful, move back and forth from foot to foot. What are they thinking? Are they meditating on the endless cycle of birth, death and rebirth that you can see in the natural world in the life rhythm of crops and that is mirrored in the Christmas story of Christ? Are they praying for the health and welfare of everyone they know? Are they praying for all of us? I think so.

The End of a Cycle

As we leave the Plaza, I find a sprig of evergreen on the ground and pick it up. It has been used in the dance, and therefore it is blessed. I hold it close to me, and then place it in our car—a very special gift. We go into the Pueblo church. On the roof are two statues of angels, and although they are Anglo, I am glad to see they have a thick head of Indian hair.

Inside, there are more white angels and white Christ figures, and pictures of the stations of the cross. Some of the saints are very life-like and very beautiful, but it still seems to me that they should have Indian features, so that at moments of intimacy and prayer the Indians get back a strong image of themselves.

We drive to Cochiti Pueblo, and it is even more sparsely populated. But it is very exciting to see the eagle dance performed on a Plaza instead of at a powwow. It is an entirely different feeling. There are about seven men and boys dancing, and they have large, long, out-spread eagle wings. The lead dancer is obviously the most seasoned, and he walks like a bird. When he spins and crouches and soars, flying to his Creator, I really see an eagle before me. The eagle dancers all wear white feathered caps with yellow eyes and beaks, and their faces are painted white, yellow and red. The dance is short so it seems like they have alighted for a moment at the Plaza and then are gone.

Suddenly I see Paul hold his breath. A long line of elk dancers appears, and it is so primitive and powerful that we have to keep saying out loud how lucky we are to be here. All of the dancers have their faces painted dark, so they look like animals, and all we can see are their eyes. They lean on two branches, so each seems to have four feet. Their posture is just like an elk, poised to run away or be caught unaware. There is a man dressed like a Plains Indian who accompanies them. He is a hunter, carrying a bow and arrows, and he dances a sober dance.

As the elk continue to dance, women come and give them gifts of soda and candy and candy canes. Some even hang the gifts on their horns. And then men appear, friends of the dancers, to gather up the gifts and keep them safe while the dance continues. How did this all get so organized? Who decided that the dancers should be blessed and then the blessings should have "keepers"? Who first chose these costumes, so that everyone looks alike? Who decided on the white knit leggings, the bare chests, the heshi and turquoise necklaces, the colorful turkey feather bustle, the colorful fringe over the hair, the evergreen headdress? How did this get so ritualized and complicated? Will I ever know the answers?

We just saw deer and elk dancing at Taos, but it was very different—the colors, the costumes, even the steps. What they have in common is that they are both other-worldly dances. The men go into the kivas to prepare. I don't know what they do in there—fasting, praying, practicing—but when they emerge, they are more than men. They aren't exactly deer and elk, but they are probably closer to the animals than they are to us. Their eyes are absent, their focus is inward, they are in an exalted state.

The next day I start making plans for our return to Los Angeles, and in the evening, thinking I will relax, we have one of our most emotional experiences in Santa Fe.

We are invited to a small dinner party at Rita and John Goodman's house. At the last moment, some old friends show up, and I ask Rita if I can bring them along. In her usual generous way, she says yes. We want to bring some Triple Sec for John, who is the world's best margarita maker, but you cannot buy liquor in Santa Fe on Sunday. Paul wanders into a great used bookstore, buys a load of cookbooks for Rita, and wraps them up in the Sunday comics. Just to add to the ungainly arrival, we take all of our laundry, two huge hefty garbage bags full, and throw it into the car to do at Rita's during the dinner party. It's tacky, we know that, but it's such a pain in the butt to sit at a laundromat for three hours.

So there we are—the extra friends in tow, the funnies-wrapped cookbooks, the laundry, and to make matters more awkward, it is freezing outside, the car won't start, and we arrive half an hour late. We walk in the door, start peeling off our layers of clothes, and suddenly *everyone* yells SURPRISE!!!!!!!! I look around and I can't understand what our very eclectic friends are doing in Rita and John's bedroom, and why they all come streaming out. Then it hits me: THIS IS A FAREWELL SURPRISE PARTY FOR US!!! I start to scream with delight and surprise. We go around the house and there is a receiving line of people. These are not just acquaintances, but friends. Amigos. People who have meaning in our lives. There are friends from the Pueblos, from southern New Mexico, from northern New Mexico—all of our Indian and Spanish and Anglo friends! Rich and poor, artists and working folk, a real cross-section. The ages range from seven to seventy-seven. It is completely overwhelming! John shoves a margarita in my face and the party begins. Everyone keeps saying: "How can you have so many friends when you have been here such a short time?" and we wonder ourselves.

We look at the buffet table: all of our friends chipped in and made the food. Then they begin to entertain for us! Flamenco songs, jazz, satirical ditties, Indian drumming, Spanish guitar. We are showered with gifts and we sit there, cracking jokes on the surface, but very moved inside. I understand something with absolute clarity now: we have found here what has always been lacking in our lives—a sense of belonging, of community. It is not healthy or normal for people to be isolated, to have to make it on their own. We need each other for physical and emotional survival.

The clock is definitely winding down now, and we set out for the next phase of our lives exactly one week and two days from tomorrow. This time it is REAL. Paul has made me promise to have the same adventurous attitude about L.A. as we have here about life. I think it is time to go home, to see our friends and family, to take care of our house. If there really has been a healing here, then it is something we will carry with us in our hearts, and no amount of urban infiltration can take it away from us.

I walk the streets of Santa Fe and already I feel nostalgic. I will miss the adobe houses and the snow-crested mountains around the city. I'll have a yen for chili every once in a while, and I'll yearn for the Pueblos. I'll miss the beauty, the beauty around us, beside us, in front of us, behind us. I'll miss the gentleness and the deep, deep humanity of this place.

Six days before our departure, we start missing our new-found friends before we have even gone. We throw a huge party at Uncle Alfie's. The little house on Osage Circle is mobbed. The gifts continue to pour in. Sage is lit and everyone is "smoked" and blessed. Joseph's daughter, little Candy Villegas, does a dance for us and then comes over and blesses my head with the sign of the cross several times. The light touch of her hand and her open heart transcend any specific religion.

Five days to go. We can't discipline ourselves to pack, so we jump in the car and ride to the Randall Davy Audubon Center. We have never hiked in the snow, so we decide to give it a try. We pass the reservoir, and we hear the rustle of leaves and the occasional cry of a bird, but other than that, it is completely silent. We walk and walk, and suddenly we hear music. A man approaches us, playing a flute, accompanied by his snow-eating dog. It is the kind of image we have come to associate with northern New Mexico. Something completely unexpected, offbeat, and charming.

When the sun sets in the familiar tones of a blood orange, we stop at a store to buy some comestibles. "You mustn't obsess," one checkout person is saying to another checkout person. "Obsession keeps your mind from being in the Now." And then she goes on to ring up the peas and couscous. I think I can learn from virtually every conversation here.

Four days to go. We drive to Ojo Caliente, the oldest indoor hot springs in North America. After the scalding baths, we go out into the cold winter air. Ojo was a settlement on the way from Chaco Canyon or Mesa Verde to the Pueblos of the Rio Grande, so I begin to search for Indian ruins.

We climb into the mountains, stomping through snow and mud. We finally make it to the top of the mesa, and the minute we get up there I find a potsherd. Soon we are surrounded by potsherds—there are so many it is overwhelming. As far as we can see, the broken pieces of painted pottery are all around us. We take a few of them, knowing we should leave them in place. I am afraid that the spirits of dead Indians are going to rise up and punish me.

Three days to go. I take two Anglo women to see the January 6th dances. It is the day when the new governors and tribunals of the Pueblos are inaugurated, and the animal dances are held to celebrate this. We go from Pueblo to Pueblo, but the information is always erroneous. There are no dances, and so we finally decide to go to San Juan, where I knew for sure the dancing is taking place. Wrong. And right. There are dances, but they are not in the public Plaza. Rather, the buffalo dancers are going from house to house, celebrating at the houses of the new officials. The only way to find them is to drive around and listen for a drumbeat.

We set out to do just that, but it is not easy. The Pueblo is large, the streets are covered with snow and mud, and finally we cross the main highway and are just going to give up and head back to Santa Fe when we hear it—the sound of a drum. We roll down the car windows and follow the sound and, amazingly, find the dancers. They are young buffalo dancers. About seven men and one buffalo woman. They are in front of someone's house, right next to a red truck, dancing their hearts out. They wear red and black facepaint, white leggings, and thick, rich buffalo headdresses.

I take a deep breath. The sun is going to set. This is the final dance of the day on the last day of dances that I will see in New Mexico. It has been magical, as usual.

When I get home, I am edgy, irritable, in a bad mood. I hate moving. I feel out of control, like I have no idea of where we are heading or why.

Two days to go. Now I am extremely anxious. Bernie Krause, who has worked for twenty years with the Nez Perce Indians, calls and tries to calm me down by talking about the natural world.

"We are not separate from nature. We are part of it," Bernie says. "The Indians, in fact, do not seem to have a word for nature, because it is such a part of their selves and their lives."

As he speaks, I look up at the moon and understand that she is doing her job, lighting the night for us. I thank her, and she tells me I am safe and well provided for.

One day to go. Rushing madly, I try to accomplish everything. At her insistence, I stop by the house of Indian sculptress Estella Loretto to take a quick look at her work. Since I have been in Santa Fe I have only exchanged about a hundred words with her. When I leave, she stuns me by handing me a gift of a bronze frog sculpture, with its focus inward where it gains sustenance. She also places cornmeal in my hand and in Paul's hand for a safe voyage and transition. She keeps looking me in the eyes and telling me in a husky voice to make *my* schedule the only schedule that counts, and that I need not rush and give in to the pressures of the outside world. I clutch the frog, hardly finding the words to thank her.

"You will return," she whispers to me. "I can feel it. I know you will be back."

Now it is time to unplug the computer, which has served me so well for all these months. I pull the plug, and all of my feelings come bubbling to the surface. I am aware that the place you live in IS important, and the people you live with are even more important. There are spots on earth where the soul can soar, and others where you are bogged down, or where your wings are clipped. I have known real freedom in Santa Fe, and, at times, real peace. I have known how it feels to be fully functional, and to be effective as a human being. I have fallen in love with the sky, the mountains, the birds, the flowers, and with my husband Paul all over again. We have shared something so deep that a word or a look suffices to call back the memories and evoke the feelings. We have been part of a chain of connection, an extended family of our own choosing. We have said YES to life on every level.

And now we reenter. We come back into our former life. Will I slip back, or will I be okay? I look up at the sacred peaks that surround Santa Fe, and I know in my heart that everywhere on earth is sacred. "Indian Country" is not only in the Southwest, or in places where Indians live. It is anywhere we are, all around us. Right now. At this moment. We just have to look for it.